Where Art Meets Nature

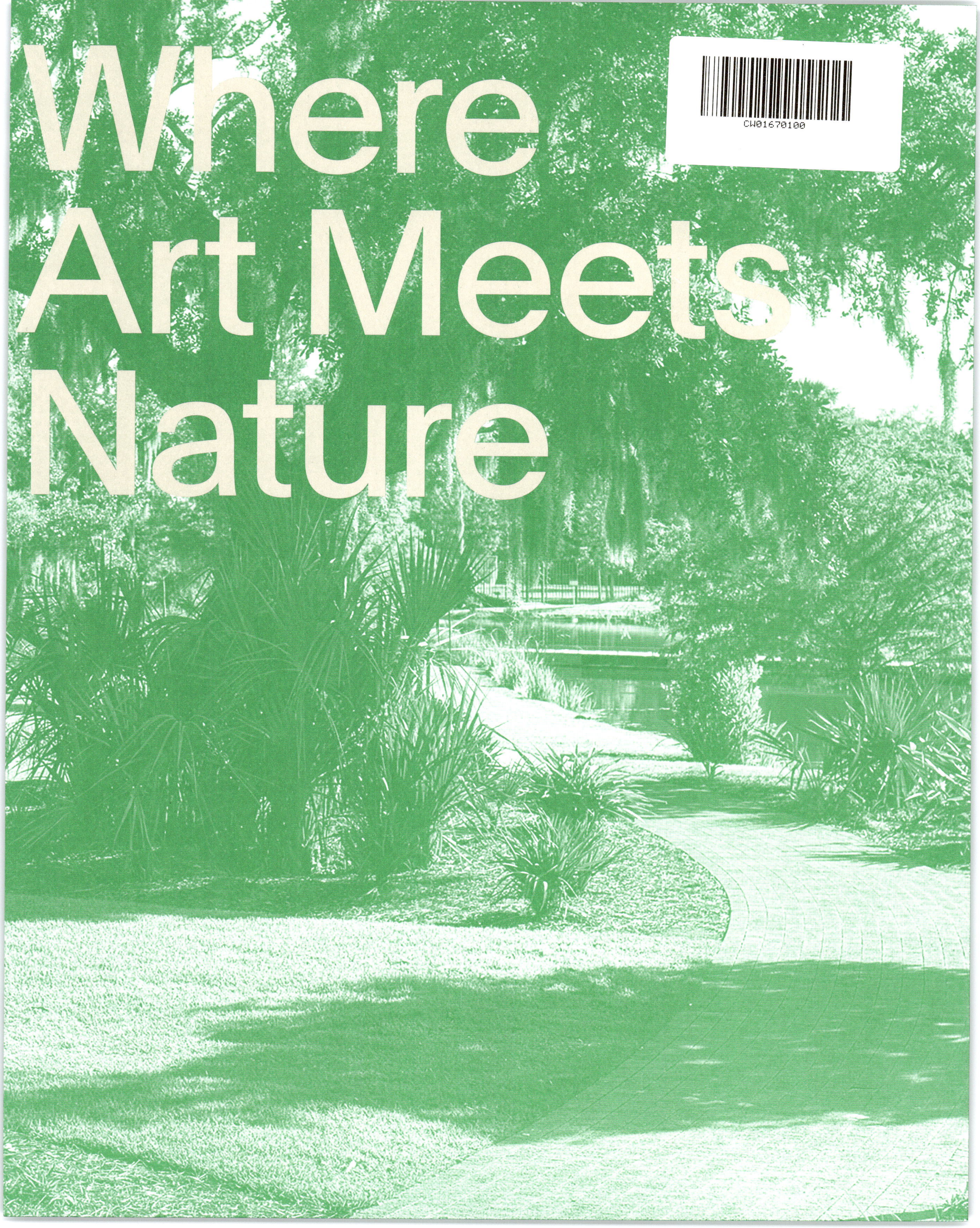

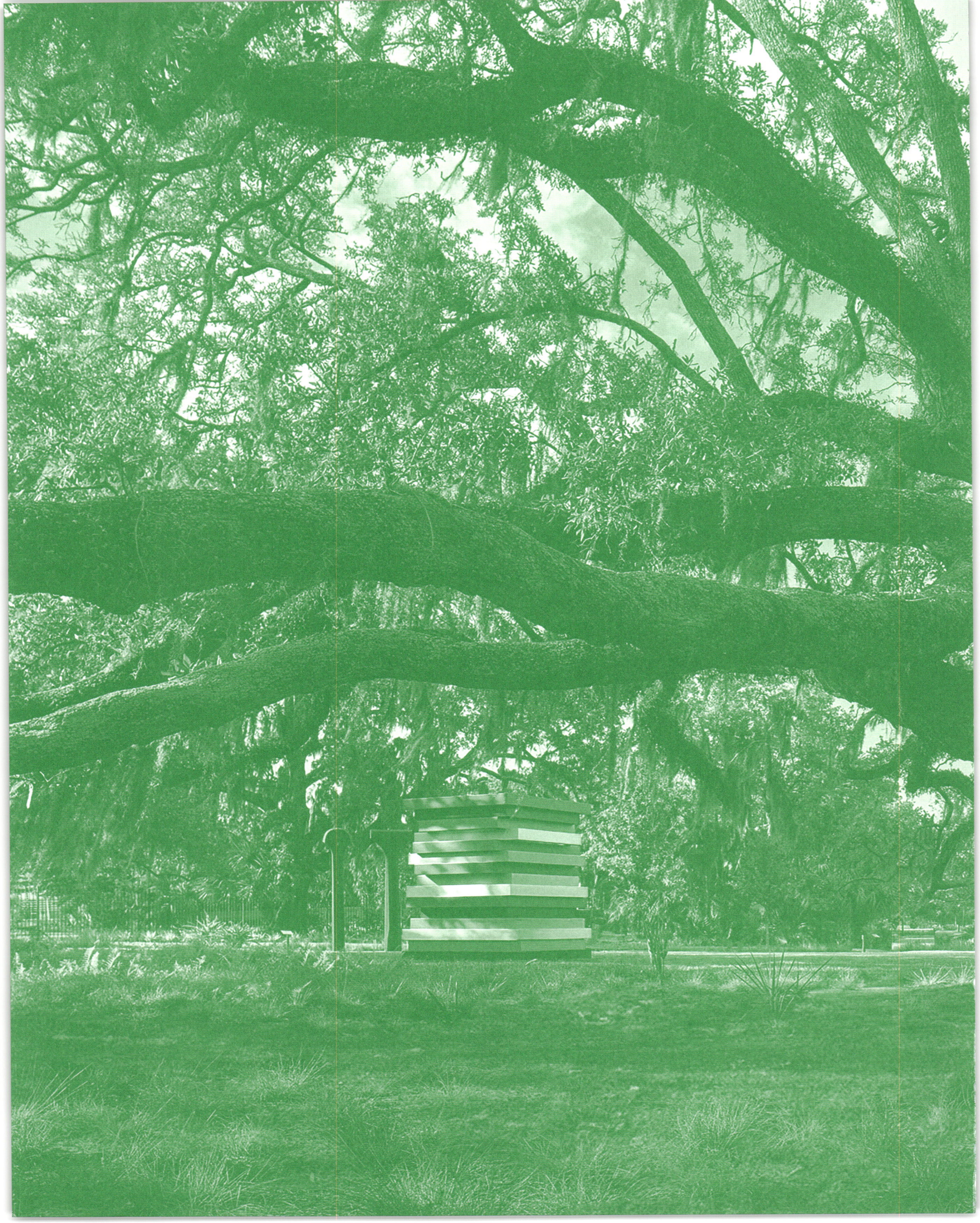

Where Art
Meets Nature

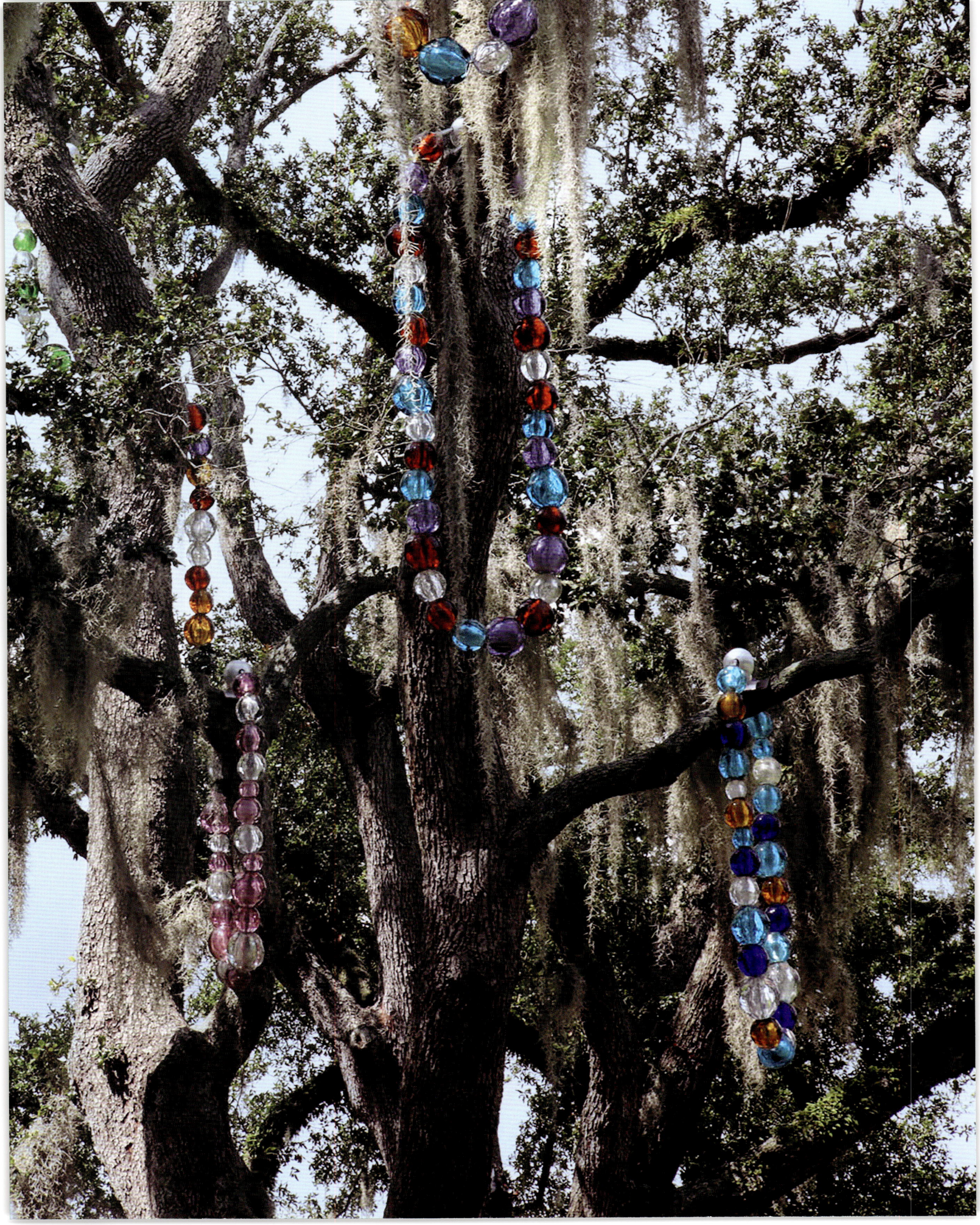

Where Art Meets Nature

The Sydney and Walda Besthoff Sculpture Garden

Foreword by Susan M. Taylor

Introduction by Suzanne Turner

Walda Besthoff and Susan M. Taylor: In Conversation

Text contributions by
Maddie Hampton, Juliana Mascolo,
and Adam M. Thomas

New Orleans Museum of Art

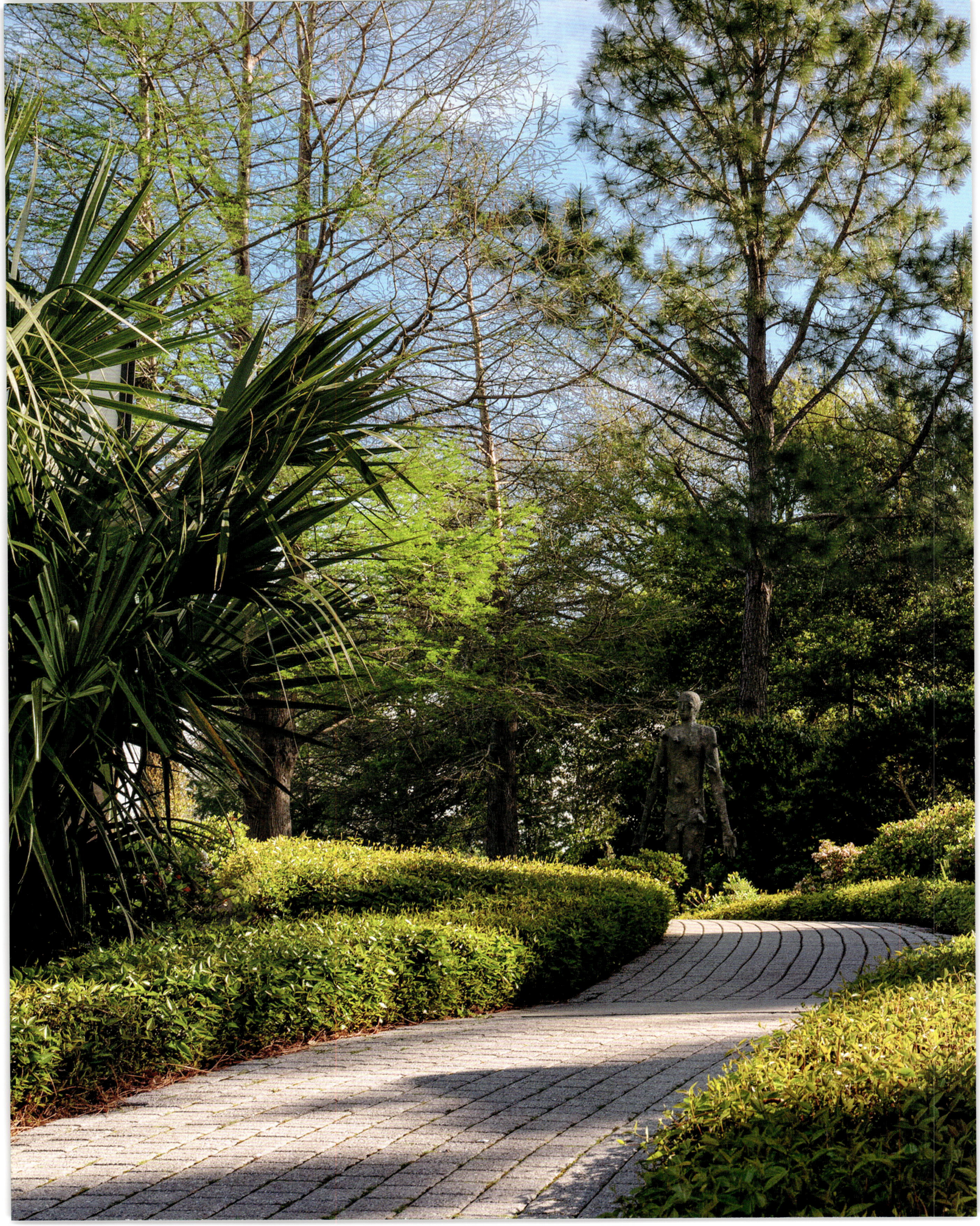

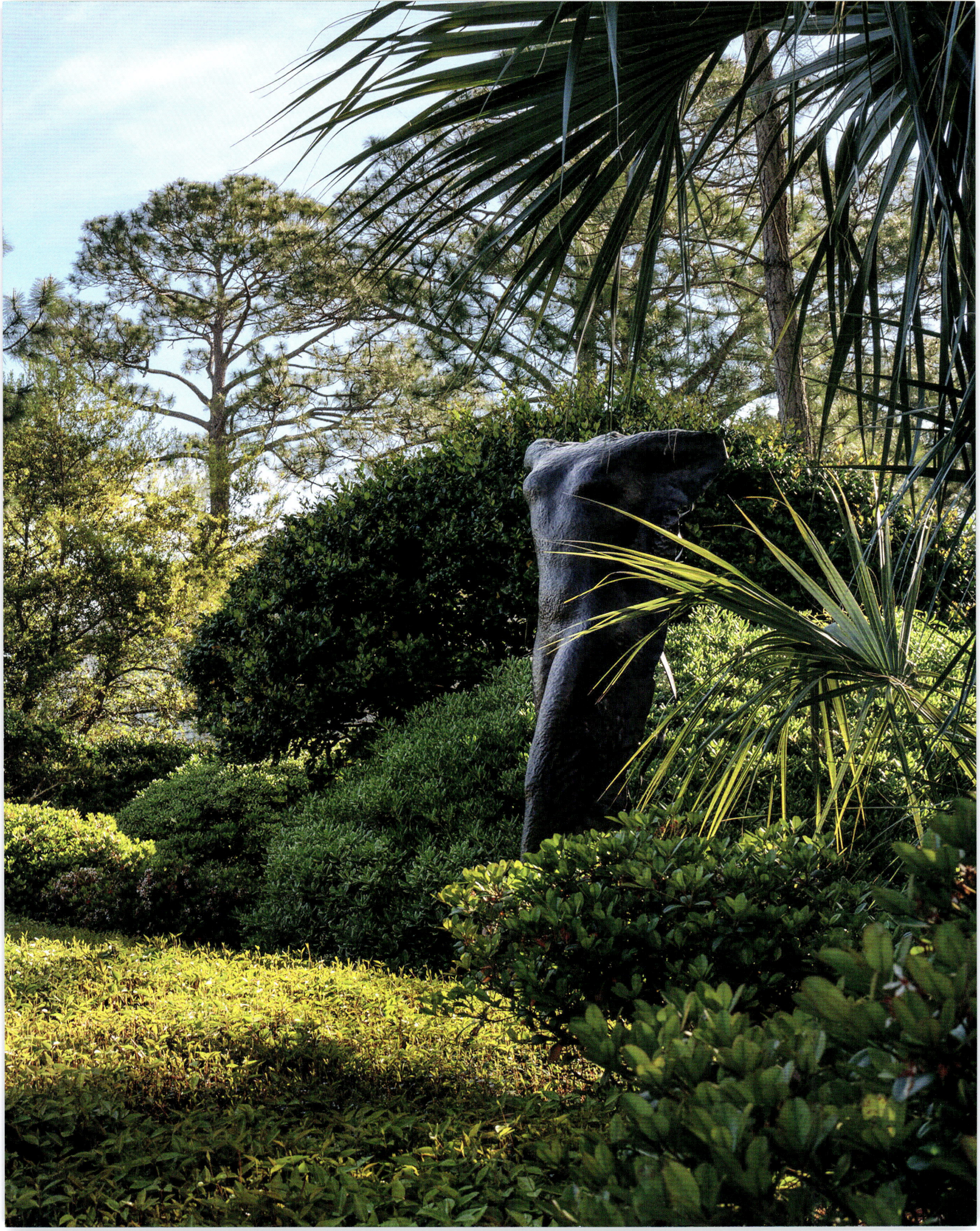

Contents

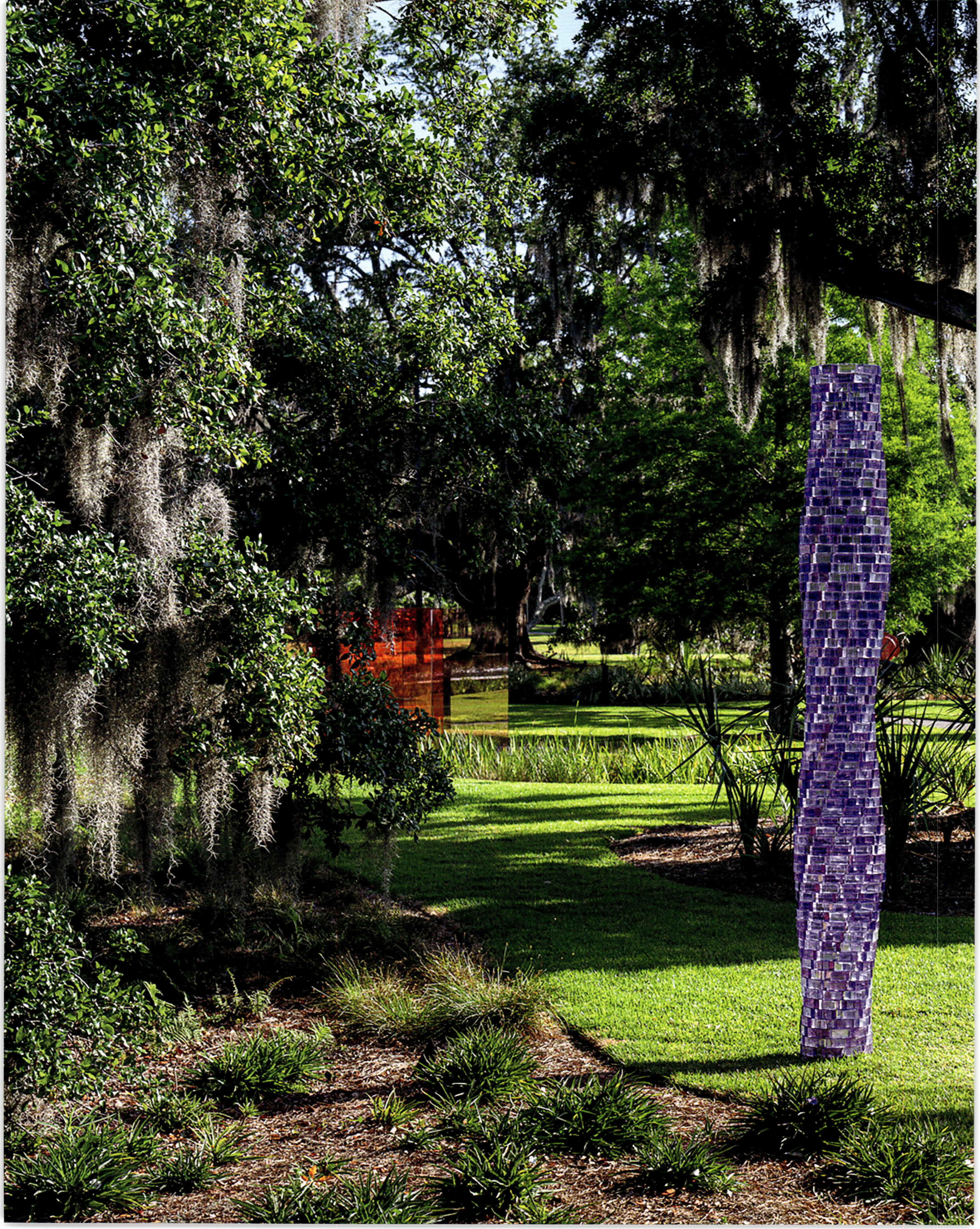

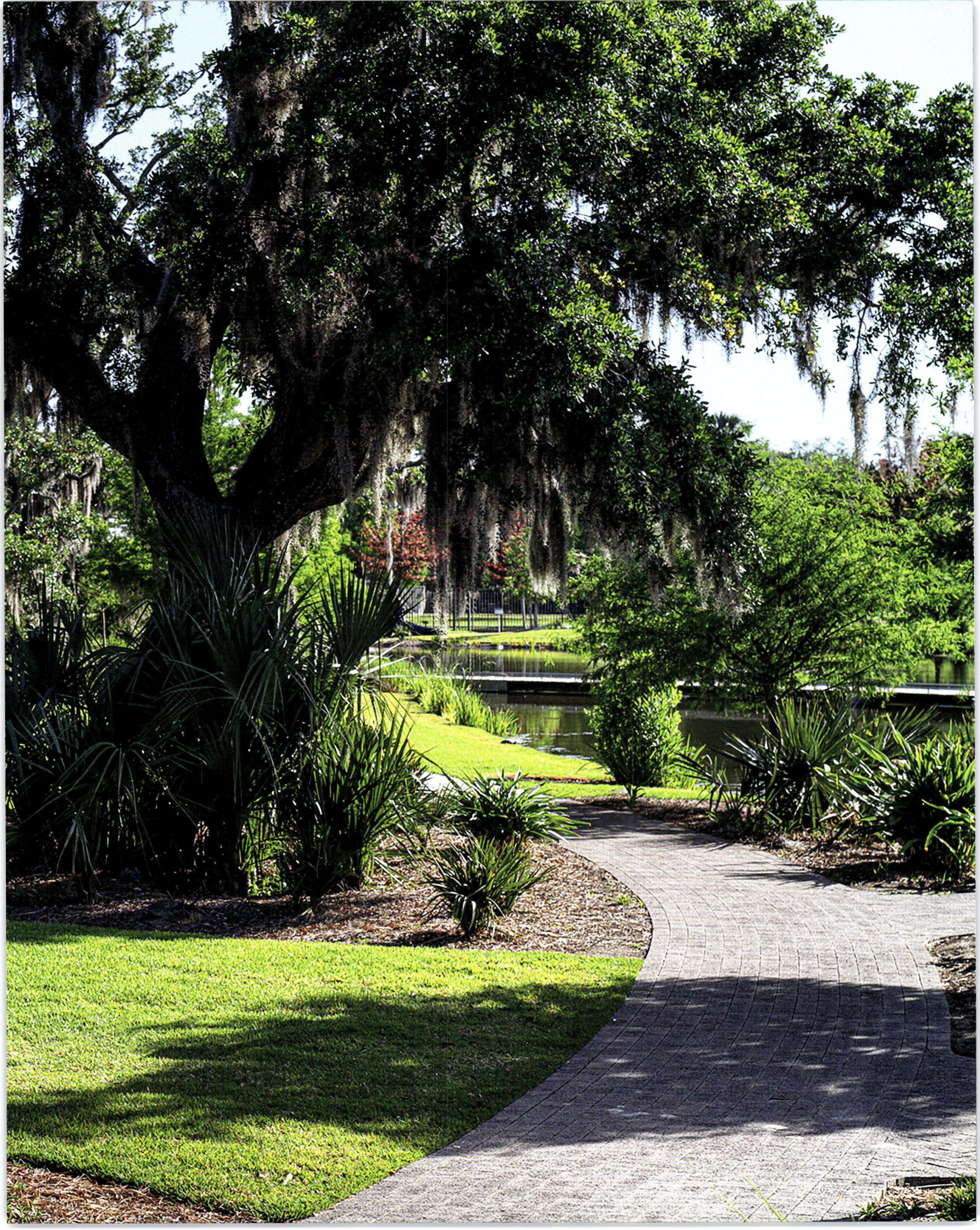

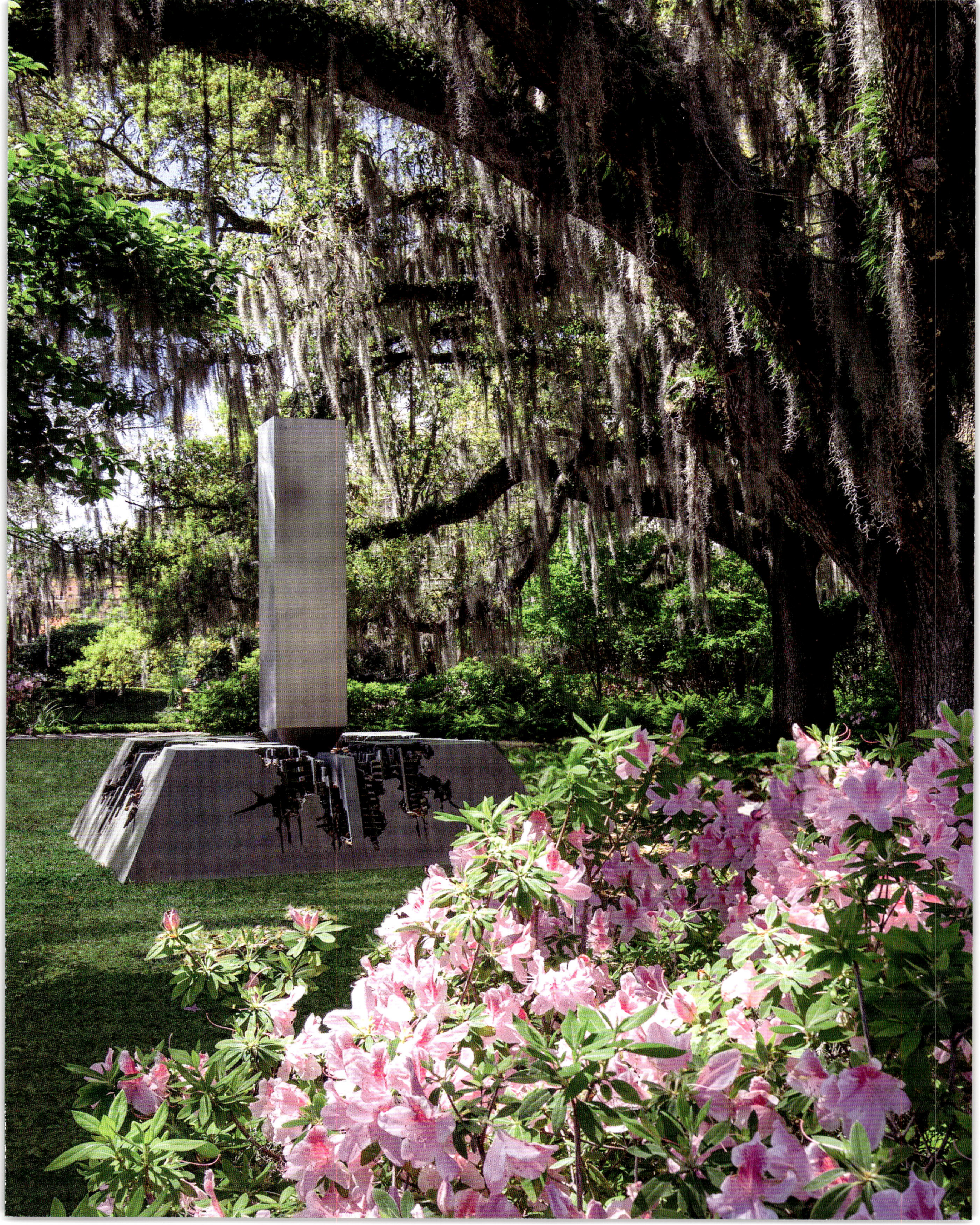

Foreword

Susan M. Taylor
The Montine McDaniel Freeman Director, NOMA

Where Art Meets Nature is a celebration of twenty years of the Sydney and Walda Besthoff Sculpture Garden at the New Orleans Museum of Art, and a tribute to the generous philanthropists who created this stunning public garden. Sydney and Walda Besthoff's unwavering vision and commitment distinguishes New Orleans as home to one of the most important sculpture gardens in the world.

A successful New Orleans business executive and philanthropist, Sydney Besthoff (1927–2022) began his long relationship with NOMA in 1992 when he was first appointed to the board of trustees. In 1998, he started conversations with then NOMA Director John Bullard, and others, about what would become the Sydney and Walda Besthoff Sculpture Garden.

Some of my fondest memories of the Besthoffs are going from gallery to gallery on our trips to New York City, pacing ourselves to make the most of our time, then talking enthusiastically about what we had seen over a quick lunch so we could get back to the art. Sydney loved the chase. He often found works that weren't readily available on the market and made the deal. Private dealers, auctions, and galleries were all part of the hunt. It was thrilling—the pursuit of important work, always striving for excellence and quality. I have never worked with anyone more focused on realizing the full magnitude of such an important project than Sydney and Walda.

The excitement was even more palpable when a work, loaded on a flatbed truck, was delivered to the garden, ready for installation. Sydney and Walda would be the first to arrive, warmly greeting the crane operators from American Machinery Movers. We would all stand by, watching as the works soared above us, landing precisely on the proposed site. Sydney and Walda's vision, passion, and dedication paved a new way for NOMA to expand and broaden its audience in a natural setting.

The garden, a manifestation of the Besthoffs' outstanding devotion to the visual arts, has made a lasting impact on the New Orleans Museum of Art and our city. Twenty years after its founding, we celebrate the legacy that Sydney and Walda created, and embrace Walda's ongoing commitment to the art of today. Their lasting legacy is a garden that is free and open to all.

Opposite
Arnaldo Pomodoro, *Una Battaglia (A Battle)*, 1971

Previous spread
(sculptures from left to right) Larry Bell, *Pacific Red (VI)*, 2016–17; Shirazeh Houshiary, *Exuviae*, 2016–17

Introduction

Suzanne Turner

In the early 1980s, American sculptor Frank McGuire's *Stool* was installed on the median of St. Charles Avenue near (then) Lee Circle—just outside of Katz & Besthoff (K&B) Plaza in New Orleans, Louisiana. The bronze stool-like sculptures, a nod to the waiting area of a public bus stop, were sited where no bus would stop, and no one could sit. This was my first introduction to Sydney and Walda Besthoff as connoisseurs of modern sculpture; art collectors whose humor, dedication, and love of public sculpture was immediately evident.

As an art historian and urban designer, I appreciated the genius of selecting this whimsical McGuire piece both as an installation and as a means of showcasing the power of sculpture to the broadest possible public. The Besthoffs' commitment to art continued on; they spent the last quarter of the twentieth century amassing a collection of important large-scale sculpture, and in 1998 they began discussions with John Bullard, then the director of the New Orleans Museum of Art, about a possible home for their collection.

A sculpture garden in New Orleans City Park seemed almost preordained. The forms of the ancient live oaks communicate strength and sinuosity in this primordial landscape—nature's own sculptures. Given the site's location between Lake Pontchartrain and Bayou St. John, swampy conditions and water are constants, with the curving, flowing lines that inspired the park's ultimate design.

Two important moments in City Park's history set the stage for the sculpture garden. First, in 1910, local businessman Isaac Delgado helped fund the creation of an art museum within a monumental Beaux Arts building located at the terminus of a ceremonial boulevard into the otherwise picturesque landscape—today, the New Orleans Museum of Art. This triggered the commission of a long-term plan in 1922 to balance the classicism in architecture with the romanticism in landscape design and ensure a coherent park design.

The second pivotal event involved the Works Progress Administration (WPA), the federal relief program created in response to the Great Depression. Because their 1922 plan provided a list of "shovel-ready" projects, City Park received support from the WPA that brought much of the plan to fruition. The collaborative team of architect Richard Koch, landscape architect William Wiedorn, and sculptor Enrique Alferez developed a kit-of-parts (a system of predesigned, standardized components that can be assembled in various combinations to create structures, thus saving time and reducing waste) that celebrated the diversity of the existing landscape of ancient trees and waterways, while capitalizing on its spatial and sculptural possibilities. Although there had been sculptural elements added to the park over the years, in the WPA projects—including the Botanical Garden (opened in 1936) and numerous bridges, structures, and thoroughfares—sculpture ultimately became a hallmark.

Starting in the late 1990s and over the course of the next two decades, the twelve-acre Besthoff Sculpture Garden would be created in two phases, both made with a commitment to engage only the best designers for the project. Landscape architect Brian Sawyer and architect Lee Ledbetter worked on the first phase, which culminated in the garden's opening in 2003. In 2019, landscape architecture firm Reed Hilderbrand completed a major expansion with Ledbetter and the ongoing input of associate Chris Loudon.

Sawyer's design takes advantage of the amazing family of mature pines at the entrance to the garden. They provide a high filtered canopy, and the lines and texture of the trunks form an intricate backdrop for sculptures. Beyond, historic live oaks create a lower and denser shade, their monumental trunks echoing the mass of the more significant pieces. The effect is one of peace, reflection, and verdure created using many native Louisiana flora.

With the addition of Reed Hilderbrand's planning, the NOMA building and its modern wings feel more integral to the park, their mass more balanced. The garden invites movement, play, laughter, and people-watching. The design celebrates the constancy of water both in the broader Louisiana landscape and in City Park specifically by reshaping an existing lagoon to emphasize its open expanse and reflective potential. A broad palette of native plants secures the lagoon's sloped banks, filtering runoff from nearby areas. These banks, and the use of weirs to slow the flow of the stream that leaves the large lagoon, remind the visitor of the impact of Hurricane Katrina (August 2005) on the city and the park and how both have continued to persevere.

Since the Besthoff Sculpture Garden first opened in 2003, it has served as a public locus for pleasure, learning, and wonder. The Besthoffs' decision to move such an important part of their lives' work into NOMA's collection and into the landscape of a historic and beloved urban park was one of generosity and brilliance. The capacity of sculpture to move the human spirit was all important to the creation of the Besthoff Sculpture Garden at the New Orleans Museum of Art. Their vision created much more than a world-class sculpture garden; it is a true gift to the city of New Orleans.

Following Spread
(sculptures from left to right) Beverly Pepper, *Split Ritual II*, 1996; Sean Scully, *Colored Stacked Frames*, 2017; Ursula von Rydingsvard, *Dumna*, 2015

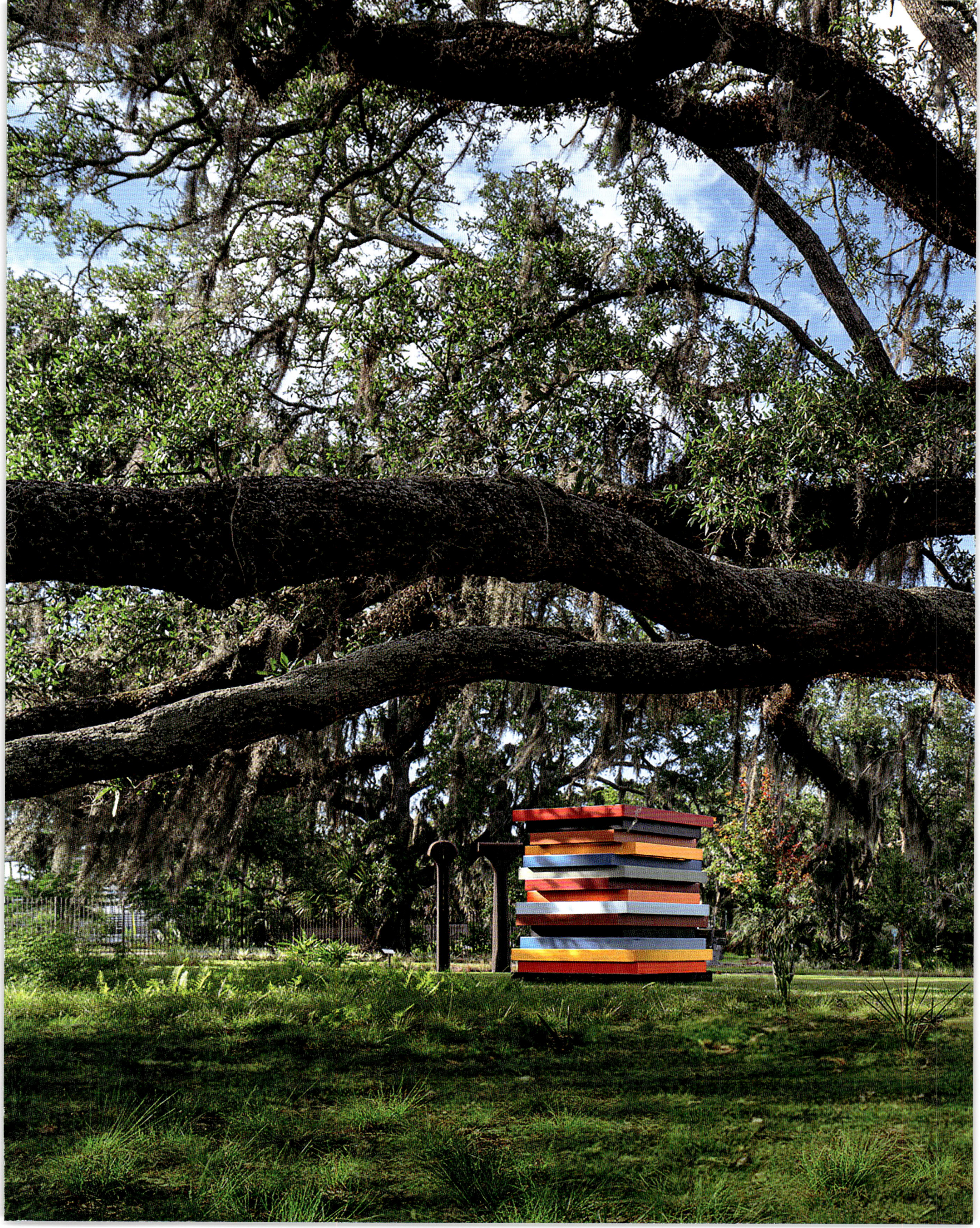

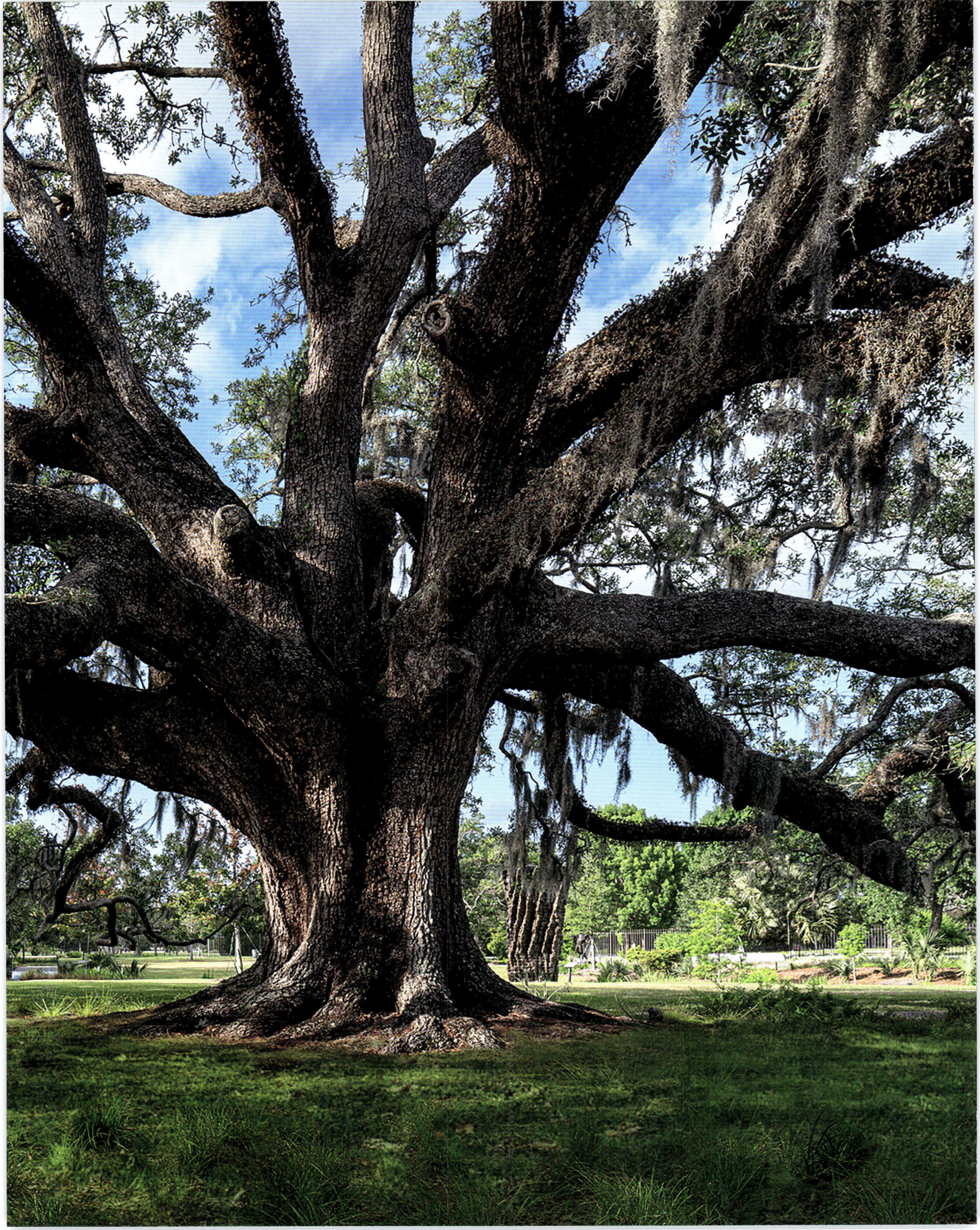

Walda Besthoff and Susan M. Taylor: In Conversation

Walda Besthoff The idea for collecting sculpture came about after Sydney, my husband, bought an office building for K&B [Katz & Besthoff pharmacies] in 1973. It's a prize-winning Skidmore, Owings & Merrill building from the 1960s, and on the plaza was a huge stone Isamu Noguchi sculpture.

When Sydney occupied the office, he thought, *This is very exciting*, and *maybe it would be nice to have another sculpture*. At that time, George Rickey had just left New Orleans, where he'd been a professor of art at Newcomb College at Tulane. So, Sydney consulted with John Bullard, then director of the New Orleans Museum of Art, and in 1978 they decided to go forward with commissioning Rickey to create a twenty-nine-foot sculpture for the plaza.

Sydney was very excited about that, and thought, *Well, this looks great. Maybe I'll add another one*. Sydney was the type of person who believed if it was worth doing, it was worth overdoing.

Susan M. Taylor And worth doing well.

WB And worth doing well. So we continued to buy sculpture, and we had Bullard's input, approval, and counsel. I got involved shortly after, and it was a wonderful project. After we had maybe ten or twelve good pieces [at the office], Bullard said, "You know, this is museum-quality art. You should think about putting these pieces in a sculpture garden at the museum." And he said it repeatedly over several years. We kept buying sculptures, and Bullard kept saying, "We need to have a sculpture garden. The New Orleans Museum of Art can get the land next to the museum with the help of Bob Becker [head of City Park at the time]."

Becker said, "Sure, we'll give you five and a half acres if that's what you want," which was just amazing. So that was it. Everything fell into place. It was a seamless endeavor. We contributed money toward it, but the museum raised money through naming opportunities and other gifts to help bring it to fruition. And of course, the sculpture had mostly already been bought by our business, which had established a foundation. It was just wonderful.

And that was how we started—we grew from a plaza at K&B with a few select works to the initial five-and-a-half-acre footprint of the sculpture garden, which opened in 2003. If we'd had to buy the land, that would have been the end of it. If we'd had to buy all the sculptures at once, that would have been the end of it. But we had this wonderful seed to grow from. These beginnings can be seen in the garden today, particularly in contrast to the newer expansion, which gave us the possibility of more site-specific installations to even further emphasize the relationship between art and nature.

SMT: There was a rigorous design process to both sections of the garden in terms of how they came to be and how they were imagined to operate. The design principles for the landscape underscore visitors' experience of sculpture.

The sculpture garden's growth over time has allowed it to expand the experience of the museum—first and foremost, because the sculpture garden is free and open to the public. It invites visitors to explore art beginning in the nineteenth century and continuing through the twenty-first century. It's an experience that is self-directed, as well as contained within a pleasing and inviting natural environment. Visitors feel connected to both the landscape and the art.

For the museum, it's important that the sculpture garden creates a narrative through sculptures embedded in a series of spaces connected with one another through pathways designed to minimize disruption to the viewing experience. Because of the nature of a garden, that narrative is not always linear, but rather filled with discovery, and sometimes surprises, as you walk along the meandering paths.

WB And the garden has grown significantly since your arrival at NOMA.

SMT One of the first things that happened when I arrived at NOMA in 2010 was a conversation with Sydney and Walda. Sydney asked me to compile a list of the artists with whom I would like to work. Having come from a background of site-specific sculpture and outdoor commissions, I was excited about the possibilities. I wrote down my aspirational list of sculptors to acquire; he showed me his. There was so much overlap!

It was an extraordinary opportunity to work with you both to continue to build a collection through our conversations about contemporary art, and to refine the story that the museum would tell through the sculpture garden. We began adding works to the garden: Do Ho Suh's *Karma* was the first; Anish Kapoor's reflective work *Untitled* was the second. And then Mimmo Palladino's *Caduto a ragione [Fallen to the Ground]*. In front of the museum, we also installed Yinka Shonibare's *Wind Sculpture V* [now located in the garden].

WB Eventually, Sydney and you wanted more space. We were all keen on acquiring more sculpture and bringing the quality of art up to the nanosecond we find ourselves in now. We wanted art ahead of its time.

SMT At that point, we began planning for the expansion. It seemed daunting at first. We were able to secure land from City Park, but the landscape and live oaks had been severely compromised during Hurricane Katrina. Our first priority was to bring them back to health and determine how to deal with the lagoon, which had been ignored for many, many years. We had to figure out how to be the best possible stewards of this land before we could begin the project.

The concept for this expansion was rooted in our desire to include new, twenty-first century work by living artists and our ambition to continue assembling a cohesive, world-class collection that is reflective of the current moment and engages emerging artists.

WB And I think that largely accounts for the success of the garden visually. There was such a community of minds between us. It wasn't remarkable that Sydney and I were thinking alike. We didn't come from art backgrounds, but we were exposed to art at the same time, and we learned together. And you, Susan, brought your experience to the project. We didn't have the exact same perspectives, but we did have similar paths that we wished to follow. There was a real meeting of the minds.

SMT There is an overarching strategy behind the types of sculptures that we chose to include in the garden. I think it was already well established in the first phase of the sculpture garden because of the range of nineteenth- to twentieth-century works. But in planning for the newer part of the garden, which opened in 2019, there were several driving forces that informed the selection of artists and [the works'] placement.

First, the expansion was designed both to celebrate certain pieces that we knew would anchor the garden and to accept new additions of art over time. We wanted to develop several areas of distinct character to maximize opportunities to locate sculpture.

Second, you both were adamant that it had to be a twenty-first-century garden. By that, I mean we were looking for works that represented artists who were thinking about their own work in relationship to the properties of three-dimensionality, mass, and space. Finally, we wanted opportunities for new site-specific works. There are also artists in the garden who are not primarily sculptors: the architect Frank Gehry and Sean Scully, a painter, as examples.

WB And Anselm Kiefer, who is known for his large-scale abstract paintings. But [in the garden], we had the opportunity to present a sculpture by Kiefer that touches on themes from throughout his career, but in a different form.

SMT Yes, all these artists had a moment when they were thinking about their work in different contexts.

WB Inadvertently, if you walk through the sculpture garden, you're getting an education from the late nineteenth century to the twentieth century to the twenty-first century; so many students come through [and learn about the history of art].

That wasn't planned in a definitive way, although I'm sure there was something unconscious operating in our minds. As you enter the garden, there's the nineteenth century [with Auguste Rodin and Augustus Saint-Gaudens] staring you right in the face. But nobody ever said, "Let's put the nineteenth century pieces here." Most visitors will immediately recognize some of the artists' names and sculptures, just as Sydney and I did when we were first learning about art. [It's] a safe bet that visitors will appreciate them in the future.

Continued on p. 20 >

Opposite
(sculptures from left to right) Jesús Bautista Moroles, *Las Mesas Bench*, 1989;
Arman, *Pablo Casals's Obelisk*, 1983

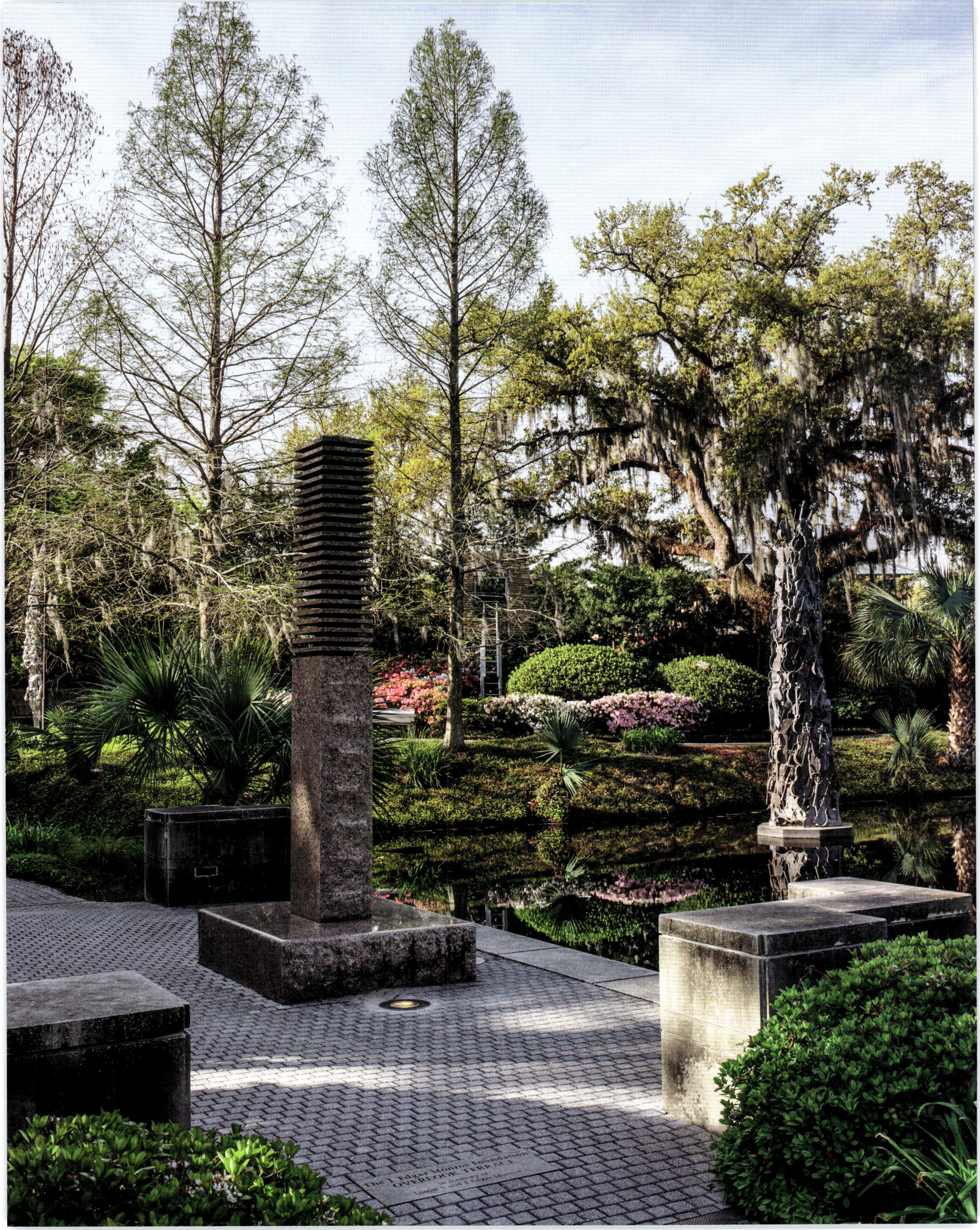
The J. Edgar Monroe Foundation
OVERLOOK TERRACE

SMT They are the classics.

WB When we expanded, we all wanted the opportunity to balance those works with cutting-edge, twenty-first-century pieces. We weren't sure how the public would respond to them. They're what's out there in the world *now*. Sculpture, I'm afraid, becomes dated more easily than painting. And our hope is that they will become timeless.

What we haven't mentioned enough is the setting—it's so beautiful. It's like putting a diamond in a gorgeous setting that will really enhance the ring.

The Louisiana landscape offers so much to the experience. We have three-hundred-year-old oak trees with Spanish moss, two lagoons, eleven and a half acres of wonderful pathways. It's a magical setting that is very romantic and welcoming. We are so fortunate that we can take advantage of it.

SMT It was important for us to unite the garden and the iconic landscape of City Park, which surrounds our museum campus. We thought about how to create a distinct garden experience while opening up physical and visual connections to the historic park landscape beyond.

Water is also an important feature in the design for both phases of the garden. The relationship of water to land, and sculptures' proximity to water, is important. Arman's *Pablo Casals's Obelisk* rises up and out of the bayou. Katharina Fritsch's oversized skull *[Schädel (Skull)]* inspired the creation of an island for her work.

WB We call it Skull Island.

SMT The sculpture was really meant to be sited in this very specific way. Architecture and landscape also became an integral part of the experience. The pathways and the boardwalks, the bridges, the outdoor amphitheater, and even the pavilion are all part of a broader design that's meant to create moments for engagement within the landscape.

WB What do you think has made our garden so successful?

SMT When I think about the qualities of successful public sculpture, it seems that the work should be in conversation with the landscape. There must be a relationship, both spatial and contextual. I love the installation of the Kiefer, for example. The original siting of it in France was in an idyllic, forested landscape. We don't have a forest in the sculpture garden, but we wanted a site that was intimate and personal, surrounded by greenery. And I think the placement amongst the trees and Spanish moss has worked well. It's a clear demonstration of how we think about the art in the landscape.

WB It works really well. And one of its counterparts in the earlier area of the garden is Louise

Bourgeois's *Spider*, which looks like it just fell out of the tree. All these years later, it's still a little startling when I see it. I think visitors feel that moment of excitement, too. Just as they experience the Jean-Michel Othoniel glass beads strung in the trees as if left behind from Mardi Gras.

There could be so many different successful types of public sculpture. Sydney and I have always been attracted to things that have a very fine finish.

SMT Visitors often first become engaged with a work because of the way it's made, the appreciation of its form, its three-dimensional qualities. But a work that has staying power has more and more layers.

WB A lot of the artists in the garden are working with really serious ideas that you can understand or engage with on many different levels. For instance, Do Ho Suh, is making a statement [with *Karma*] about people living closer together, one on top of the other, with each figure covering its eyes, implying blind faith.

On the one hand, this may be a detrimental way to live, and on the other hand, people are holding each other up and supporting each other.

SMT I agree that the Do Ho Suh work is that kind of impactful piece. So are Wangechi Mutu's sculptures [*The Seated III* and *Crocodylus*], which have a metaphorical resonance that evolves with your perspective.

WB Looking at good sculpture is a mental discipline. It makes you think. It makes you wonder. It makes you speculate. It's good for the brain.

Susan, where do you see the garden in another twenty years?

SMT The garden has grown so dramatically, in footprint and design, over the past two decades. For the next two decades, I envision great programmatic growth within the garden exploring opportunities found in the variety of spaces that we created—the amphitheater, the pavilion, individual lawns and tree groves. We want to be able to activate the landscape even more fully with music, performance, dance, and other ways to create connections between these different artistic mediums and the landscape.

WB I feel as though we have truly enjoyed a confluence of talent over the years. We really do have a wonderful group of people who have contributed. Most importantly, the garden will keep inspiring new art lovers. That's very gratifying, because we're enriching people's lives. That's the most important.

This interview has been edited for length and clarity.

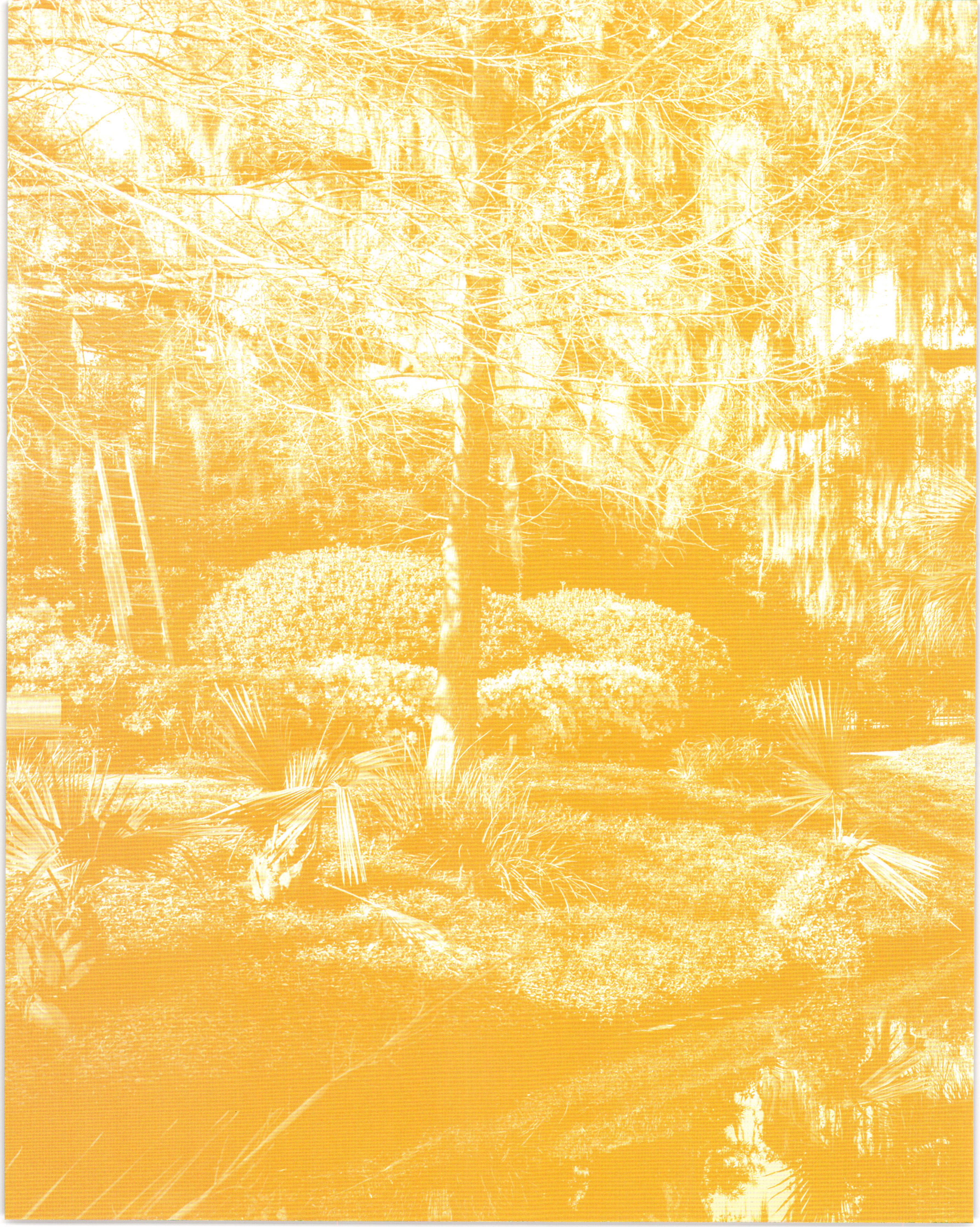

A—B

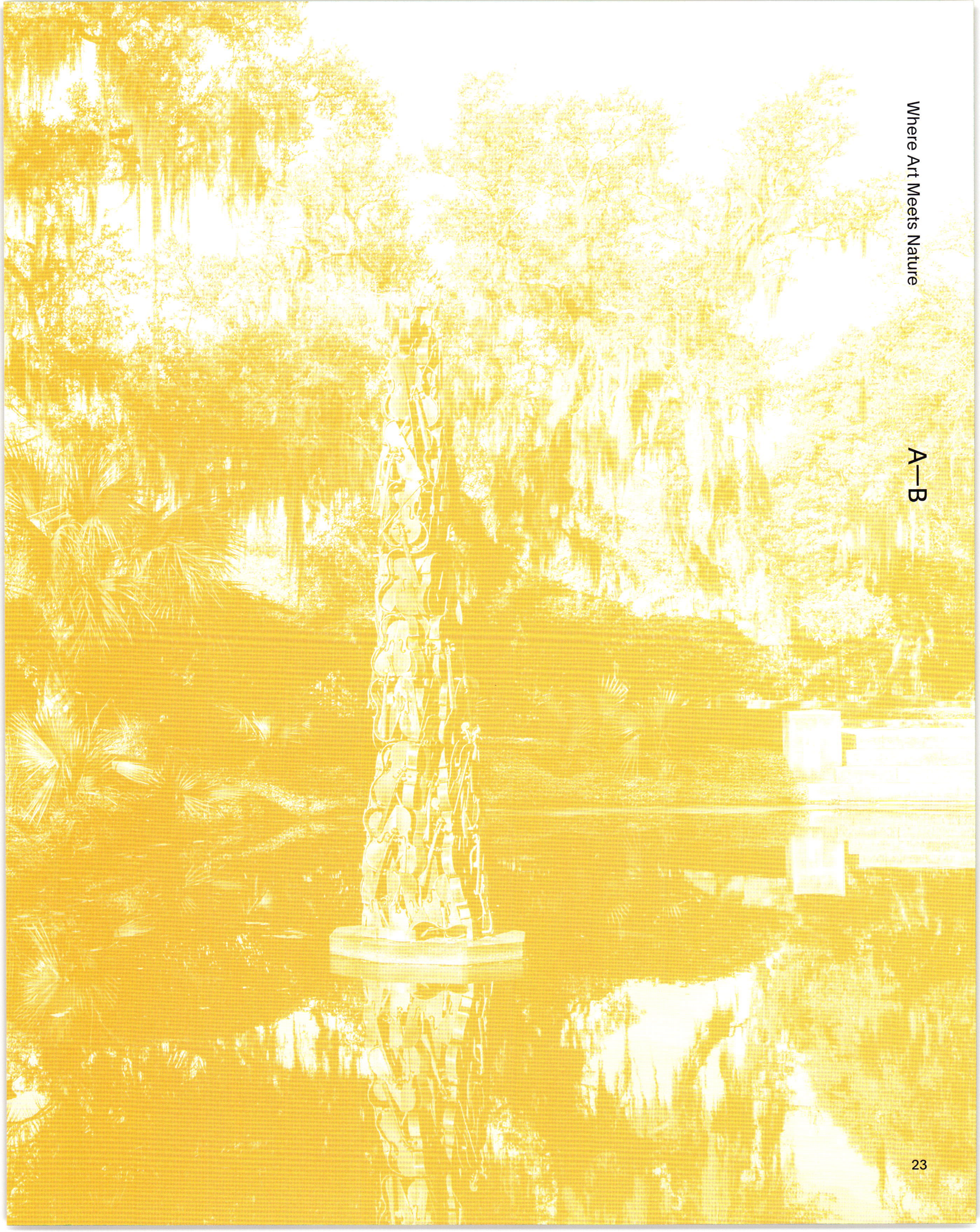

Yaacov Agam

Open Space, 1970

A pioneer in the Kinetic and Op art movements, Yaacov Agam (b. 1928) was born in Rishon Le-Zion, present-day Israel, and studied in Jerusalem at the Bezalel Academy. In 1946, he moved to Zurich and traveled extensively throughout Europe before settling permanently in Paris in 1951, where he enrolled at the Atelier d'Art Abstrait and the Académie de la Grande Chaumière. During these years, he came into contact with the aesthetic conventions in Western art, including the Bauhaus pedagogy of design, philosophies of color theory, and Wassily Kandinsky's (1866–1944) principles on mysticism. The son of a rabbi, Agam was exposed to religion at a young age, further enhancing his interest in the junctions of art and spirituality. These encounters coalesced to inform Agam's creative vision and animate his experiments in optical perception and chromatic energy.

Agam rose to prominence in Paris in the 1950s, first with a solo presentation at Galerie Craven in 1953 and later for his participation in the trailblazing exhibition *Le Mouvement* at Galerie Denise René in 1955. The influential group show presented early examples of Kinetic art and featured international artists such as Alexander Calder (1898–1976), Marcel Duchamp (1887–1968), and Victor Vasarely (1906–1997), placing Agam among the leading voices of the Parisian art scene. Over several decades, Agam focused on producing lithographs, paintings, and moving sculptures that reflected his fascination with perceptual phenomena through an emphasis on light, mobility, and sound. His art often implicates the viewer in examining the visual and subjective properties of motion and space. Agamograph—one of the artist's most famous series—sees the artist employing a technique called lenticular printing to convey shape-shifting compositions and impressions of depth and progress.

Open Space epitomizes Agam's long-standing investigations into geometry, movement, and pictorial acuity. Executed in stainless steel and relying on simple linear forms, the sculpture is comprised of broken rectangular outlines that intersect when viewed from different perspectives. Thus, the viewer's active physical involvement becomes a vital component of the sculpture. Denying the work a static identity and challenging traditional compositions, Agam demonstrates art's ability to transcend visual barriers and social contexts.—*JM*

Stainless steel, 108 × 96 × 96 in. (274.3 × 243.8 × 243.8 cm),
Gift of the Sydney and Walda Besthoff Foundation, 1998

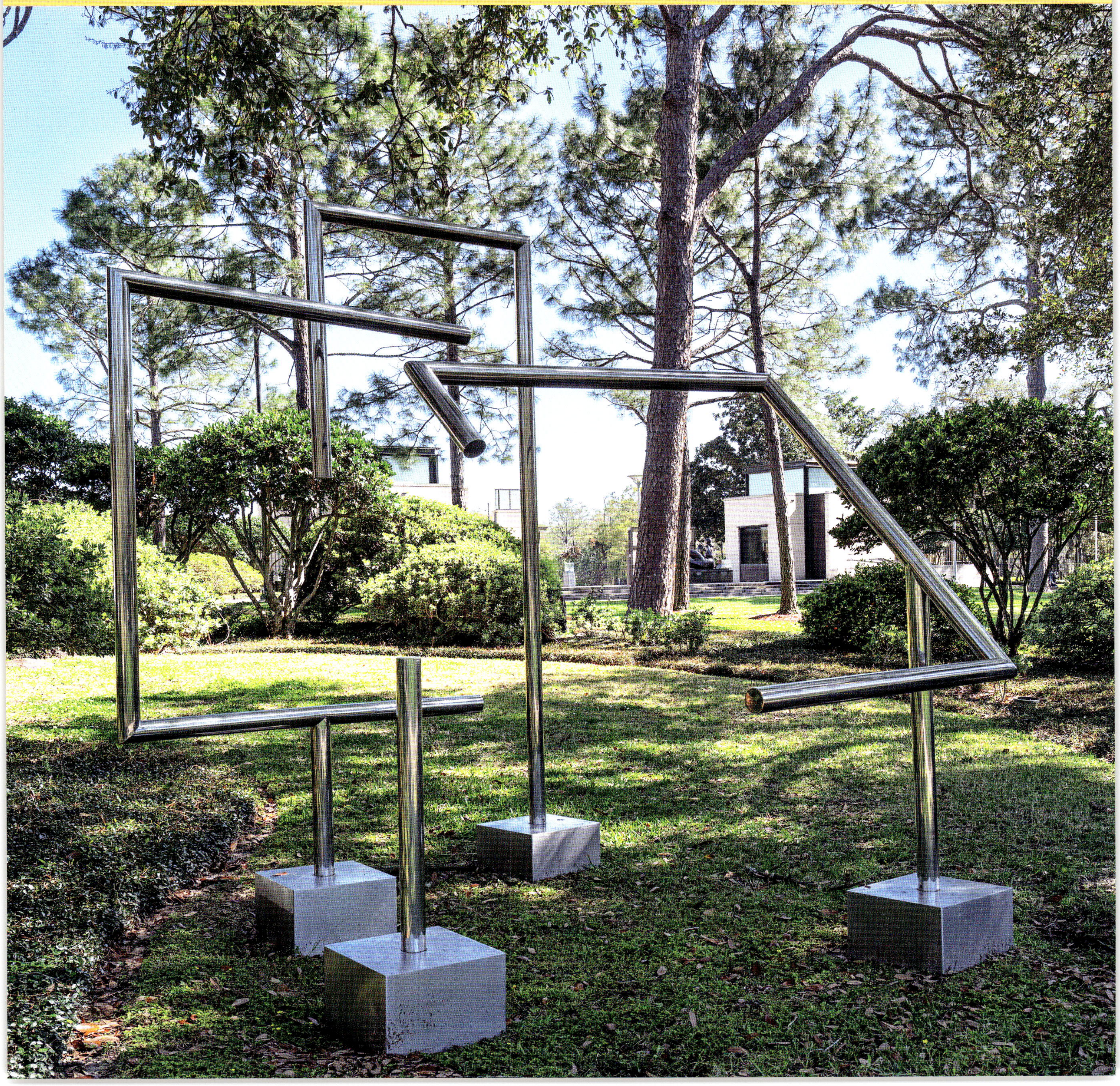

Siah Armajani

Elements #29, 1991

Collaged from incongruous fragments of architecture, *Elements #29* epitomizes Siah Armajani's (1939–2020) lifelong interest in public spaces. An ardent believer that quality of maintenance and care for the public domain serves as a litmus test for the health of a democracy, Armajani dedicated much of his artistic practice to understanding how "public" is defined architecturally. In his hands, the doorway leading to nowhere and the grounded balcony railing become political metaphors for the frustration of unrealized potential, the slug of bureaucracy, and the fractured idealism of citizens and immigrants caught in-between. Born out of his earlier series, Dictionary for Building,—which similarly combines recognizable building components such as staircases, arches, and doorways into impossible and unnavigable tabletop sculptures—Armajani's series Elements has an eerie edge. Entirely inaccessible, the spaces nevertheless appear inviting, thus transforming them into a searing critique of both the physical and metaphorical public sphere.

Born in Tehran in Iran, Armajani's family sent him to Minneapolis in 1960, fearing their son could face retribution for the political collages he had been making and distributing throughout the previous decade. He enrolled in Macalester College in Minnesota, immersing himself in the writings and philosophy of Ralph Waldo Emerson (1803–1882) and Walt Whitman (1819–1892), as well as early studies in art history. In the Russian Constructivist's conception of the artist-worker, Armajani found a welcome historical precedent for his burgeoning ideas around the practical role of the artist and art in society. Public space gradually became his artistic domain, and he approached it with critical distance. He constructed civic sculpture and infrastructure—such as the Irene Hixon Whitney Bridge (1988) at the Walker Art Center in Minneapolis—that proposed a hospitable public sphere and an engaged political body as necessary building blocks for a functioning democracy. Through time, Armajani's practice became increasingly political, and the Elements series is in many ways emblematic of his light, but insistent critical touch. Never an outright rebuke, Armajani's work nonetheless evokes an ineffable, melancholy tinge of what could be, while persistently and optimistically advocating for a realization of the democratic ideal.—*MH*

Painted steel, 114 × 80 × 79 ½ in. (289.6 × 203.2 × 201.9 cm),
Gift of the Sydney and Walda Besthoff Foundation, 1998

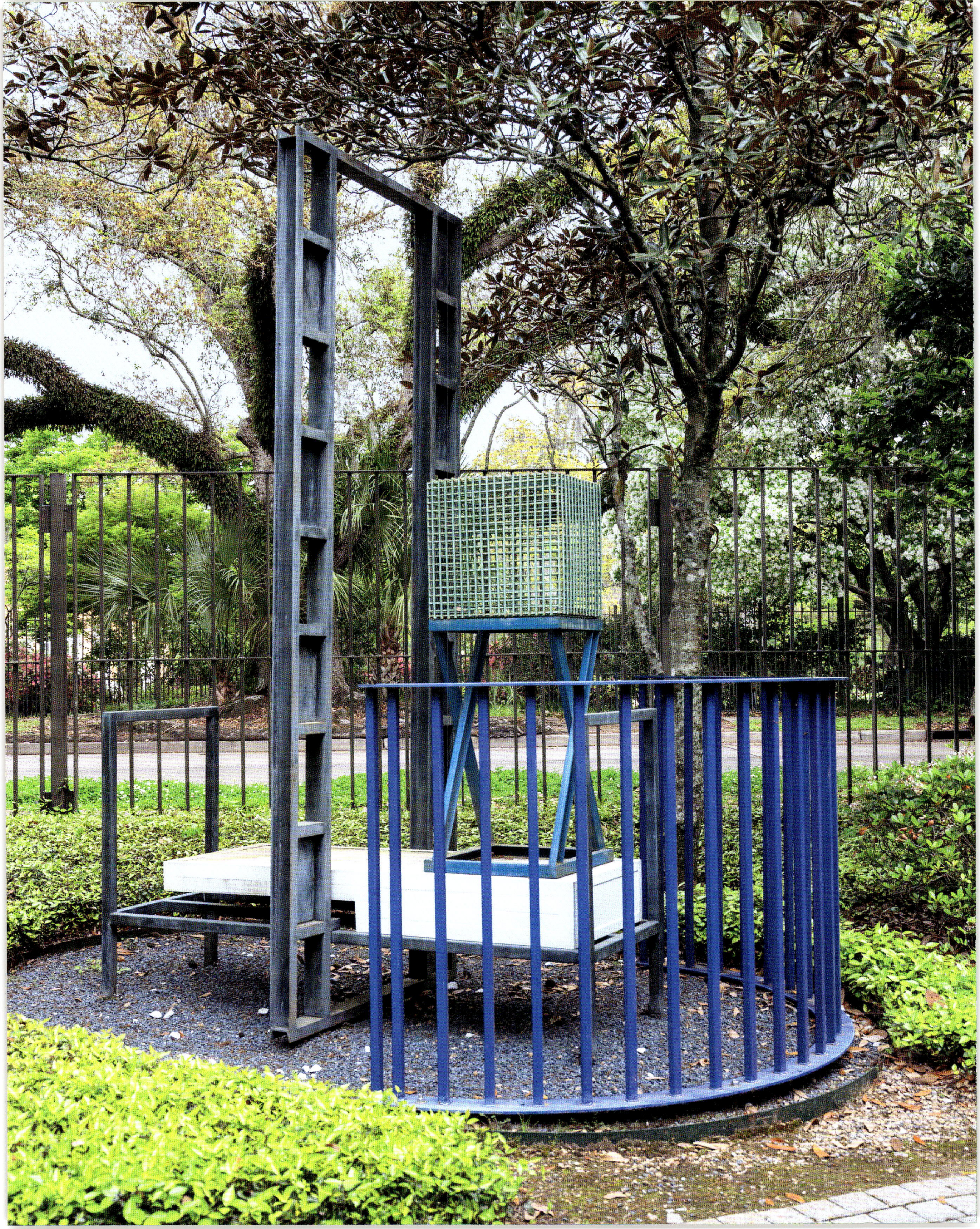

Arman (Armand Fernandez)

Pablo Casals's Obelisk, 1983

A founding figure of Nouveau Réalism, Arman (1928–2005) is widely recognized for his combine-like sculptures of objects, often instruments, assembled as collages, perched in display cases, or cast in clear resin. Inspired equally by the Dadaist Readymades of Marcel Duchamp (1887–1968) and the punchy, provocative critiques of modern consumer culture rippling through both British and American Pop art, Arman used found, discarded, and destroyed objects to investigate the aura of things. While his practice frequently critiques humanity's ever-increasing and thoughtless consumption, Arman's best works also speak to a profound love of objects and their expressions.

Born Armand Pierre Fernandez—the artist famously dropped the *d* from his name following a printing error on a gallery handout—Arman's father was an antique dealer and amateur cellist who instilled in him a respect and appreciation for artistry that would go on to inform his best works. Drawing on Cubist assemblage and the collaged works of Kurt Schwitters (1887–1948), Arman initially began as a painter before moving into three-dimensional space, eventually adding instruments directly into his works. In 1959, he began making freestanding sculptures, rocketing to notoriety the following year for a solo gallery exhibition titled *Le Plein*, or "the full," in which he filled the space floor to ceiling with refuse, making it so that the work could only be viewed through the windows from the city street below.

Constructed from cast bronze cellos, the towering form of *Pablo Casals's Obelisk* mimics the monuments of ancient Egypt and serves as an homage to the renowned Spanish cellist Pablo Casals (1876–1973). An outspoken opponent of Franco's fascist government, Casals boycotted music between 1946 and 1950, when global leaders' recognition of Franco passively legitimized his regime. Installed above the pond in the Besthoff Sculpture Garden, the work relies on the iconic Arman motif of the string instrument, overlapping in a lofty accumulation that speaks paradoxically to the power of art and the latent hum of materialism.—*MH*

Bronze, 20 ft. × 84 in. × 60 in. (6.1 m × 213.4 cm × 152.4 cm), Gift of the Sydney and Walda Besthoff Foundation, 2000

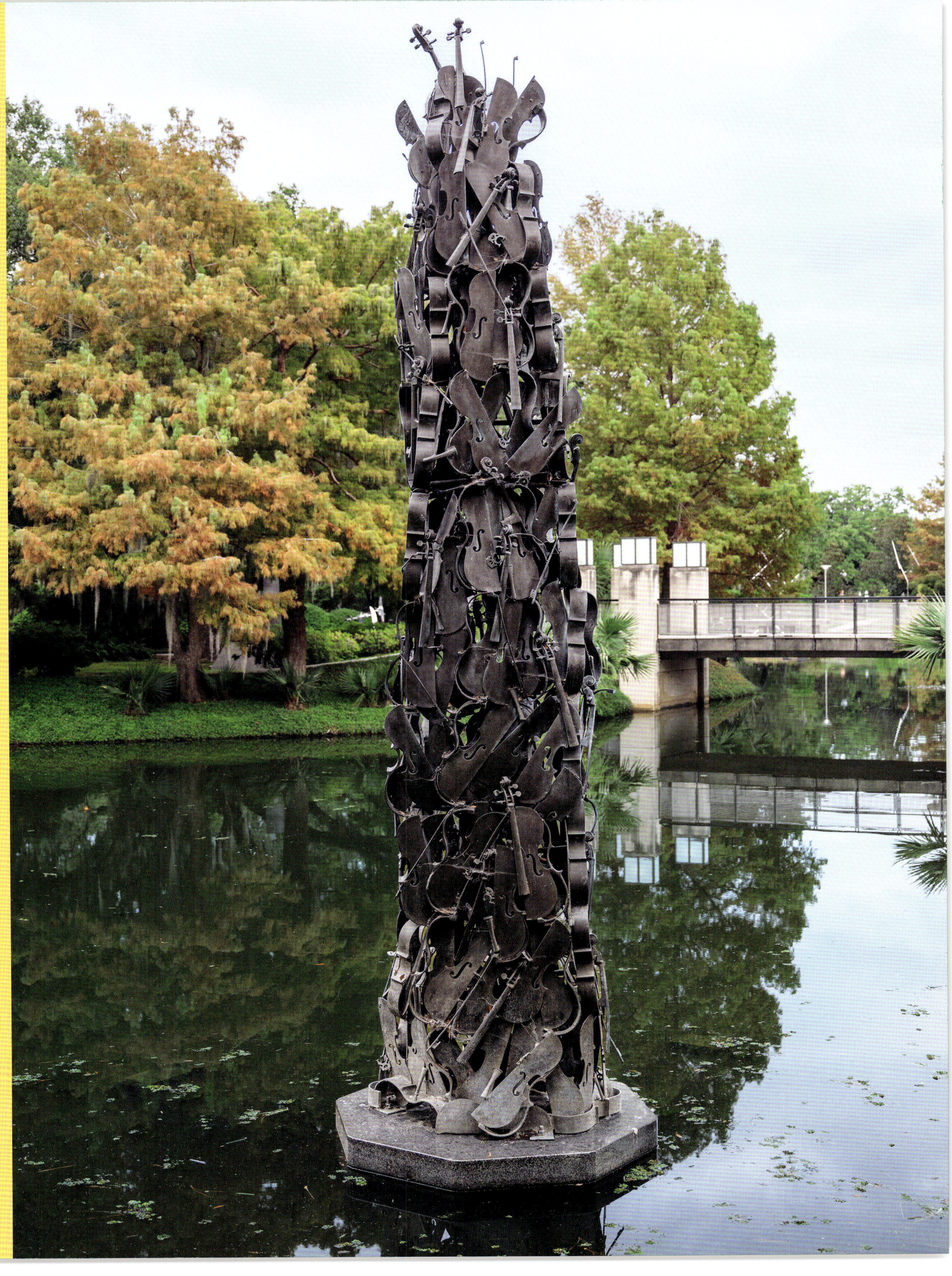

Saul Baizerman

Aurora, 1950–57

Although born and raised in Russia, Saul Baizerman (1889–1957) built his artistic career in the United States. Fleeing his home country as a teenager to escape imprisonment, in 1910 he settled in New York, where he remained for the rest of his life. A prolific artist, Baizerman became widely acclaimed for his figurative sculptures realized through an arduous and inventive use of pounded metals. The son of a harness maker, he was introduced to hammering practices at an early age. He studied in Paris and toured Europe in the 1920s, where he came across the art of Julio González (1876–1942), whose soldering and cutting skills motivated Baizerman and developed his vision. While casting small bronze statuettes, Baizerman discovered his preference for an unusual technique, which involved beating sheets of copper simultaneously from both sides to achieve natural impressions of light, shadow, and motion. He continued to master this method for the remainder of his career, interrogating the human body and its parallels to environmental occurrences. Having been directly involved with the Bolshevik Revolution, his subjects and methods were also socially and politically engaged. Though he is perhaps more recognized for illustrating female nudes in heroic proportions, Baizerman also produced a series of sculptures of urban labor, amplifying his allegiance to and solidarity with the working class.

Baizerman often looked to Greco-Roman mythology and biblical themes to title his monuments. *Aurora* is named after the Roman goddess of dawn, who re-created herself each morning for the sun's arrival. While not explicitly engaging with the environment in this piece, Baizerman depicts a personification of a naturally occurring phenomenon through subject. *Aurora* is captured emerging from a plain of copper and assertively pacing forward. Despite an unassuming semblance, her pose emanates an elegant confidence. The headless representation calls to mind ancient statues, also contributing to a feeling of timelessness. Although it appears heavy, the figure is actually comprised of a thin metal sheet and a hollow interior, a structure used regularly by the artist. *Aurora* was created just years before Baizerman's death and epitomizes a unique dynamic between the human form, movement, and material.—*JM*

Hammered copper, 78 × 35 × 20 in. (198.1 × 88.9 × 50.8 cm), Gift of the Sydney and Walda Besthoff Foundation, 2000

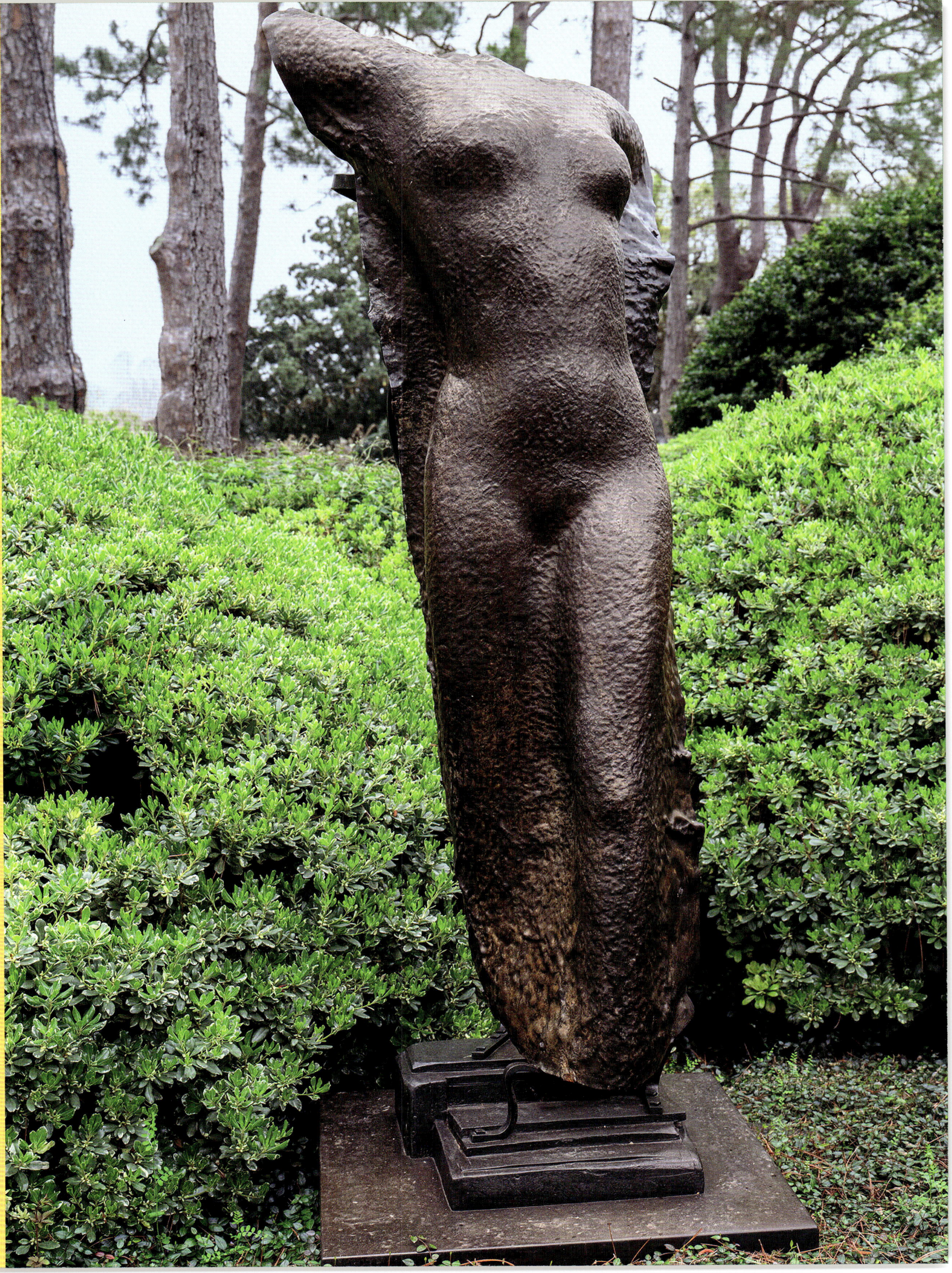

Leonard Baskin

Ruth and Naomi, 1978

Although working in various media, American artist Leonard Baskin (1922–2000) was best known for his lithographs, woodcuts, and illustrations fuelled by questions of mortality, the human spirit, and individual introspection. The son of a rabbi, Baskin articulated imagery from biblical sources and imbued his work with a steadfast concern for Jewish heritage and culture, employing various materials and techniques to draw upon history, mythology, and poetry.

Despite working at the height of the Abstract Expressionist movement, Baskin focused almost exclusively on figurative and representational art, examining the complexities of ethics and integrity. His allegorical depictions are characterized by a distinct linear quality and simple yet lyrical compositions. During his studies at the Yale University School of Fine Arts, he founded the Gehenna Press—one of the first fine art presses in the United States. He illustrated several books, including *Crow* (1970), a collection of poems by Ted Hughes, for which he rose to national prominence for his artistic work. Though perhaps most celebrated for his illustrations and works on paper, Baskin was also hired to create numerous private and public sculptures, including a Holocaust memorial in Ann Arbor, Michigan, and a bas-relief at the Franklin Delano Roosevelt Memorial in Washington, D.C.

In the displayed bronze sculpture, the artist portrays two women from the Old Testament, Ruth and Naomi. Following the death of Naomi's husband and sons, Naomi returns to Bethlehem to be with her daughter-in-law, Ruth, who faithfully elects to stay with Naomi and secure the family's prospects by marrying Boaz. The biblical story underscores themes of loyalty and devotion, demonstrating that honorable acts can lead to resolute blessings. Baskin captures the two female figures in an embrace of shared grief, their legs united by a single base. Deploying traditional casting techniques and recalling Sumerian statuary and German Expressionist sculpture, Baskin emphasizes the overall structure of the monument rather than focusing on intricate details, highlighting the symbolic and religious significance of collective unity over individual desires.—*AMT*

Bronze, 52 × 30 × 14 in. (132.1 × 76.2 × 35.6 cm), Gift of the Sydney and Walda Besthoff Foundation, 1998

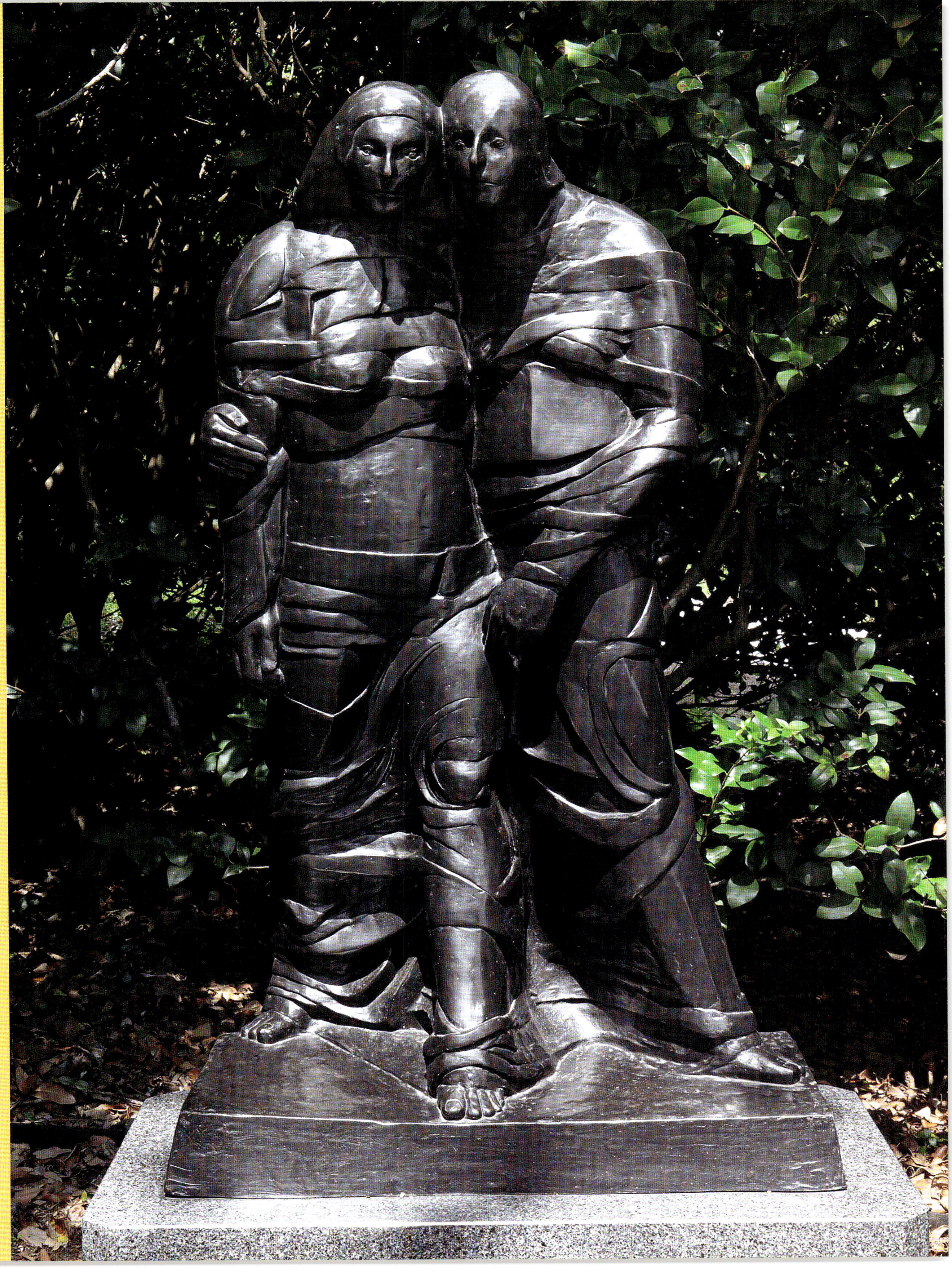

Larry Bell

Pacific Red (VI), 2016–17

The cube has preoccupied Larry Bell (b. 1939) since the early 1960s. After attending the Chouinard Art Institute from 1957 to 1959, now the California Institute of the Arts, Bell explored cubic forms in paintings, into which he incorporated reflective materials such as glass and mirror. He created constructions and reliefs, but soon moved away from the wall altogether, adopting a freestanding sculptural vocabulary predicated on the manipulation of light through glass. Through his pioneering use of the vacuum tank, Bell was able to apply a mineral coating to glass that changed its color, reflectivity, and transparency.

Aside from a brief interlude in New York in the mid-1960s that included successful gallery exhibitions and contact with Minimalist contemporaries, Bell has been a staple of the Los Angeles art scene and a key figure in the Light and Space movement. Rooted in improvisations of industrial technology, his glass sculptures have the clean, hard-edged, Finish Fetish look likewise associated with the work of fellow Southern California artists Robert Irwin (1928–2023) and Doug Wheeler (b. 1939). The trio showed together in *Three Artists from Los Angeles* (1970) at the Tate Gallery in London—both Bell's first museum exhibition in Europe and a pivotal moment in the reception of West Coast art abroad. Since the early 1970s, he has divided his time between his studio in Venice, California, and his home in Taos, New Mexico.

Finding infinite possibilities in glass, for several decades, Bell has experimented with different gradients, degrees of opacity, and subtle color variations. Earlier nested boxes—*Made for Arolsen (Pink/Blue)* (1992/2016), for example—anticipated the format of *Pacific Red (VI)*, whose walls are the same dimensions. The featured artwork was one of six laminated glass cube-like structures, each without faces on the top and bottom, that debuted as part of the 2017 Whitney Biennial in New York. The optically seductive sequence was arranged on one of the museum's roof terraces as a line of different tinted shades of red.—*AMT*

Opposite and following spread
Glass, 72 × 96 ¼ x 96 ¼ in. (182.9 × 244.5 × 244.5 cm), overall, Museum purchase with funds provided by Sydney and Walda Besthoff, 2019

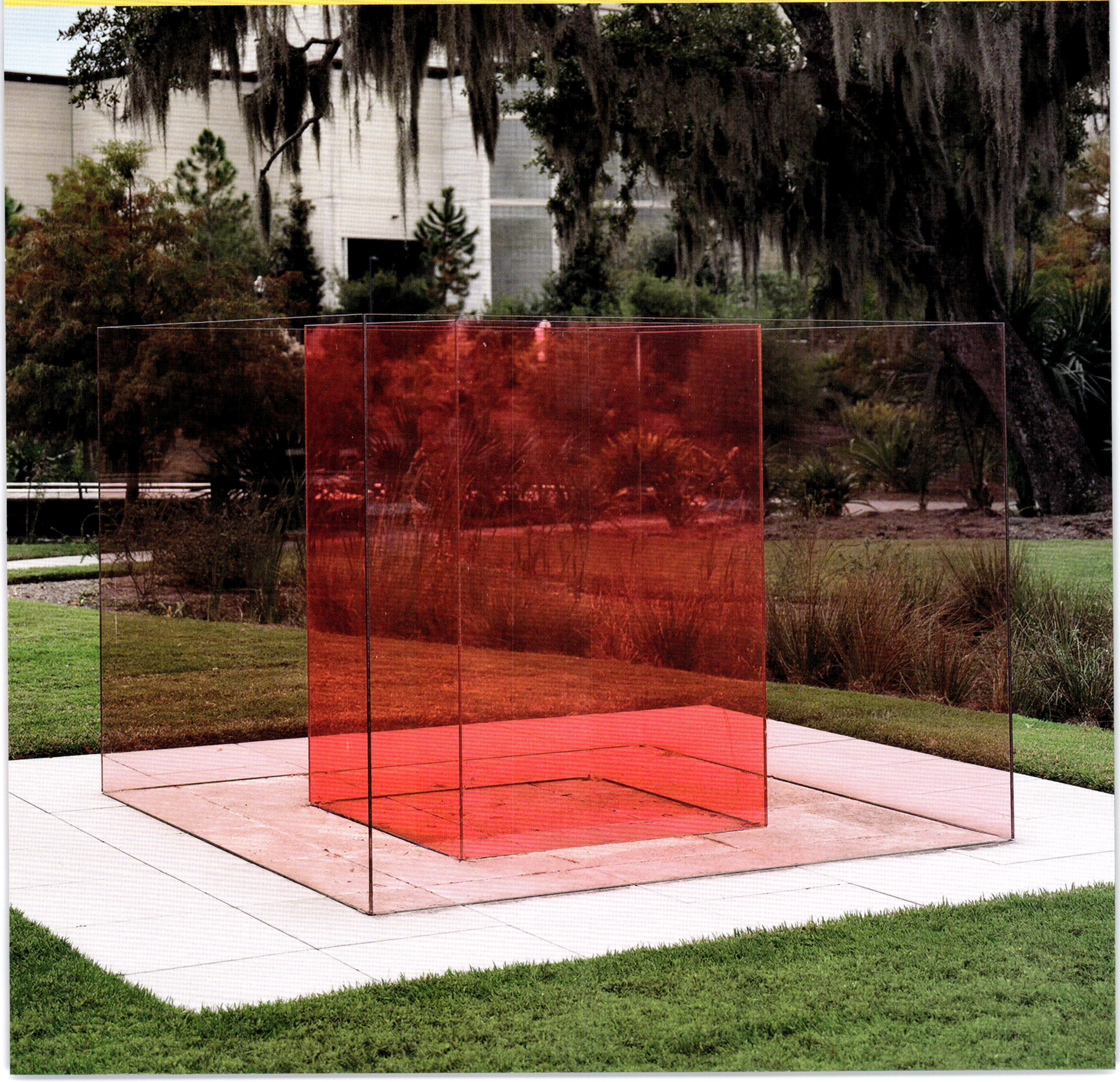

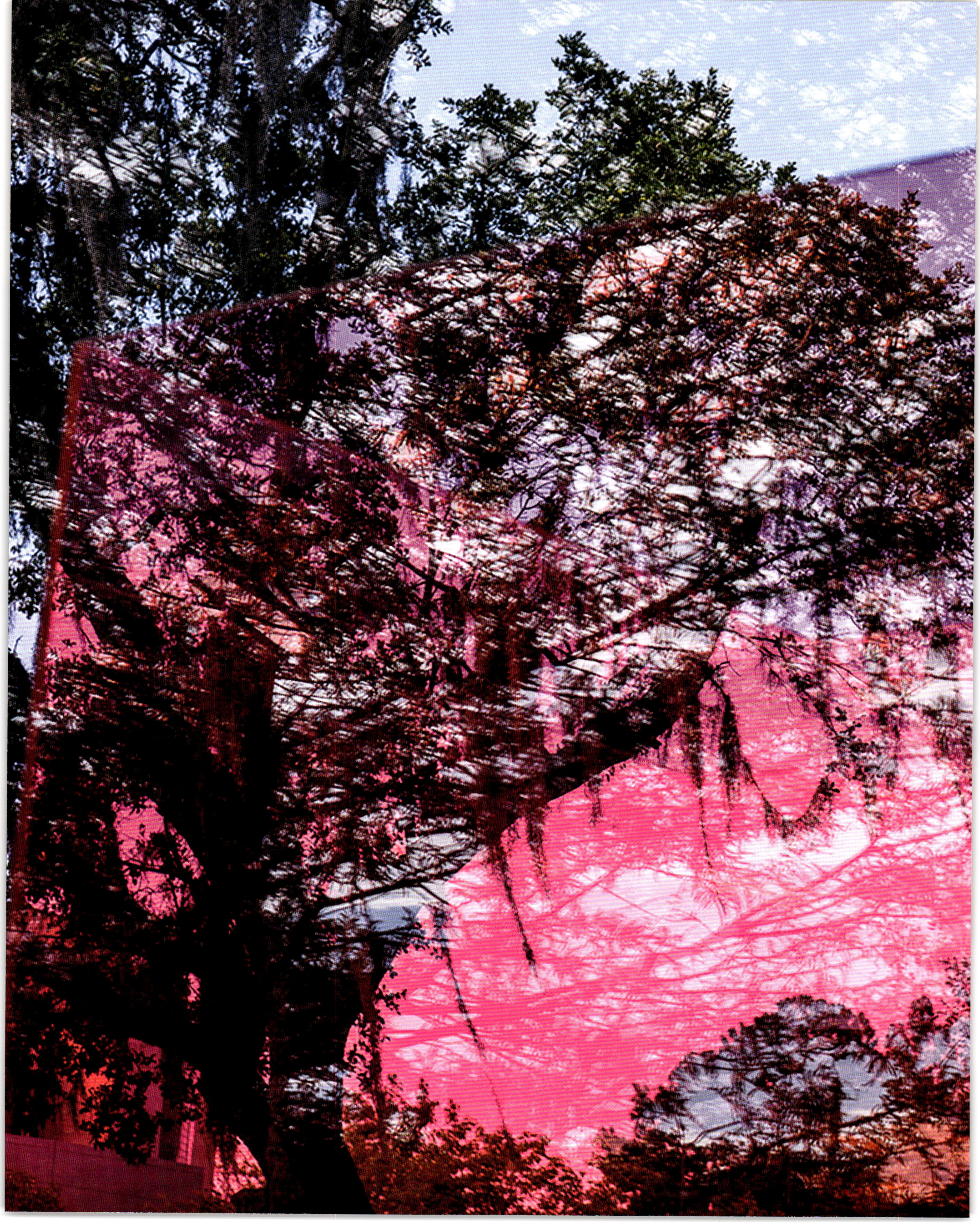

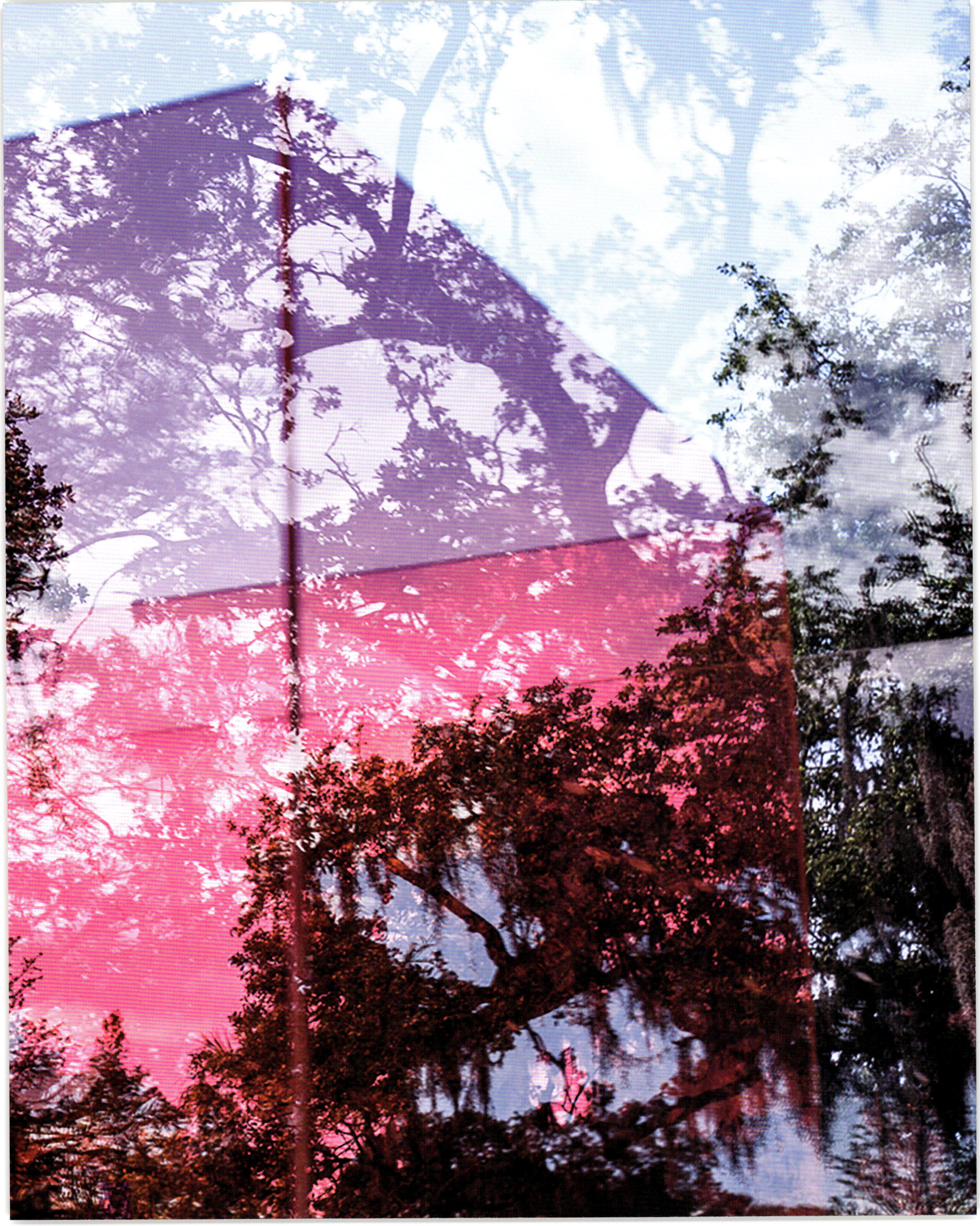

Fernando Botero

Mother and Child, 1988

With a distinguished career spanning more than five decades, Fernando Botero (1932–2023) has grown to become one of the most important artists in Latin America. Playfully inflating the volume of his subjects to explore meaning, Botero's depictions of robust characters have become instantly recognizable across both the art world and mainstream culture. Although perhaps most famous for his buoyant pictures of bourgeois life set against Colombian folkloric backdrops, Botero also portrayed prominent figures and politicians in his singular style, infusing his paintings with satirical connotations and humorous undertones. Such politically engaged work functioned to condemn the indelible effects of violence and human rights violations in his native country and abroad.

Born in Medellín, Colombia, to a humble family, Botero was initially enrolled to become a bullfighter but found a passion for drawing and painting in the bullfighting ring instead. As a teenager, he not only sold his early watercolor scenes of the spectacular sport but also illustrated them for local newspapers. At the age of nineteen, following his first solo exhibition of paintings, Botero relocated to Bogotá, Colombia. He traveled to Europe the subsequent year, namely to Spain, Italy, and France, where he encountered paintings by Old Masters and Renaissance titans such as Giotto (d. 1337) and Francisco de Zurbarán (1598–1664). In addition, Botero visited Mexico in 1955, and the monumentality of the Muralist movement left a lasting mark on his creative vision. In 1960, Botero moved to New York, at a time when gestural abstraction was favored over representation. Though Botero asserted he never formally studied fine arts, all of these experiences contributed to the development of his figurative practice.

Botero began producing bronze sculptures after settling in Paris in the early 1970s. Since then, the artist's massive statues have been widely exhibited around the world. *Mother and Child* reinterprets a biblical scene in Botero's signature rotund style and echoes the iconic religious imagery that the artist might have seen in Italy. In this work, the voluptuous mother stands gracefully atop a significantly smaller woman, holding an animated baby. The child reaches towards her head, yet the woman's facial expression is apathetic, creating tension between the figures. Her body is bare, and despite the epic scale and erect posture, the form emits a tender sense of fertility. Through this contrasting representation of feminine strength and maternity, Botero joins countless artists who have aspired to deconstruct conventional readings of motherhood.—*JM*

Bronze, 81 × 45 × 27 in. (205.7 × 114.3 × 68.6 cm),
Museum purchase, Sydney and Walda Besthoff Foundation Fund, 2003

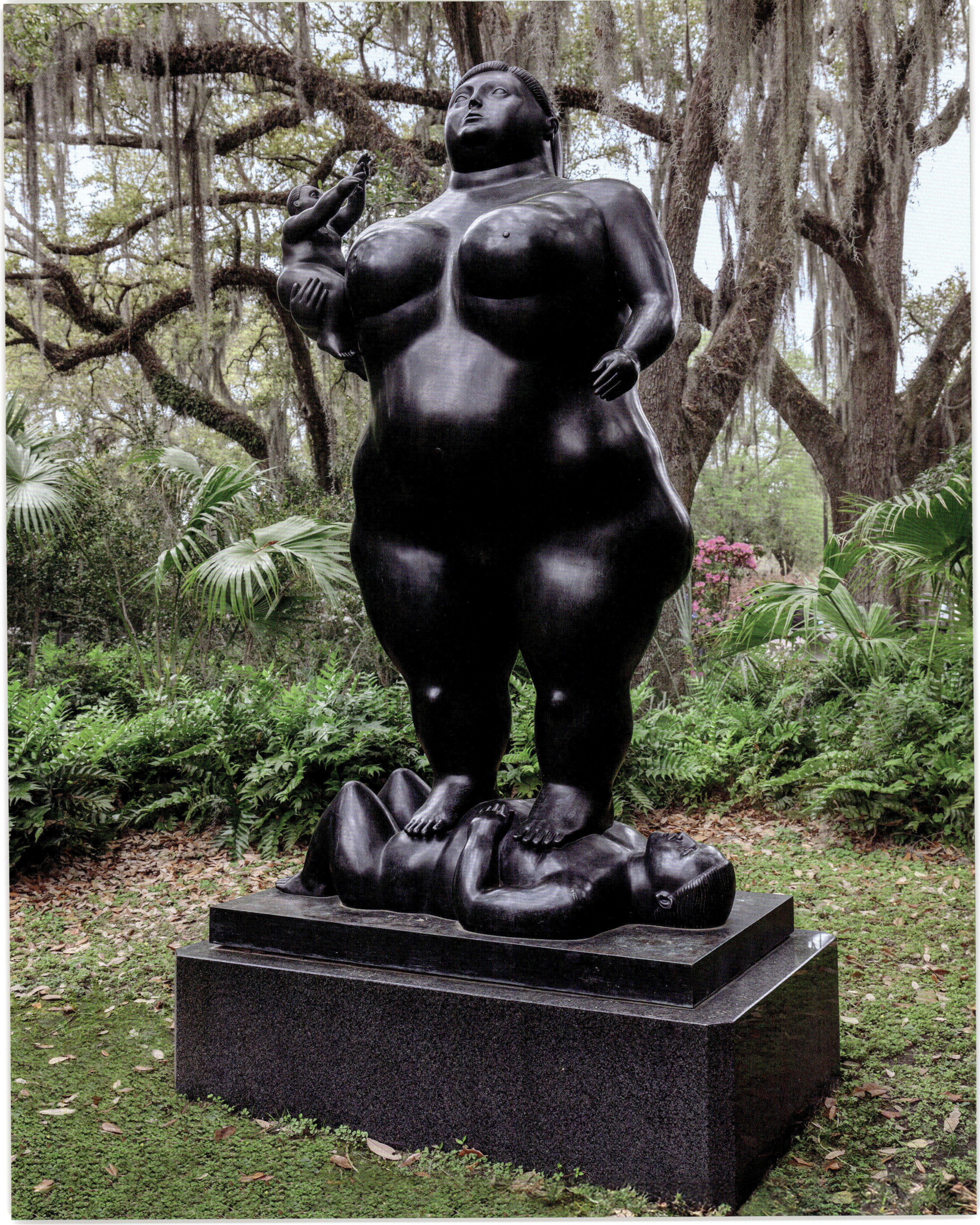

Antoine Bourdelle

Hercules the Archer, 1909; cast 1947

A collaborator and friend of Auguste Rodin (1840–1917)—whose work is also featured in the Besthoff Sculpture Garden—and teacher of Alberto Giacometti (1901–1966), French artist Antoine Bourdelle (1861–1929) achieved commercial success throughout his lifetime, however, his art goes unnoticed today compared to that of his contemporaries. He is best known for his work as a sculptor and educator, surveying forms and subjects inherited from medieval statuaries and Roman mythology. Arriving in Paris in 1884 after studying at the École des Beaux-Arts in Toulouse, France, he exhibited in the Salons des Artistes Français in 1885 and the Exposition Universelle in 1889.

Working as Rodin's assistant and marble carver for fifteen years, his practice acquired a similar craftsman-like approach. For years, he was dedicated to a series of more than eighty tormented busts of the legendary composer Ludwig Van Beethoven (1770–1827). Yet after receiving acclaim for *Hercules the Archer* in 1910, he moved away from realist conventions and focused on neoclassical themes and aesthetics. Emphasizing flat and simplified shapes, he completed critical public commissions both in France and abroad, including reliefs for Théâtre des Champs-Élysées in Paris in 1912 and *Monument au général Alvéar* in Buenos Aires in 1926. Through these monuments, the artist showed his interest in building on the classical tradition to traverse sculpture and architecture.

Hercules the Archer is Bourdelle's most eminent piece and required seven years to complete. Inspired by the Greco-Roman myth of Hercules and his twelve labors, the artist chose to depict the sixth, where the hero is tasked with slaying man-eating Stymphalian birds. Bourdelle cast Hercules from the body of military chief and accomplished sportsman Paul Gustave André Doyen-Parigot (1864–1916), although he changed the head at the model's request to stay anonymous. The original piece was commissioned by patron and financier Gabriel Thomas (1854–1932). This particular version was cast after Bourdelle's death, under the guidance and direction of his widow, Cléopâtre Sevastos (1882–1972), who was also a sculptor.—*JM*

Bronze, marble, 98 × 94 ¾ x 49 ½ in. (248.9 × 240.7 × 125.7 cm), Museum purchase, 1949

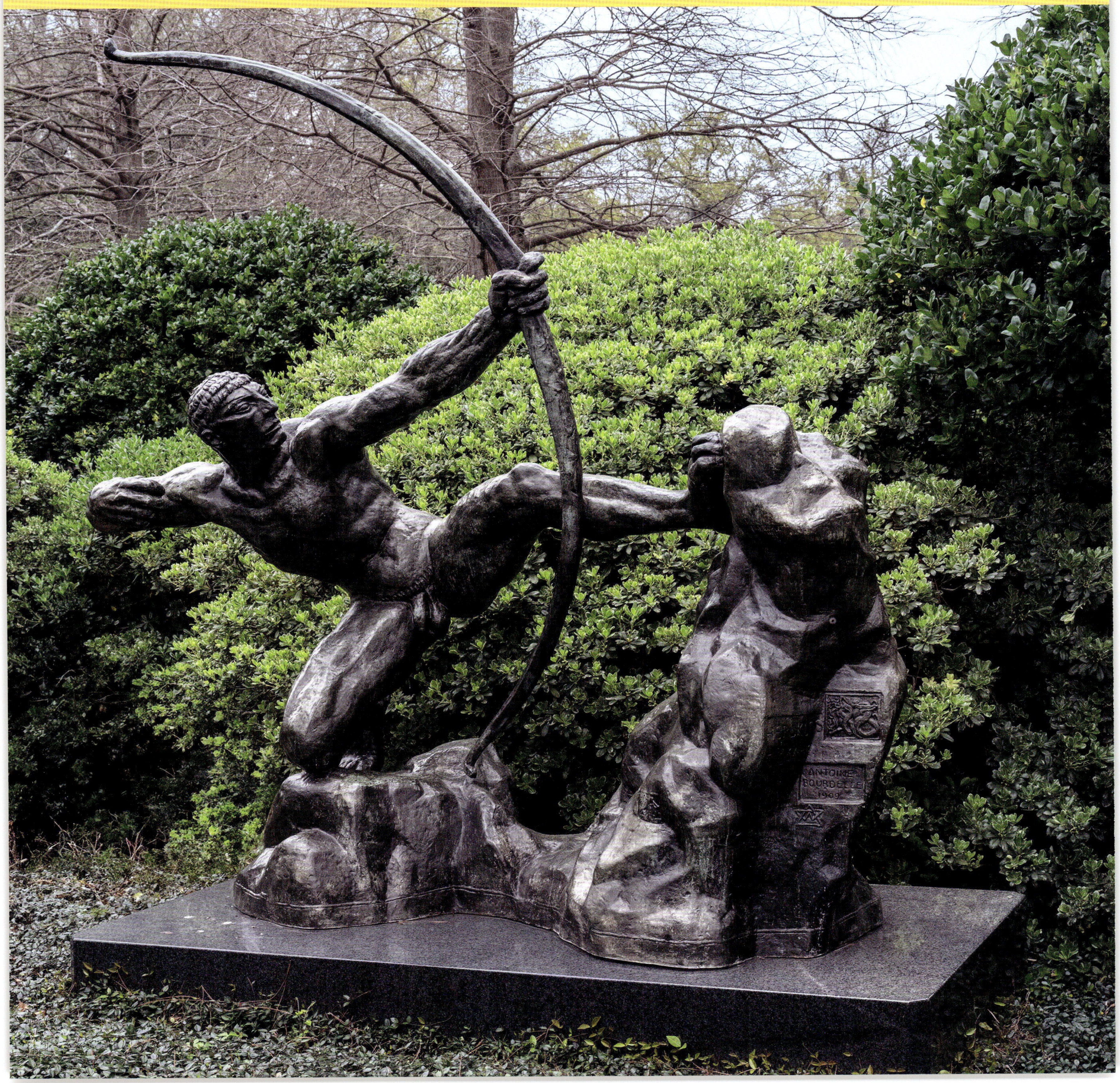
ANTOINE
BOURDELLE
1909

Louise Bourgeois

Spider, 1996

From brooches of a few inches to sculptures rising more than thirty feet, later in her life, metal spiders became Louise Bourgeois's (1911–2010) central motif. Although her career officially began in the late 1930s, the artist had a notable burst of activity in 1994, while in her eighties. That year alone she produced multiple versions of single spiders in either iron, bronze, or steel, also sometimes adding glass or marble. They sat on tabletops and filled rooms. Bourgeois had dabbled with arachnid forms in two ink and charcoal drawings from 1947, but the forceful emergence of this protagonist in the 1990s constituted a new direction. She increased the size of her spiders, built environments for them, made them from cloth, and set them outside. As was so often the case in Bourgeois's work, the creature was bound up in personal history, family dynamics, and heightened emotional states. In her telling, the spider, an industrious weaver, alluded to her mother, a tapestry restorer. But motherhood for Bourgeois, an artist known for plumbing the deepest depths of psychological tensions and traumatic memories, was seldom one-sided. *Spider* is then, reassuring and protective while simultaneously menacing and ferocious—a symbol of both feminine creativity and destruction.

The French-born Bourgeois had a penchant for anthropomorphism and ambivalence, which can be found in many of her sculptures, the earliest of which date to the late 1940s. After training in Paris, she moved to New York in 1938 to study at the Art Students League and focused, for a time, on painting and printmaking. "The two dimensions do not satisfy me," Bourgeois said in a 1993 BBC interview, "I have to have the reality given by the third dimension." The idiosyncratic and varied nature of her sculpture demonstrates her ability to repeatedly reinvent herself. Often exploring psychosexual ideas, alluding to the body, and underpinned by Surrealism, Bourgeois's practice encompassed virtually every type of material. A brief sample: animistic wood slats in the 1940s and 1950s; globular wax, latex, and plaster protuberances in the 1960s; voluptuous and headless marble figures in the 1980s; and stuffed fabric dolls and masks in the 2000s. The immensity of her fraught libidinal world continues to astound.—*AMT*

Bronze, 127 in. × 24 ft. 7 in. × 23 ft. 2 in. (326.4 cm × 7.5 m × 7.1 m), overall, Museum purchase, Sydney and Walda Besthoff Foundation Fund, 1998

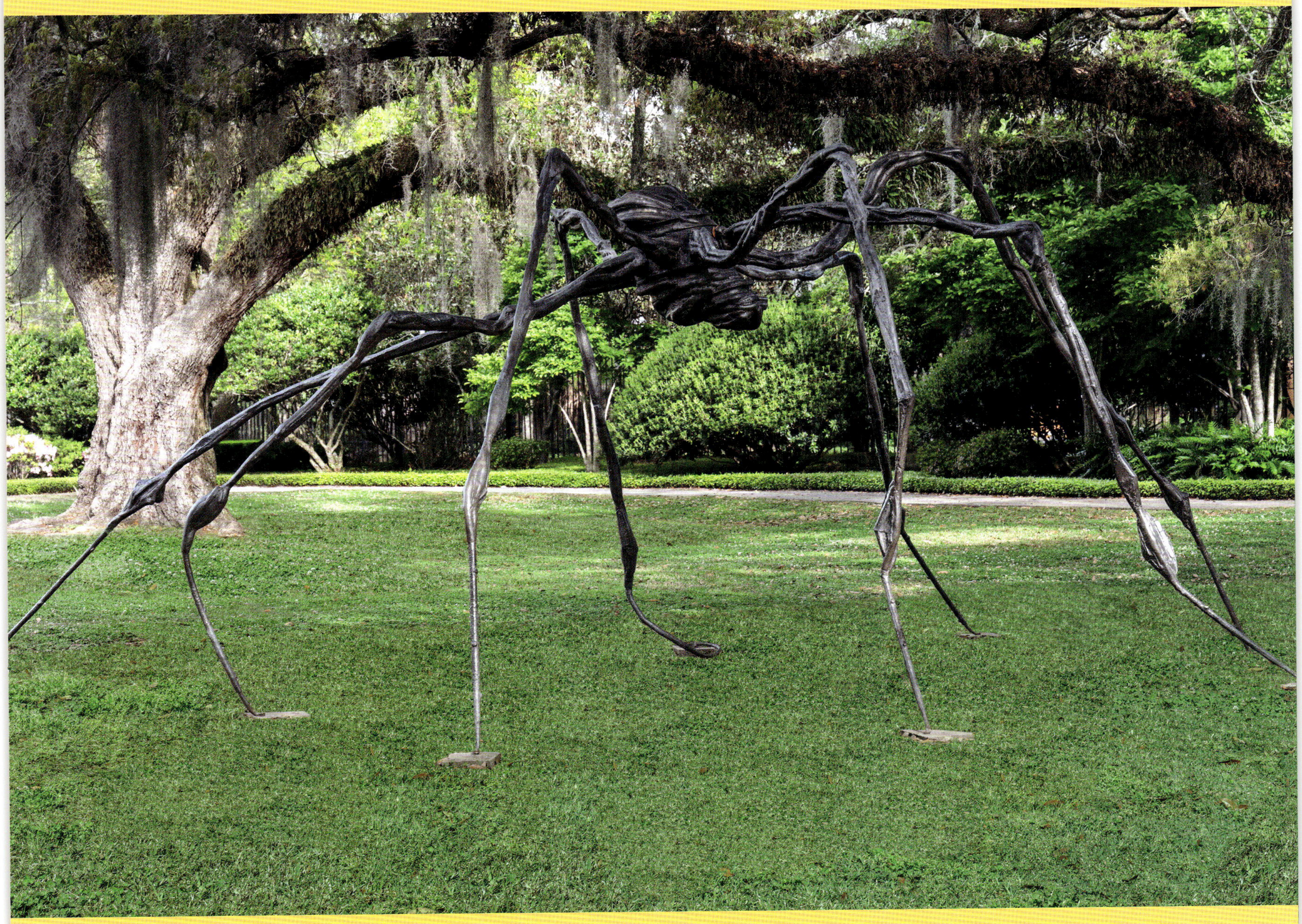

Carol Bove

Mood, 2017

The curved and crinkled sculptures of Bove (b. 1971) can feel both beautiful and brutal, from appearing like the contortions of a gymnast to the wreckage of a catastrophe. Her subtle manipulations of stainless steel are aided by various mechanisms and tools, some purpose-built for her precise and personal process. Bove's light touch makes a solid and strong material look soft and supple. She has noted a resemblance to fabric and paper and in this vein calls her most plentiful body of work of the last decade "collage sculptures." The twisted tubes and beams achieve an almost uncanny effect—one sometimes enhanced by their bright colors and playful titles, such as *Horse Lover* (2016), *Baby Fat Pants* (2017), and *The Séances Aren't Helping* (2021), the last of which was a set of four sculptures commissioned for niches on the facade of the Metropolitan Museum of Art in New York.

The Swiss-born, California-raised Bove moved to New York in the early 1990s and in 2000, earned an undergraduate degree in education from New York University, where she would go on to teach some years later. Bove's assemblages of books, shells, and other found objects displayed on wall-mounted shelves recall the lyrical conglomerations of ephemera in Joseph Cornell's (1903–1972) midcentury boxes. In 2012, Bove started what she calls her "glyphs," tubular white powder-coated steel corkscrews and loops. These sculptures—*Celeste* (2013), which was shown on the High Line in New York City, and *Mood*, among them—have been compared to noodles and Slinkys. The exuberance of these associations belies the tedious labor involved in producing the immaculate finish of each sculpture. Bove's surface treatment, that is, seems to change how the material it covers is understood. In addition to her sculptural practice, Bove has helped curate exhibitions devoted to artists Felix Gonzalez-Torres (1957–1996) at the Foundation Beyeler in Basel in 2010 and Harry Smith (1923–1991) at the Whitney Museum of American Art in New York in 2023.—*AMT*

Opposite and following spread
Stainless steel, urethane paint, 93 ½ × 124 × 95 in. (237.5 × 314.9 × 241.3 cm), overall, Museum purchase with funds provided by Sydney and Walda Besthoff, 2020

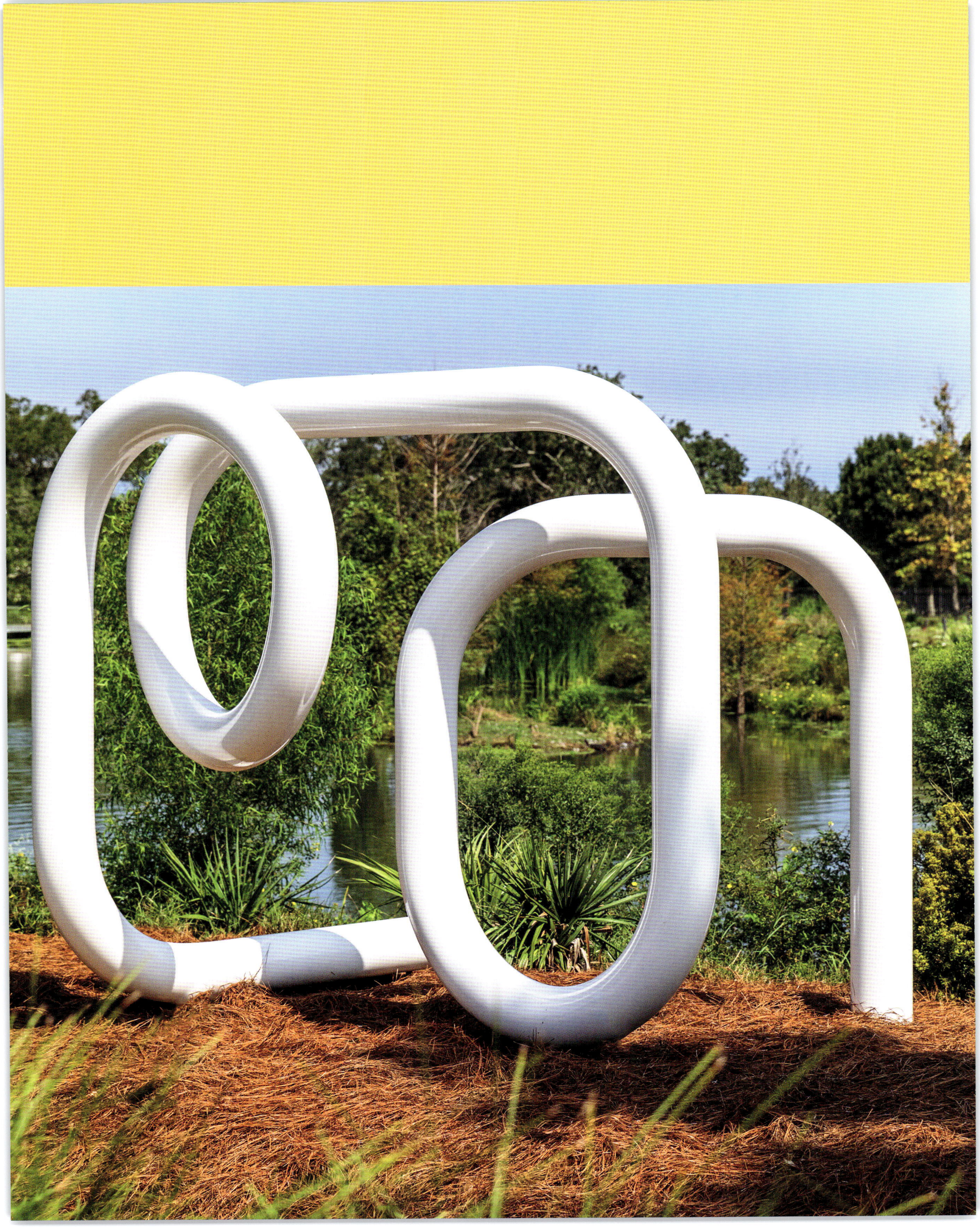

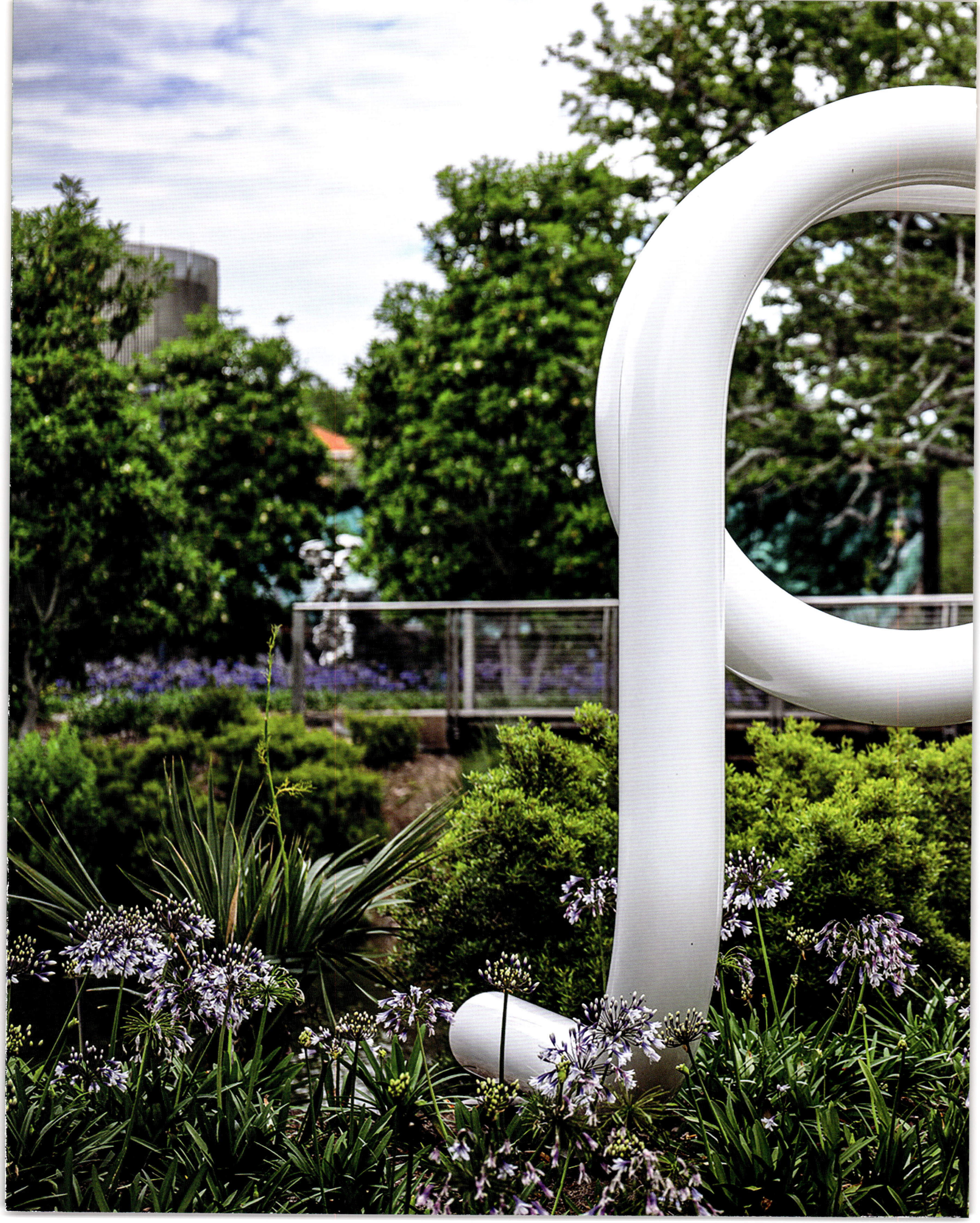

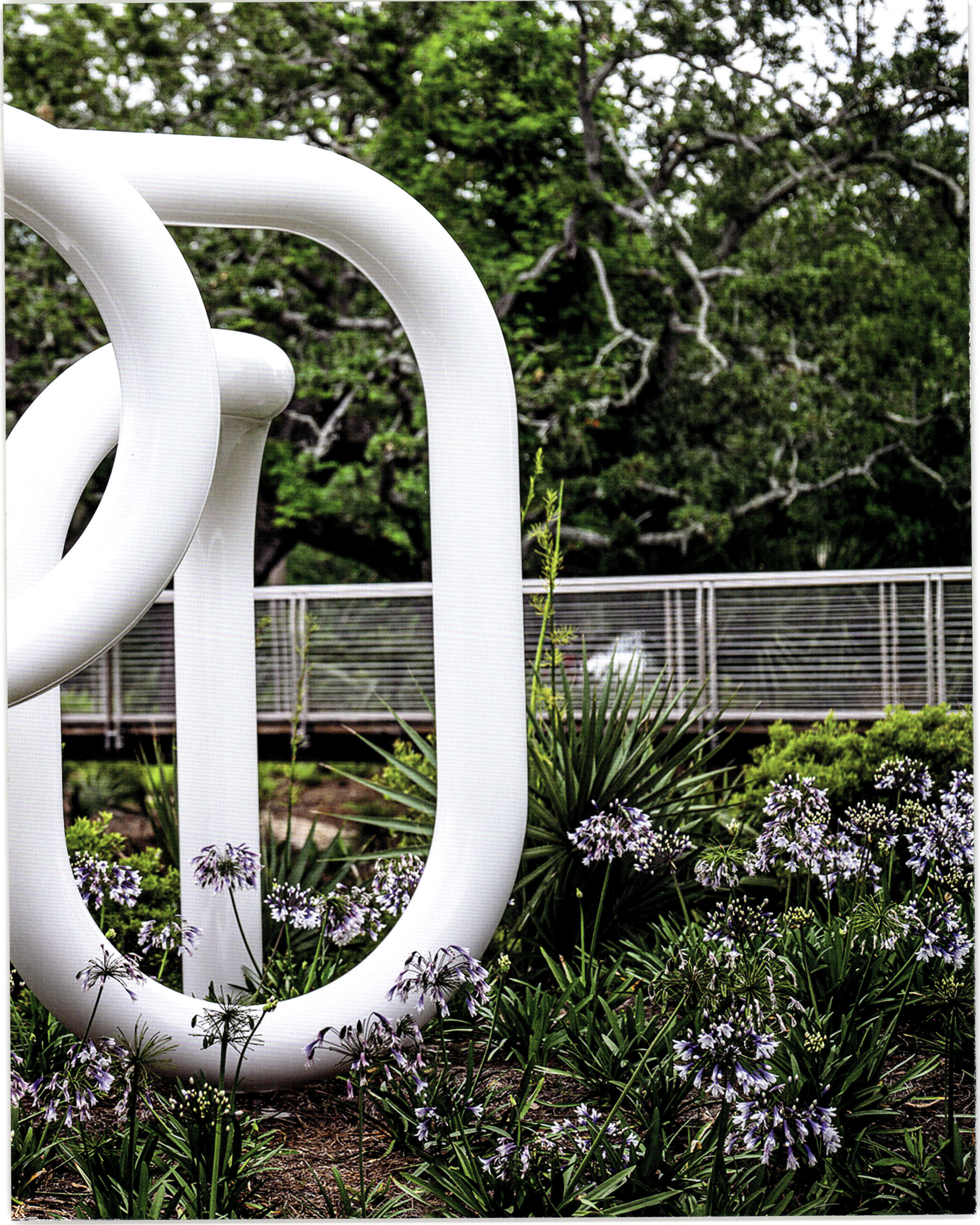

Fritz Bultman

Barrier (Big Bird), 1967–70

New Orleans-born Fritz Bultman (1919–1985) charted an artistic path from an early age. Inspired by the example of modernist painter Morris Graves (1910–2001), who stayed with his family when he was just thirteen, Bultman studied in Munich, Chicago, and then with Hans Hoffman (1880–1966) in New York during the 1930s and early 1940s. He lived between Manhattan and Provincetown, Massachusetts, for much of his career, which initially, largely comprised gestural and pictographic abstract paintings. Part of the so-called Irascibles, the group of twenty-eight New York School painters who protested the exclusionary policies of the Metropolitan Museum of Art in 1950, he was the only member hailing from the South. Bultman missed their famous 1951 *Life* magazine photo shoot because, thanks to a grant from the Italian government, he was studying the art of bronze casting in Florence.

After this first foray into sculpture, Bultman moved effortlessly between various media until his death. For Bultman, his method of making sculptures was closely related to that of collage: he began by creating small wax pieces, which he then joined together and cast via the lost-wax process. He received grants, including a Fulbright, that helped fund the considerable expense of casting bronzes. In 1976, an exhibition of his bronze sculptures from 1963 to 1975 opened at Martha Jackson Gallery in New York. In the catalog, Bultman reflected, "My sculpture is the geometry of interior sensations, the intuitive engineering of making weight levitate, of overcoming the inertia of gravity." *Barrier (Big Bird)*, which was included in the show, captures that sense of flight or upward momentum. The dual spread of undulating curves suggests both cresting waves and upraised wings, with areas of the surface roughly worked to approximate feathering. As here, Bultman often addressed themes of aggression and rebirth through depictions of totemic forms, spanning from the elemental to the bodily. The terms "wave" and "barrier" appear in many of the titles of his collages, paintings, and sculptures in subsequent decades. Bultman was the subject of a major retrospective at the New Orleans Museum of Art in 1993.—*AMT*

Bronze, 66 × 96 × 30 in. (167.6 × 243.8 × 76.2 cm), overall,
Gift of Jeanne Bultman, 2003

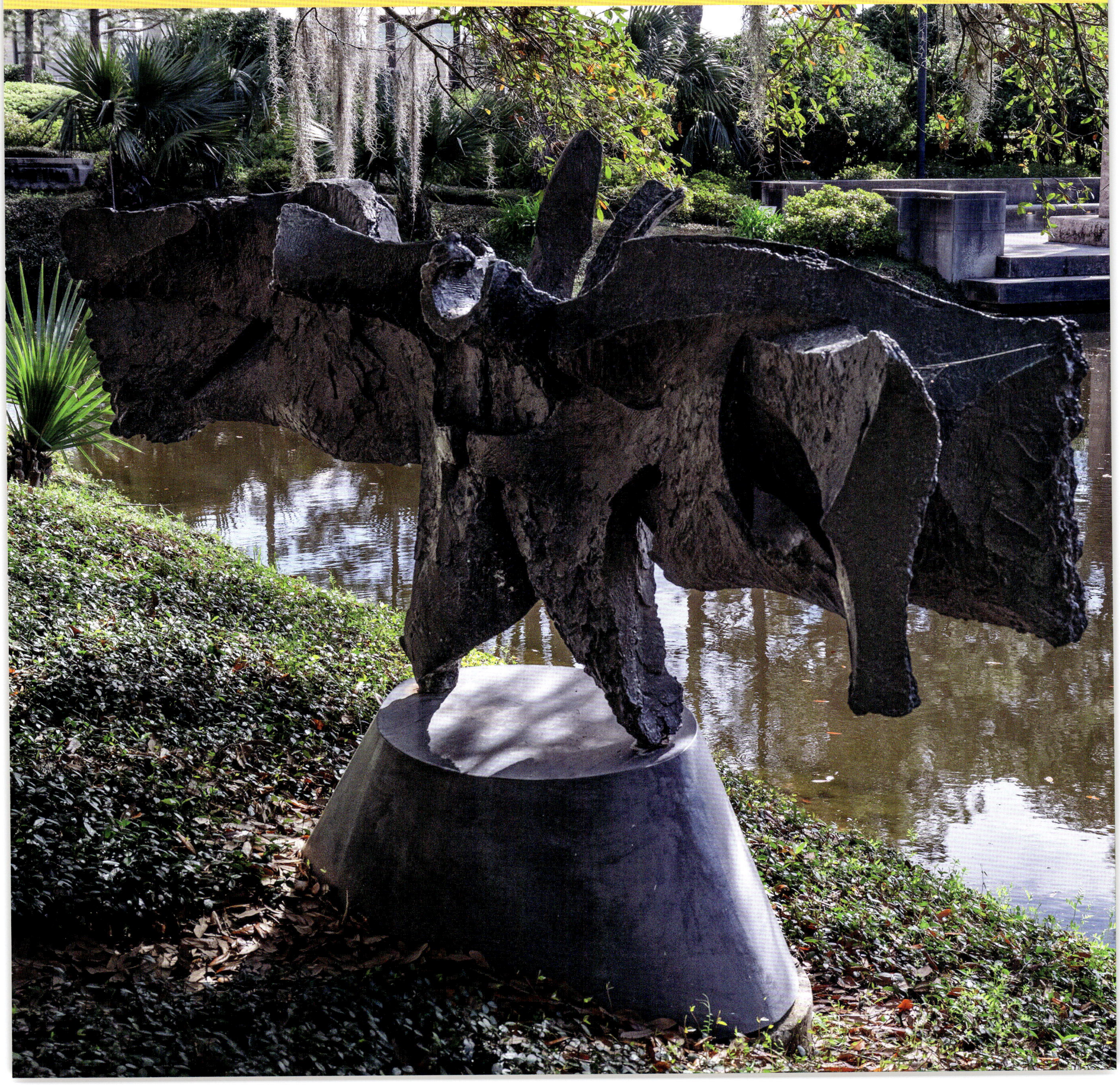

Scott Burton

Right Angle Chairs (Pair) and *Settee*, 1983

Renowned for his hybrid objects understood as both sculpture and furniture, Scott Burton (1939–1989) ardently believed in the value of public art, and explicitly made pieces designed to be touched, interacted with, and used. Informed by early performance art, his practice strove to counter the Minimalist sculpture that was, at the time, emerging as central to the New York art scene. Burton leaned into the provocative edge of his sculptures, preferring to blur the line between informal functionality and austere art object.

After a brief stint studying painting at Hans Hofmann's (1880–1966) art school in Provincetown, Massachusetts, Burton moved to New York, where he worked as a critic and editor for *Art in America* before committing to making art full time. His earliest pieces were staged performances, but quickly, the artist found himself more interested in his audience than his own actions. Observing how his viewers encountered his performance and interacted with the space sparked a fascination with interactivity that would go on to inform the rest of his artistic output. In the early 1970s, Burton started experimenting with furniture-as-sculpture, which he first used as props before abandoning his performance practice to prioritize the objects completely. As he moved deeper into working physically with materials, Burton continually fought back against the austerity and distance of Minimalism. Inclined instead to underscore the utility of his objects, Burton adopted the Russian Constructivist view that the social function of an artwork was of prime importance to its essence.

Staged like a welcoming living room in the Sydney and Walda Besthoff Sculpture Garden, Burton's stone seats invite the viewer to linger. Inspired equally by the design objects of De Stijl artist Gerrit Rietveld (1888–1964), and the classic silhouette of an Adirondack chair, the seating featured here is comprised of interlocking blocks of polished granite. As familiar objects, they encourage interaction, providing a resting place and transforming this public space into one of leisure. As with much of Burton's sculpture, the piece serves a clear use—designed to put the body at ease, the stone seats argue for artwork to have both an action and an aesthetic.—*MH*

Opposite and following spread
Granite, chairs: 38 × 20 × 27 in. (96.5 × 50.8 × 68.6 cm); settee: 34 × 57 × 36 ½ in. (86.4 × 144.8 × 92.7 cm), Gift of the Sydney and Walda Besthoff Foundation, 1998

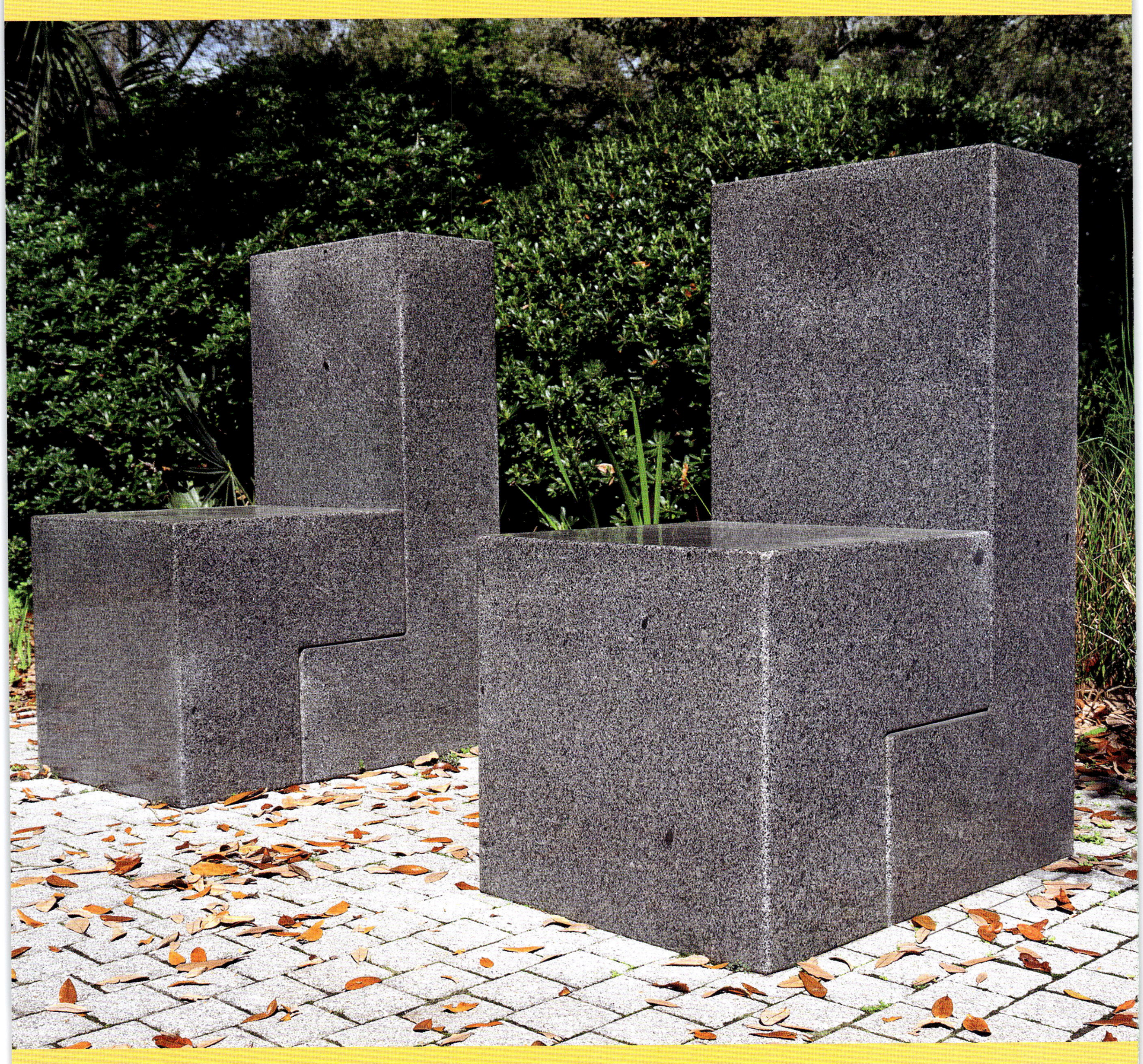

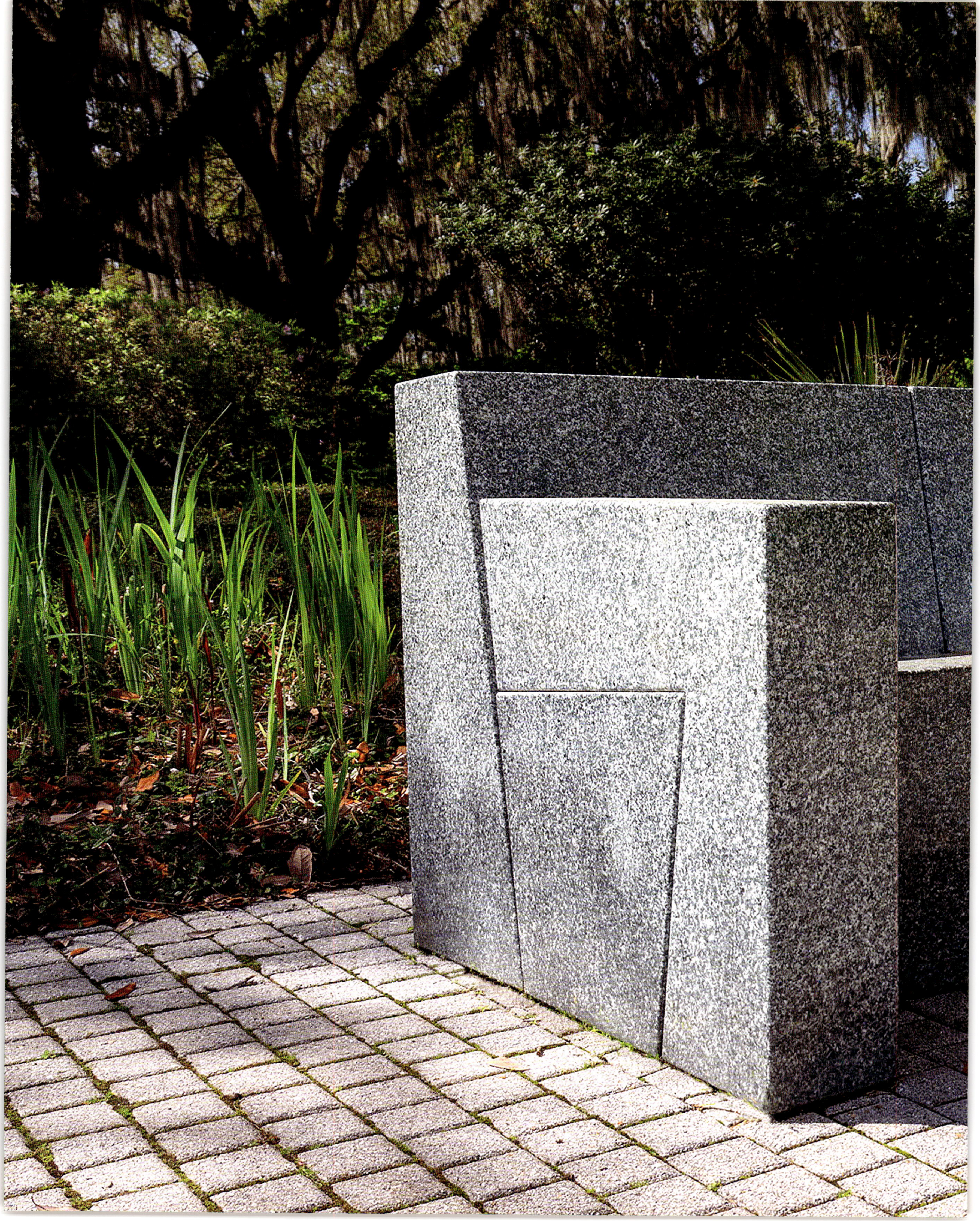

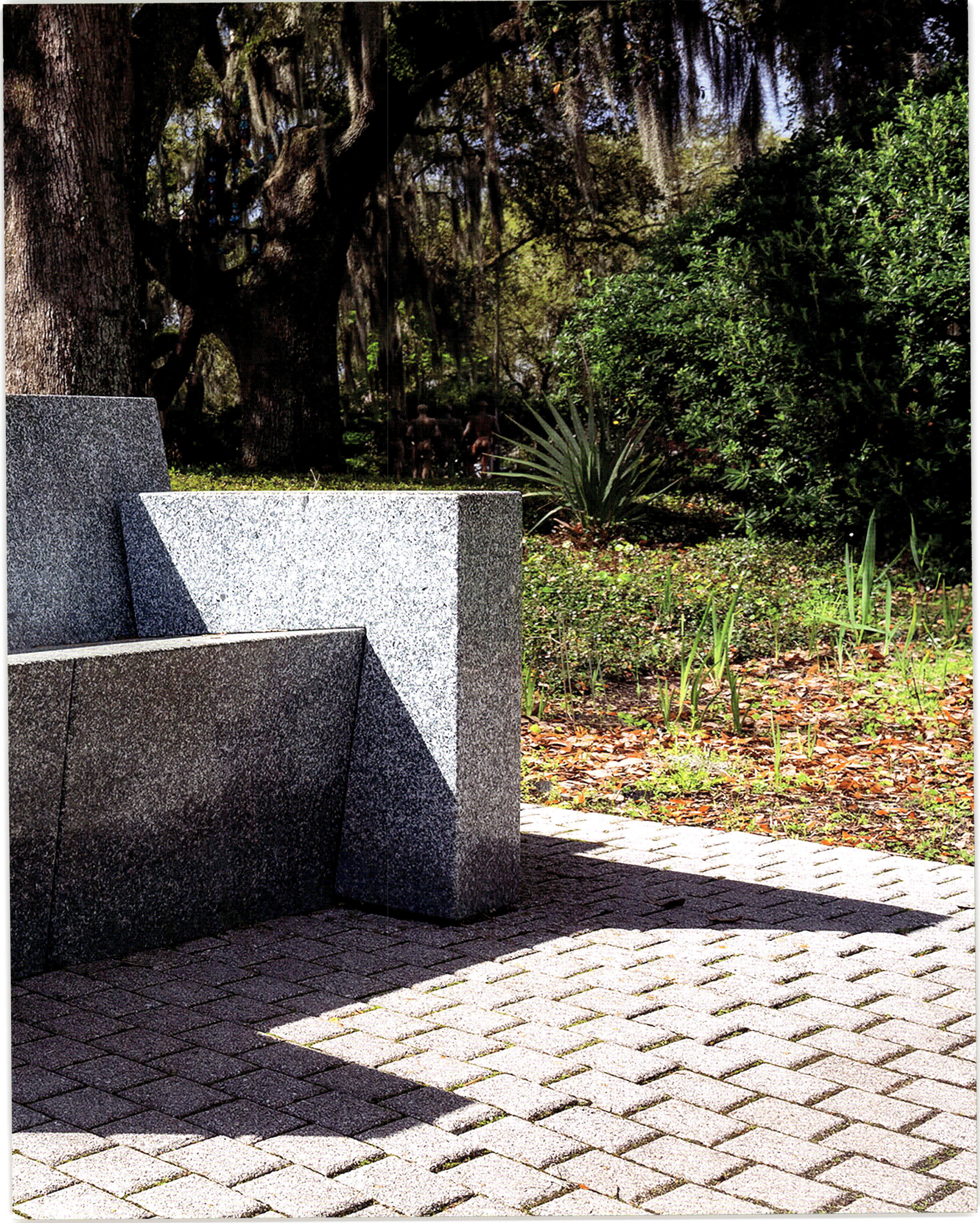

Deborah Butterfield

Restrained, 1999

Centered on semi-abstract representations of horses, Deborah Butterfield (b. 1949) has developed a cohesive sculptural output. Born and raised in San Diego, California, where she pursued equestrianism, the artist initially envisioned studying veterinary medicine, yet eventually specialized in ceramics, receiving a fine arts degree from the University of California, Davis.

Originally creating more realistic pieces, Butterfield began producing life-sized animals when she moved to a ranch in Montana in 1979, utilizing simple components and natural materials such as mud, sticks, and straw. A year later, the artist started incorporating detritus, scraps of metal and steel, and considering the potential of these resources by manipulating them through different techniques such as welding, hammering, and denting, among others. Butterfield eventually arrived at a notably ingenious process, for which she assembled the skeleton of her sculptures from found branches and wood. She casts the preliminary wooden structures in bronze and achieves a complex yet rustic patina, rendering an extraordinarily realistic resemblance to wood. Butterfield's innovative use of medium and form is exemplified in *Restrained*; the work's semblance invokes an organic quality, while the bronze appears timeless and everlasting.

The artist's remarkable understanding of the equestrian allows her to accurately evoke the spirit and muscle structure of the horses she depicts. Although exuding force and vigor through its heroic proportions, the steed in *Restrained* comes across as delicate and poised, with a bowed head and subdued resting stance. From prehistoric cave paintings to avant-garde movements such as Cubism, horses have steadily appeared in the history of art, often included in battle scenes and political portraits to symbolize military power and prestige. Also playing a central role in artworks illustrating sports and athletic competitions, horses likewise indicate strength, endurance, and speed. Yet Butterfield's steeds are often in peaceful and vulnerable positions, insinuating stillness and tranquility, and emulating a sensitivity decidedly different from the emotions horses typically embody. Using them as vehicles of the human condition, Butterfield taps into universal truths.—*JM*

Cast bronze, 86 × 99 × 46 in. (218.4 × 251.5 × 116.8 cm),
Gift of the Sydney and Walda Besthoff Foundation, 2000

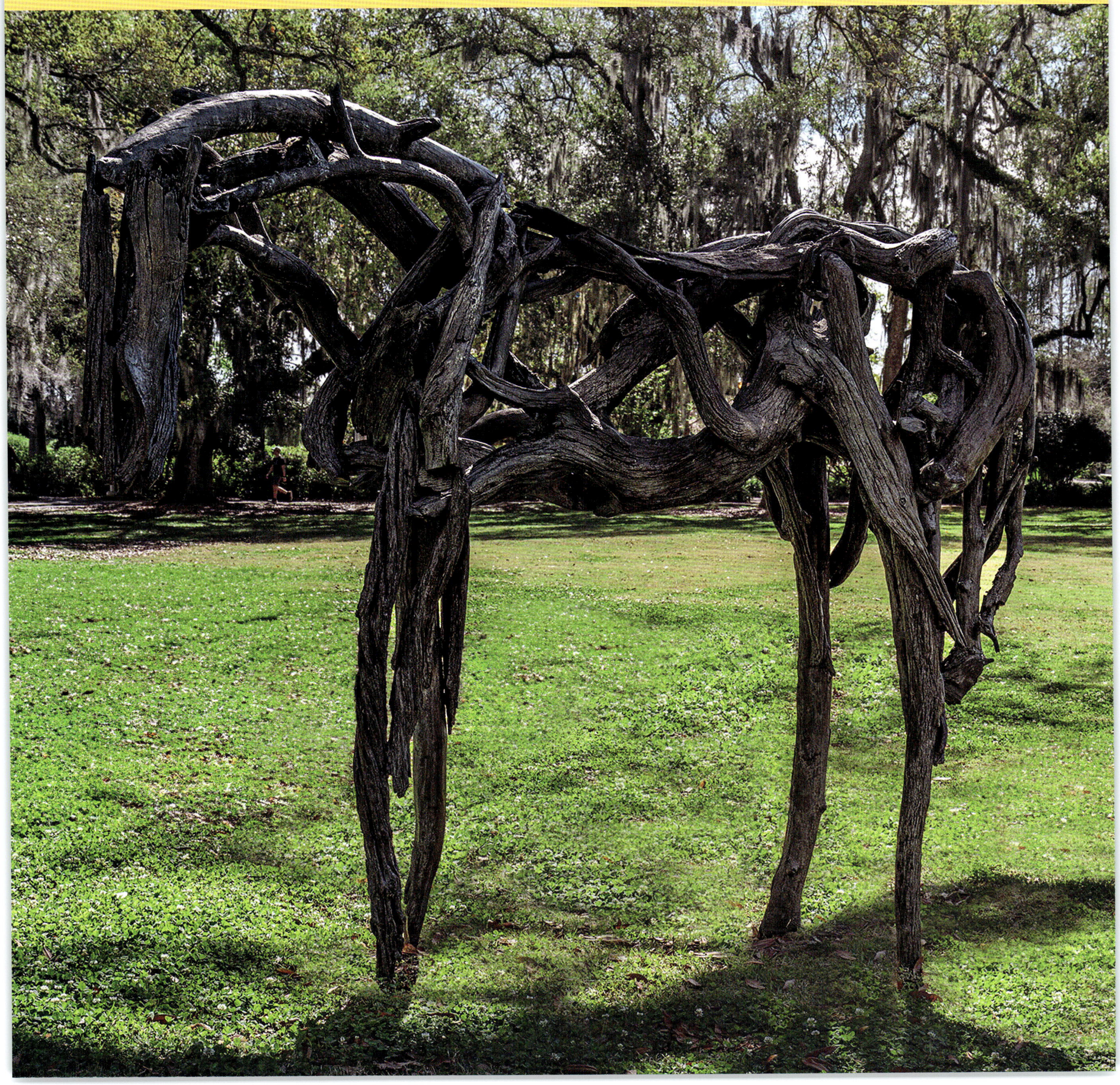

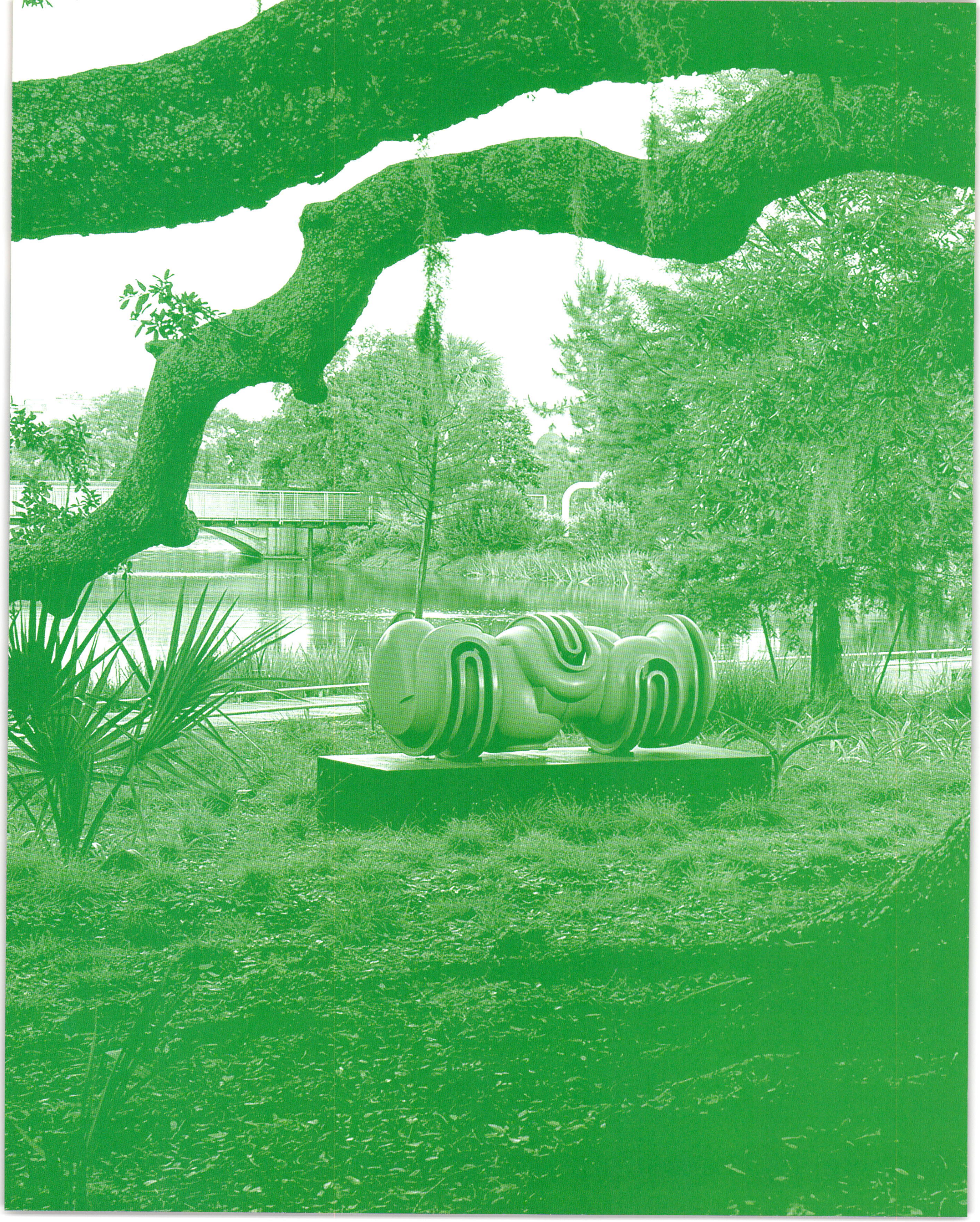

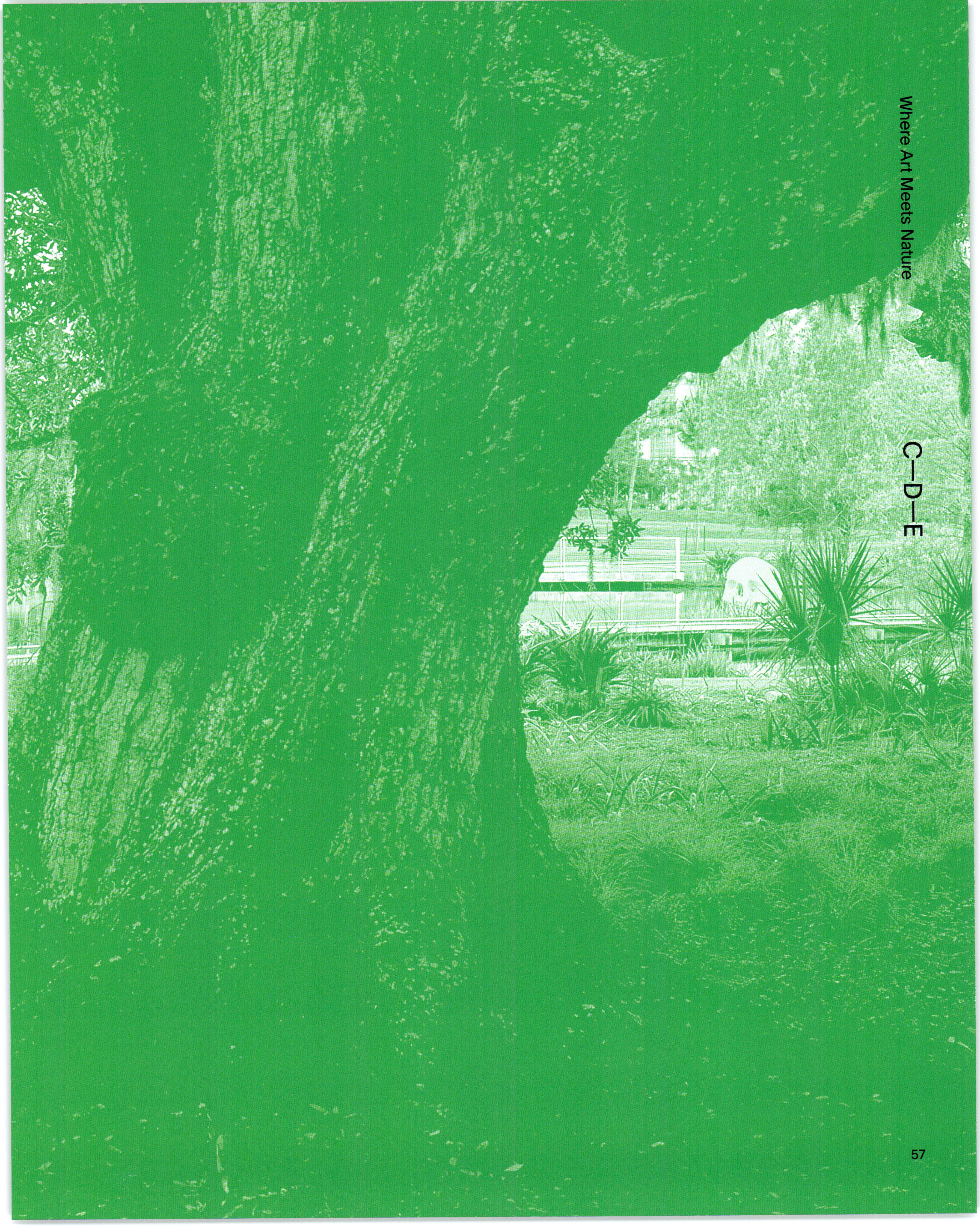

C—D—E

Saint Clair Cemin

Acme, 1990

Born and raised in Brazil, but currently residing between Hydra, Greece, and Connecticut, USA, Saint Clair Cemin (b. 1951) has built an illustrious international career through a multidisciplinary practice that disrupts conceptions of the everyday. At the age of twenty-two, he moved to Paris where he studied at the École Nationale Supérieure des Beaux-Arts, focusing on printmaking and illustration. In 1979, soon after completing his degree, he relocated to New York, where he became involved in the East Village art scene. That same year, a Guggenheim retrospective of the German artist Joseph Beuys (1921–1986) prompted Cemin to experiment with different mediums. Switching his attention to sculpture in 1983, the artist has since produced a diverse and prolific body of three-dimensional work.

Informed by mythology, philosophy, and a preoccupation for art history, Cemin has developed a comprehensive visual lexicon, in which elements of classicism, Art Nouveau, and Surrealism intersect to awaken familiar and uncanny feelings alike. Working with various materials including bronze, glass, and marble, and utilizing traditional sculpting techniques, Cemin's artistic output yields myriad forms, sizes, and textures. Relying on the imagery of commonplace items—such as furniture, statuettes, and toys—many of his works interrogate the functional elements of art objects and explore paradoxical conditions, both physical and psychical. Cemin's humorous reframing of mundane possessions gives his oeuvre a playful and sometimes even mischievous spirit.

The featured work, *Acme*—taken from the Greek word for a high point—has a vertical composition that alludes to a peak. With a polished finish and pristine form, ceding the artist's hand invisible, the work's appearance is typical of Cemin's metal sculptures. The composition gives prominence to the eroticism of the body, illustrating a phallic pinnacle, yet the surface and finish of the piece radiate an unnatural feeling. Abstract and associative, the work creates contrasting reactions and manifold interpretations, bringing to the forefront a unique reciprocity between object and subject and leaving little space for final proclamations.—*JM*

Copper, 54 × 44 × 44 in. (137.2 × 111.8 × 111.8 cm), Gift of the Sydney and Walda Besthoff Foundation, 2000

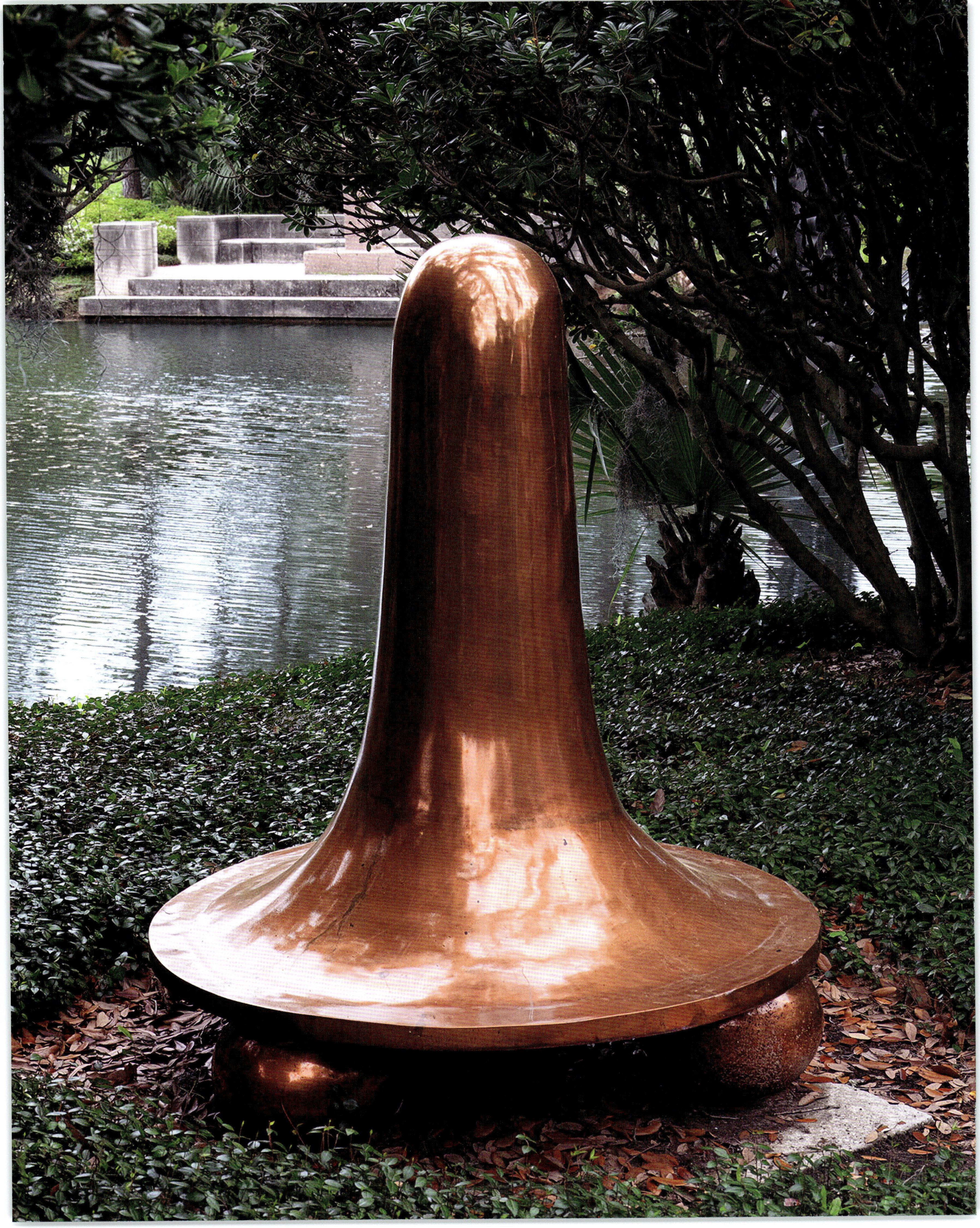

Lynn Chadwick

Sitting Figures, 1979–80

Instead of attending art school, during his twenties, Lynn Chadwick (1914–2003) worked as a draftsman for London architects. After serving in World War II, his first mobiles, comprised of wood and wire, were conceived as constructions for design projects rather than sculptures. In 1950, Chadwick, then a freelance designer, received significant commissions—a mobile in a restaurant and a stabile in a garden—that led him to learn how to weld. His subsequent semiabstract shapes in metals suggested fantastic beasts and small birdlike creatures that were both ominous and playful. His inclusion in the 1952 Venice Biennale aligned him with the Geometry of Fear, a group of young British sculptors nominally responding to the angst of the war's aftermath.

In the mid-1950s, his sculptures became winged, dancing figures on spindly tapered legs, ranging from a couple of feet to more than six feet in height. Chadwick's style evolved further so that his still angular forms—sometimes paired or in clusters of three or more—appeared humanoid and erect. The heavy, blocky domes of his figures of the late 1960s persisted into the next decade: heads in the shapes of diamonds, triangles, squares, and rectangles.

Chadwick's large-scale outdoor bronzes of the 1970s were soon in reclining, walking, or resting positions. *Sitting Figures* is part of the expanded range of permutations on which Chadwick settled. Slightly leaning toward each other, it is as if the two figures are in conversation, while the cloaked bodies emphasize the air of mystery. Their manner is at once inwardly engrossed and outwardly watchful. He returned to the subject of the seated pair some fifty times. Although actively collected and exhibited in England until near the end of his life, Chadwick's sculptures were less widely appreciated in the United States.—*AMT*

Bronze, 66 × 33 × 56 in. (167.6 × 83.8 × 142.2 cm), Gift of the Sydney and Walda Besthoff Foundation, 1998

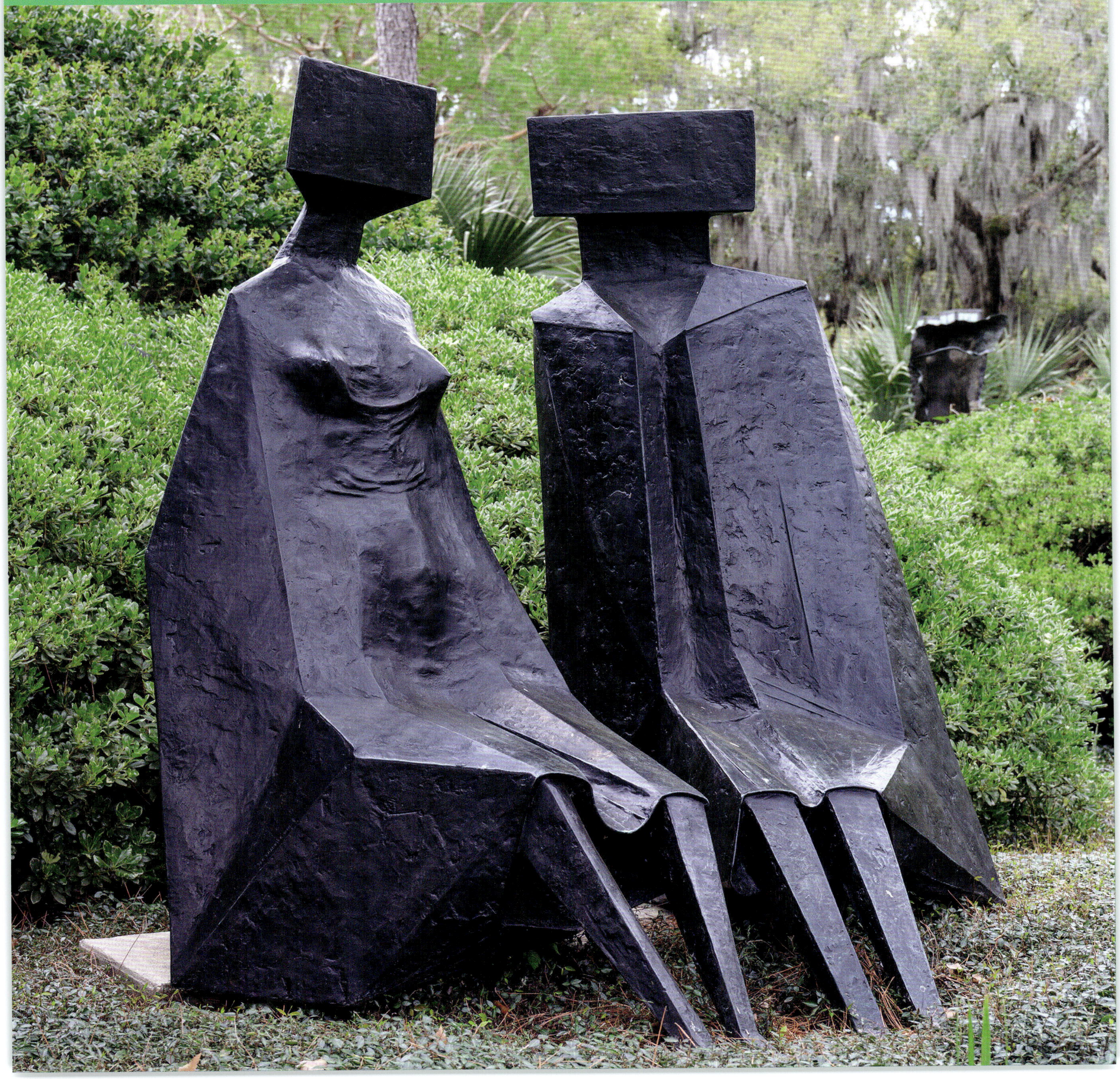

Sandro Chia

Figure with Tear and Arrow, 1982

An Italian artist, Sandro Chia (b. 1946) has developed an expansive visual practice that is comprised of painting, drawing, and sculpture. Combining references to ancient and modern art, notably the Italian Renaissance, Chia is renowned for creating universally understood scenes of melancholy, eroticism, and violence. The artist was born in Florence, where he studied at the Instituto d'Arte and the Accademia di Belle Arti, and presently lives between Rome and Miami, Florida.

Emerging in the 1970s at the height of the Conceptual movement, Chia initially experimented with installation and performance. Unconvinced by the intellectual formalism of Conceptual art, he became involved with the Italian Neo-Expressionist group Transavanguardia in the early 1980s. Along with fellow affiliated members, including Francesco Clemente (b. 1952) and Enzo Cucchi (b. 1949), Chia sought to break from abstraction and minimalism, and favored a return to figurative representation through vigorous palettes and gestural brushstrokes. Chia's early pieces are devoted to depictions of collective experience and are often peopled with young, muscular men much like himself. Although his later works are more subdued in composition and design, the artist maintains a passionate interest in the art historical canon and humankind's relationship to nature.

An early work by the artist, *Figure with Tear and Arrow* shows a reclining body rendered in exaggerated marks and robust shapes. Here, Chia oscillates between the past and the present in both content and material. A traditional subject, the woman can be viewed as passive and exposed. Her curvy outline suggests vitality and fertility, while the bronze coating brings art from Classical antiquity to mind. Nevertheless, the abstract representation and dynamic contours create an energetic form and point to contemporary interpretations of the female build. Garish and potent, the woman's body comes into being through an expressive jumble of marks and lines. Chia's sculpture resonates with the forward-thinking art of the Italian Futurists, whose fragmented forms and critical examination of time and space embodied a dynamic celebration of modernity.—*JM*

Bronze, 72 × 38 × 53 in. (182.9 × 96.5 × 134.6 cm), Gift of the Sydney and Walda Besthoff Foundation, 2000

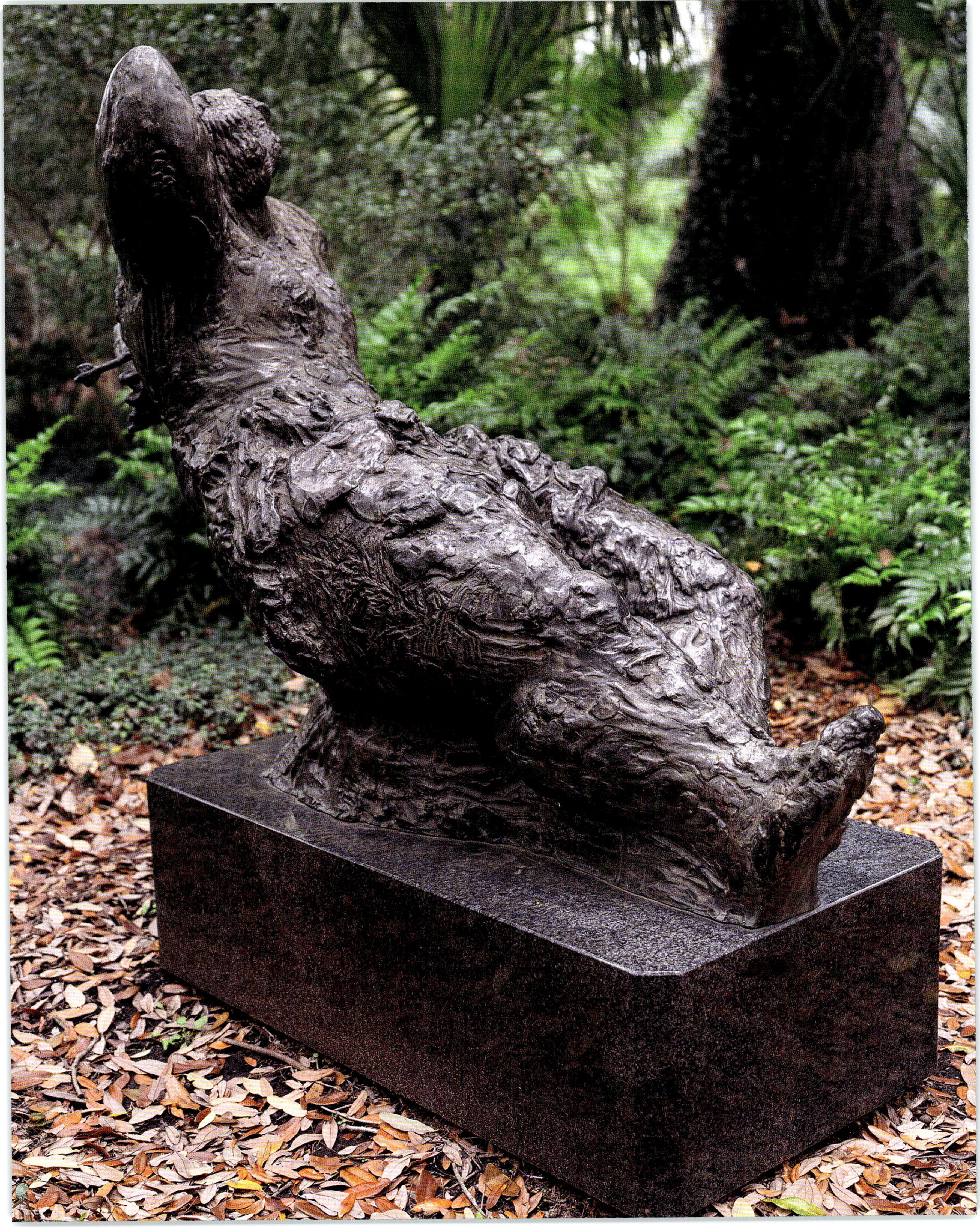

Pietro Consagra

Conversation with the Moon, 1960

A central figure in postwar Italian art, Pietro Consagra (1920–2005) helped usher in a new emphasis on abstraction and socially conscious aesthetics during the second half of the twentieth century. He believed strongly in Marxist philosophy and pushed his sculpture to embody the same cooperative ethos that fueled his politics. Though he worked in several materials throughout his career—from stone to iron and bronze to cloth and found textiles—Consagra is best known for his Colloqui (Conversations), series of the 1950s and 1960s, in which he sought to flatten sculpture and decentralize its focal point. Sculpture, he believed, should invite a dialogue with the viewer rather than create a hierarchy. These works are defined by their sheetlike shapes and layered surfaces, exemplified by the dynamic white exterior of *Conversation with the Moon*, held in the Sydney and Walda Besthoff Sculpture Garden.

Desperate to find the pulse of Italian art, Consagra moved to Rome in 1944, where he quickly fell in with the creative set. Two years later, he traveled to Paris and immersed himself in the French avant-garde, further energizing his desire to merge his art with his politics and make a drastic aesthetic declaration. Upon returning to Rome, he founded Forma Uno alongside Piero Dorazio (1927–2005), and in 1947, the group drafted a manifesto for formal abstraction. Working under their newly established aesthetic guidelines, Consagra attempted to remove the center of sculpture, flattening it, and in his eyes, transforming it into an equalized object. For Consagra, the center of a sculpture in the round represented an authoritarian force, which he continually tried to neutralize through his ever-evolving experimentations with streamlined, textured surfaces. As he gained increasing critical and curatorial attention, Consagra exhibited at the Venice Biennale, the São Paulo Biennial, and the Hermitage Museum in Saint Petersburg, Russia; and though his affiliations with different movements evolved, his dedication to the social angle of art never wavered.—*MH*

Cast in white stone and bronze, 49 ½ × 50 ¼ × 4 in. (125.7 × 127.6 × 10.2 cm), Gift of John W. Lolley, 1999

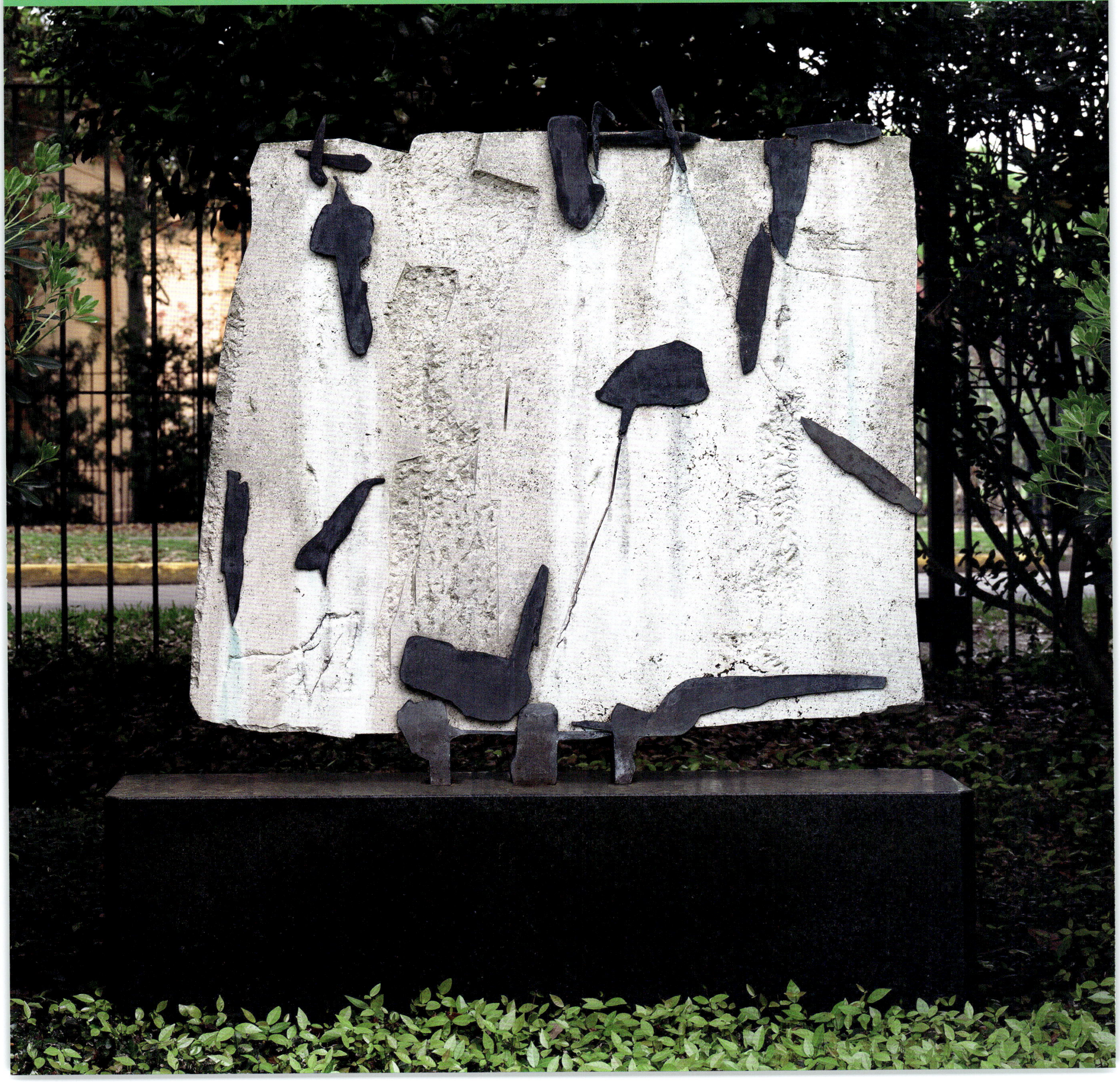

Tony Cragg

Runner, 2017

Throughout his decades-long career, Tony Cragg (b. 1949) has developed an expansive sculptural practice rooted in natural evocations, scientific investigations, and their intersections with the human world. Prior to his rise as a visual artist, Cragg, who is passionate about science and geology, worked in a laboratory—an experience that proved fundamental for his subsequent creative journey. A British artist, he studied at the Wimbledon School of Art and the Royal College of Art in London before relocating to Wuppertal, Germany, where he has lived since the late 1970s. Inspired by Land art and performance art, Cragg's work is concerned with environmental and archaeological themes.

In the 1980s, he rose to prominence for configurations of amassed found objects and garnered international recognition as part of the New British Sculpture group. He won the revered Turner Prize for outstanding contributions to British art in 1988. Since then, he has continued to push artistic boundaries, experimenting with new methods to conduct vertical assemblies through a variety of media, including stone, steel, wood, and fiberglass, and an overlapping diversity of forms and styles, such as rigid lines, smooth surfaces, and undulating contours.

Utilizing industrial supplies, Cragg is perhaps best known for creating biomorphic objects that are reminiscent of naturally occurring phenomena. In 2005, he founded the Waldfrieden Sculpture Park in Wuppertal, where visitors can view several of the artist's works and experience his creative vision.

Drawing from both natural realms and synthetic schemes, *Runner* resembles an ecological formation akin to a stalactite mineral or geological stratification, rendered from highly processed stainless steel. The work's reflective properties invoke aquatic currents or chemical processes, while its upward-moving structure suggests an allusion to perpetual transformation. Investigating the limits of mass, malleability, and material, Cragg's art embodies contrasts between the rational and the emotional, the artificial and the organic, encouraging viewers to reflect on the interplay of the natural world and the human condition.—*JM*

Stainless steel, 68 ½ × 43 ⅛ × 22 ⅞ in. (173.9 × 109.5 × 58.1 cm), overall, Museum purchase with funds provided by Sydney and Walda Besthoff, 2017

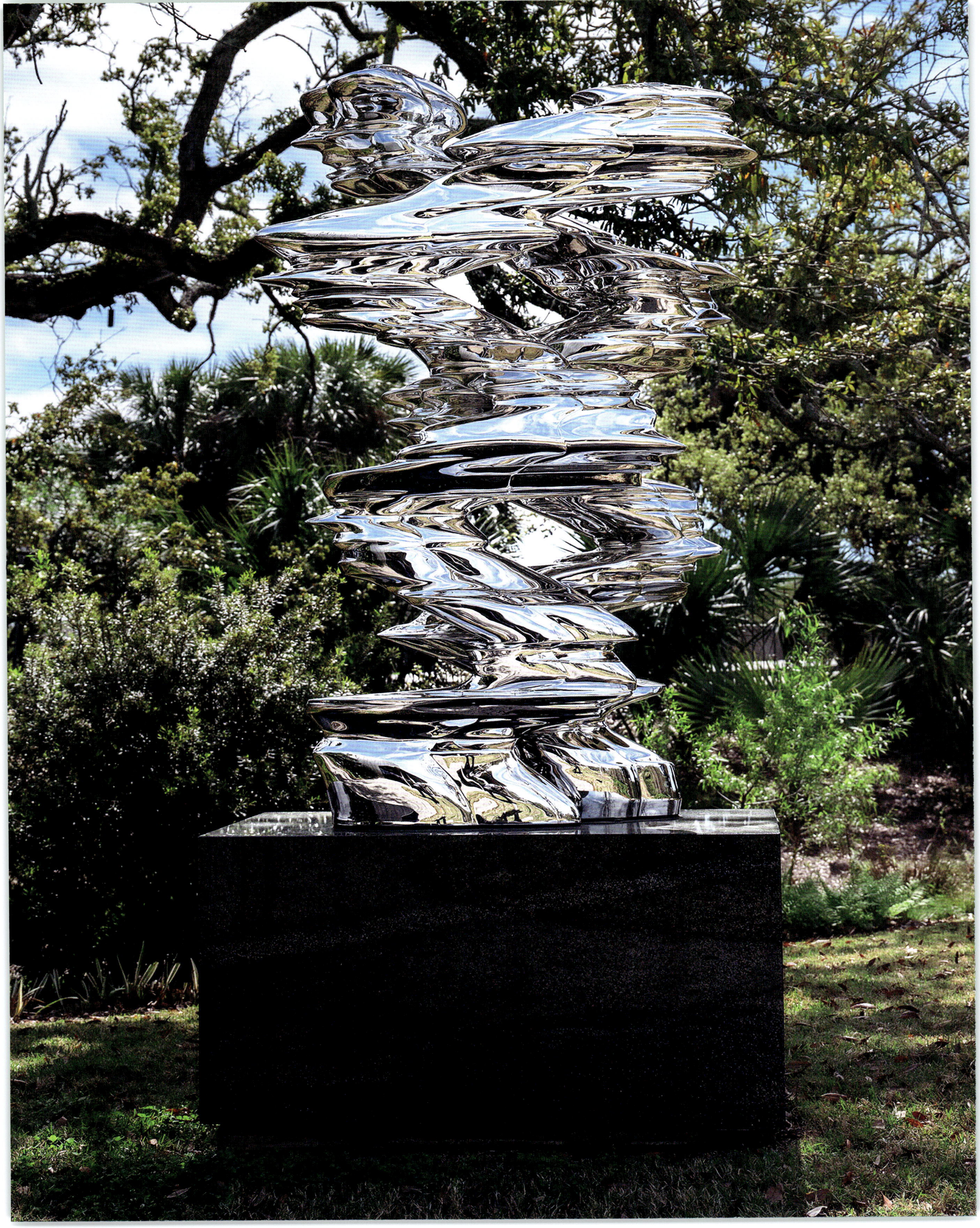

Tony Cragg

Sinbad, 2000

Through an innovative sculptural practice, Cragg investigates the potentials and limits of various materials. At the center of Cragg's art lies a deep concern for science and the environment. Employing industrial materials, Cragg creates rippling patterns and fluid shapes that resemble geological formations, dwelling on the relationship between the natural and the artificial.

The artist's early works—for which he deployed found objects—observed a stacking technique he would continue to use throughout his career. Implementing stone, steel, wood, and fiberglass, the artist is continuously attempting to alter different mediums through technological processes to render organic silhouettes and hard edges alike.

In the 1980s, Cragg briefly entertained the possibility of outsourcing production to a foundry but ultimately insisted on remaining involved in fabrication, preferring to collaborate with assistants in his studio and oversee all facets of assembly—a practice he continues to uphold today.

Sinbad, part of a larger series of bronze sculptures, reflects the artist's lasting fascination with the medium's molten viscosity as well as its enduring resilience to environmental factors. The sculpture exudes a mechanized quality—the smooth patina and slick lines, for example—while giving prominence to the organic through negative space, sinuous forms, and an undulating silhouette. Embedded in Cragg's scientific background as a lab technician, *Sinbad* challenges conventional notions of form and material whilst demonstrating the artist's exploration of dichotomies—whether static or dynamic, rigid or graceful, orderly or organic.—*JM*

Bronze, 33 ⅛ × 77 ⅛ × 32 in. (84.1 × 195.6 × 81.3 cm), Gift of the Sydney and Walda Besthoff Foundation, 2016

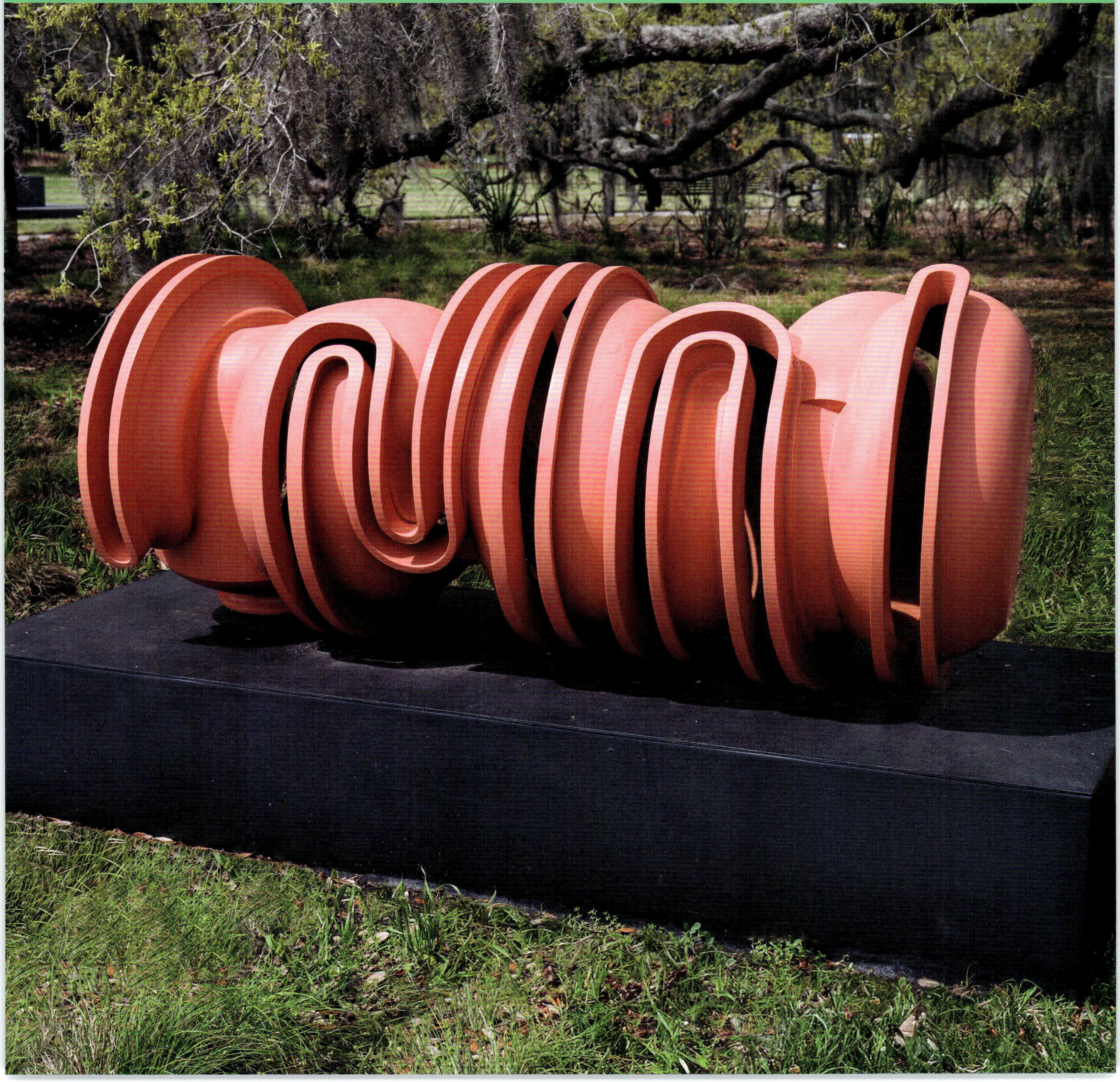

Johan Creten

Massu II, 2015

Now a sculptor working almost entirely with clay and bronze, Johan Creten (b. 1963) was originally trained in painting and performance art. Based in Paris but actively creating work from various cities around the world—including Miami, Monterrey, Nice, and Rome—Creten is credited for elevating the legitimacy of ceramic which, at the time, was a historically underused and overlooked medium within the art world. After graduating in 1985 from the Royal Academy of Fine Arts in Ghent, Belgium, Creten made a name for himself by opting for the unusual medium of clay, a stark contrast to the Conceptual and Minimalist art movements dominating the scene. Since then, he has realized a unique approach to sculpture through a practice focused on materiality and allegorical figuration.

Inspired by mythical narratives, Old Masters, classical music, and literature, Creten has developed an idiosyncratic visual vocabulary in which symbols and anthropomorphic bodies converge to become a supernatural world open to the viewer's interpretation. His objects tend to be covered by several layers of glazes a myriad colors, revealing an ornate complexity that highlights tactility and the process of making. In addition to examining personal and universal themes, Creten's lyrical works often interrogate social injustices and political issues taking place beyond gallery walls.

Although immediately appealing to viewers for its balanced proportions and tactile form, *Massu II* nonetheless releases a prominent sense of menace due to its jagged projections. A seemingly organic figure, the piece has a bronze patina susceptible to material changes over time, granting the work a historic quality. Still, a futuristic current runs throughout the seamlessly undulating column that looks out of place within the leafy garden setting. The work is monstrous and towering, yet shapely and majestic. Like many of Creten's sculptures, *Massu II* blurs impressions of past, present, and future, and invokes a pattern of artificial exchanges between nature and humanity.—*JM*

Bronze, 13 ft. 9 in. × 11 ½ in. × 11 ½ in. (4.2 m × 29.2 cm × 29.2 cm), Gift of Sydney and Walda Besthoff, 2015

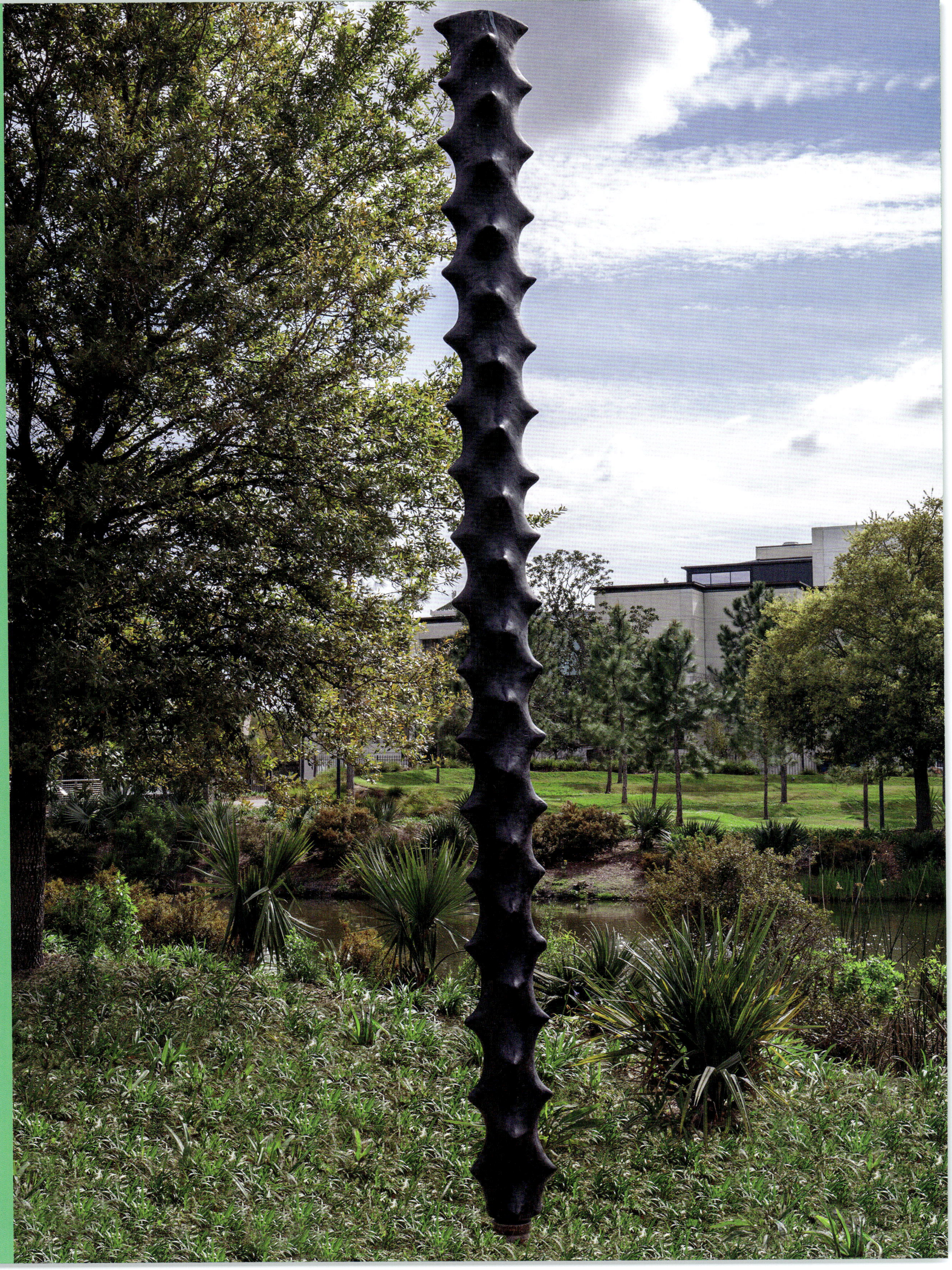

Stephen De Staebler

Standing Man with Outstretched Arm, 1987

With a career spanning decades and a celebrated interdisciplinary practice, Stephen De Staebler (1933–2011) is praised for his semiabstract sculptures that prompt a profound emotional response. Although originally from Missouri, De Staebler settled in California in the 1950s and played an integral role in the Bay Area art scene, in which he became an avid advocate for the use of clay and ceramics despite historically being regarded as merely mediums of craft. He maintained a concern for representing the human body, even at the height of the Abstract Expressionist movement in the United States, where a nonrepresentational approach was favored over figurative styles.

De Staebler studied archaeology, art history, and religion at Princeton University, and subsequently spent time at Black Mountain College, North Carolina, before completing a master of fine arts with a focus on ceramics at the University of California, Berkeley. Inspired by his cultural surroundings and theological studies, De Staebler developed a practice where classical antiquity and religious iconography conflate to conjure a mixture of phenomenological emotions such as melancholy, spirituality, dread, and alienation.

Initially employing clay exclusively, De Staebler postponed casting his works in bronze until later in his career, as exemplified by *Standing Man With Outstretched Arm*. Even when working with glossier materials, the artist retained the splintered, fractured, textural qualities of earthen mediums to grant his objects an organically rustic finish. The exhibited totemic statue shows a thin, headless man standing precariously on one toe. Despite the unusual balancing pose, the sculpture conveys no movement. Withered and battered, the dismembered subject—placed in a cross-like composition—elicits religious connotations, contributing to the overall elegiac character of the work. Evoking a ghostly instability, *Standing Man With Outstretched Arm* is a metaphor for resilience, nostalgia, and ephemerality, and bespeaks an interrelation between the human body, nature, and faith.—*JM*

Bronze, 86 ½ × 50 ½ × 35 ½ in. (219.7 × 128.3 × 90.2 cm),
Gift of the Sydney and Walda Besthoff Foundation, 2000

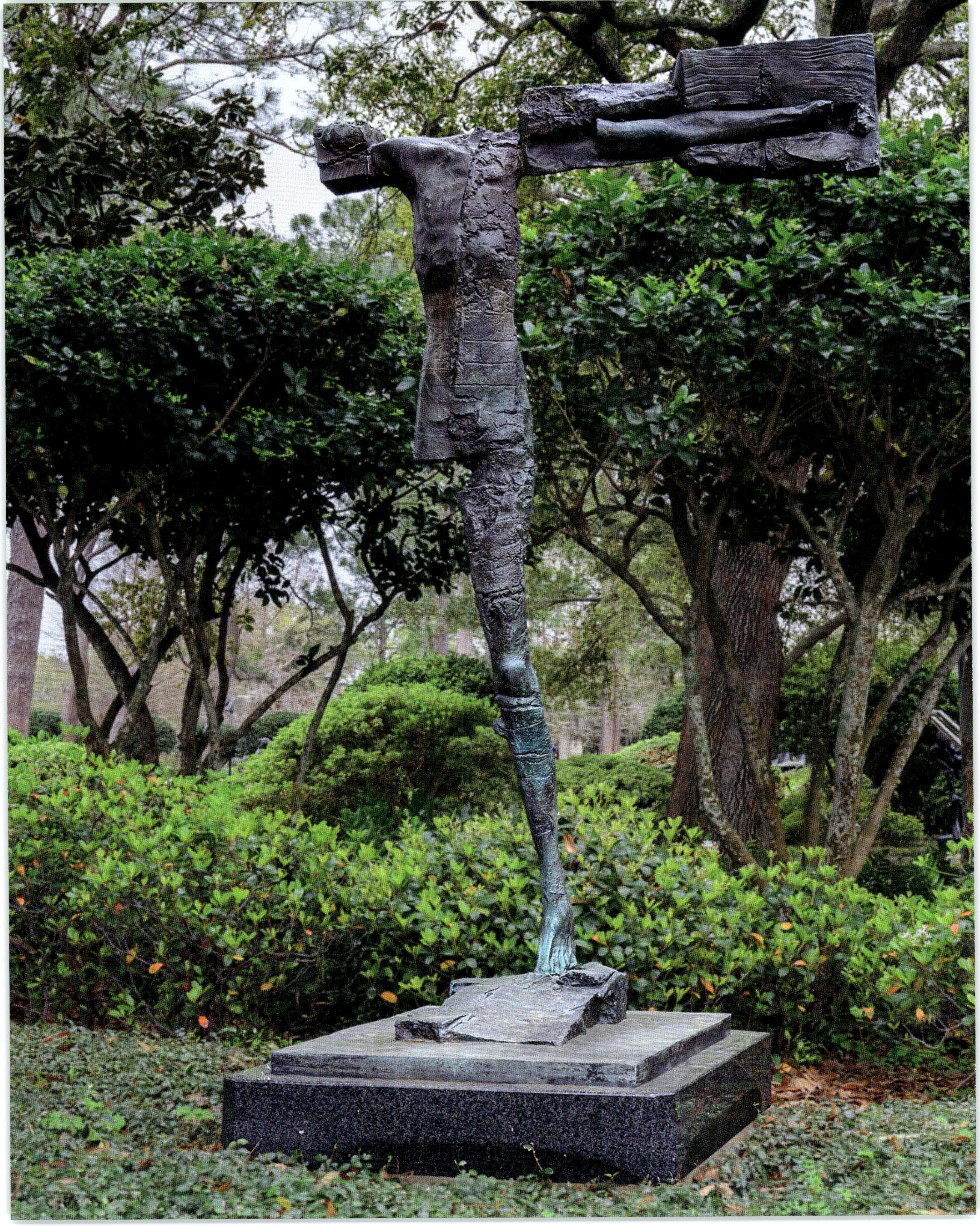

Lesley Dill

Standing Man with Radiating Words, 2006

Words are integral to the art of Lesley Dill (b. 1950). A voracious reader as a girl growing up in Maine, an English major at Trinity College in Connecticut, and a passionate devotee of the poet Emily Dickinson (1830–1886), Dill has been incorporating words into her various practices since the 1990s. In drawings, prints, photographs, performances, and sculptures, the artist quotes, fragments, transforms, and plays with language. "I have spent my life shaping words and images," reflects Dill in the exhibition catalog for *Wilderness: Light Sizzles Around Me* (2021). Her imagery often depicts or alludes to the human form—isolated body parts, ghostly outlines, and flowing dresses recur, for example. Today, the artist is based in Brooklyn, New York. Throughout her practice, she uses an eclectic mix of materials, from the unorthodox and delicate, such as horsehair and thread, to the traditional and durable, like bronze and wood.

Standing Man with Radiating Words is one of several, unique life-sized cast bronze sculptures that Dill produced in the 2000s. Barefoot and rumpled, the striding figure carries block letters on his back as though cargo. They spill out in different sizes and directions—uncontainable as they burst forth. As in Dill's bronze *Divide Light* (2003), in which letters seem to sprout from a seated woman's body, the letters are an unreadable jumble in *Standing Man with Radiating Words*. Although the text amounts to something—"How ruthless are the gentle," an opening line of a Dickinson poem—the poetic utterance is just out of reach. Both burden and resource, in these sculptures the alphabet soup operates as a kind of word bubble. Dill is often interested in the relationship between language and the divine—specifically, the types of expressions that summon, or act as guides to, invisible realms, such as chant, mantra, prayer, song, and speaking in tongues. *Standing Man with Radiating Words* and other bronze figures are a clear prelude to her more recent series (2017–21) of textile and paper effigies featuring abolitionists, literary icons, and spiritual crusaders, likewise animated with words, including John Brown (1800–1859), Mother Ann Lee (1736–1784), and Sojourner Truth (c. 1797–1883).—*AMT*

Unique cast bronze, 61 × 35 × 28 in. (154.9 × 88.9 × 71.1 cm), overall, Museum purchase, Sydney and Walda Besthoff Fund, 2007

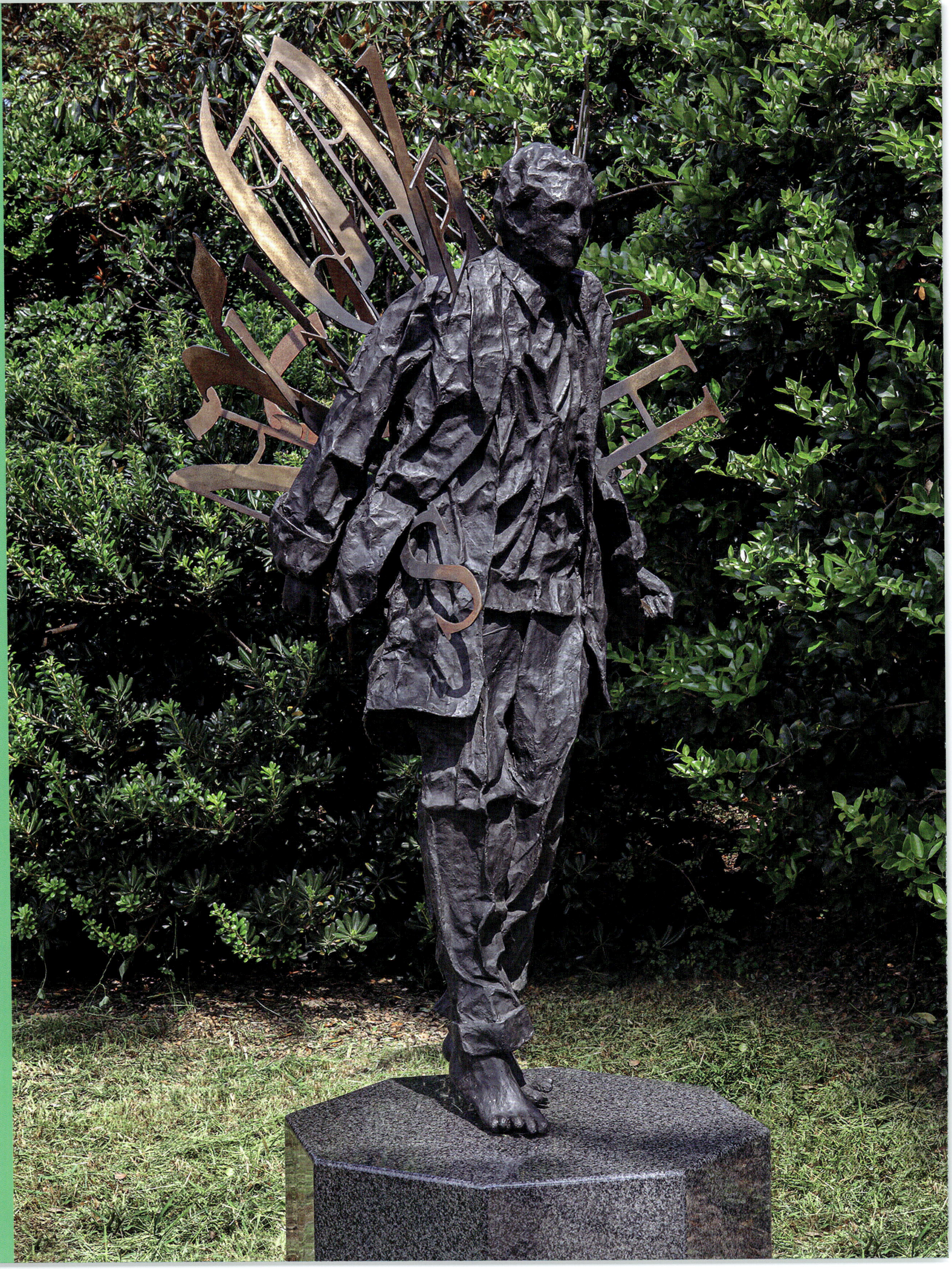

Elmgreen & Dragset

Maybe (Not), 2022

Based in Berlin, Michael Elmgreen (b. 1961; Copenhagen, Denmark) and Ingar Dragset (b. 1969; Trondheim, Norway) have been working together as an artistic duo since 1995. They are internationally renowned for radically redefining the art experience, producing large-scale sculptures and environments that simultaneously embody and challenge the everyday. Their works demand participation and performance, and often defy their surroundings, raising questions around the complexities of public spaces, social systems, and institutional models. At times presented in unexpected locations, Elmgreen & Dragset's sculptures are instantly recognizable for their reconditioning of ordinary objects—such as drained swimming pools mounted upright, twenty-four-hour ATMs rendered useless, and staircases abruptly destroyed halfway through. As a result, their art evokes contrasts of beauty and decay, splendor and chaos, wonder and fear.

Short Cut (2003), initially installed in the Milanese Galleria Vittorio Emanuele II, was an uncanny scenario in which a camper trailer attached to a Fiat Uno seemingly broke through from underneath the marble floor of the high-end shopping gallery. With a penchant for the absurd, Elmgreen & Dragset consistently challenge the familiar and explore themes of identity and desire through a wry application of elementary forms, architectural installations, and minimalist aesthetics.

A recurring motif in Elmgreen & Dragset's world, the diving board first appeared in their practice in 1997, when they installed a springboard (*Powerless Structures, Fig. 11*) inside the Louisiana Museum of Modern Art in Denmark. It is rendered nonfunctional by extending, illogically, through the glass of a window overlooking a body of water.

The established motif continues in *Maybe (Not)*, which was specially commissioned for the lagoon in the Besthoff Sculpture Garden. The white, eighteen-foot-tall diving board features two figures at the very top: one of them stands at the edge of the board, preparing for the plunge, while the other dangles their feet from the side, calmly contemplating the view from atop. Although in close proximity, the figures appear disengaged from and unaware of one another. Perhaps acting as a metaphor for the individual experiences that often transpire in civic and communal spaces, *Maybe (Not)* draws attention to the parallels and intersections of the private and public realms.—*JM*

Bronze, stainless steel, lacquer, 18 ft. x 10 ft. 7 ½ in. x 24 in. (5.5 m x 3.2 m x 60.9 cm), overall, Museum Purchase with Gifted Funds from the Sydney and Walda Besthoff Foundation, 2024

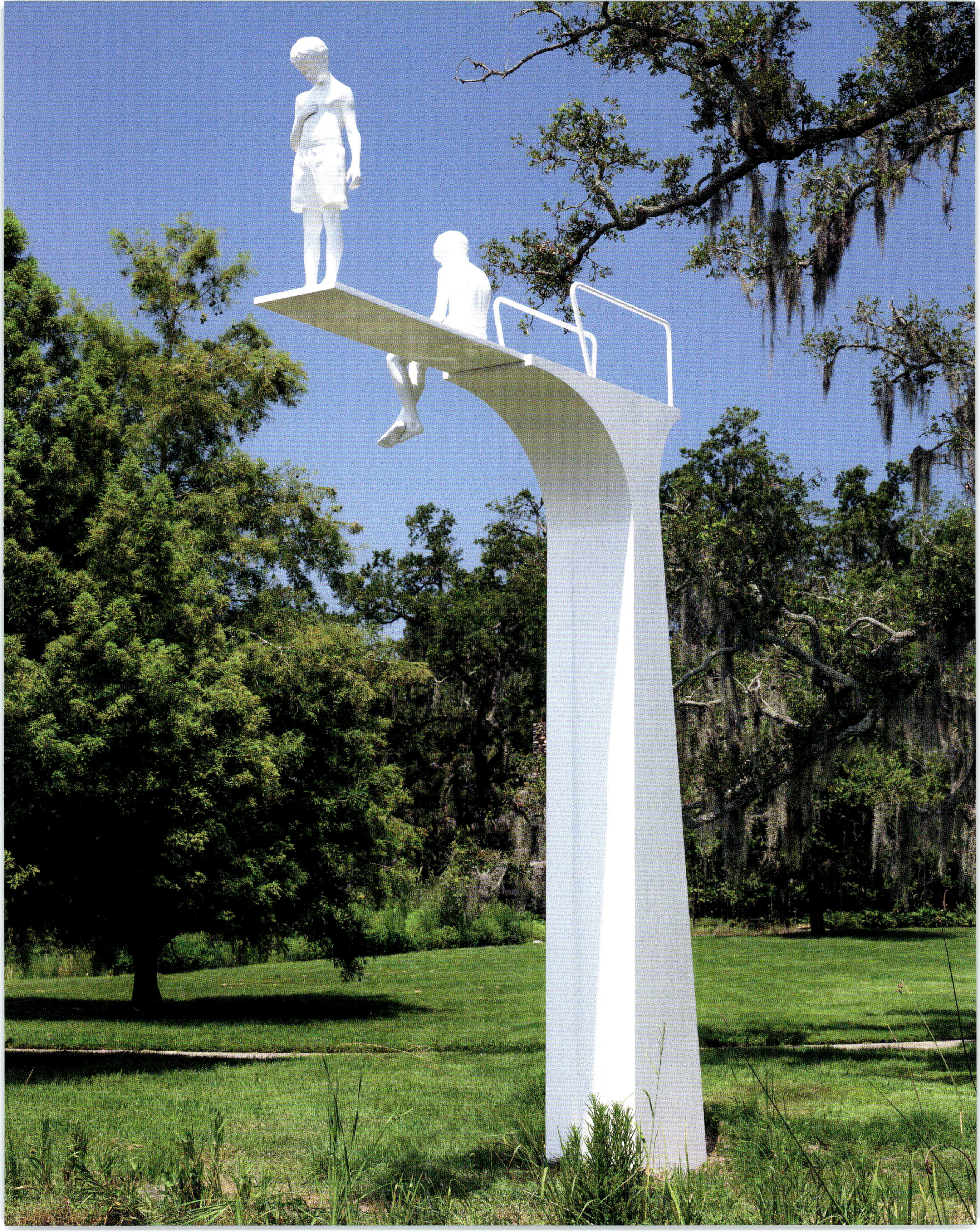

Lin Emery

Wave, 1988

An influential figure in kinetic sculpture, Lin Emery (1926–2021) is best known for her fluid, geometric abstractions made from highly polished aluminum. Born in Larchmont, New York, she never received a formal arts degree but was attracted early on to the beautiful and the aesthetic, spending hours of her childhood drawing various objects from her father's art collection. She bounced between universities before settling in Paris at the end of the 1940s where she took a job at a local newspaper. Emery moved into a flat directly opposite the sculpture studio where Ossip Zadkine (1888–1967) was then teaching courses for students on the GI Bill. Wandering through one day, she was completely taken in with the three-dimensional forms. She returned to the studio daily, shaping and molding clay figures after a live model. At the end of each week, along with her fellow students, Emery would destroy her work, a ritual which only underscored that their immense effort was all merely practice—a study in line, shape, and gravity aimed towards the hope of mastery.

On returning to the United States, Emery settled in New Orleans, taking work sculpting biblical figures for churches across southern Louisiana. More than the figures, she was interested in the underlying armature that supported the sculptures. Soon, she had abandoned any pretense of the figure, opting to focus on the angular, architectural scaffold inside. Equipped with a modernist appreciation for material, Emery always maintained a hand in the fabrication of her work, frequently welding elements together herself and preferring to let the characteristics of the material dictate how it morphed into an artwork. Though she took plenty of inspiration from the natural world—especially after she began working with ball bearings, allowing her sculptures to rotate in the wind—the properties of the metal always took precedence in determining how her forms came to be.

The tensions between ideation and material are visible in *Wave*. A lithe, weightless arc, the sculpture immediately recalls its namesake. The neat, abstract wedges convey both the random and the routine, that so often coexist inexplicably in nature; but the gleaming aluminum surfaces nevertheless remain, first and foremost, an homage to the physicality of the metal itself.—*MH*

Polished aluminum, 14 ft. × 15 ft. × 108 in. (4.3 m × 4.6 m × 274.3 cm), Gift of the Frederick R. Weisman Company, 1988

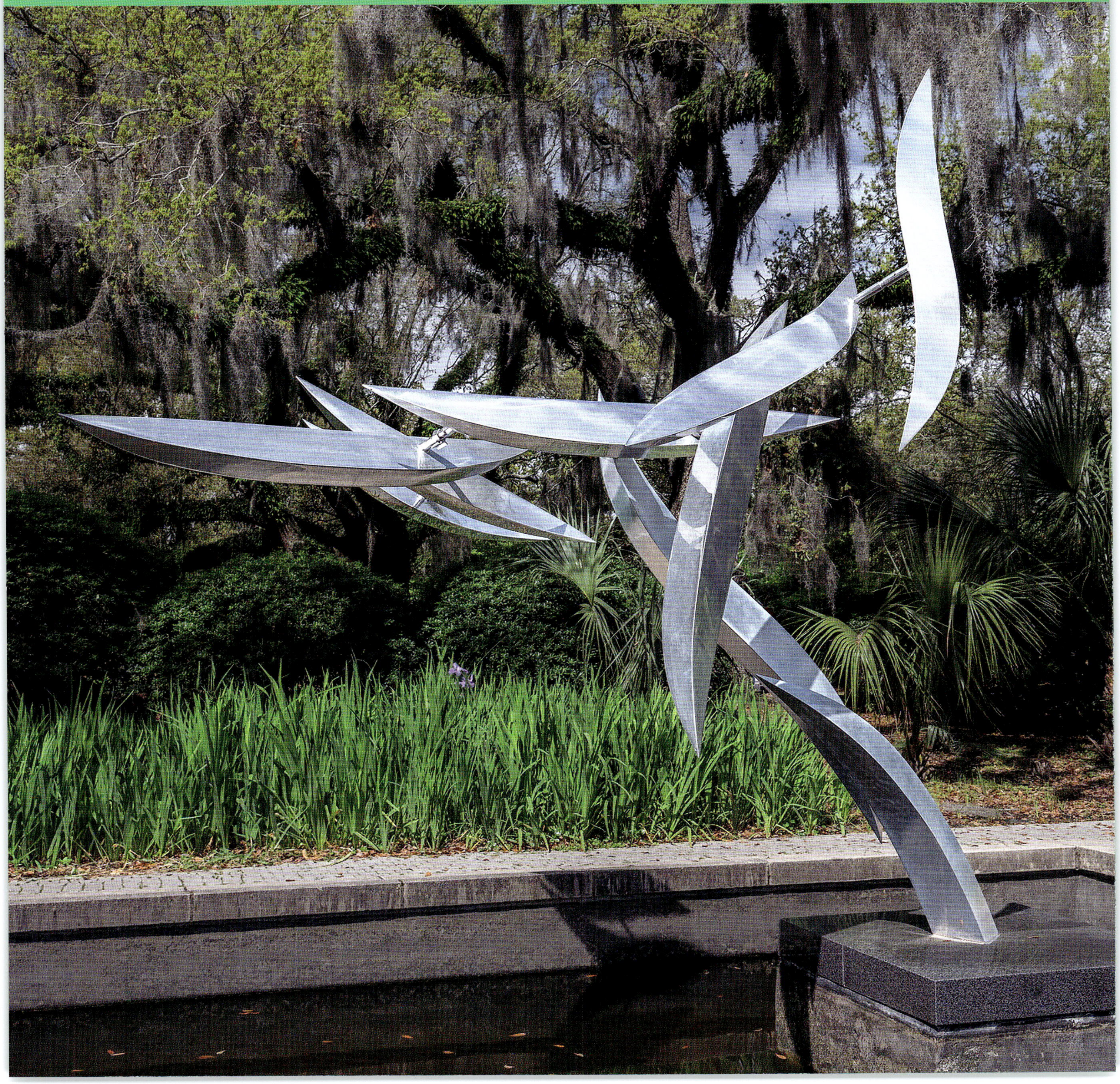

Leandro Erlich

Window with Ladder - Too Late for Help, 2008

Blurring the lines of reality to exude the uncanny, Leandro Erlich (b. 1973) leads his audience into realms of ambiguity through expansive architectural simulations. Born in Argentina and dividing his time between Buenos Aires, Paris, and Montevideo, Uruguay, the artist gained international acclaim following a series of successful exhibitions, fellowships, and residencies in the late 1990s and early 2000s. At the young age of 26, he crafted one of his most iconic pieces: an immersive installation that beckoned viewers to step inside the illusion of a swimming pool seemingly filled with water. Since then, Erlich has used conventional spaces and mundane fixtures—beauty salons, subway cars, and classrooms, as well as windows, elevators, and revolving doors—to disrupt conceptions of the everyday.

Drawing inspiration from film and literature, particularly from the work of Jorge Luis Borges, Alfred Hitchcock, David Lynch, and Luis Buñuel, Erlich's imaginative practice conjures sensations that are both familiar and peculiar, oscillating between the emotive domains of art and life. His works, often described as dreamlike environments for their disparate essence and allusions to themes of childhood and domesticity, give form to emotions that concurrently manifest and question reality.

Window with Ladder – Too Late for Help is imbued with a profound sense of danger and vulnerability. Defying basic laws of physics, a ladder leans against a floating building facade. The title speaks of an irretrievable situation when support might be sought, but any potential relief has passed its expiration. A hypothetical accident bestows the sculpture with a disturbing dimension and contributes to the supernatural agent that runs throughout. Despite inferring ominous implications, the installation intrigues viewers, tempting them to ponder the possibility of climbing the rungs, peering into the display, and becoming part of the artwork. Through an unassuming subversion of reality, *Window with Ladder – Too Late for Help* activates a unique corporeal awareness and triggers a powerful psychological reaction. Showcasing a cunning character that is at once playful and sinister, Erlich's construction demonstrates his unparalleled ability to wrestle with our unconscious, recondition the ordinary, and embrace the unknown.—*JM*

Metal ladder, steel underground structure, fiberglass, aluminum frames, 14 ft. 8 in. × 63 in. (4.5 m × 160 cm), Museum purchase, Frederick R. Weisman Company Fund and De-Accession Fund, 2009

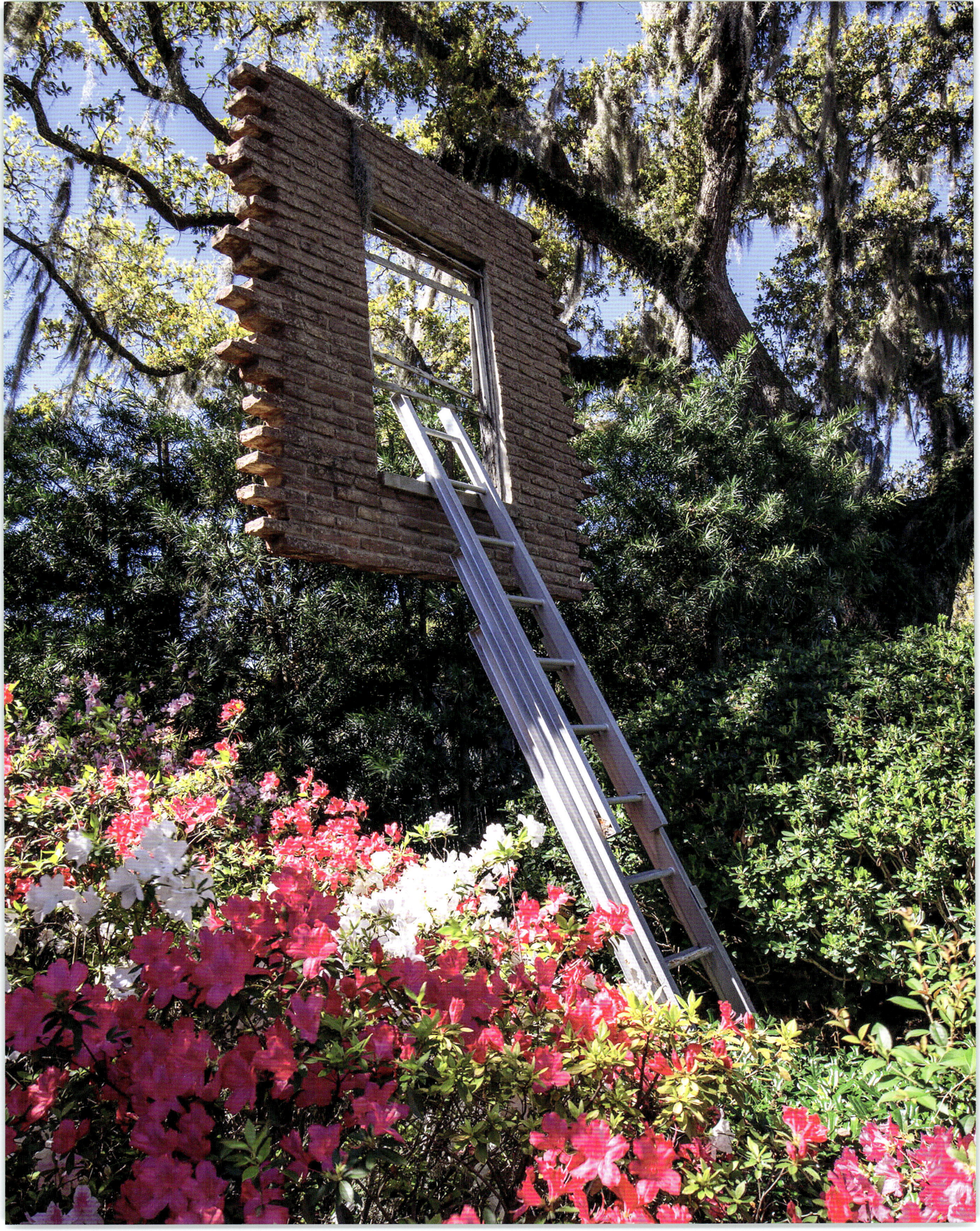

Sorel Etrog

Large Pulcinella, 1965–67

Drawing inspiration from Cubist collage and the direct carving method championed by modern British sculptors Barbara Hepworth (1903–1975) and Henry Moore (1898–1986), Sorel Etrog's (1933–2014) geometric sculptures combine faintly figurative elements with resolutely abstract forms. His first three-dimensional shapes were carved from wood or shaped in terra-cotta and plaster, but as he moved into working with looser, more biomorphic shapes, Etrog began exclusively casting his sculptures from bronze.

Born in a Romania to a Jewish family, Etrog's childhood fissured after Ion Antonescu's authoritarian government officially allied with the Nazi party. Confronted with unspeakable violence, his family survived through the end of World War II, but the community he grew up in was decimated with swaths of people having been either murdered or displaced. Etrog fled his homeland just as the Soviet government established itself in Romania, settling in Tel Aviv and beginning a life of exile.

In 1958, Etrog received a scholarship to study at the Brooklyn Museum, New York, where he encountered the African and Oceanic artworks that had originally spurred the Cubism he so admired. Up until the late 1950s, Etrog's practice was dominated by his Painted Constructions series of largely two-dimensional painted canvas or wall reliefs, but in 1959, he began experimenting with sculpture in the round. With the support of a Canadian patron, Etrog left New York for Toronto and he quickly made a name for himself with his unique, semiabstract forms.

Large Pulcinella dates from a particularly productive moment in the artist's career when, following his presentation at the Venice Biennale, international interest in his work was at its peak. Typical of Etrog's practice, the work evocatively stitches together the bodily and the abstract, resulting in a collage-like form that echoes the synthetic and analytic Cubism of the early 1900s. The shape shifts under our gaze, becoming both mechanical and organic and pushing the boundaries of three-dimensional space.—*MH*

Bronze, 113 × 51 ½ × 27 in. (287 × 130.8 × 68.6 cm),
Gift of the Sydney and Walda Besthoff Foundation, 1998

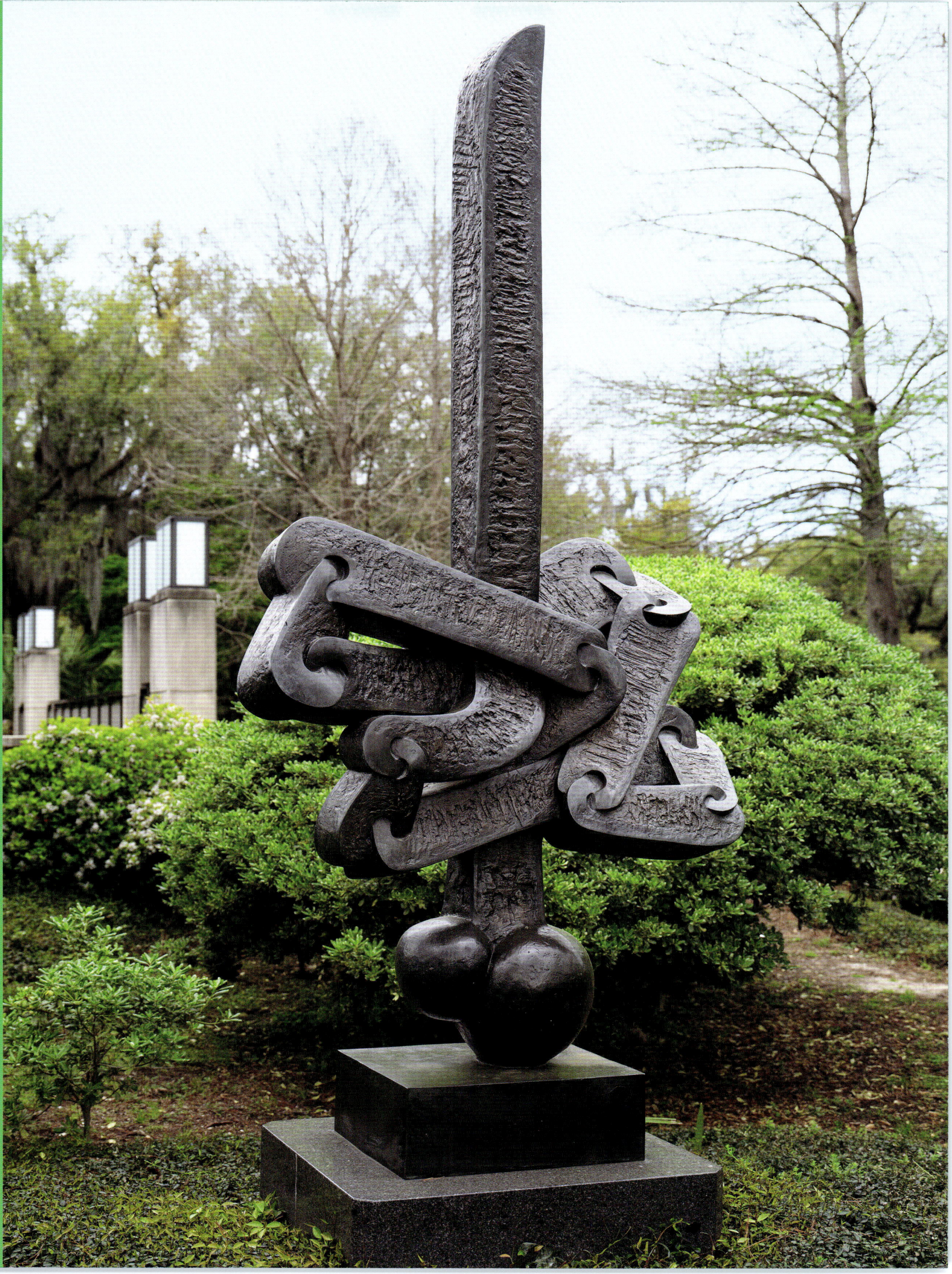

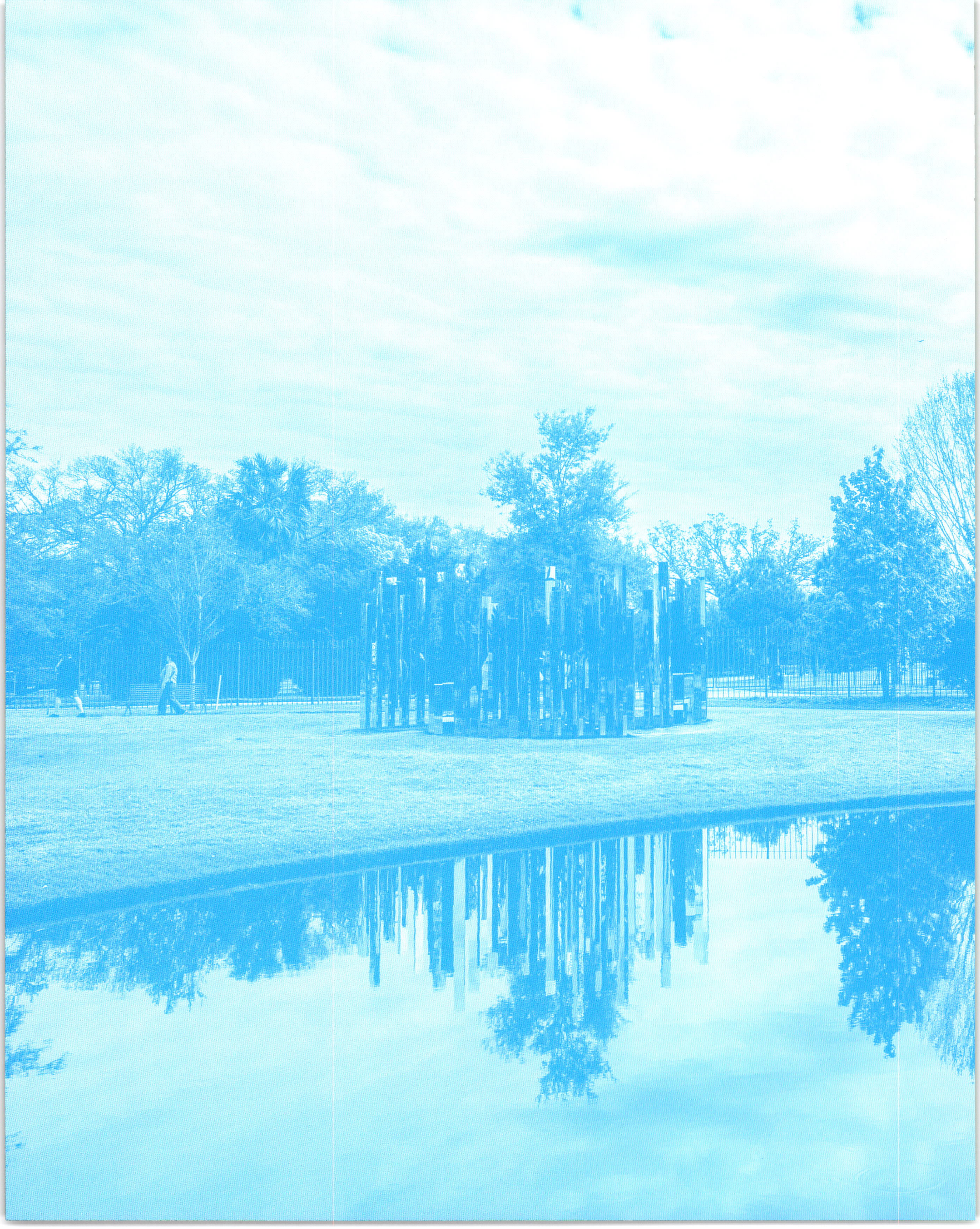

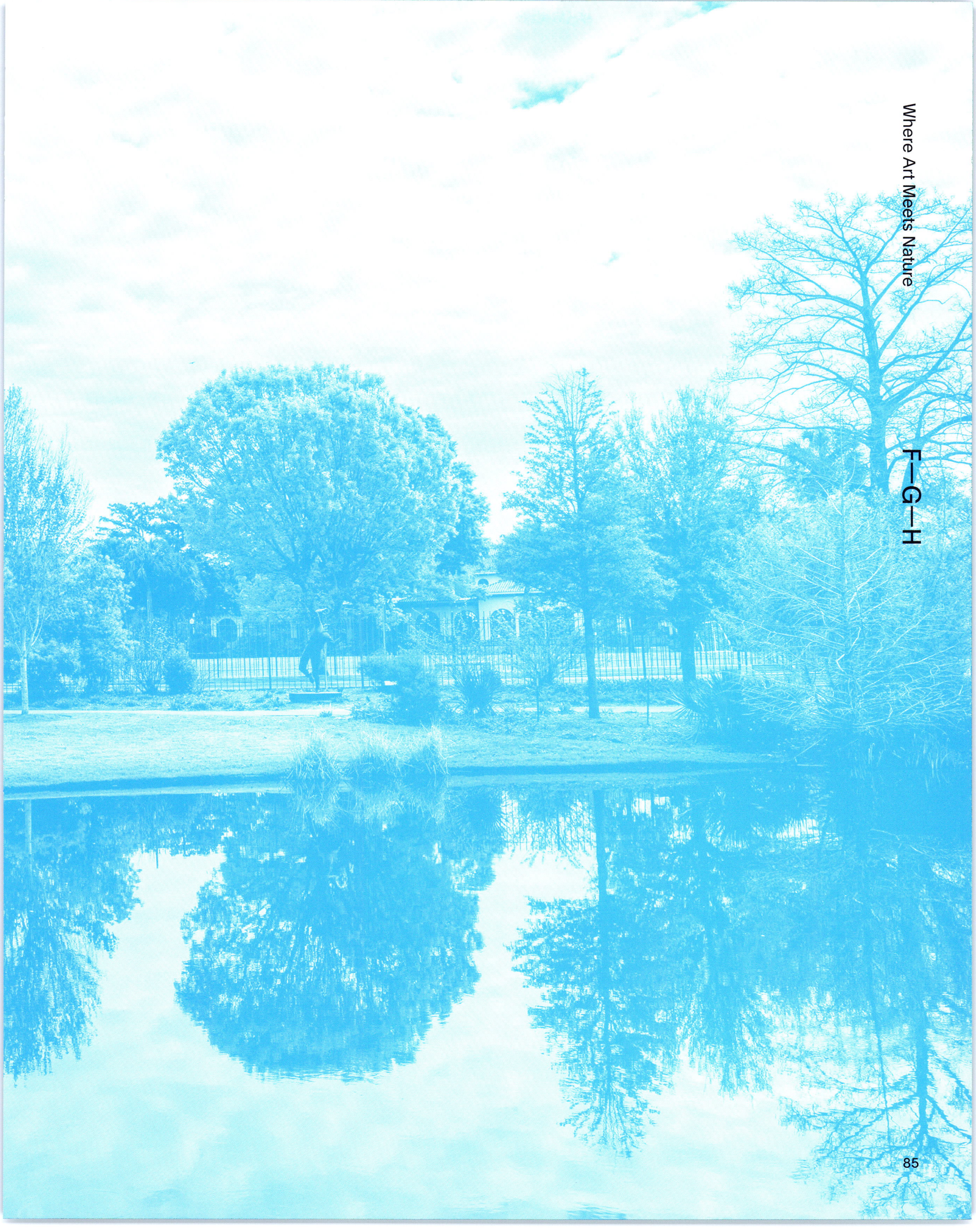

Luciano Fabro

Il giorno mi pesa sulla notte V (Day Weighs Heavily on My Night V), 2000

A central figure in Arte Povera, Luciano Fabro's (1936–2007) sculpture practice was consistently determined by the materials he worked with. Coalescing after World War II, Arte Povera was a critique by Italian artists of the industrial consumer culture being taken up by the Nouveau Réalisme movement then blossoming in France and the Pop art of both Britain and the United States. Working in what they deemed 'poor materials,' the group created art destined to be impermanent. Designed to degrade over time or to appear physically weak or immaterial, pieces were made impossible to consume in order to subvert commodification. Though he graduated from the fragile, ephemeral materials the movement was famously associated with—eventually incorporating gold, fabric, and marble—Fabro never lost his connection to medium. He believed that the material substance of a sculpture would guide the spontaneous creation and its final form.

Heavily inspired by the classical history of Italy, and equally interested in the political divisions that had gripped the country throughout the twentieth century, Fabro adopted a unique view of history—preferring to think of events not as past, or "historic," but as continuously informing and altering the landscape of the present. In much the same way that the materials dictated the ultimate shape of his sculptures, for Fabro, history was constantly designing contemporary life. He believed to call it "the past" was an obvious misnomer. In *Il giorno mi pesa sulla notte V (Day Weighs Heavily on My Night, V),* the fluted exterior of the white marble dial instantly evokes the columns of classical Greco-Roman architecture. The marble, a medium that might appear decadent in certain contexts, is presented as practical and purposeful. A commonplace material in Fabro's home country, the marble functions as a direct reference to centuries of artistic and aesthetic innovation that, though specific to that geography, were born of overlapping cultures and societies that well predate the nation of Italy itself.—*MH*

Fior di pesco marble, Rosa Portogallo marble, 36 ¼ x 78 ¾ x 59 in. (92 × 200 × 150 cm), Gift of Sydney and Walda Besthoff, 2006

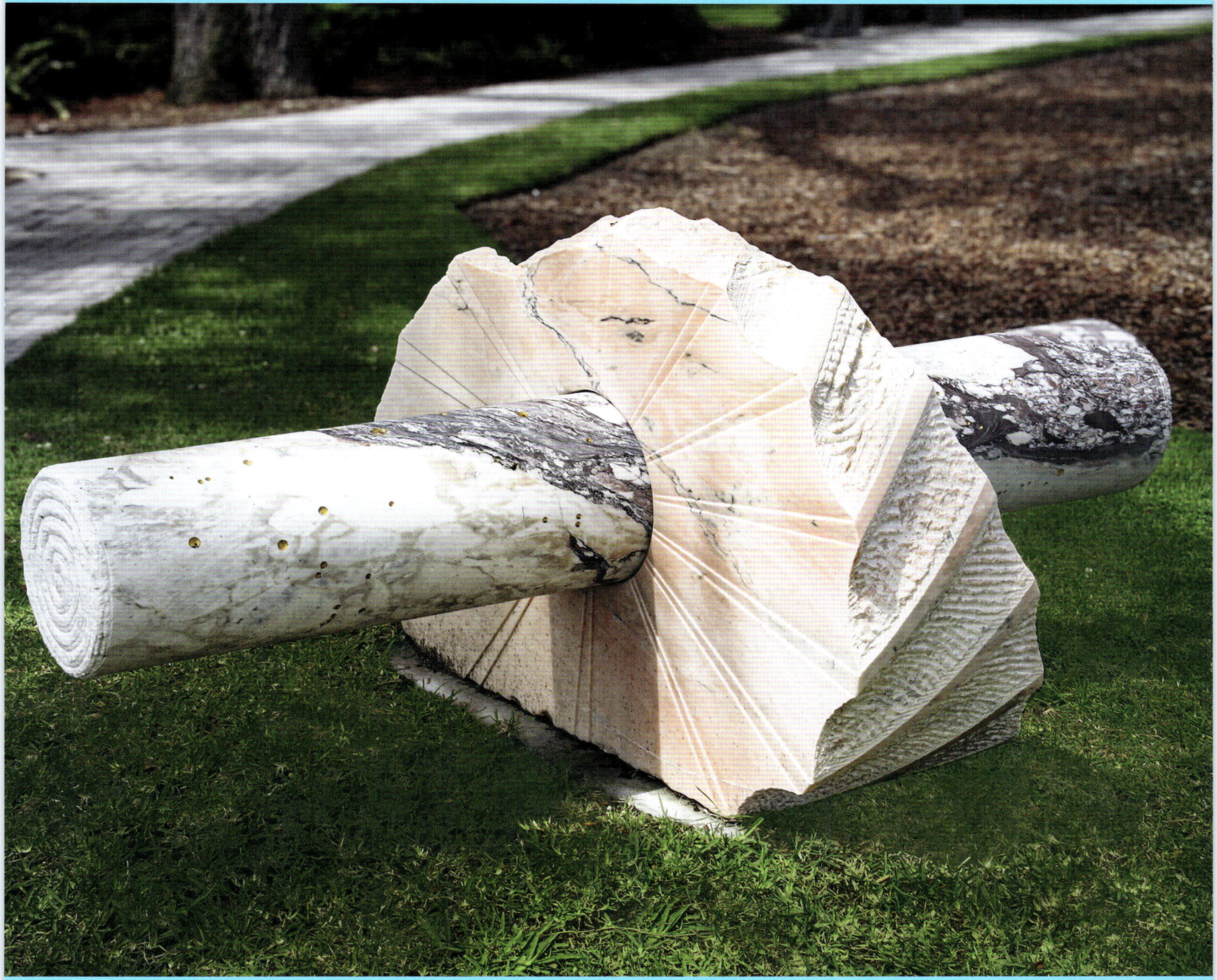

Teresita Fernández

Viñales (Mayombe Mississippi), 2019

Teresita Fernández's (b. 1968) work is characterized by a conceptual interrogation of environmental, historical, and physical landscapes, achieved through an inventive use of material and scale. Emphasizing art's spiritual dimension and deriving inspiration from genres of traditional landscape painting and Land art, Fernández's practice subtly yet powerfully tackles themes of ecological exploitation and colonial models that abuse nature as a resource. Place, memory, and visibility synthesize in her cosmic work to shed light on oppressed narratives. Engaging with unexpected media such as gold, charcoal, volcanic rock, and mirror-polished metals, Fernández questions these resources' convoluted histories and associations. She has garnered international recognition for her sculptural installations that evoke the sublime qualities of organic phenomena through perceptual experiments and intimate exchanges. Born in Miami to Cuban parents, Fernández currently lives and works in Brooklyn, New York, and holds degrees from Florida International University and Virginia Commonwealth University.

Viñales (Mayombe Mississippi) was commissioned for the Besthoff Sculpture Garden and serves as a striking gateway for visitors entering the pavilion. The sixty-foot-long mural executed in thousands of handmade tesserae glazed in hues of brown, blue, and green, mirrors viewers' reflections and shimmers with changes in the surrounding environment. This titanic mosaic is part of a series started in 2015, in which Fernández alludes to Cuba's provincial countryside, Viñales, a valley once home to Taíno communities and a refuge to runaway enslaved people. Despite echoing the verdant terrain of Cuba, the depicted scenery was acquired from the imagery of a malachite mineral native to the Democratic Republic of Congo. Amplifying proportions, Fernández transforms otherwise microscopic petrologic patterns into an immensely luminous panorama, creating parallels between the physical landscapes and their histories. Through a methodically layered approach, she intertwines references to her family's homeland, images of extracted crystals in Africa, and the historical significance of Congo Square in New Orleans, once the hub of the slave market. Described by the artist in a *New York Times* article in 2019 as a "stacked landscape," the work represents "multiple times and places happening simultaneously" and illustrates Fernández's ability to offer renewed visions of our past while nurturing philosophical shifts in thinking about our contemporary relationship with Earth and its elements.—*JM*

Opposite and following spread
Glazed ceramic tiles, 51 × 17 ft. (15.5 × 5.2 m), overall, Museum purchase with funds provided by Sydney and Walda Besthoff, 2019

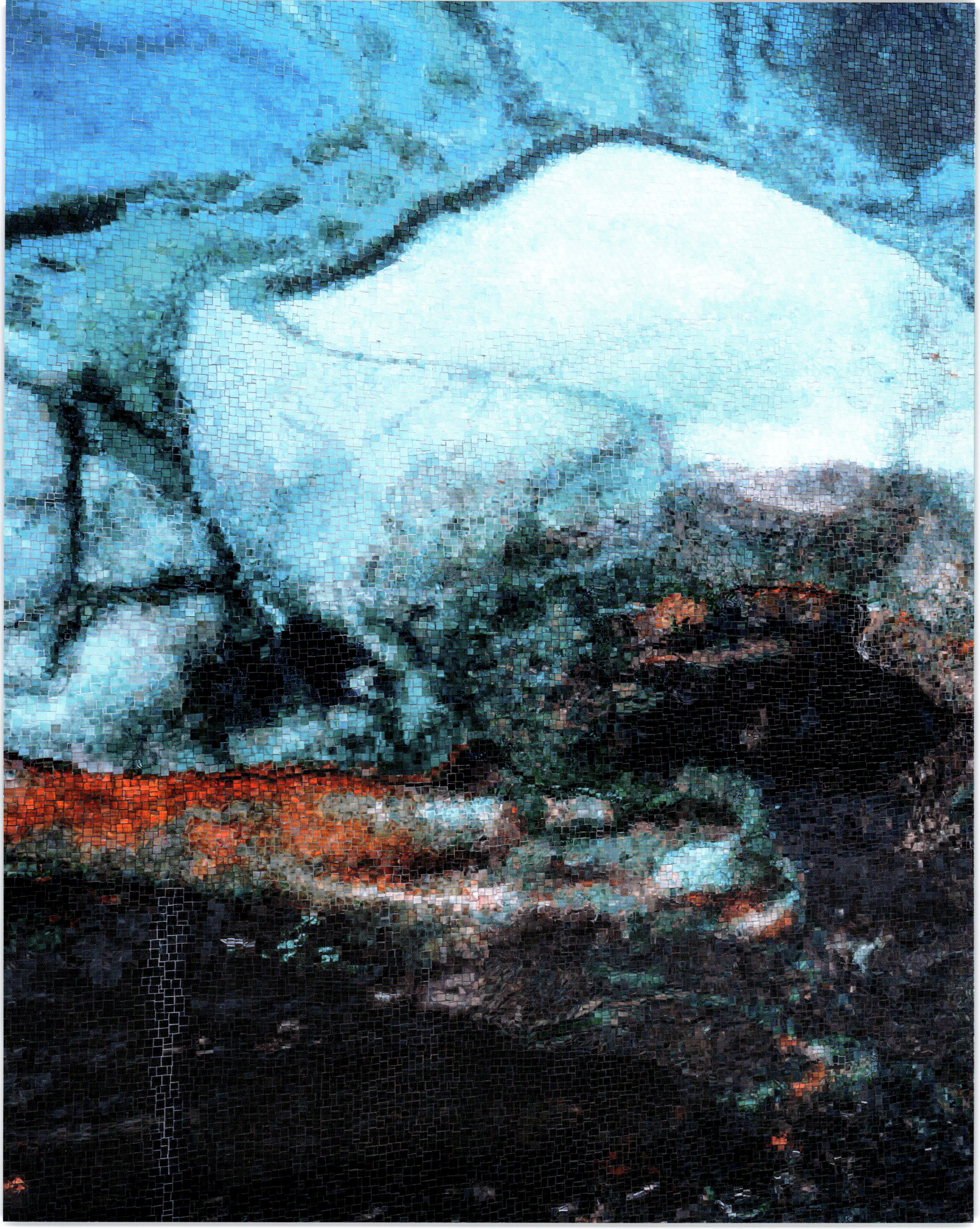

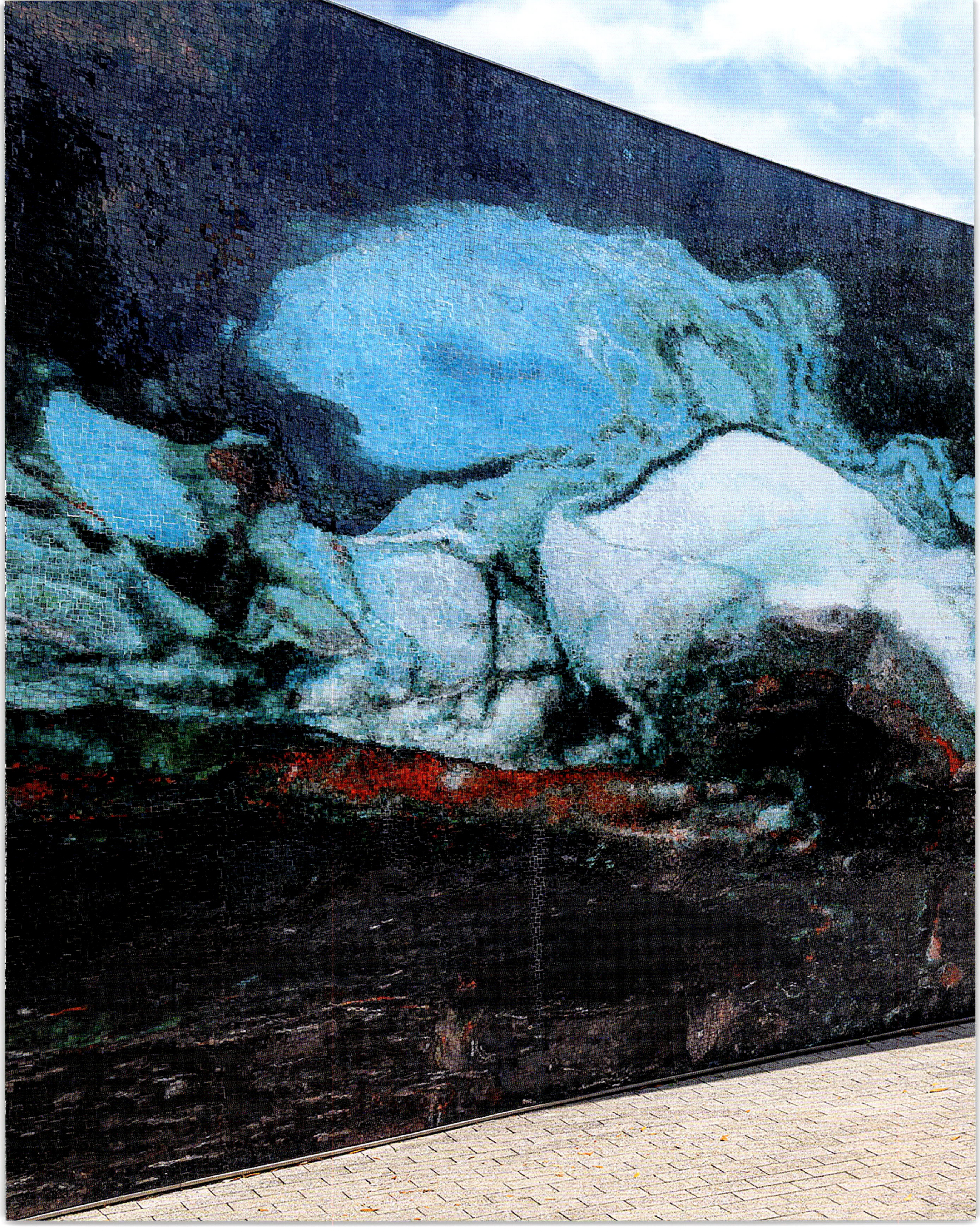

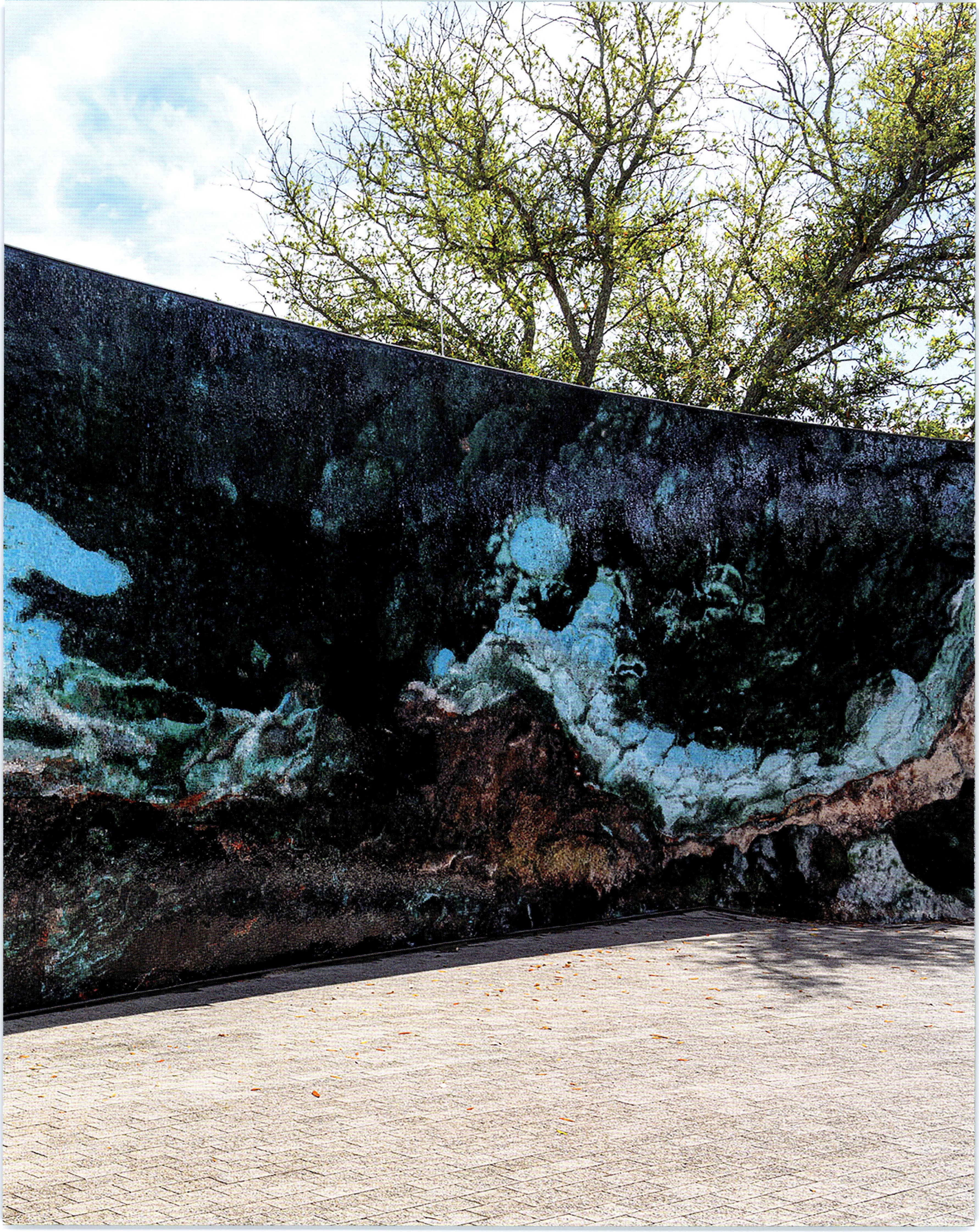

Audrey Flack

Civitas, 1988

An Abstract Expressionist painter in the 1950s, a Photorealist painter in the 1970s, and a sculptor of monumental figural bronzes since the 1980s, Audrey Flack (1931–2024) has pursued a career marked by striking transformations. She began studying at Cooper Union in New York, her native city, and then switched to Yale University, where she graduated in 1952. Returning home, her subsequent training in anatomy at the Art Students League would prove fundamental for her later turn to figural sculptures, a medium in which she was essentially self-taught. Flack was one of the first artists to use photographic sources as the basis for paintings and the most significant woman among a coterie of men producing hyper-realistic work. Her *vanitas* still lifes of the late 1970s in particular—crowded with perfume, cosmetics, and jewelry—investigated the construction of femininity through objects of the beauty regimen.

Flack's various bronze guardians and goddesses extended her feminist concerns into three dimensions. Acting as counter monuments to the long history of public sculpture that honors "great men," her pantheon of mythic and historical women exudes independence, pride, and power. Inspired by classical sculpture and nineteenth-century academic realism, Flack aimed to create archetypes and beacons of hope that people could relate to. She would make tabletop-sized sculptures first, then spend months refining larger versions at the foundry. *Civitas*, a personification of citizenship, shared responsibility, and community, relates to a group of four larger sculptures she installed as a gateway to Rock Hill, South Carolina, in 1991. With fluttering drapery and raised heels, this ethereal yet athletic, figure seems to levitate above the spherical base as the gold surface shimmers in the sun.—*AMT*

Patinated and gilded bronze with cast glass flame and attached marble base, 57 ½ × 12 × 17 in. (146.1 × 30.5 × 43.2 cm), Gift of Susan P. and Louis K. Meisel, 2002

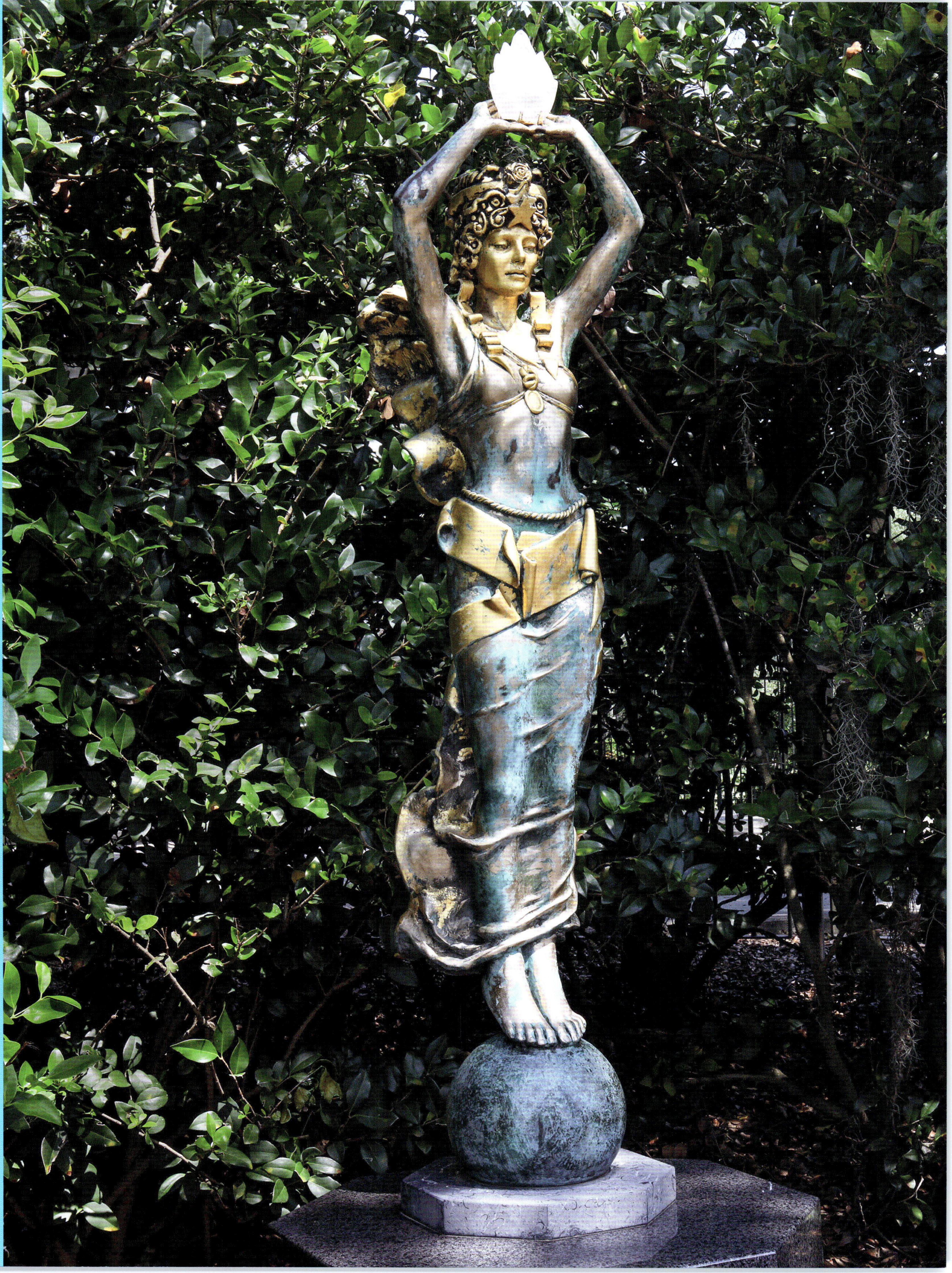

Elisabeth Frink

Riace Warriors, I, II, III, IV, 1983–88

Infusing the existential precarity of the postwar years into her textured bronze sculptures, Dame Elisabeth Frink (1930–1993) often depicted birds, horses, and mythic hybrids between human and animal, but her most enduring theme was the tension of masculinity itself and man's perennial need for violence. Born into a military family in Suffolk, England, Frink's childhood was spent outdoors, from learning to ride horses, to roaming the countryside, to shooting small animals to supplement wartime rations. As with many artists of her generation, the shadow of World War II and the dawn of nuclear threat loomed over Frink's practice, and out of it, she developed a unique style of sculpture that defies clean categorization within any of the artistic movements then taking hold in Britain. Carnal and often menacing, her work speaks to the worst side-effects of aggression.

Frink earned early critical acclaim for a series of bird sculptures, and at just twenty-two years old, she had her first solo exhibition, with the Tate Gallery subsequently acquiring one of her sculptures. At the time, Frink worked in a Giacometti-like style, building her maquettes from a mixture of wet and dry plaster to create a roughly hewn, highly varied surface. In the 1960s, however, she moved to France and her sculptures grew more smooth, textured only by shallow chisel marks such as the abrasions visible across the chests and bodies of *Riace Warriors*. Modeled on two fifth-century Greek bronzes that had been excavated from the sea off the coast of Calabria in 1972, Frink's *Riace Warriors* are typical of the artist's portrayals of brutish violence. The original Greek bronzes were thought to represent mercenaries who could be hired to commit terrible acts of brutality. The figures' bodies are perhaps the most true-to-life of the artist's sculptural oeuvre, though their white masked faces—a clear reference to the Aboriginal art Frink had seen firsthand while traveling through Australia—abstract the men and anonymize them. Hovering larger than life, their classically beautiful physiques appear paradoxically magnificent and threatening, their advancing stature ominous.—*MH*

Patinated bronze, 83 × 84 × 48 in. (210.8 × 213.4 × 121.9 cm), overall, Gift of the Sydney and Walda Besthoff Foundation, 1998

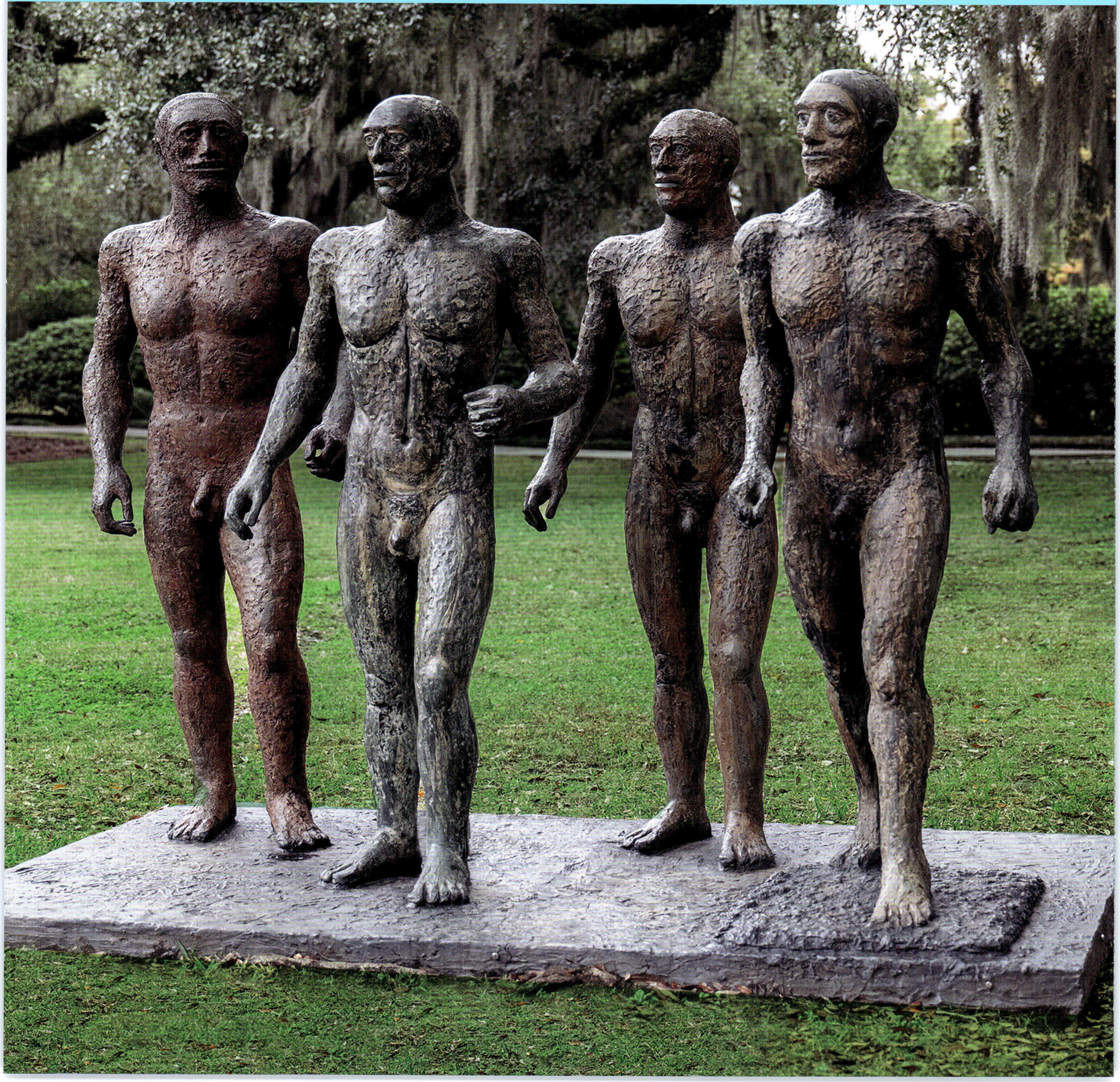

Katharina Fritsch

Schädel (Skull), 2017

Distorting her subjects through clever manipulations of scale and palette, Katharina Fritsch (b. 1956) depicts animals, human figures, and quotidian objects in a larger-than-life format, painted with matte finishes in vivid, unnatural hues. She pulls inspiration for her subjects, equally, from daily life—with examples including strawberries, umbrellas, and roosters—and the symbolism of fairy tales and religion, specifically the stories of the Brothers Grimm and Catholic iconography. Through the juxtaposition of scale, color, and subject, Fritsch situates her sculptures squarely between the humorous and the cryptic, speaking to her long-standing fascination with the subliminal and the unconscious.

Fritsch began her formal arts education at the renowned Kunstakademie in Düsseldorf. At the time, Germany's contemporary art scene pulsed with the subversive iconoclasm of Joseph Beuys (1921–1986), whose influence permeated every level of the local artistic community. Fueled by this ruleless spirit, Fritsch's first foray into the three-dimensional took the form of early experimentations with readymades, in which she painted found objects in solid shades of color. In 1987, she broke through, however, and pioneered her trademark style with a life-sized Madonna painted entirely in electric yellow, realizing a surreal combination of color, scale, and subject that would go on to become emblematic of her work.

Despite their visual perfection, Fritsch's sculptures are in fact molded by hand. Each shape is reworked through a number of plasters before it is cast either in bronze or polyester resin. The matte paint, fabricated from Fritsch's own custom-mixed pigments, absorbs light, preventing any reflections from catching in the sculptures' surfaces and adding to their uncanny ability to appear both in and out of place. Painted white, *Schädel (Skull)*, is part of a series that began in the 1990s. A solemn subject, the monumental skull not only nods to the art historical trope of the memento mori, but also evokes a handful of the themes Fritsch is known to explore: what defines the self, the possibility of life beyond death, dreamworlds existent only in realms outside our own. Ultimately, the sculpture opens more questions than answers—a telltale sign of Fritsch's best work.—*MH*

Bronze, paint, 45 5/8 × 57 7/8 × 37 in. (115.9 × 147 × 93.9 cm), Museum purchase with funds provided by Sydney and Walda Besthoff, 2018

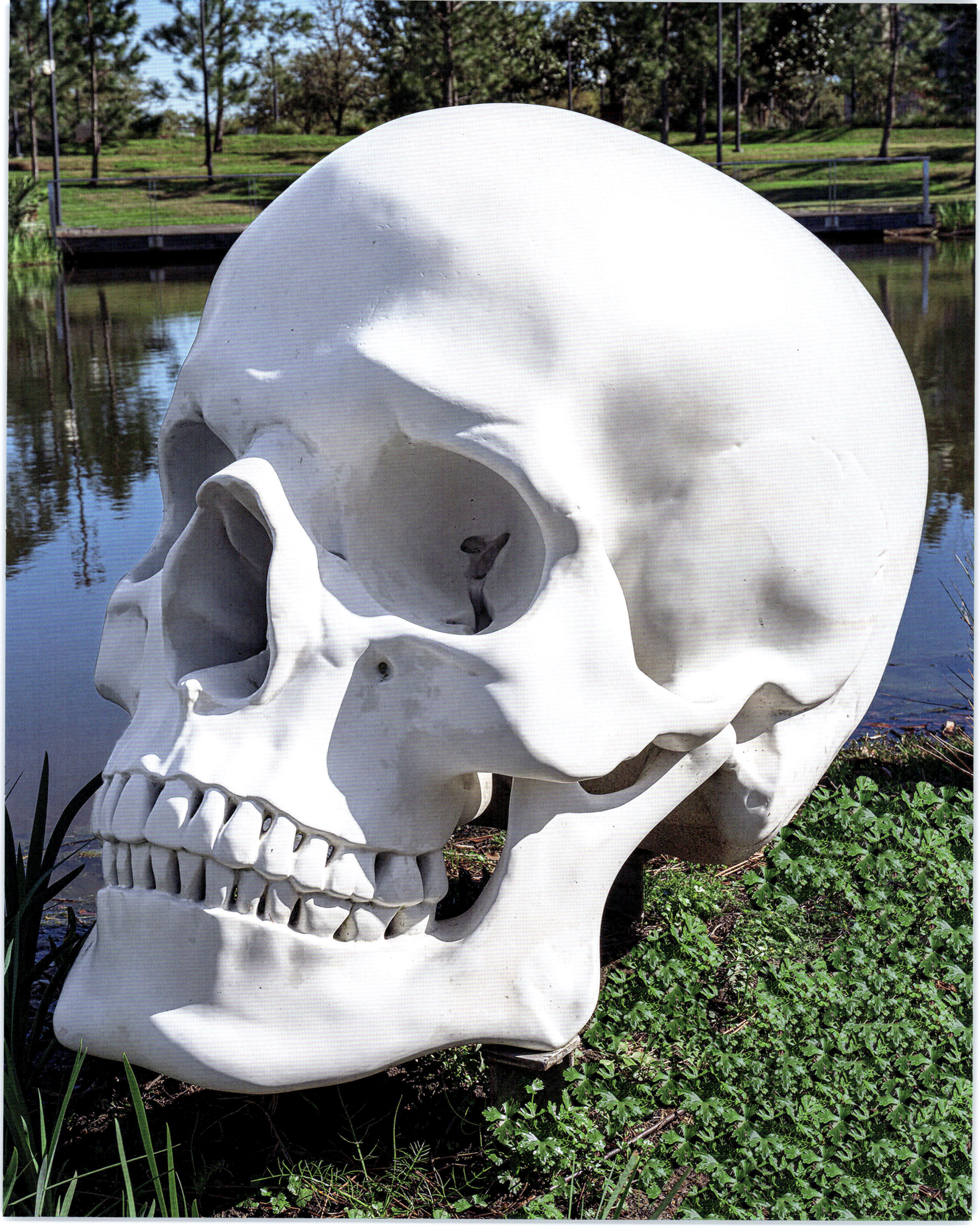

Frank Gehry

Bear with Us, 2014

Despite being considered one of the most influential architects from the twentieth and twenty-first centuries, Frank Gehry (b. 1929) is also a prominent artist and designer. With an illustrious career spanning more than fifty years, Gehry has left an indelible mark on urban landscapes worldwide, designing vast buildings that have become instantly recognizable and continue to astonish the public today.

Born and raised in Toronto, Gehry studied architecture at the University of Southern California and urban planning and design at Harvard University. In 1961, he relocated to Paris and encountered the avant-garde world of pioneering architect Le Corbusier (1887–1965) before returning to Los Angeles the following year. During the 1960s and 1970s, Gehry integrated into the cultural milieu of Santa Monica, establishing a modest architecture firm and befriending artists such as Edward Kienholz (1927–1994) and Ed Ruscha (b. 1937). Gehry first received national acclaim for a series of furniture pieces titled Easy Edges (1969–73), for which he transformed utilitarian and inexpensive materials, such as corrugated cardboard, into durable yet sophisticated objects. However, it was the 1978 restoration of his Santa Monica bungalow using industrial supplies that marked his ascent to prominence. Since then, Gehry has honed a trailblazing vision with a decades-long commitment to articulating movement and probing the contextual roles of form and function in architecture. Some of his most remarkable projects include the Guggenheim Museum in Bilbao, Spain (1997), the Neuer Zollhof in Dusseldorf (1999), and the Walt Disney Concert Hall in Downtown Los Angeles (2003). Interrogating the complexity of new materials and pioneering new technologies, the strength of Gehry's inventive process lies in drawing unexpected parallels between art and architecture.

Gehry's sculptures are a testament to his unique creativity. They embrace the shapes and materials he favors in his buildings, often incorporating unconventional techniques. *Bear with Us* is a playfully named work constructed from stainless steel in which the titular animal is drawn from fluid lines and tectonic planes that mimic the effects of a creased sheet of aluminum. Despite the resulting jagged relief, the bear's endearing character remains intact. Gehry's *Bear with Us* exemplifies the artist's deft manipulation of new and unusual materials and highlights his ability to captivate viewers through ludic subjects and form-shifting compositions.—*JM*

Stainless steel, 45 ½ × 84 ¾ × 45 ¾ in. (115.6 × 215.3 × 116.2 cm), overall, Museum purchase with funds provided by Sydney and Walda Besthoff, 2019

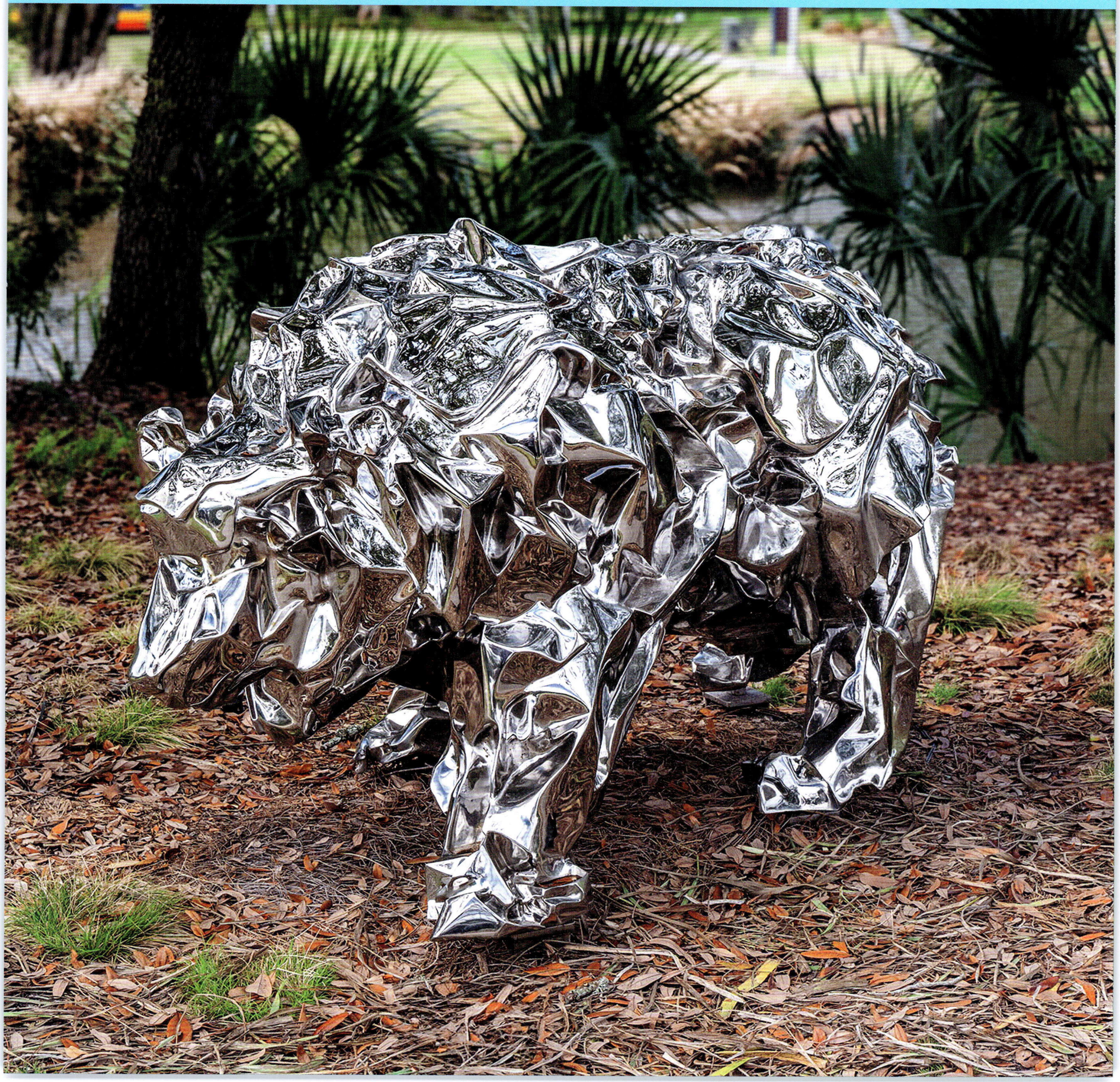

Robert Graham

Source Figure, 1991

Although rising to prominence for his civic monuments and public sculptures, Robert Graham (1938–2008) spent most of his career surveying the female form through multidisciplinary sculpture. Born in Mexico City, the artist moved to California in 1948 and studied at San José State University before completing a degree at the San Francisco Art Institute in 1964.

Despite mainly living in the United States, Graham credits the art he saw during his early years in Mexico—murals and paintings by Diego Rivera (1886–1957) and David Alfaro Siqueiros (1896–1974), among others—as a vital source of inspiration. In addition to producing major private commissions, Graham worked on important public sculptures including the Olympic Gateway for the 1984 Los Angeles Olympics, the Franklin Delano Roosevelt Memorial in 1997, and the National Medal of Arts for the US Congress in 1984.

During the late 1960s, Graham produced miniature architectural scenes in plexiglas boxes containing hyperrealist wax models. Voyeuristic in nature, most of the displays portrayed the figurines in the nude, often in sensual positions or carrying out mundane acts, casting an erotic light on their bodies. After spending four years in London, where the revered Whitechapel Gallery hosted an exhibition of these dioramic works, Graham settled permanently in Venice, California, in 1972. By the mid-1980s, he was experimenting with new techniques and utilizing 3-D scanners. Eventually, his practice evolved, shifting his fascination with the human form to create bronze statues in various scales, including *Source Figure*.

The pictured piece, installed in the Cascade Garden Pool, shows a nude female figure gracefully standing atop a coral-like column that is protected at its base by large-clawed crabs, evoking marine or aquatic undercurrents. With her eyes gently shut, the woman's hands are clasped in front of her abdomen as if presenting a sacred offering to the viewer. The heightened support grants the smaller-than-life woman an elevated stature, both physically and symbolically. Even though many of Graham's statuettes were named after their models, here we have a title that alludes to a new beginning. Demonstrating the artist's sustained interest in the female form, *Source Figure* incorporates mythical elements while exploring collective concerns inherent to human nature.—*JM*

Bronze, figure: 40 in. (101.6 cm); diameter: 24 5/16 in. (61.81 cm); 106 in. (269.2 cm), overall, Gift of the Sydney and Walda Besthoff Foundation, 2000

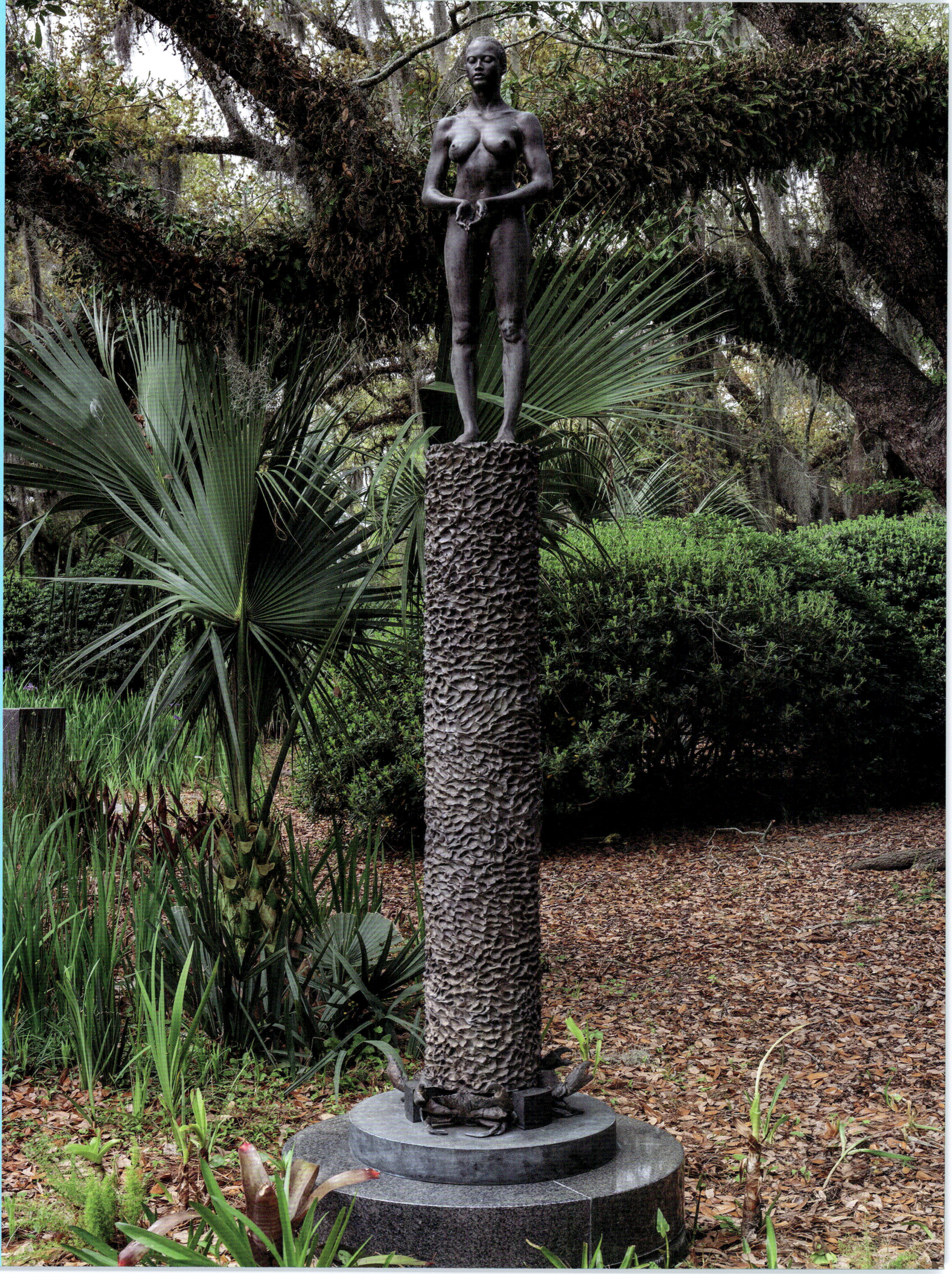

Jeppe Hein

Mirror Labyrinth, Besthoff Sculpture Garden, 2017

Eclipsing conventional sculptural practices, Jeppe Hein's (b. 1974) work consists of experiential pieces that defy perceptual boundaries and demand an active and psychological commitment from the viewer. Through the use of materials with reflective surfaces and the incorporation of dynamic text and sound, Hein warps the lines between object and subject and, by extension, art and life. Championing conceptual and minimalist art language from the 1970s, with his wry humor Hein transforms unassuming objects into immersive experiences that astonish and delight audiences.

A buoyant reinterpretation of the everyday is central to his creative practice, in which he playfully converts and distorts commonplace items such as benches, balloons, and streetlamps. In many instances, Hein's interactive works are presented in communal areas and feature movable elements or mazelike configurations, and therefore, his art frequently engages with tenets of architecture and technology.

The artist studied at the Royal Danish Academy of Arts in Copenhagen and the Hochschule für Bildende Künste-Städelschule (Städelschule Academy of Fine Arts) in Frankfurt, and is presently based in Berlin and Copenhagen. Some of his best-known installations have been exhibited at prominent international public spaces, including the Brooklyn Bridge Park, New York; Freilager Platz, Basel; and the Royal Fort Gardens, Bristol, England.

Made from freestanding polished steel panels positioned to form interlocking arcs, *Mirror Labyrinth* creates a narrow path for viewers to discover. Together the rhythmic, multifaceted elements create a fragmented reflection, an optical illusion that changes with movement, light, and shadow. Mounted at different heights, the repeated panes in the installation further interact with their surrounding environments and participating visitors, generating a lush kaleidoscope of the Besthoff Sculpture Garden and playfully stretching the limits of our visual perception. Through masterful and spirited tactics, Hein introduces audiences to a new relationship with the art object and the world beyond.—*JM*

Opposite and following spread
Steel, mirror, dimensions variable, Museum purchase with funds provided by Sydney and Walda Besthoff, 2019

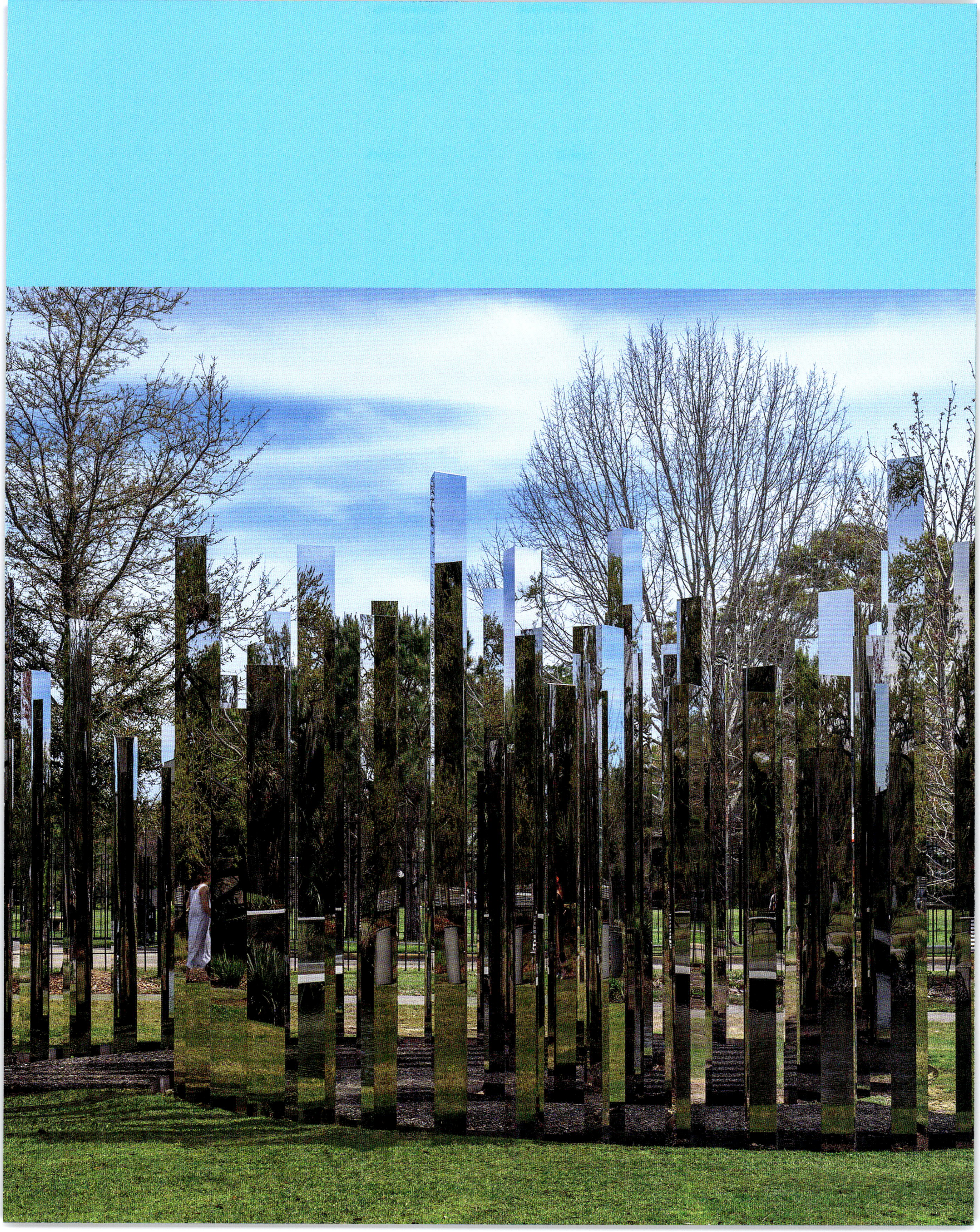

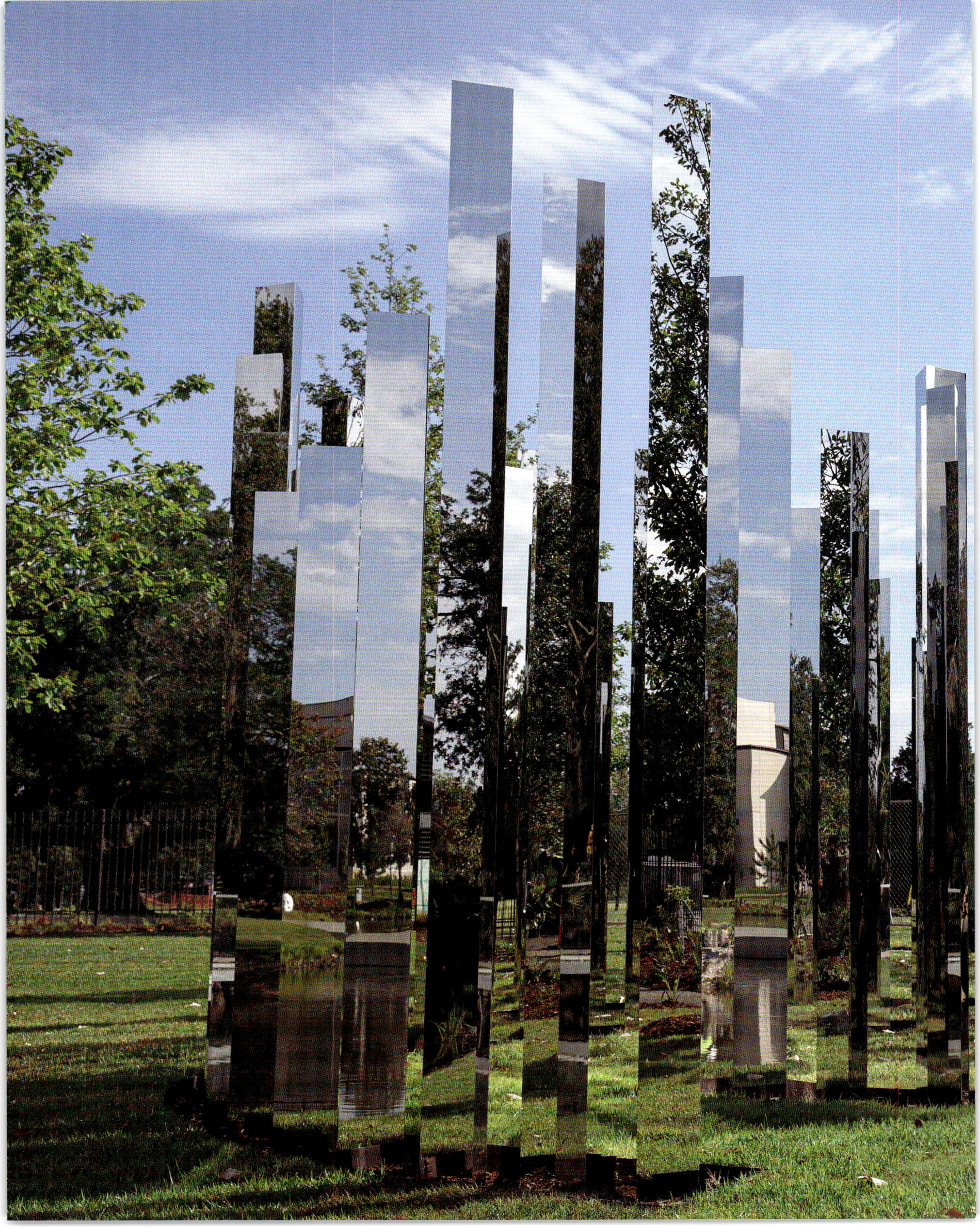

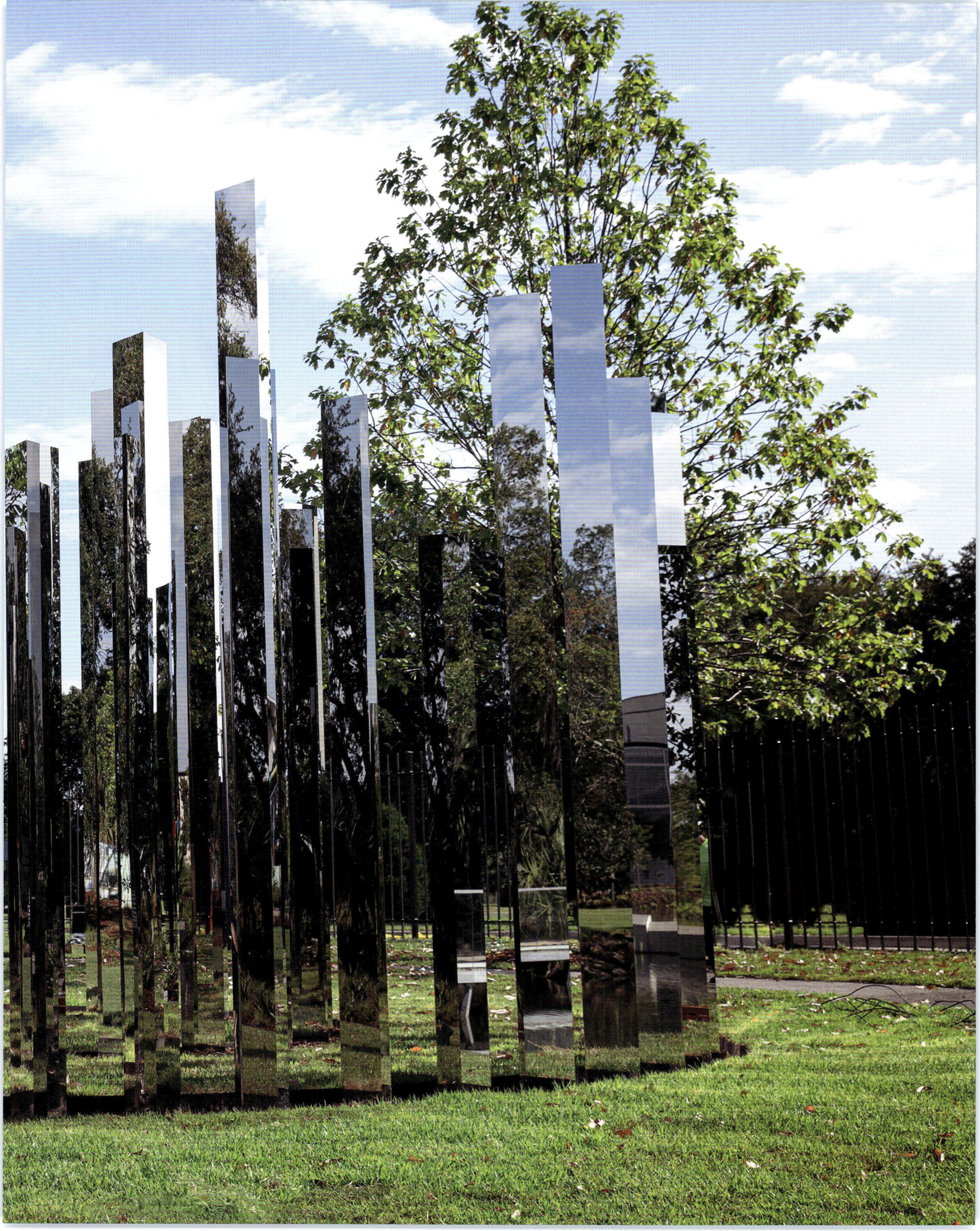

Barbara Hepworth

River Form, 1965

One of the most prominent British sculptors of the twentieth century, Barbara Hepworth (1903–1975) pioneered a new language of abstraction in England. Known for carving directly into her materials, she often worked in rounded, ovoid shapes that play continuously with volume, form, and the voids created by negative space. Above all, however, her biomorphic forms are the product of the medium she sculpted with, and her profound understanding of both wood and stone.

Hepworth was fascinated by sculpture and shape from an early age, and at the age of sixteen enrolled in the Leeds College of Art, where she befriended the artist Henry Moore (1898–1986). The two subsequently went on to study at the Royal College of Art, spurring a healthy rivalry that developed into a mutual respect and shared comradery over their lifetimes. Both artists were working in the direct carving method, first introduced by Constantin Brancusi (1876–1957) in 1906, and their respective artistic experiments became important references for one another. Though she had initially incorporated figurative elements into her work, by the 1930s Hepworth was working entirely in abstraction. In 1932, she made her first pierced sculpture, a development that would lead her towards a more pronounced play of negative space and shadow. Following the outbreak of World War II, Hepworth relocated to Cornwall with her second husband, the artist Ben Nicholson (1894–1982). There, the pair became active members in a flourishing arts community, and Hepworth's sculpture oriented itself increasingly towards the beauty of the natural landscape that surrounded her.

Initially a carving made from American walnut, *River Form* began to split shortly following completion, prompting Hepworth to carefully cast the shape in bronze. The oblong form, open on one side and pierced through with three holes, incorporates the compositional elements Hepworth is best known for, the negative space at the center of the sculpture creating a womb-like interior. The patina of the bronze exterior is carefully patterned to mimic the grain of the original walnut, a testament both to Hepworth's precision and to her enduring respect for the materials she worked with.—*MH*

Bronze, 33 ½ × 74 × 32 ½ in. (85.1 × 187.9 × 82.6 cm),
Gift of the Sydney and Walda Besthoff Foundation, 1998

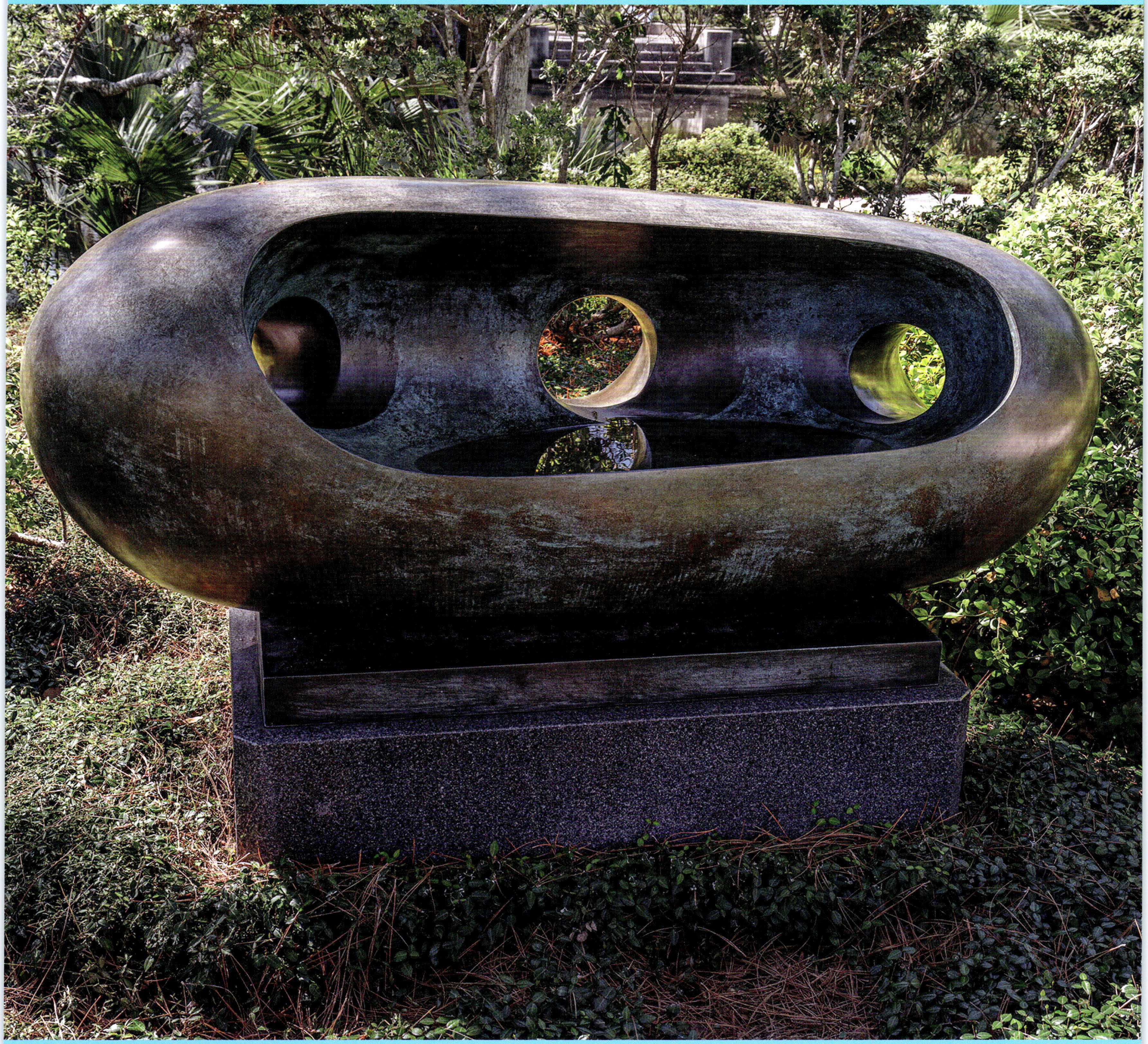

Georg Herold

Liver of Love, 2013

Fascinated by the limits of language, Herold's brassy, audacious, and often humorous style has earned him a reputation as a bombastic conceptualist. Known for his sculptures, but also his paintings and mixed-media works, Georg Herold's (b. 1 947) signature cheeky bravura is perhaps most apparent in the titles he gives his pieces. They often have the feeling of a suspended punch line, and emphasize the discrepancy between what can be seen and what is being described, effectively highlighting their own incompetence.

Herold came up in the late 1970s and 1980s with a generation of provocative, iconoclastic German artists that included Albert Oehlen (b. 1954), Werner Büttner (b. 1954), and Martin Kippenberger (1954–1997). After several years at the Academy of Fine Arts in Munich, Herold moved to Hamburg, where he studied under Sigmar Polke (1941–2010).

Emboldened by Polke's approach to conceptual art, and equally affected by his divided childhood in Germany—growing up in the East and coming of age in the West—Herold experimented freely with unconventional materials. He applied mediums that were nevertheless political and symbolic of either socialism or capitalism, working with everything from bricks and caviar to mattresses, roofing tiles, and baking powder.

Cast in bronze, the figure in *Liver of Love* derives its form from a construction of wood which Herold bound in wet canvas, a process that compacts the structure as the fibers dry, creating a firm solid that can then be coated in bronze, followed by one of the artist's signature lurid colors. Part of a series of larger-than-life, elongated figures, the sculpture sits right at the edge of abstraction. Its form and angles remain inscrutable, their construction, and their very reason for being, mysterious. While clearly a figure in repose, the shape and form of the body are obviously secondary to Herold's top priority: the manipulation of the material. Both the work and the larger series exude Herold's telltale nonconformism as he takes a familiar trope from the art historical canon and repurposes it, in a way that is playful though not entirely innocent.—*MH*

Lacquered bronze, 41 3/8 in. × 12 ft. 4 in. × 69 in. (105.2 cm × 3.8 m × 175.26 cm), Museum purchase with funds provided by Sydney and Walda Besthoff, 2017

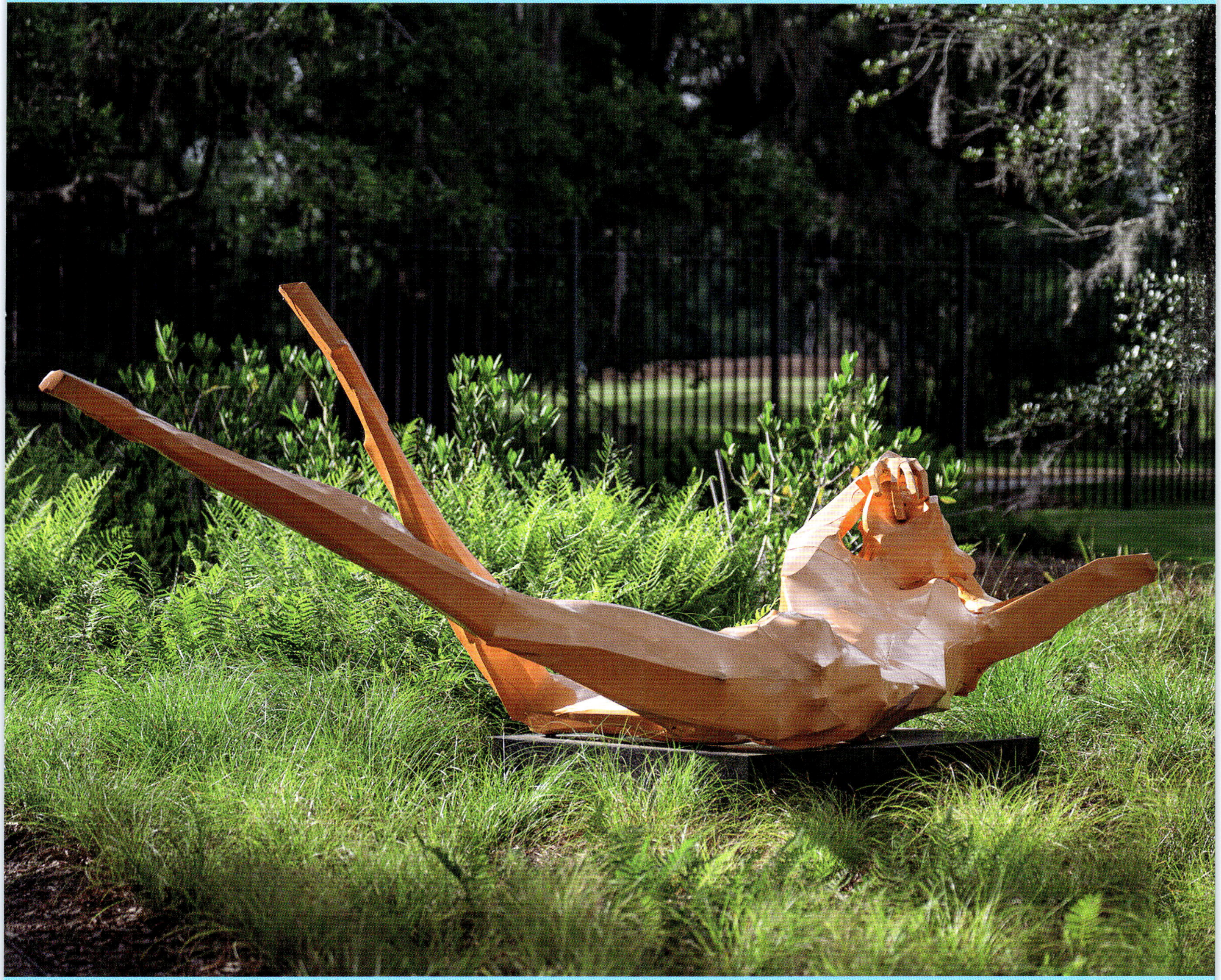

Thomas Houseago

Striding Figure (Rome I), 2013

Characterized by a singular permutation of materials and references, Thomas Houseago's (b. 1972) sculptures embody a new conceptual understanding of the human form that recalls modern art, classical statuary, and popular culture. Houseago was born and raised in the United Kingdom and lived in Belgium and the Netherlands before permanently moving to Los Angeles in 2003. He studied art, first in London at Central Saint Martins and later in Amsterdam at De Ateliers. His titanic figures and oversized masks, made from carved wood, clay, plaster, and bronze, among other media, draw inspiration from a wide range of sources, including science fiction, tribal art, and pop music. At once substantially imposing, structurally precarious, and seemingly incomplete, Houseago's paranormal beings appear to emerge from a dystopian world. His raw, bulky bodies are bound together by multidimensional planes and rods, rendering their insides visible and conveying a delicate state of decomposition. Also traversing drawing and painting, Houseago has recently produced two-dimensional works that investigate the expressive and perceptual properties of color.

Often, the artist works preliminarily with clay before casting his bronze sculptures, resulting in raw and unfinished contours, as typified in *Striding Figure (Rome I)*. Disparate dabs and strokes make up the monster's broad shoulders and stocky limbs, exposing rough surfaces and imparting a dilapidated and archaeological undercurrent. The piece's colossal magnitude and anatomical structure exude a divine vigor. Physical dominance and symbolic strength are standard in the historical tradition of monuments, and here, Houseago parallels a legacy of oversized statues that imposed political, religious, and colonial control. Additionally, the work invokes Egyptian icons and their archetypal treading pose. Yet closer inspection reveals that the figure's thighs are hollow and its stance precariously propped up. Although assertively conveying movement and might, the inclined position is rigid and awkward, leaving the heavy body susceptible to collapse. Bridging past, present, and future and building on existing customs of abstraction and figuration, Houseago creates new mythologies and reimagines contemporary notions of fragility and power.—*JM*

Bronze, figure: 142 ½ × 70 × 91 ¼ in. (361.9 × 177.8 × 231.8 cm); base: 14 × 62 × 94 in. (35.6 × 157.5 × 238.8 cm), Museum purchase with funds provided by Sydney and Walda Besthoff, 2017

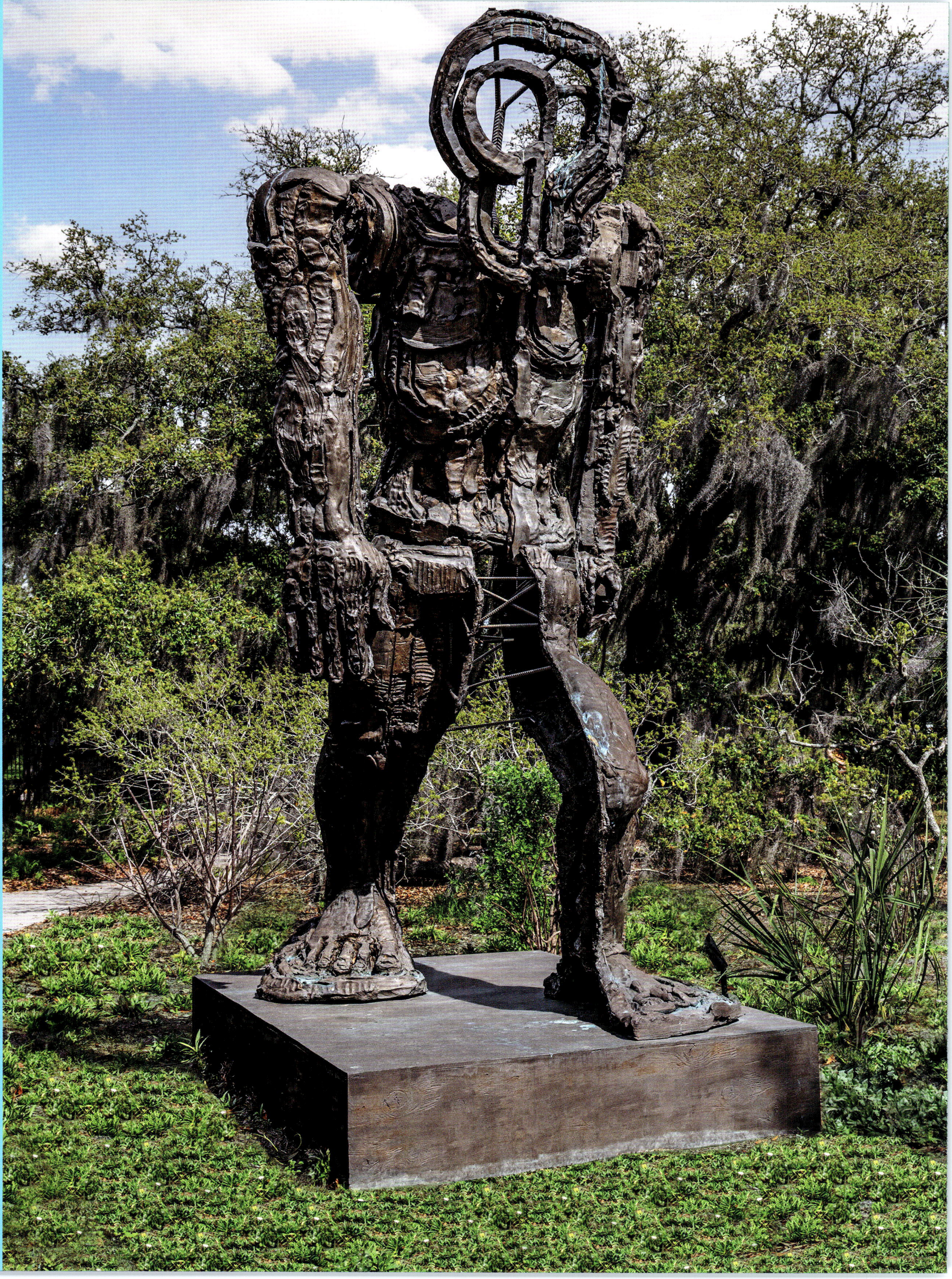

Shirazeh Houshiary

Exuviae, 2016–17

The first non-white woman nominated for the prestigious Turner Prize in 1994, Shirazeh Houshiary (b. 1955) has called London home since moving there from Iran in 1974. She graduated from the Chelsea School of Art in 1979 and rose to prominence as a part of the New British Sculpture generation, who reacted to their minimal and conceptual forebears in the 1980s. Houshiary, however, has questioned nationality as an organizing principle and attempts to classify her work generally. "I don't want to fit into any category," stated Houshiary in a profile in *ArtNews* from 2013, "I want to be an individual, with a mind and ideas, who can connect to the bigger picture of who we are as human beings."

Whereas Houshiary's early sculptures were made of clay, wood, and straw, she began to use various metals as her primary materials in the mid-1980s. *Exuviae* is among the many spiral towers she has created since the 1990s. The first—and several feet taller than the featured work—*The Extended Shadow* (1994) was composed of cast lead blocks and gold leaf and was initially installed in Cass Sculpture Park in Sussex, England. The white glazed limestone bricks of *Breath* (2004), another variation, rose twenty feet from a plaza in Battery Park in Manhattan and emitted sounds from different religious traditions: Islamic call to prayer, Buddhist meditation, Jewish song, and Christian chant. This spiritual hybridity informs much of Houshiary's work, including her monochrome, cobweb-like paintings with meticulous, yet indecipherable, script selected from Arabic, Hebrew, Sanskrit, or Latin. Although her spiral sculptures have graced indoor as well as outdoor spaces, the site-specific towers, such as *Exuviae*, reflect and play with natural light most effectively so that the forms seem to disappear and reappear. Cast glass, in an array of iridescent colors, became a prominent component of these towers in the 2010s. Recalling forces—both infinitesimal, the twisting double helix of DNA, and vast cyclones, comets, and solar flares—*Exuviae* and other related sculptures invite meditation on metaphysical dualities: being and nonbeing, physical and immaterial, life and death.—*AMT*

Glass, stainless steel, 114 7⁄8 × 14 3⁄4 × 11 in. (291.8 × 37.5 × 27.9 cm), overall, Museum purchase with funds provided by Sydney and Walda Besthoff, 2018

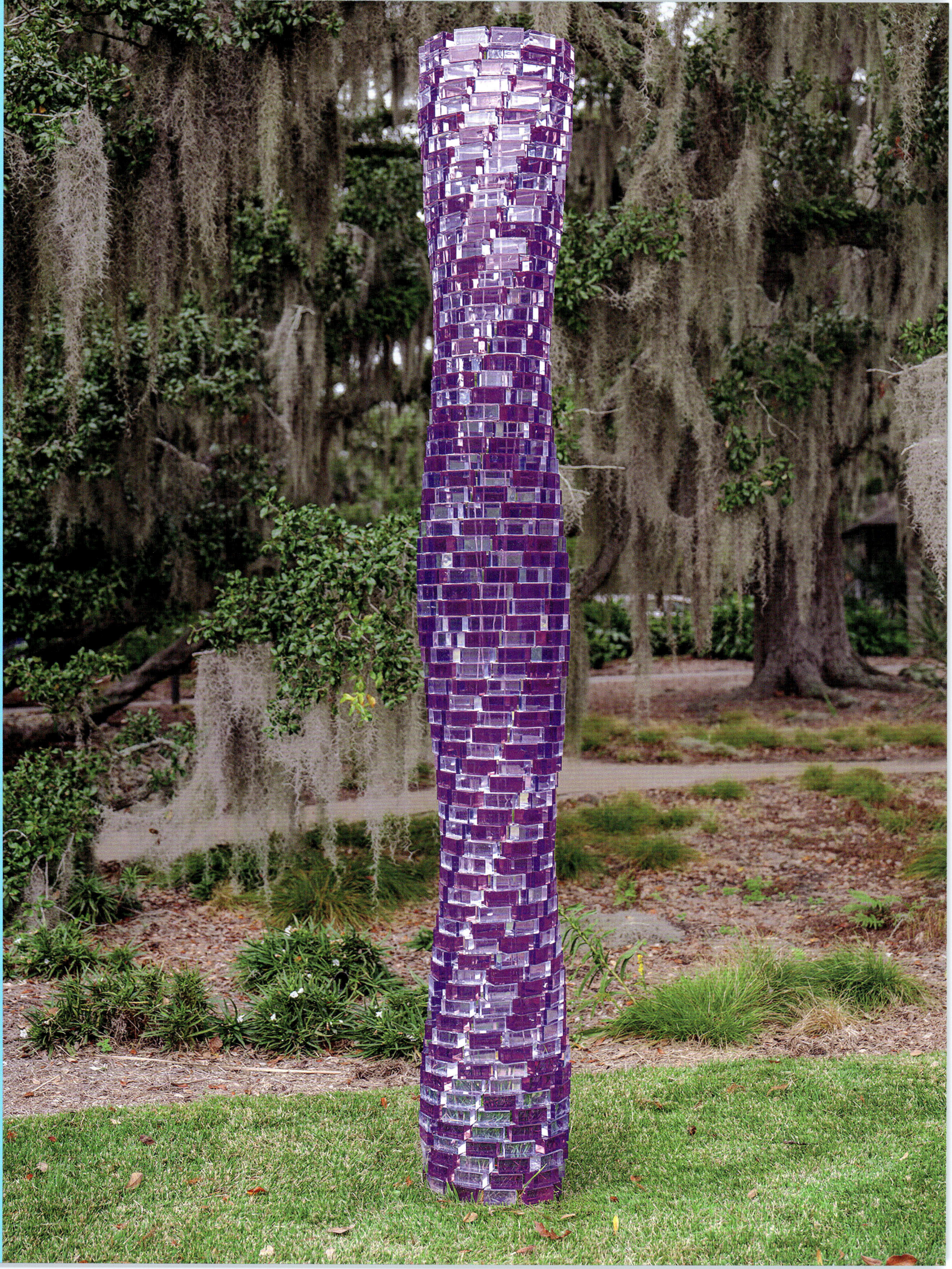

Linda Howard

Sunyatta, 1979

Based on simple geometric principles, Linda Howard's (b. 1934) curvilinear sculptures are constructed from aluminum poles, steadily repeated and methodically spaced to create rounded, illusory shapes. Combining mathematics and aesthetics, the artist's monumental designs are carefully calibrated to play with the viewer's perception of shape and solidity. The works' metal surfaces, buffed to a deliberate shine, catch and reflect any changes in the light, making them appear variably substantial and ephemeral.

Influenced in part by memories of her earliest years wandering beaches and forests, Howard first encountered writings on the calculated patterns of the environment while a graduate student at Hunter College, New York. The new knowledge instantly reframed her childhood memories: now the minute designs of petals or the spines of a crustacean could be understood as equations. Howard quickly began exploring the intricacies and implications of such principles in her work, applying a mathematical lens to her burgeoning sculpture practice.

Each form is developed by drawing on concepts central to Eastern philosophy and physics. For Howard, the two disciplines intersect and share crucial commonalities. Both frameworks offer methods for describing the mechanics of nature—albeit from drastically different perspectives—and Howard derives her richest material from these earthly and human phenomena. Drawing on the cognitive states of meditation as well as the mathematics undergirding the natural environment, Howard's work ultimately attempts to bridge the gap between the metaphysical and the concrete, the emotional and the numerical.

Taking as its title the Sanskrit word meaning "emptiness," *Sunyatta* combines two identical arched forms. Assembled from aluminum rods, the two forms meet at their mirror edge, creating an incomprehensible whole. From every angle, *Sunyatta* presents myriad distinct shapes and patterns, existing as an evolving, spectral object, that is at once of this world and, at times, appears entirely like a dream.—*MH*

Brushed aluminum, 100 × 72 × 102 in. (254 × 182.9 × 259.1 cm), Gift of the Sydney and Walda Besthoff Foundation, 2000

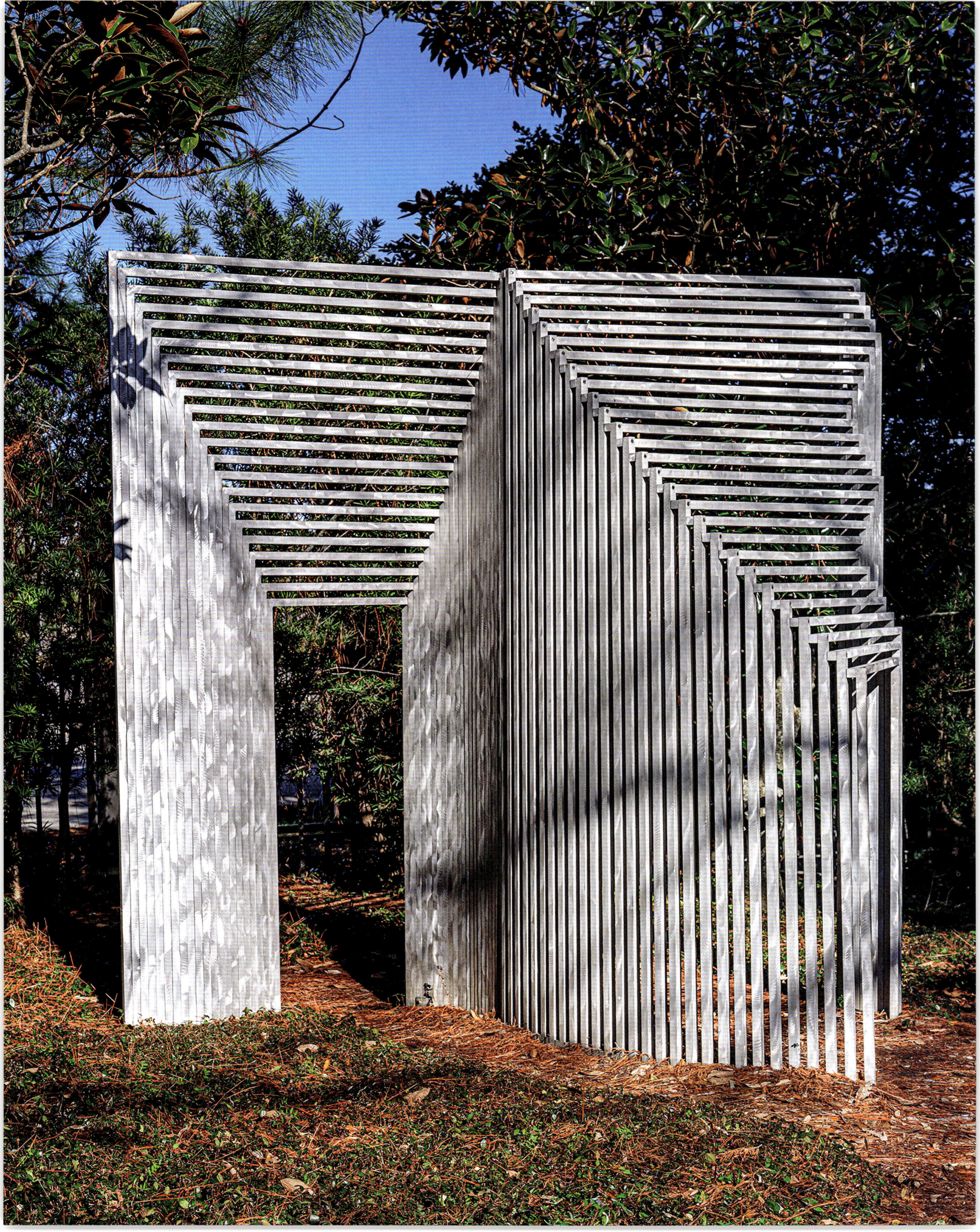

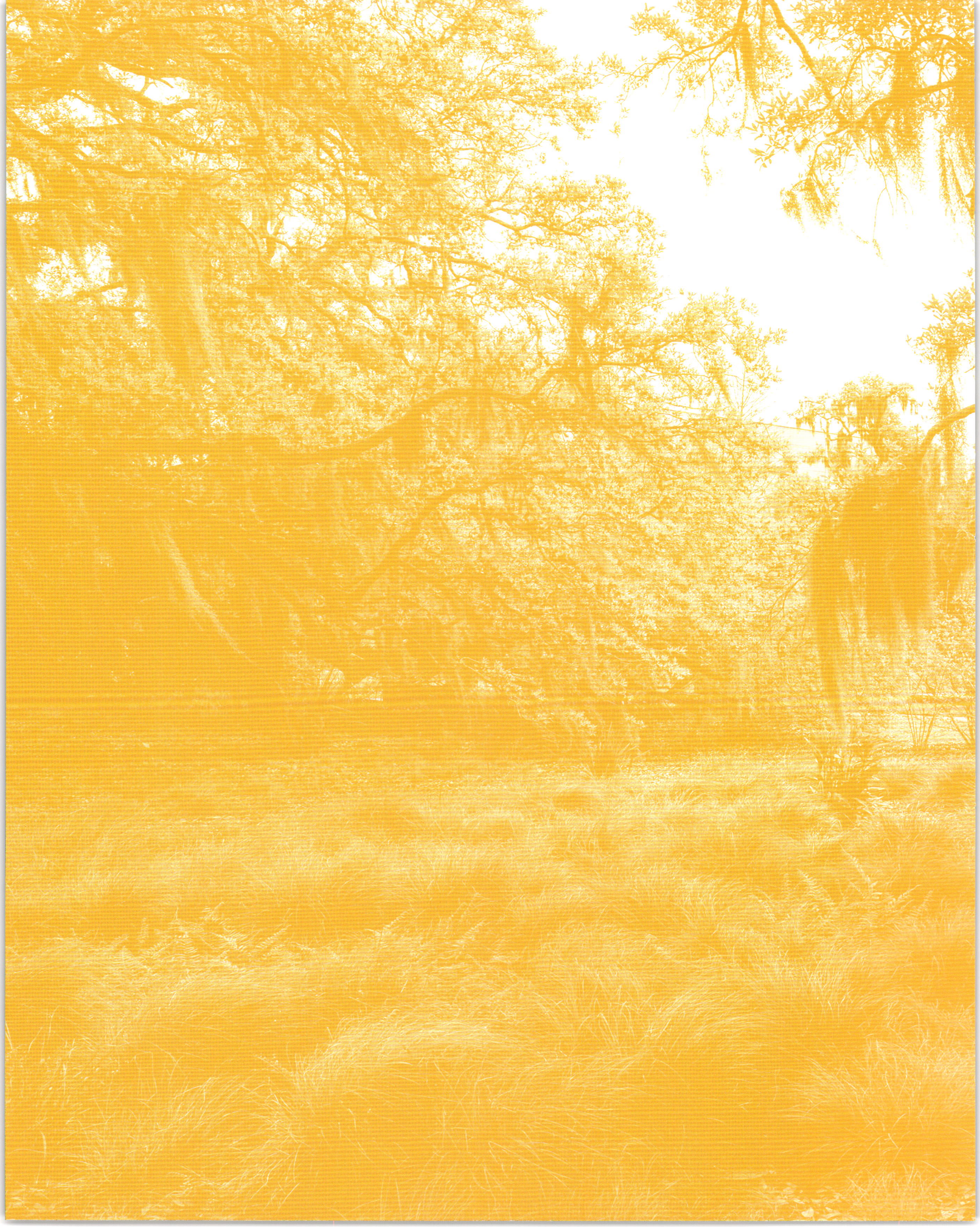

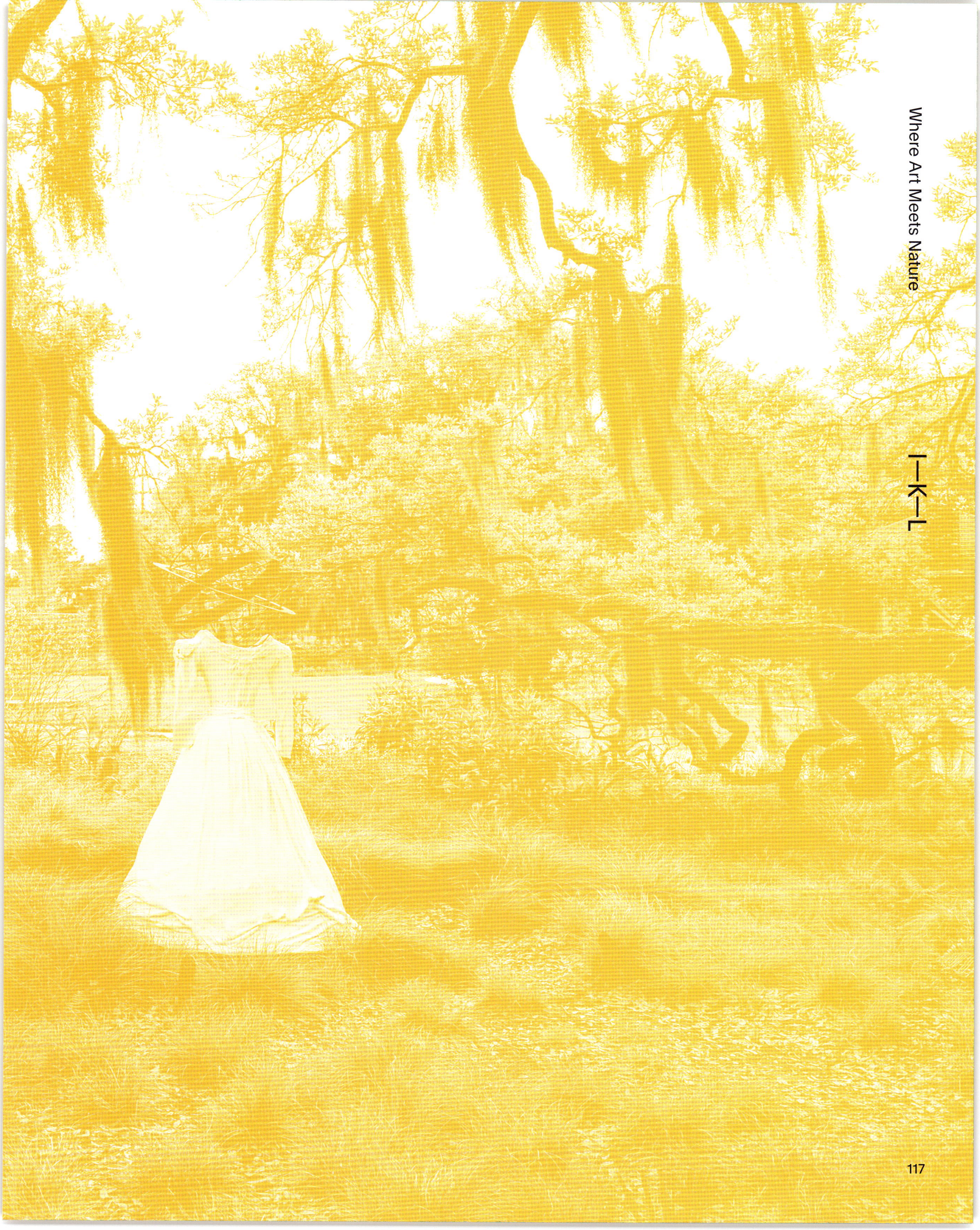

Robert Indiana

LOVE (red outside violet inside), 1966–97

One of the most prominent artists in postwar American art, Robert Indiana (1928–2018) expanded the boundaries of both assemblage sculpture and abstraction, but is perhaps best known for his graphic, bold text paintings and early contributions to Pop art. Working with simplified shapes and punchy, evocative phrases, Indiana combined the cold silhouettes of Hard-edge painting with bright, idealized symbols of Americana. His artworks became emblematic of an evolving New York art world as the dominance of Abstract Expressionism splintered into a number of the different movements that would come to define the postwar era.

Born Robert Clark, Indiana changed his name shortly after landing in New York. Arriving by way of three years in the US Air Force, followed by a formal education at the Art Institute of Chicago; the Skowhegan School of Sculpture and Painting in Madison, Maine; and the Edinburgh College of Art, Indiana garnered early attention for his combine works assembled from found objects. In 1956, he met Ellsworth Kelly (1923–2015), beginning a vital but turbulent romance that would continue to propel both artists' practices long after their relationship ruptured. At Kelly's suggestion, Indiana moved to Coenties Slip, a group of buildings off one of Manhattan's old shipping ports that had become an informal artists' community, home to Agnes Martin (1912–2004), James Rosenquist (1933–2017), Jack Youngerman (1926–2020), and Kelly himself. The move and the proximity to like-minded artists had a massive impact on Indiana's work and he experimented freely while enjoying the intellectual and emotional support of his friends and fellow artists.

Indiana's LOVE motif is arguably one of the most iconic of the late twentieth century. Initially created in 1961, Indiana iterated the design across numerous paintings and drawings, until it lit fire when it appeared on the Museum of Modern Art's Christmas card in 1965. An oblique reference to Kelly, the work was a jab at his disavowal of Indiana's use of text. For Kelly, lettering was too representational, but Indiana insisted that language could be a productive subject. The motif caught on, appearing on U.S. postage stamps, and has since been printed on nearly every other object imaginable. Still, the original ethos of the design holds, and the sculpture is a graphic, bold manifesto for language as an artistic subject—one that has proved enduring and evergreen.—*MH*

Aluminum and acrylic polyurethane enamel, 72 × 72 × 36 in. (182.9 × 182.9 × 91.4 cm), Museum purchase, Sydney and Walda Besthoff Foundation Fund, 2004

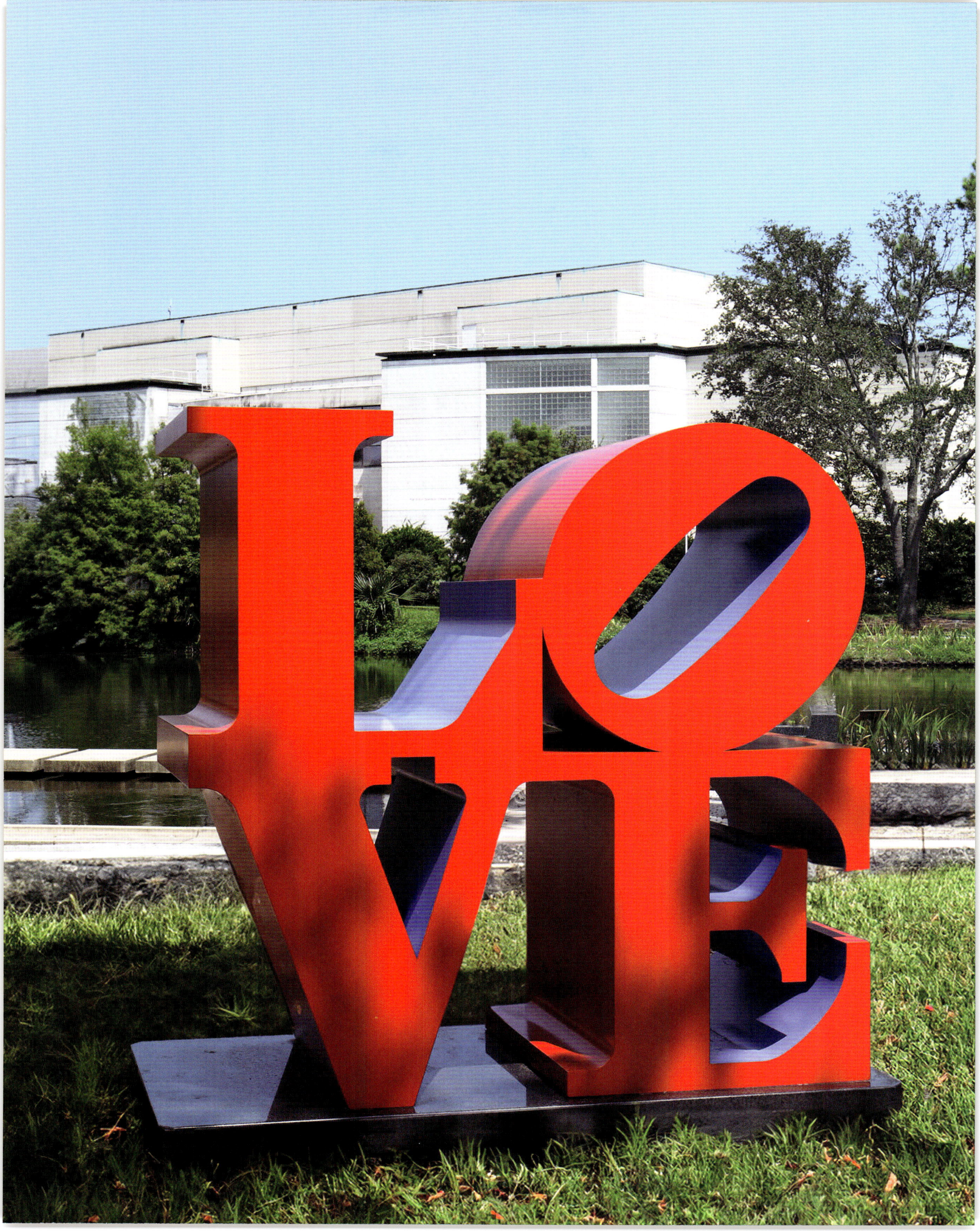
LO
VE

Jean-Robert Ipoustéguy

Grand Val de Grâce, 1977

Born in the French village of Dun-sur-Meuse, Jean-Robert Ipoustéguy (1920–2006) came of age during the interim period between World War I and II. After moving to Paris in 1938, a brief two-year art course was interrupted by the onset of the German invasion. Relocated to the South of France, Ipoustéguy was mobilized into iron and cement construction, and the skills he acquired during this labor would inform his sculptural practice. Ipoustéguy completed his studies at the war's end and focused his early artistic career on drawing and painting.

His official journey as a sculptor began in 1949, when he set up a studio on the outskirts of Paris and experimented with pure geometric forms. He became fascinated with the human body following a trip to Greece, where he encountered classical nude statues from antiquity. Contrary to the preferred aesthetics of the time, he shifted his attention to representation and eventually arrived at his signature style, in which figuration and abstraction met to render public monuments rooted in the nature of opposites. Themes of life, death, and resurrection were achieved through juxtapositions of rough and polished surfaces, factual and fantastical subject matter, and straight and sinuous lines.

While broadly acclaimed in France and Europe, Ipoustéguy's work has been largely overlooked in the United States, and therefore, *Grand Val de Grâce* is of unique value. At the heart of the piece stands a naked male form. His left thigh is chiseled, and his lower limb is distorted to rest on an inclined base. His arms are reaching outward in a gesture that resembles both a warm salute and a desperate call for help. A withered torso dangles from the central body, suggesting a shedding layer or symbol of a past life. Ominous cylindrical structures sustain the figures. *Grand Val de Grâce* was a commission for the military hospital in Paris of the same name. The sculpture reveals a fascination with the human form and typifies the incongruous poetics of Ipoustéguy's world, where anatomy and surrealism intersect.—*JM*

Bronze, 90 × 54 × 60 in. (228.6 × 137.2 × 152.4 cm), edition 5 of 8, Gift of the Sydney and Walda Besthoff Foundation, 1998

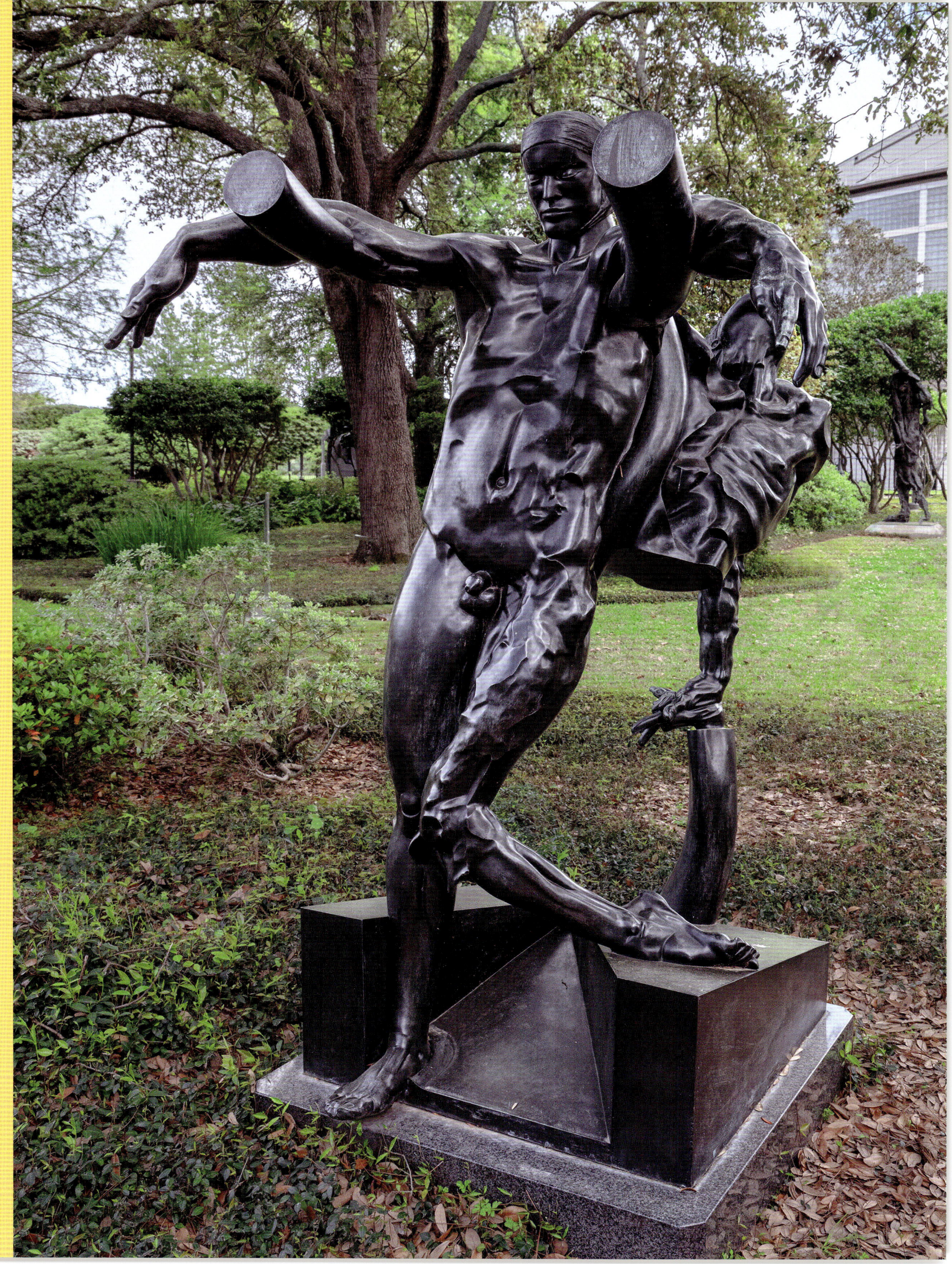

Menashe Kadishman

Open Suspense, 1968

Menashe Kadishman (1932–2015) studied art in Tel Aviv for three years before moving to London in 1959, where he first attended Saint Martin's School of Art and then Slade School of Fine Art. Having studied with the critically acclaimed British artist Anthony Caro (1924–2013) in the late 1950s, Kadishman embraced a minimalist articulation in his early sculptures, constructing geometric shapes and gracefully balancing them in positions appearing to defy the laws of physics. Often deploying glass or sheets of plastic in addition to steel, his inventive methods could achieve almost incomprehensible structures. Concerns with nature and religion later infiltrated the artist's practice. Between 1950 and 1953, Kadishman worked as a shepherd in Israel and this experience inspired much of his later work. Beginning in the late 1980s, after representing Israel in the 38th Venice Biennale, Kadishman turned his attention to illustrating motifs from wildlife, namely depictions of sheep. These colorful paintings and drawings express the tension and bonds between the personal and the collective, while recalling biblical themes and spiritual associations.

Kadishman's architectural sculptures such as *Open Suspense* elicit a unique spatial awareness in viewers through material, volume, and composition. More than three-meters high, the artwork is composed of a rectangle and disklike figure performing a balancing act on a quadrilateral base. A playful rebellion against the rules of gravity, the structure stimulates a paradox by creating a threatening anticipation of collapse. There is a rustlike patina across the entirety of the structure which is made of COR-TEN steel, a metal created to corrode naturally with exposure to the elements and therefore eradicate the need for priming. Although a clear rejection of figurative expression, *Open Suspense* triggers a powerful bodily reaction through an elementary vocabulary of forms. Employing industrial materials and working with simple shapes, Kadishman manifests viewers' intrinsic vulnerability to external forces while reminding them of nature's fickle predicament.—*JM*

COR-TEN steel, 120 ½ × 87 × 15 in. (306.1 × 220.9 × 38.1 cm),
Gift of the Sydney and Walda Besthoff Foundation, 1998

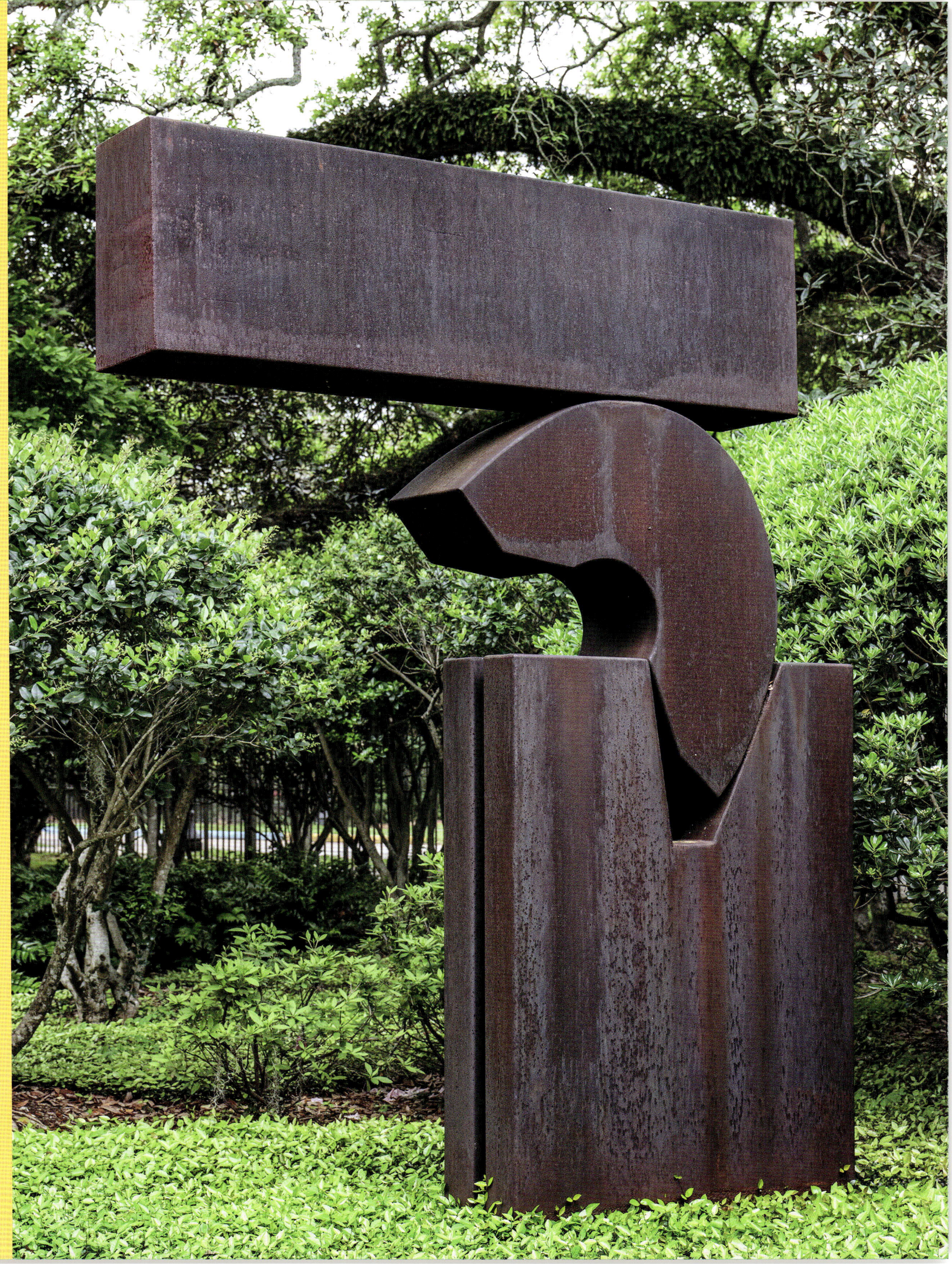

Anish Kapoor

Untitled, 1997

Born in Mumbai but now living between London and Venice, Anish Kapoor (b. 1954) is internationally renowned for his public sculptures that destabilize perception and inspire an introspective experience. Since the late 1970s, Kapoor has engaged his audience through a subversive practice, employing various mediums to test the potentials of color, light, and scale. He completed his education in London, first at Hornsey College of Art and later at the Chelsea School of Art and Design, where he studied under the Romanian-born artist Paul Neagu (1938–2004) and experimented with new technologies.

Initially investigating geometric monochromatic forms in the early 1980s, Kapoor's constructions became grander and heavier in the 1990s when he started utilizing industrial resources such as cement, granite, marble, PVC, and steel. Since then, his artistic output has become intricately embedded in its surroundings, at times disrupting the seemingly neutral nature of institutional environments to create far-reaching kinetic installations. Examining the implications of primary colors, especially red, Kapoor also deploys pigments and wax in his work, drawing from ancient mythological references to contrast splendor with chaos, intimacy with monumentality, and presence with absence.

Often Kapoor utilizes materials with mirror-like properties, employing stainless steel to create and distort reflections, which he achieves through concave bends and curvilinear forms. Such is the case in *Cloud Gate* (2006), publicly pronounced as *The Bean*, the centerpiece sculpture located in Millennium Park, Chicago, for which the artist received global recognition. Similarly, in *Untitled*, a rectilinear mirror-like block is disrupted through a convex hole on one of the box's polished surfaces. Enveloping the viewer through its rounded reflection, *Untitled* creates a warped rendering of the sculpture's backdrop, playfully deforming our tangible reality. The dark cavity in the center intimately transmits a paradoxical sense of both awe and danger. Through optical illusions and active participation, Kapoor's art redefines our rational awareness of space and invites a meditative experience that ruptures perceptual boundaries.—*JM*

Stainless steel, 78 × 39 × 39 in. (198.1 × 99.1 × 99.1 cm),
Gift of Sydney and Walda Besthoff, 2011

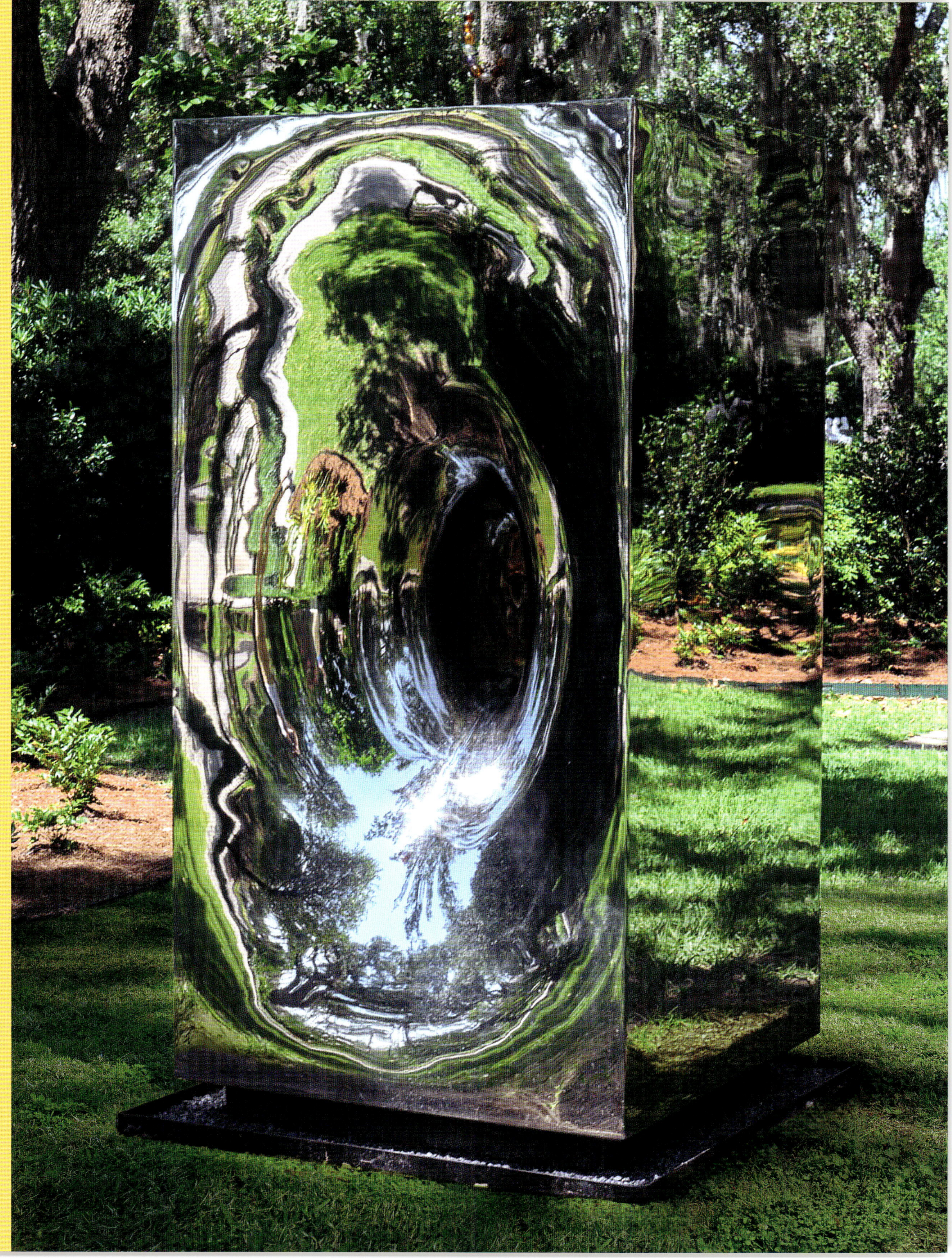

Anselm Kiefer

Ptolemaïs, 2019

The trauma of World War II and the Holocaust haunts much of German artist Anselm Kiefer's (b. 1945) work. Born in the waning months of the war, Kiefer grew up amid the ruins of West Germany. He studied art at institutions in Freiburg, Karlsruhe, and Dusseldorf. But just as pivotal was Kiefer's acquaintance with the artist Joseph Beuys (1921–1986), who he met in 1971 and who encouraged his early work, which was sometimes controversial. As in Beuys's performances and sculptures, history and personal experience are often intertwined for Kiefer.

In the 1970s, he painted on an increasingly grand scale and grappled with grim themes—guilt, memory, national identity, collective denial, and abuse of power. His dark, wrecked landscapes are encrusted with unconventional materials such as broken glass, wire, and straw. In 1980, his nightmarish paintings shared the German pavilion at the Venice Biennale. Such examples figured prominently in transnational debates about the ongoing relevance of painting as a medium and the maximalist tendencies of Neo-Expressionism in the 1970s and 1980s. Kiefer moved from Germany to the South of France in 1992 and then to Paris in 2008. His critical reputation there exceeds that in his home country—until recently, he was the only living artist allowed an exhibition at the Louvre Museum.

Kiefer's excavations of history are often complemented by an array of intellectual sources drawn from myth, religion, poetry, and theories of the cosmos. In the late 1990s, for example, Kiefer painted a series of star constellations from the Milky Way. During that period, he also began a sculpture series of women's dresses in a variety of materials. Atop spectral white drapery, objects and symbols take the place of a head. Sometimes the title of these artworks names an ancient historical figure, such as the poet Sappho, or a mythological goddess, such as Nemesis; other times they are more arcane, seeming to embody abstract ideas or allegories. These two strands come together in *Ptolemaïs*. The attribute, an armillary sphere, refers to Claudius Ptolemy (c. 100–c. 170 CE), the second-century astronomer and mathematician known for his influential, but inaccurate, geocentric model of the solar system. But the name also suggests Ptolemais of Cyrene (dates unknown), the only identified female musicologist of antiquity.—*AMT*

Cast bronze with white patina and metal, 76 ¾ × 49 3/16 × 19 3/16 in. (194.9 × 124.9 × 48.7 cm), overall, Museum Purchase with Gifted Funds, 2022

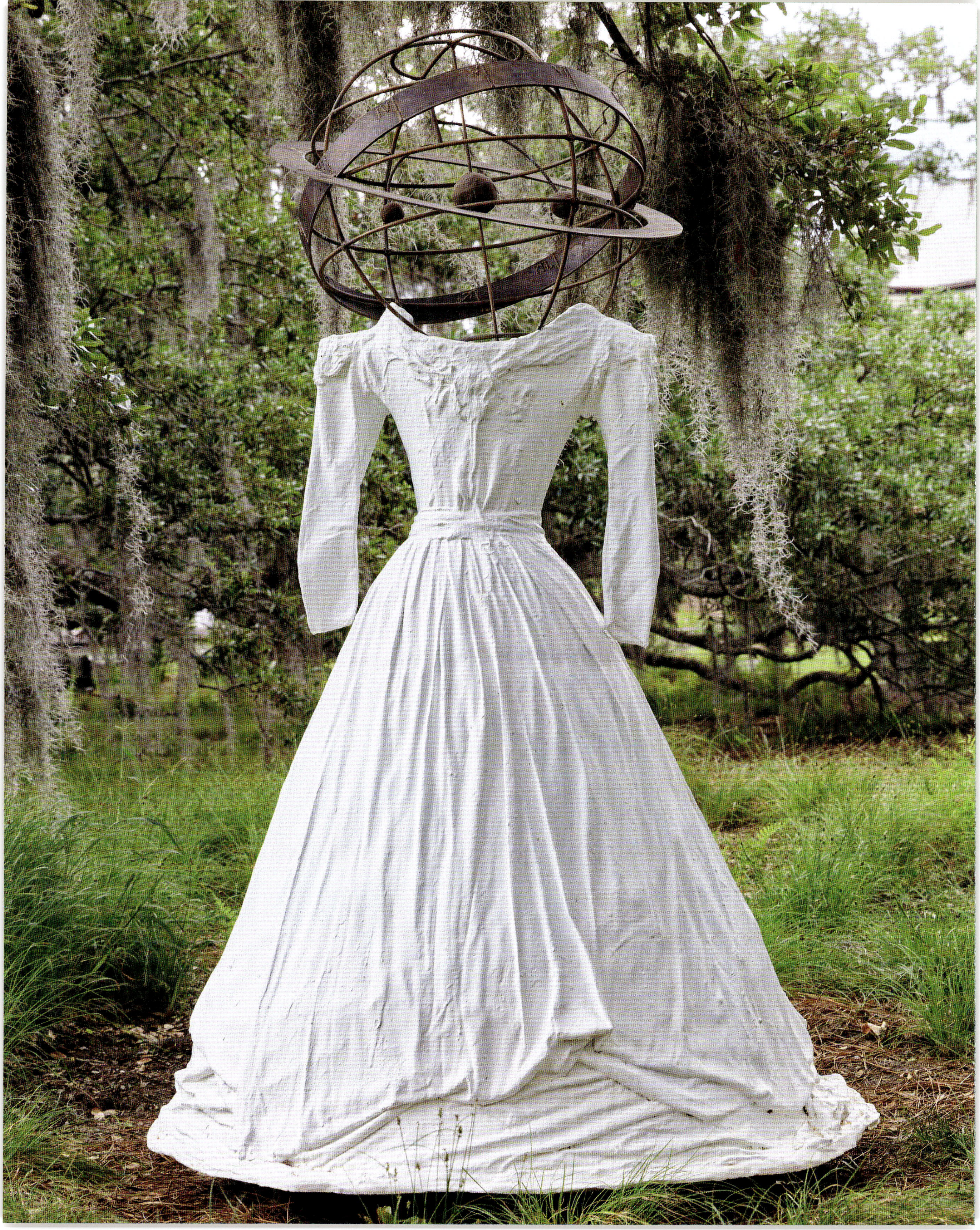

Ida Kohlmeyer

Rebus 3D-89-3, 1989

The youngest child of Polish-Jewish immigrants, Ida Kohlmeyer (1912–1997) did not become an artist until her late thirties. After earning an MFA in 1956 from Newcomb College (now Newcomb-Tulane College) in New Orleans, her home city, and studying with Hans Hofmann (1880–1966) in Provincetown, Massachusetts, that summer, Kohlmeyer gradually developed a distinctive abstract painting style charged with bright colors, scribbly strokes, and hieroglyphic-like symbols organized in a loose grid format. She had a solo gallery show in New York in 1959 and would continue to exhibit there periodically, but it was in her native New Orleans that Kohlmeyer continued to live, work, and garner the most attention. She later taught at her alma mater. The Newcomb Art Gallery at Tulane devoted the largest retrospective to her in 2004.

Kohlmeyer's paintings, drawings, and prints tend to overshadow her sculptures, which she experimented with in the late 1960s but seriously committed to in the 1980s, after receiving several highly visible local commissions. In 1981, her work was selected for the new Equitable Life Assurance Society Building in downtown New Orleans. Completed in 1983, Krewe of Poydras, a series of five more than forty-foot-tall kinetic sculptures, was soon followed by an even larger sculpture, *Box of Artificial Flowers #6*, in 1985. Her *Aquatic Colonnade* opened at the city's Audubon Aquarium in 1990. *Rebus 3D-89-3* is part of a series of riddlelike "rebus" sculptures in painted aluminum, her preferred medium, that Kohlmeyer produced into the 1990s. It translates her idiosyncratic shape and sign systems into three dimensions using two concentrically lined masses intercut by a horizontal slab. Seemingly both stable and precarious, the stack attains a graceful seesaw dynamism.—*AMT*

Painted aluminum, 109 ½ × 97 × 36 in. (278.1 × 246.4 × 91.4 cm), Gift of the Sydney and Walda Besthoff Foundation, 1998

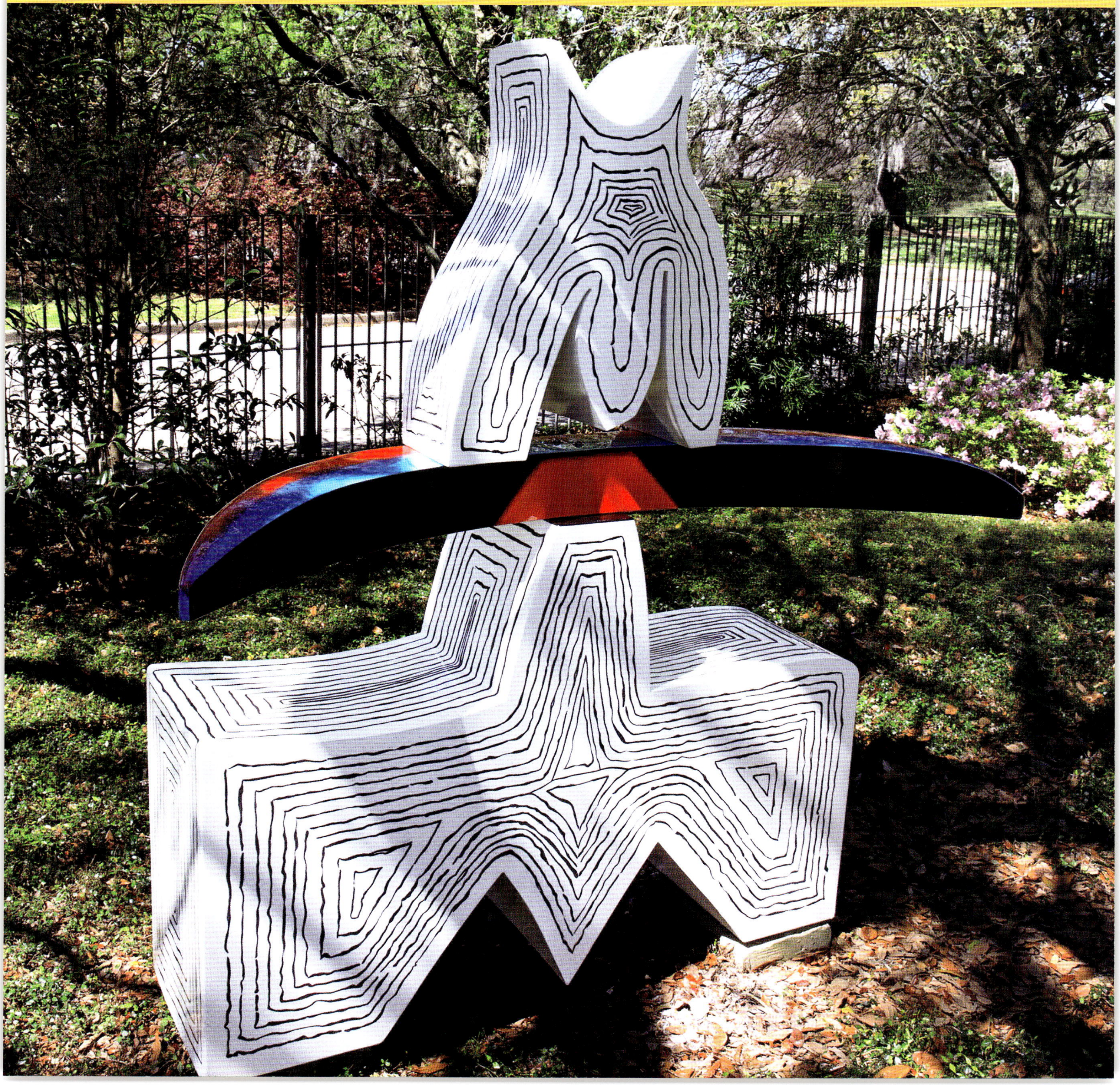

Gaston Lachaise

Heroic Man, 1930–34; cast 1993

Updating a tradition that stretched back to antiquity, Gaston Lachaise (1882–1935) vigorously committed himself to portraying the heroic nude. However, the Paris-born and -trained sculptor eschewed classical proportions in favor of his subjective, modernist vision that exaggerated and simplified anatomy. In his early twenties, he met an American woman who would become his model, his muse, and eventually his wife: Isabel Dutaud Nagle (1872–1957). Lachaise followed her to the United States in 1906, settled in New York in 1912, and never returned to France.

Primarily, the artist's reputation rests on three major larger-than-life sculptures of curvaceous women: *Standing Woman (Elevation)* (1912–27), which he first exhibited in plaster in 1918 and would not cast in bronze for another ten years until he could raise enough money; the buoyant, reclining *Floating Figure* (1927); and *Standing Woman* (1932), whose heels are down and eyes are open, differentiating her from the first "elevated" version. The radical eroticism of their swelling breasts, hips, and buttocks challenged taboos and harked back to the ample Paleolithic fertility goddess, the Venus of Willendorf (24,000–22,000 BCE).

Lachaise's *Heroic Man* is a companion of sorts to *Standing Woman*, suggesting the alliance of two archetypes. The figure's muscular frame, confident uprightness, and large hands—the right extended in a protective gesture—exude a regal ease. Lachaise composed only a small number of male nudes, all of them made near the end of his life. *Heroic Man* was the largest. He much preferred—was even obsessed with—the female form. Although Lachaise completed portrait busts of friends and associates, bas-reliefs, torso fragments, and myriad drawings, his majestic freestanding sculptures of graceful, sensuous, and buxom women were his exceptional achievement. He died suddenly a few months after his retrospective at the Museum of Modern Art in 1935, its first devoted to an American sculptor. A plaster version of *Heroic Man* was included in the show.—*AMT*

Bronze, 99 × 50 × 32 in. (251.5 × 127 × 81.3 cm), overall, edition 1 of 6, Gift of the Sydney and Walda Besthoff Foundation, 2000

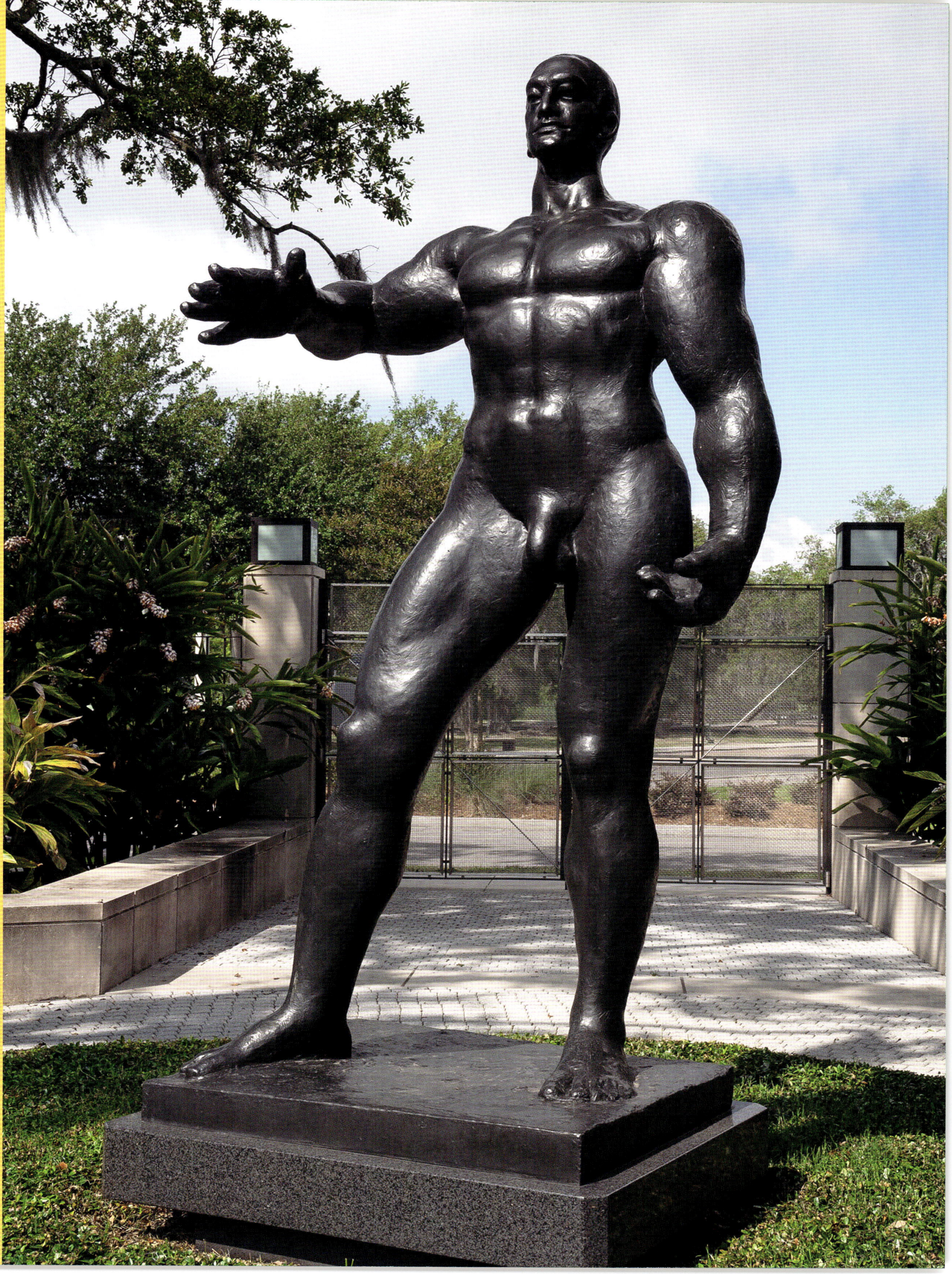

Maya Lin

Folding the Mississippi (1938), 2019

Fascinated by the effects of memory, the weighted consequences of the bygone, and the residue of the vanished, Maya Lin (b. 1959) creates poetic visualizations of the planet's interconnected—and increasingly endangered—ecologies. Using maps and data sets as her source material, Lin's work often charts an evaporating present, calling attention to the already tangible loss of landscape brought on by the climate emergency. Perhaps most famous for her monuments of remembrance, Lin has described her recurring turn towards the environment in her artistic practice as itself, a kind of memorial.

While still in her senior year as an undergraduate student at Yale, Lin won a nationwide competition to create a memorial commemorating the Vietnam War. The project drew controversy, dredging up unresolved friction and debate; but Lin's simple, understated yet effective memorial—seventy-two sheets of black granite inscribed with the name of every American soldier who fought in the conflict—smoothed the festered tension and provided a balm for those still grappling with the vivid after-effects of such a controversial war. Lin went on to complete her graduate studies in architecture before consciously devoting herself to an art practice, aware that she did not want to be exclusively defined as a maker of monuments.

In 2007, she began looking at depleted and disappearing bodies of water, research which prompted her to begin a series of works charting the losses. Working with recycled silver, glass marbles, and custom-made stainless-steel pins, Lin transcribed the historical footprint of waterways into gallery spaces, mapping out a range of rivers and lakes from Africa's Lake Chad to the Artic Ice Sheet, to the network of the Hudson River Valley in the United States.

Folding the Mississippi (1938) traces the entirety of the Mississippi River, from its genesis in Northern Minnesota to the Gulf of Mexico, in translucent turquoise marbles. Snaking up the walls and onto the ceiling of NOMA's five thousand square foot indoor sculpture pavilion, the curved surface of each marble glints in the sunlight, creating a mirage-like reflection that at once recalls the water it represents, and simultaneously creates the illusion that the sculpture too is fading before the viewer's eyes.—*MH*

Glass marbles, adhesive, 22 × 37 ft. (6.7 × 11.3 m),
Gift of Sydney and Walda Besthoff, 2020

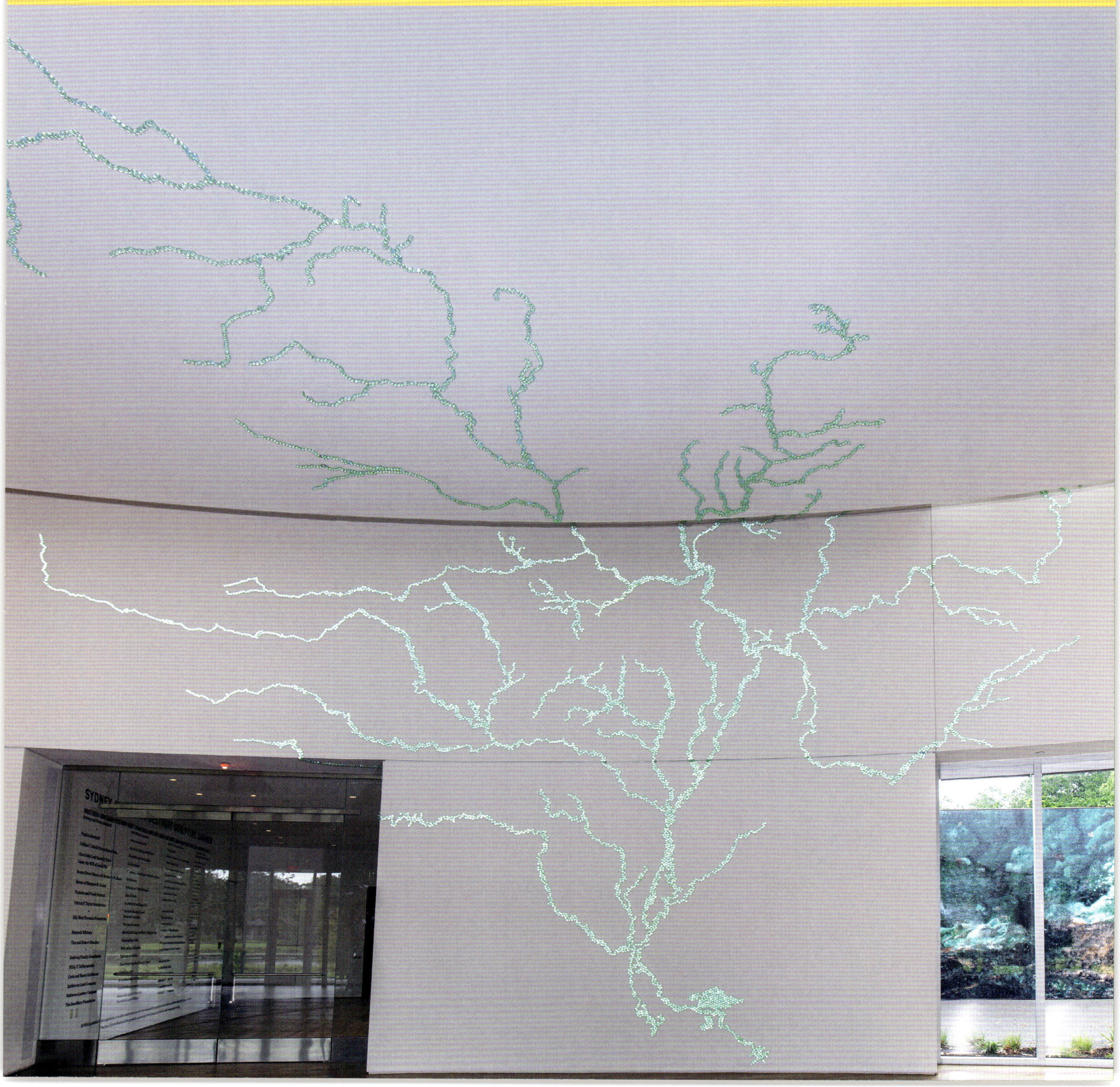

Jacques Lipchitz

Sacrifice III, 1949–57

Though he is best recognized for his early Cubist works, each chapter of Jacques Lipchitz's (1891–1973) career was marked by stylistic innovation. He continually sought out new visual languages, developing fresh aesthetic approaches to a wide array of subjects, ranging from humble still lifes to biblical scenes to mythological struggles between man and nature.

In 1909, Lipchitz moved to Paris where he fell in with the avant-garde circles active in Montmartre and Montparnasse. Friendly with Pablo Picasso (1881–1973), Amedeo Modigliani (1884–1920), and Guillaume Apollinaire (1880–1918), Lipchitz started experimenting with the angular abstraction of Cubism. Working first in bas-reliefs, his earliest pieces are defined by a contrast of light and shadow, using the physical depth of the work to communicate classic Cubist motifs of harlequins, acrobats, and domestic tablescapes. During this time he fostered an artistic collaboration with Juan Gris (1887–1927), and the two frequently drew inspiration from one another's work, often rendering the same subjects, each in their respective mediums. Lipchitz's work began to receive attention, notably from the fashion designer Gabrielle Chanel (1883–1971) and the American collector Dr. Albert C. Barnes (1872–1951), and following a particularly lucrative commission from the latter, Lipchitz in turn hired Le Corbusier (1887–1965) to build him a live-in studio and home in Boulogne-sur-Seine, France, where he moved in 1925.

Increasingly frustrated by the limitations of Cubism, he transitioned to the fluid style that would result in his famed Transparents series, a group of works in the round that emphasized the interplay of positive and negative space. As war loomed, Lipchitz's shapes became ever more curvilinear and his subjects grew progressively grander, riddled with existential themes. Both his series titled Jacob and the Angel, and Prometheus Strangling the Vulture serve as predecessors to *Sacrifice III*, which Lipchitz made on discovering the Nazi concentration camps in the aftermath of World War II. *Sacrifice III* belongs to a series of works depicting ancient Jewish ceremonies involving the sacrifice of animals, that Lipchitz had initially begun upon fleeing to the United States in 1941. The final work of the group is the most definitive: an image of atonement captured once more with a novel approach, in a mode that blends the artist's later impressionistic style with shadows of his earliest Cubist inclinations.—*MH*

Bronze, 55 × 40 × 25 in. (139.7 × 101.6 × 63.5 cm),
Gift of the Sydney and Walda Besthoff Foundation, 1998

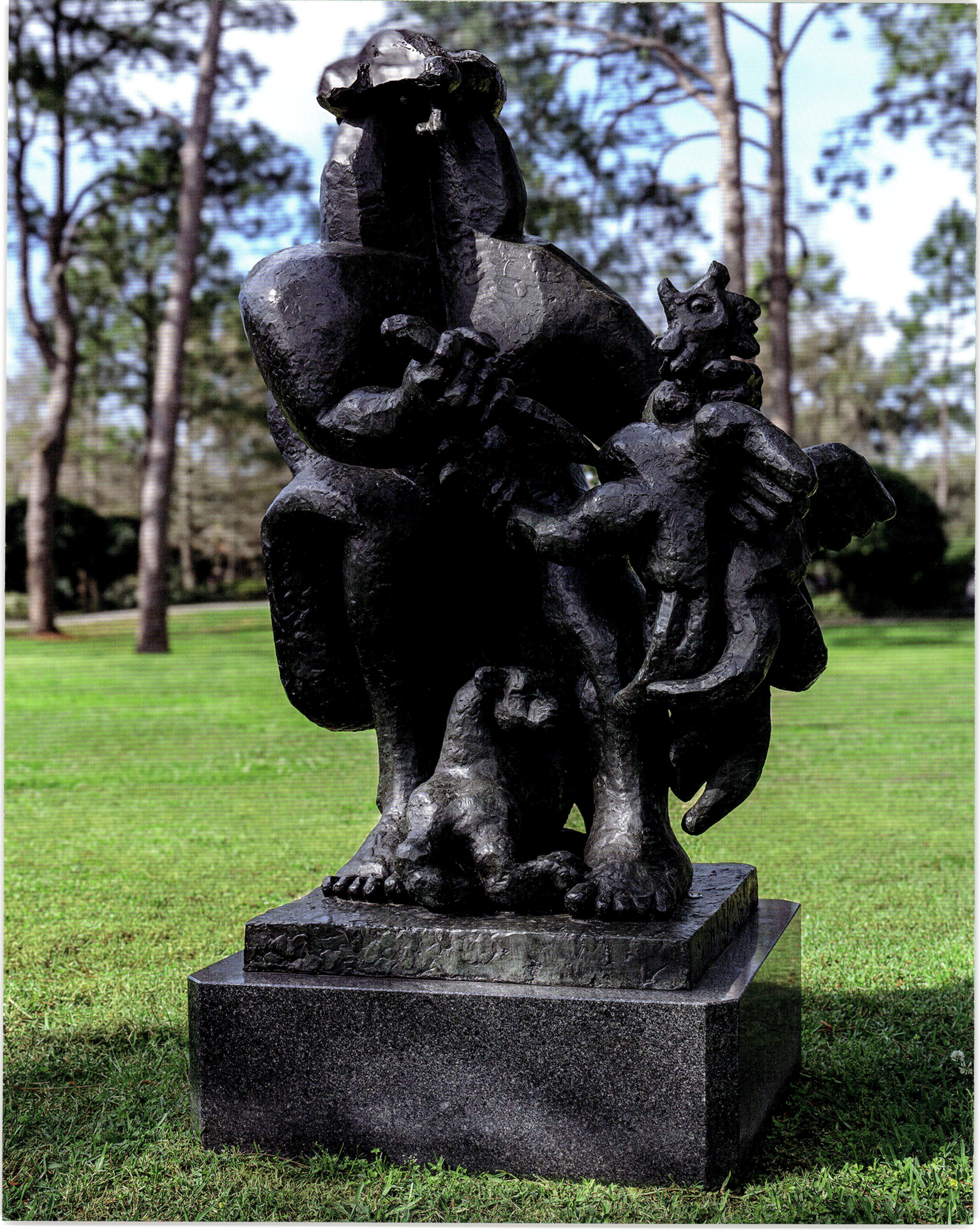

Seymour Lipton

Cosmos, 1973

A dentist-turned-sculptor in the early 1930s, Seymour Lipton (1903–1986) was basically self-taught. Initially carving agonized and contorted figures in wood, by the mid-1940s, Lipton was working predominantly with metal to create increasingly abstract sculptures. His exploration of ideas derived from psychologist Carl Jung (1875–1961)—about archetypes and unconscious forces—loosely aligned Lipton with the Abstract Expressionists, though he always remained something of an outsider.

In the 1950s, he developed a personal method of working with sheet metal and Monel metal brazed with bronze or nickel silver; this process offered a modulated surface effect to the finished works. His curvilinear, biomorphic, and twisted forms seemed especially attuned to the existential struggle and horrors of life post World War II. Partly motivated by a spiritual undercurrent, Lipton was adept at uniting opposites: evoking both danger and vulnerability simultaneously and counterposing convex and concave shapes. As quoted in his *New York Times* obituary, December 1986, "Art has a kind of sacred significance to me," he said.

Although constructing spirals nested within, or pierced by larger structures was not unusual for Lipton, *Cosmos* activates these interior voids in a particularly forceful way. A rectangular element frames the womblike recess. Opening up negative space to this degree was a new direction for Lipton and is seen later in *Winterseed* (1974) and *Guardian* (1975). That *Cosmos* featured in multiple museum and gallery exhibitions during the the 1970s—at prestigious institutions such as the National Collection of Fine Arts in Washington, D.C., and the Johnson Museum of Art at Cornell University and the Marlborough Gallery in New York—is indicative of its power and the esteem in which it was held.—*AMT*

Nickel silver on Monel metal, 70 × 73 × 36 in. (177.8 × 185.4 × 91.4 cm), Gift of the Sydney and Walda Besthoff Foundation, 1998

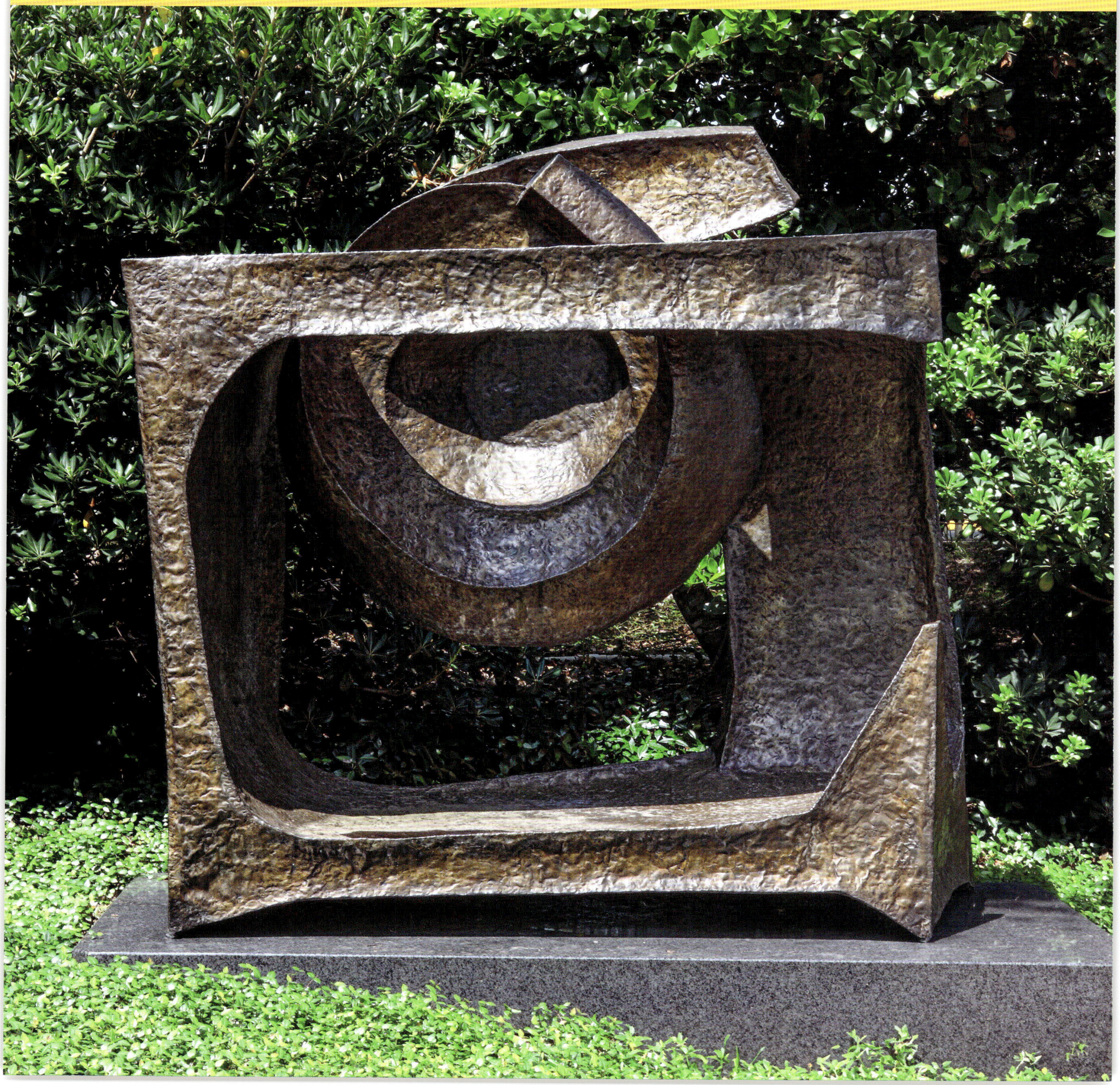

Baltasar Lobo

Grande jeune fille à genoux, 1987; cast 1994

One of Spain's most notable twentieth-century artists, Baltasar Lobo (1910–1993) primarily made sculptures representing nude female figures and motherhood. The artist first learned wood carving techniques from fellow Spaniard Ramon Núñez and briefly studied at the San Fernando Academy of Fine Arts in Madrid. Fleeing the Spanish Civil War, in 1939 he settled permanently in Paris.

Captivated by the Cubist art movement and its avant-garde approach to composition, he developed a relationship with Pablo Picasso (1881–1973), who introduced Lobo to Julio González (1876–1942), Jacques Lipchitz (1891–1973), and Henri Laurens (1885–1954). Lobo quickly integrated into the Paris art scene, where he exhibited at the Galerie Vendôme on Rue de la Paix, encountering the art of Jean Arp (1886–1966) and Constantin Brancusi (1876–1957).

Strongly influenced by their work, Lobo established his visual style predominantly creating in marble and bronze, utilizing geometric shapes to create polished and poised interpretations of the human body. Intertwining figuration and abstraction, Lobo embraced simple forms and undulating contours to capture movement, energy, and emotional meaning. Although never deviating from anatomical subjects, his practice became increasingly abstract and experimental in the 1950s.

Grande jeune fille à genoux was cast after the artist's death in 1993. Although the formal corporeal features of the seated woman are instantly apparent—thighs, feet, and belly—a modern sense of abstraction distorts any identifiable traces of her upper physique, causing a biomorphic character to prevail. The waves in the elongated torso create a harmonious rhythm and contribute to an organic sensation of motion rising from the ground. Recalling classical and Cycladic statues, Lobo emphasizes a voluptuous female body, alluding to themes of fertility and reproduction. *Grande jeune fille à genoux* epitomizes Lobo's sustained appreciation for the nude form and adept amalgamation of modernist tropes with influences from the ancient world.—*JM*

Bronze with brown patina, 84 in. (213 cm), Gift of Sydney and Walda Besthoff, 2016

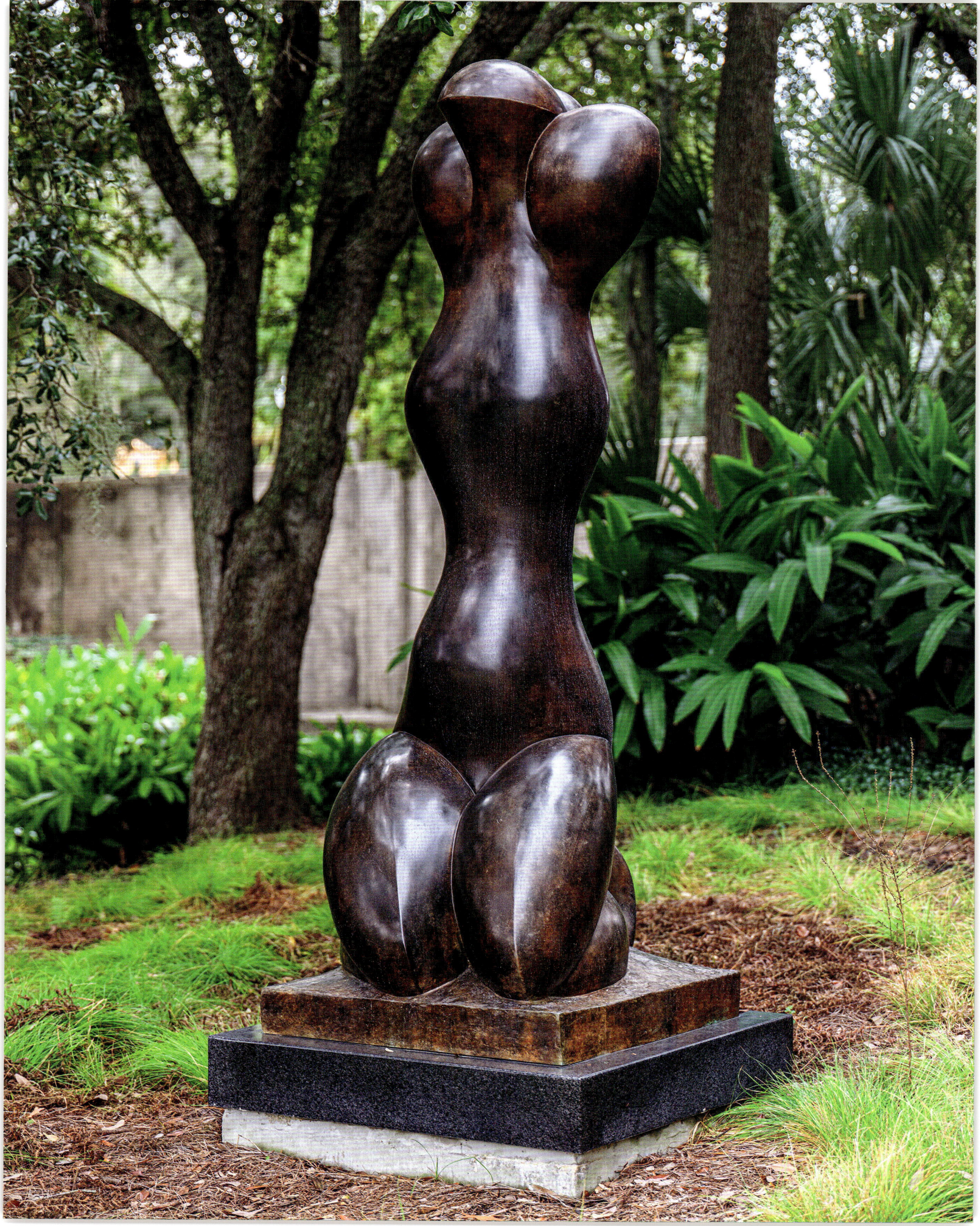

Robert Longo

Speed of Grace, 1982–83

The origin of Robert Longo's (b. 1953) multimedia series *Men in the Cities*, is a movie that captivated the artist not long after receiving a BFA from Buffalo State University in 1975. The slow-motion death scene of two gangsters in German director Rainer Fassbinder's (1945–1982) *The American Soldier* (1970), inspired Longo to make an eponymous painted aluminum wall relief of about two feet. The sculpture appeared in the seminal group show *Pictures* (1977) at Artists Space in New York and helped establish Longo among the so-called Pictures Generation—artists weaned in, and investigating an image-saturated society. Longo soon turned to drawing large-scale charcoal and graphite figures falling and floundering in the manner of shooting in the film's finale. *Men Trapped in Ice* (1978), a triptych, was the first. But subsequently, Longo photographed friends on his lower Manhattan rooftop moving ecstatically or writhing as if hit by bullets. The photographic studies served as the basis for more black-and-white drawings, the bulk of which he produced between 1979 and 1982. In some cases reaching as much as ten feet high, the hyperrealistic drawings dramatically decontextualized the besuited people from the staging and defined Longo's quintessential style.

Since Longo "wanted to make monumental drawings that [...] felt like sculptures," as he explained in a 1987 interview in *Men in the Cities: Photographs 1976–1982*, is it any wonder that actual sculptures followed? *Speed of Grace*, a phrase from Longo's description of the fluid movements of Fassbinder's characters, displays the signature spasm that is somewhere between dancing and dying. Their poses have also been likened to the jittery movements of the lead singers of New Wave bands, a significant comparison as Longo performed as a musician in the late 1970s and directed music videos in the 1980s. Nonetheless, violence, fear, and disaster—and the way our experience of them is mediated by mass culture—continued to be pressing themes in Longo's work. For instance, his drawing series *Bodyhammers* (1993–95) depicts oversized handguns, and his sculpture *Death Star* (1993) is comprised of 18,000 bullets, the approximate number of gun-related deaths in the U.S. at the time. With worsening gun violence, Longo reprised the sculpture in 2018: this time the sphere required 40,000 bullets.—*AMT*

Cast bronze, 83 × 28 × 47 ½ in. (210.8 × 71.1 × 120.7 cm), Museum Purchase with funds provided by Sydney and Walda Besthoff, 2017

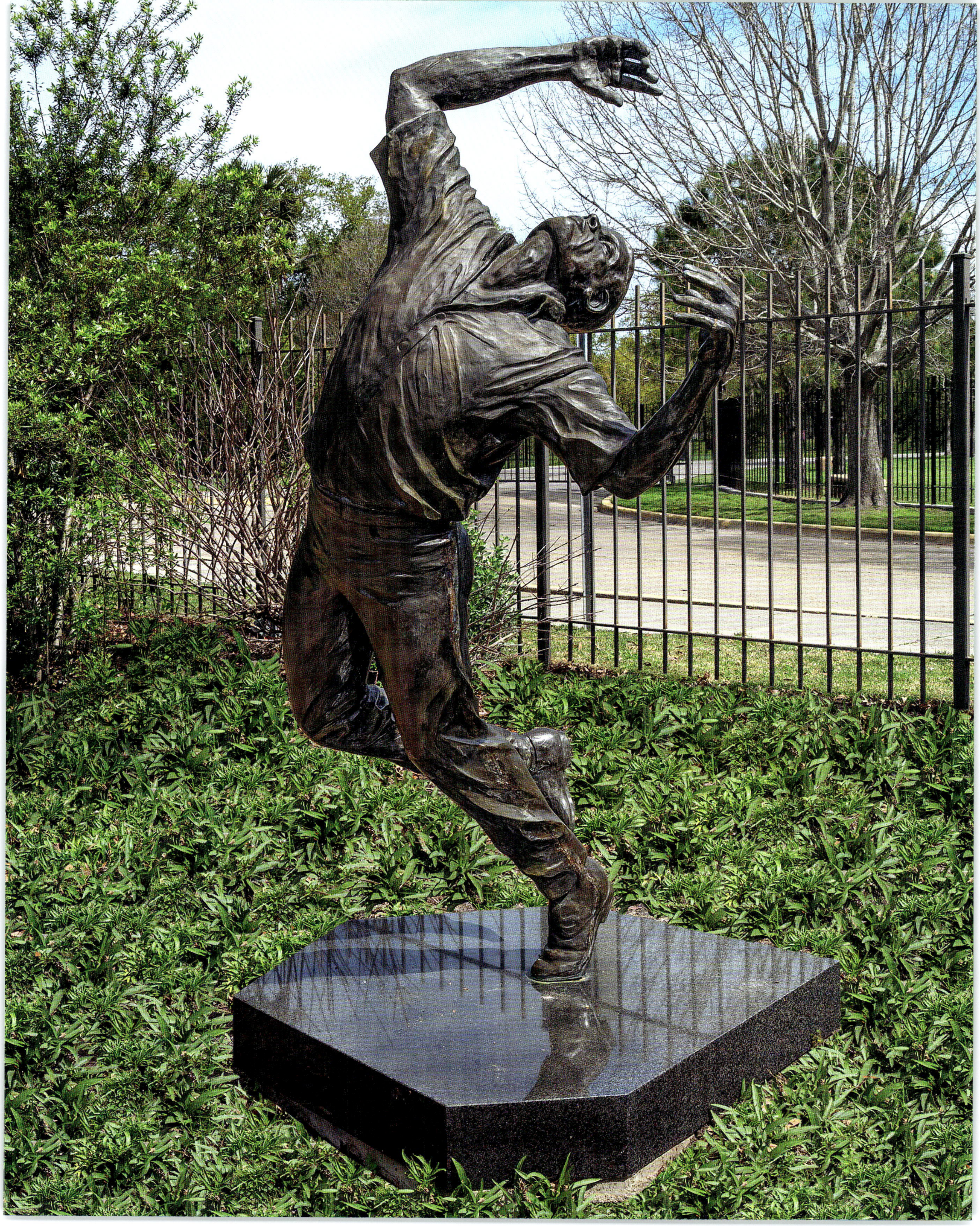

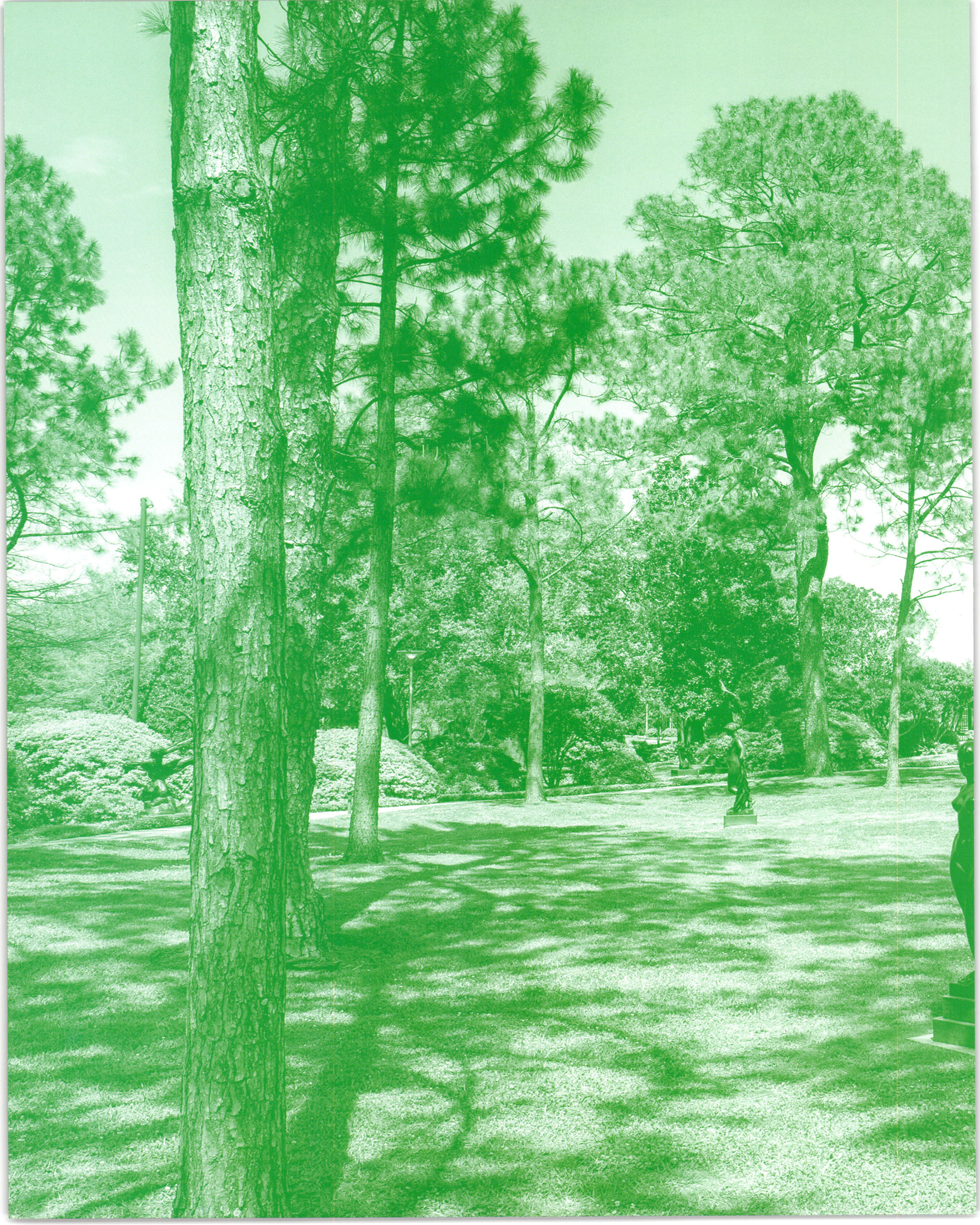

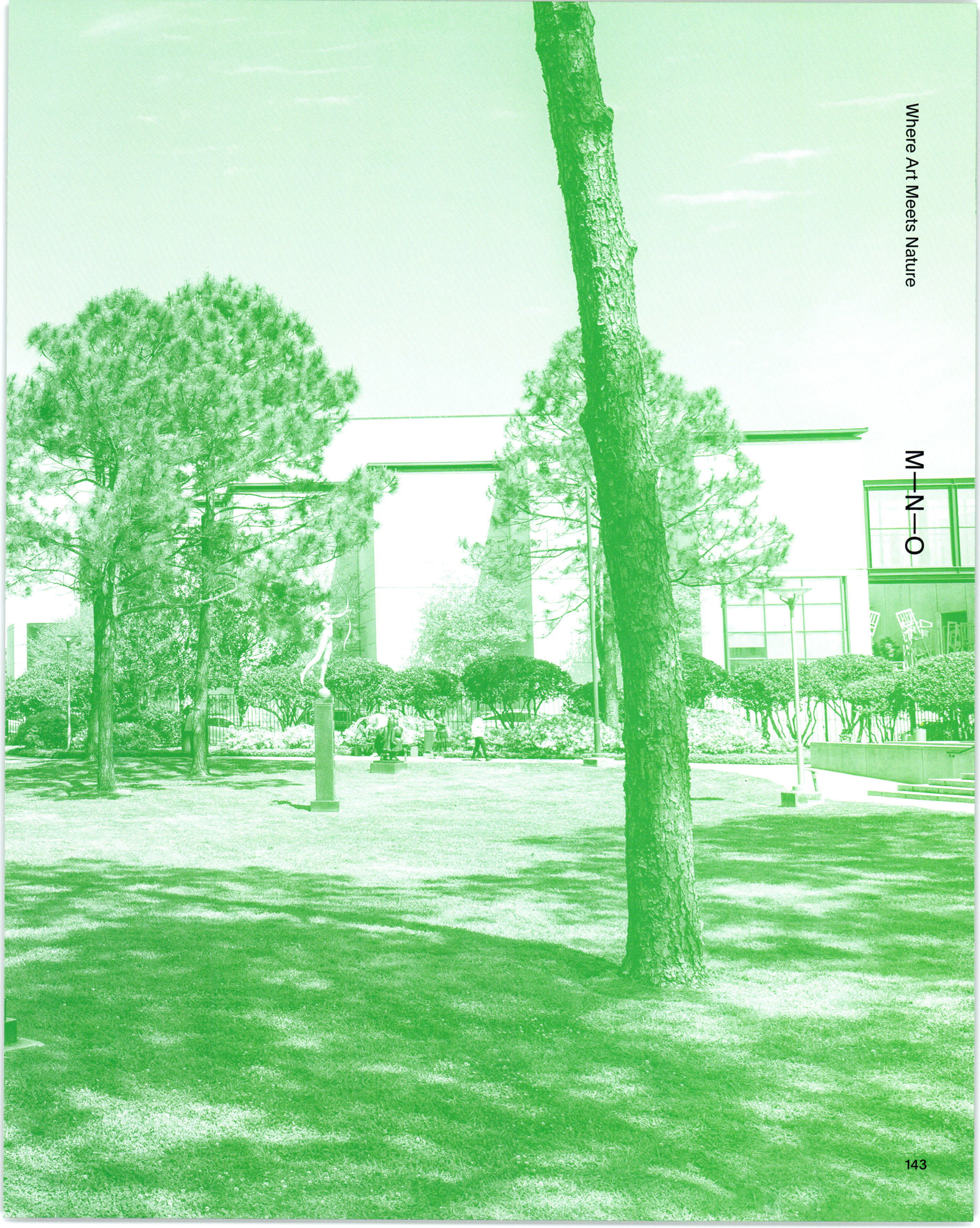

René Magritte

The Labors of Alexander, 1967

A key figure in Surrealism, René Magritte (1898–1967) is widely renowned for his delicate, poetic compositions which subtly restage the impossible within the context of the everyday. Where his contemporaries such as Salvador Dalí (1904–1989) and Yves Tanguy (1900–1955) relied on entirely fabricated worlds, often veering into near-total abstraction, Magritte located the uncanny in the quotidian, juxtaposing recognizable symbols, commonplace objects, and choice phrases of language to underscore his belief that the mysterious vibrated under the surface our daily lives. Primarily a painter and a draftsman, Magritte frequently returned to the same motifs, often revising and reworking imagery multiple times. He is famous for depictions of men in bowler hats, masked green apples, and language itself—perhaps best expressed in his iconic painting of a pipe, *La Trahison des Images (The Treachery of Images)* (1929).

Magritte's foray into sculpture resulted from a conversation with his dealer, Alexandre Isolas (1908–1987), who suggested that the artist take a handful of his best-loved and most revisited themes and collaborate with a foundry to cast them in bronze. Magritte agreed, and just seven months before his death, began the laborious process of designing three-dimensional representations and meticulous wax models for eight of his oft-repeated motifs, including *The Labors of Alexander.* In this composition, the roots of the tree stump clutch at an axe so that the trunk appears, mysteriously, to have chopped itself down. Magritte first painted the image in 1950, subsequently iterating it through a number of drawings, etchings, and gouache works on paper. Titling it on the suggestion of Julien Gracq (1910–2007), a French critic and writer, the subject evokes what he described in a 1950 letter to Magritte as "the conqueror vanquished by his conquest." Rendered three-dimensional and at a human scale, the bronze stump inserts the eerie more directly into our world, inviting us to look for the unexplainable and the enigmatic in the everyday.—*MH*

Cast bronze in two pieces: tree trunk: 25 × 60 × 41 in. (63.5 × 152.4 × 104.14 cm); axe: 52 ¾ in. (134.62 cm), Gift of Muriel Bultman Francis, 1971

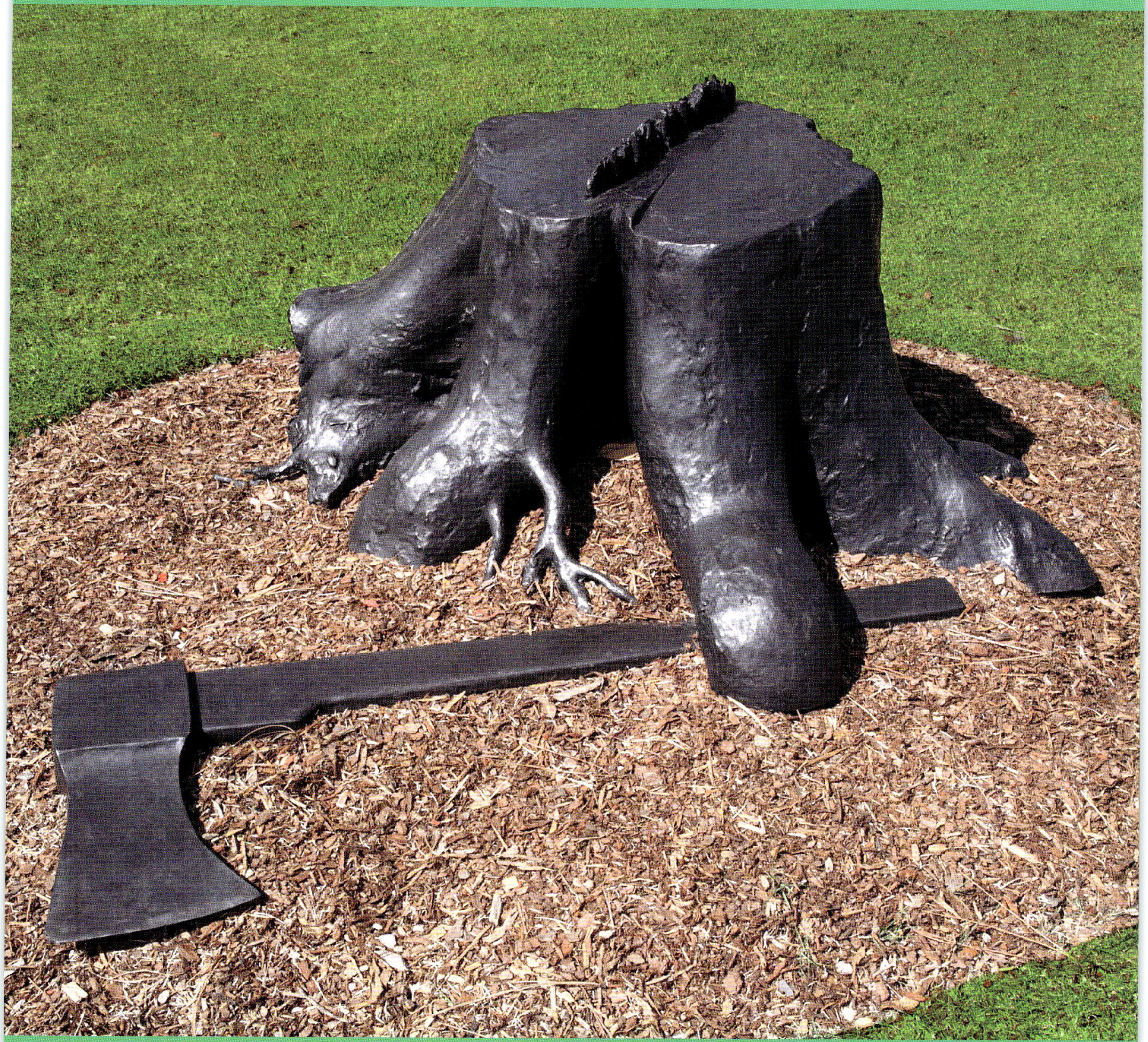

Aristide Maillol

Venus Without Arms, 1922

Best known for his sculptures of female nudes, Aristide Maillol (1861–1944) returned to the subject throughout his career, continuously reworking compositions through subtle variations in stance and scale. The subject of the goddess Venus, in particular, appears frequently across Maillol's body of work, with the artist reimagining her form over the decades.

Born in the small fishing village of Banyuls-sur-Mer, France, at an early age, Maillol moved to Paris intent on becoming an artist. In 1885, he enrolled in the École des Beaux-Arts, studying painting with Alexandre Cabanel (1823–1889) and Jean-Léon Gérôme (1824–1904). However, he quickly tired of the rigidity of academicism, and growing increasingly frustrated with its restrictive aesthetic codes, sought alternatives among the Post-Impressionists. In 1889, Maillol found a renewed sense of artistic inspiration in an exhibition of expressive, abstract paintings by Paul Gauguin (1848–1903). Completely taken by the flat picture planes and stylized compositions of the Nabis, Maillol officially joined the group and exhibited with them in both 1895 and 1896.

With his eyesight in decline, Maillol started to incorporate small terra-cotta sculptures alongside his painting practice; but by 1901, his vision had deteriorated to such a degree that he began working almost exclusively as a sculptor. Returning to naturalistic representation, and with classical Greco-Roman carvings as his primary reference point, Maillol developed a signature style of curved, broad figures whose smooth surfaces exude a certain timelessness.

In *Venus Without Arms*, Maillol makes an obvious allusion back to the *Venus de Milo*, arguably the most iconic rendering of the goddess in Western art history. In Maillol's version, Venus's gently bent knee softens her stance into a classical contrapposto; her gaze is fixed downwards and the muscles in her face are lax. For Maillol, the form of the figure was singularly important, and his smooth, rounded, and often archetypal depictions of the female nude typify his practice. This approach contrasted sharply with the then-dominant style that prized roiling tumult, and the expression of emotion and inner psychological states, best epitomized in the sculpture of Auguste Rodin (1840–1917). Maillol's attention and commitment to form would go on to influence the modern sculpture of Jean Arp (1886–1966), Constantin Brancusi (1876–1957), and Henry Moore (1898–1986), whose sculpture *Reclining Mother and Child* (1975–77), is also in the collection of the Besthoff Sculpture Garden.—*MH*

Bronze, 69 ¼ × 19 × 14 in. (175.9 × 48.3 × 35.6 cm), edition 3 of 6, Gift of Sydney and Walda Besthoff, 2006

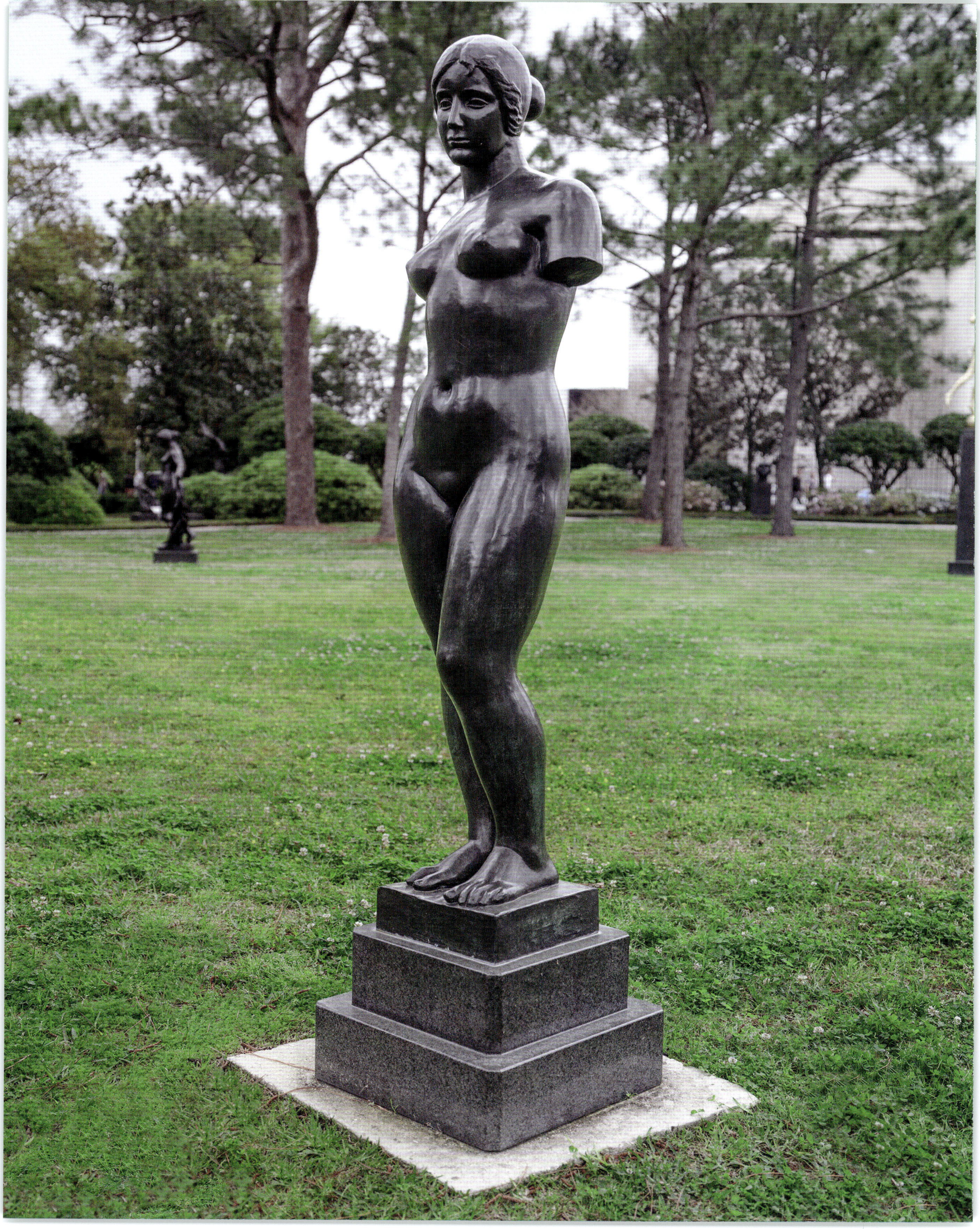

Paul Manship

Tortoise, 1916; cast 1998

Animals appear regularly in the sculpture of Paul Manship (1885–1966). Born in St. Paul, Minnesota, in 1905 he began a two-year apprenticeship with the sculptor Solon Borglum (1868–1922) in New York. For what was perhaps his earliest sculpture, he created a miniature (c. 1906) of Borglum's sleeping Dalmatian as a gift to his mentor. In 1907, Manship studied at the Pennsylvania Academy of the Fine Arts (PAFA) in Philadelphia with animalier Charles Grafly (1862–1929). A scholarship to the American Academy in Rome allowed him to travel abroad. Several years in Italy and Greece were crucial to his artistic development. Borrowing freely, his subsequent sculptures, almost always in bronze, were a stylized, ahistorical fusion of archaic Greek, Roman, Egyptian, Assyrian, and Indian art that served him as a significant transitional figure between academic and modernist artistic trends. Adept at a style characterized by sharp lines, sleek volumes, and a sense of movement, Manship became associated with Art Deco in the interwar years.

In the 1910s, most often when he sculpted animals they were included with human figures. For instance, his life-sized *Duck Girl* (1911), won a prize at PAFA in 1914 when it was first exhibited and was later installed in a Philadelphia park. Although never realized as a fountain, the fish that circle the pedestal were intended to have water spurting from their mouths. Manship's *Dancer and Gazelles* (1916) is another, more complex combination of human and nonhuman actors. His large figural groupings often refer to mythological stories, which he treated in fresh and dynamic ways. Sometimes the animals and humans are in harmonious companionship, as in *Diana and a Hound* (1925). Other times, humans and animals conflict, as in *Hercules and the Cretan Bull* (1956), one of Manship's several representations of the labors of Hercules.

The circumstances that led to *Tortoise* are not well documented, but it may be his first full-sized solitary animal sculpture. A trio of static, forward-facing tortoises flank the entrance gate of the Bronx Zoo, a project he began in 1926 and dedicated in 1934. Manship's preparations for the design yielded many animal bronzes. His extensive collection from 1932 includes numerous birds, now in the Smithsonian American Art Museum: *Crowned Crane*, *Flamingo*, *Goliath Heron*, *Concave-Casqued Hornbill*, *Pelican*, *Adjutant Stork*, *Black-Necked Stork*, and *Shoebill Stork.—AMT*

Bronze, 25 × 49 × 26 in. (63.5 × 124.5 × 66 cm), overall, edition 1 of 12, Gift of the Sydney and Walda Besthoff Foundation, 2000

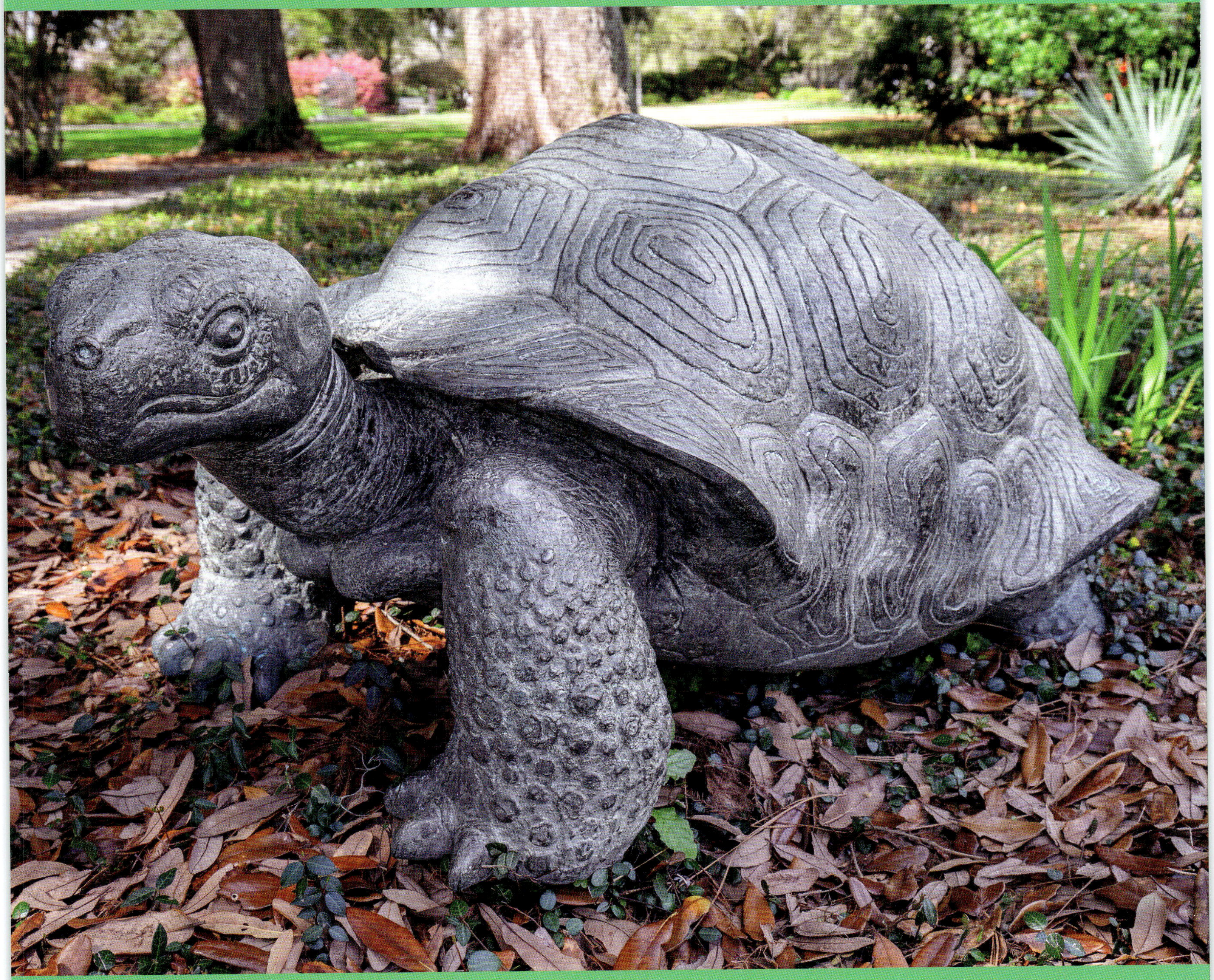

Giacomo Manzù

Grande Cardinale Seduto (Large Seated Cardinal), 1983

Internationally celebrated for his streamlined sculptures of the human form, Giacomo Manzù (1908–1991) grew up the son of a shoemaker in Bergamo, Italy. His hometown was a bustling hub for the Catholic church and as a boy, Manzù frequently encountered religious figures adorned in full vestments parading through the local streets, early memories which evolved into source material for his most famous series of cardinal sculptures. From a young age, Manzù apprenticed with a number of craftsmen, learning how to mix and mold plaster alongside the proper carving techniques for both wood and stone; but it wasn't until he happened across a book illustrated with the sculptures of Aristide Maillol, that he turned his attention fully towards art. Taken with the reduced lines and classical compositions, the voluptuous figures reproduced in the book marked his initial encounter with more modern theories and methods of representation.

In 1929, he received a commission for a chapel at the Catholic University in Milan, catalyzing a new turn in Manzù's work. The subject matter came naturally to him after a childhood spent in close observation of the clergy. Throughout his career, Manzù insisted on his detachment from religion, claiming to see bible scenes as motifs like any other, merely an artistic subject rather than a devotional. His fascination with the iconography and symbolism of the church came to a head when, on a visit to St. Peter's Basilica in Rome, he became enchanted by the silhouettes of two cardinals seated flanking the pope. Four years later, he sculpted the first successful and surviving cardinal, launching the famed series that Manzù would continue to iterate over three hundred times in different variations until his death.

Both cast in bronze and carved in marble, the conical shape of the cardinal's robes remains consistent across scale and medium, and the resulting triangular seated form has become synonymous with Manzù's oeuvre. Except for a single portrait of Cardinal Giacomo Lercaro (1891–1976), the artist's figures are always fictional, anonymous characters, reinforcing that for Manzù, the allure of the cardinals never had anything to do with the religion they represented, but rather the otherworldly outline their robes cut against the world around them.—*MH*

Bronze, 87 × 44 ¾ × 58 ⅛ in. (220.9 × 113.7 × 147.6 cm), Museum purchase, Walda Besthoff and the Edgar Stern Family Fund, 2009

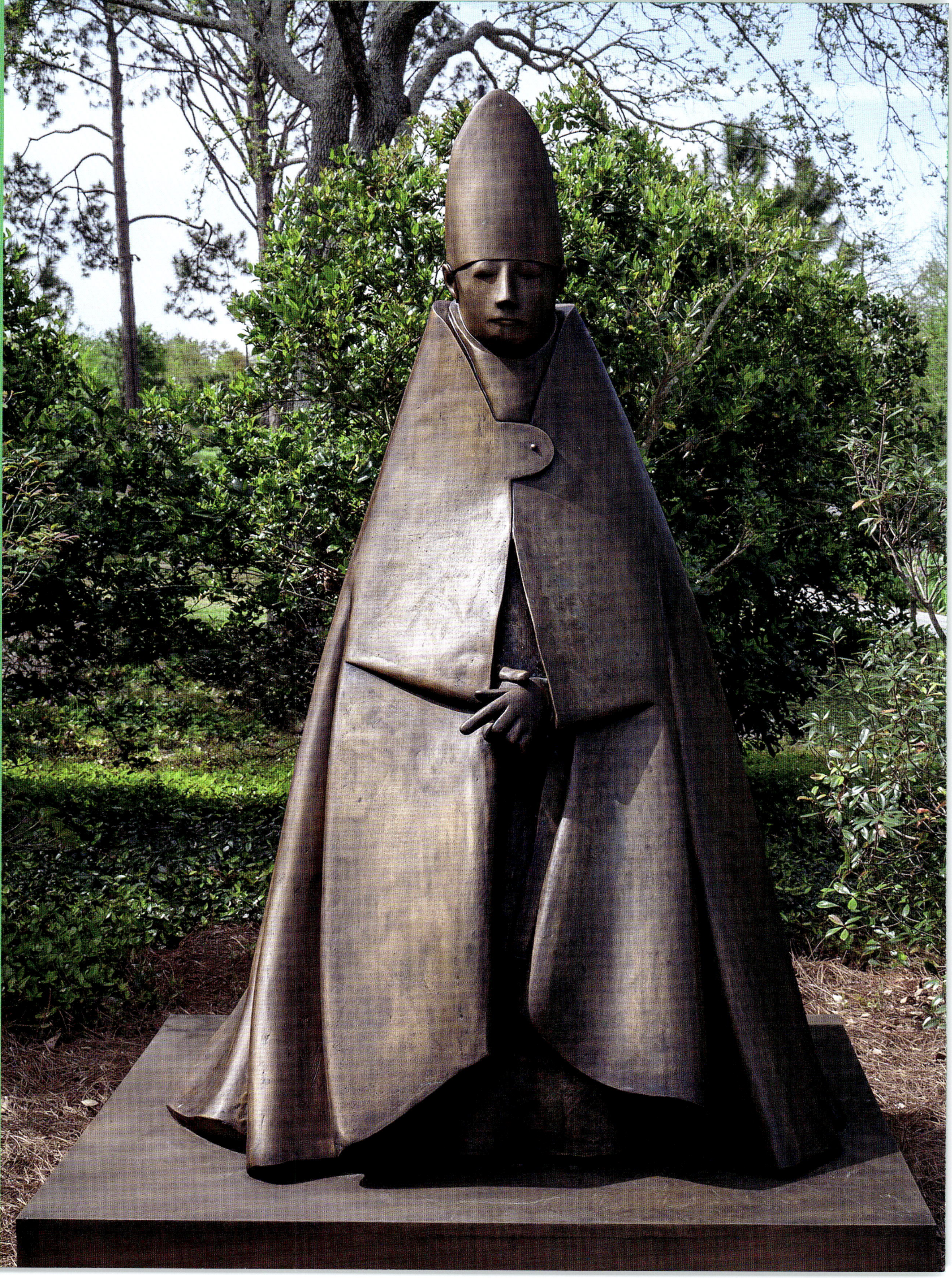

Allan McCollum

Perfect Vehicles, 1988

The first brightly-colored, six-and-a-half-foot-tall urn by Allan McCollum (b. 1944) appeared alone in a group show at Leo Castelli Gallery in New York in the spring of 1988. Then, that summer, a group of six lined a cavernous hall in a section for emerging art at the Venice Biennale. Continuing to multiply, that fall, twelve took over Brooke Alexander Gallery in New York and sixteen occupied galleries at the Ringling Museum of Art in Sarasota, Florida. The *Perfect Vehicles* owe their form to Chinese ginger jars, as McCollum has acknowledged. Though vaguely implying ceramic vessels, they are distanced from historical and functional specificity. The top is not a lid—there is no opening. The inside is not hollow but three-hundred pounds of solid concrete. Identical, except for commercial paint colors, the *Perfect Vehicles* obey the logic of mass production and suggest the illusion of consumer choice. That these inert and enigmatic sculptures frustrate our efforts to understand them or to assign them meaning, is partly the point.

For McCollum, who had no formal artistic training, the questions they raise are philosophical. The title, a phrase used in the film industry to describe an actor landing the ideal role, suggests how, in the absence of a fixed identity, we project meaning onto the sculptures. McCollum's initial works for *Perfect Vehicles*, from 1985, were smaller—just over one and a half feet—and sat on pedestals. Since the late 1970s, McCollum's concerns, informed by Dada, Conceptual art, and Pop art legacies, have revolved around how the meaning and value of works of art depend on social, economic, and psychological contexts, among others. Two of his other best-known series, *Surrogate Paintings* (1978–81) and its offspring *Plaster Surrogates* (begun 1982) address similar conundrums about institutional conditions, commerce, and the cult of uniqueness. Uniform simulations of prop-like paintings, these works comprise matte black voids in traditional frames, existing as tokens of desire or stand-ins for consumerist objects. Born in Los Angeles, McCollum relocated to New York in 1975, where he still resides.—*AMT*

Acrylic paint on concrete, 78 × 36 × 36 in. (198.1 × 91.4 × 91.4 cm), each, Gift of the Sydney and Walda Besthoff Foundation, 1998 and 2010

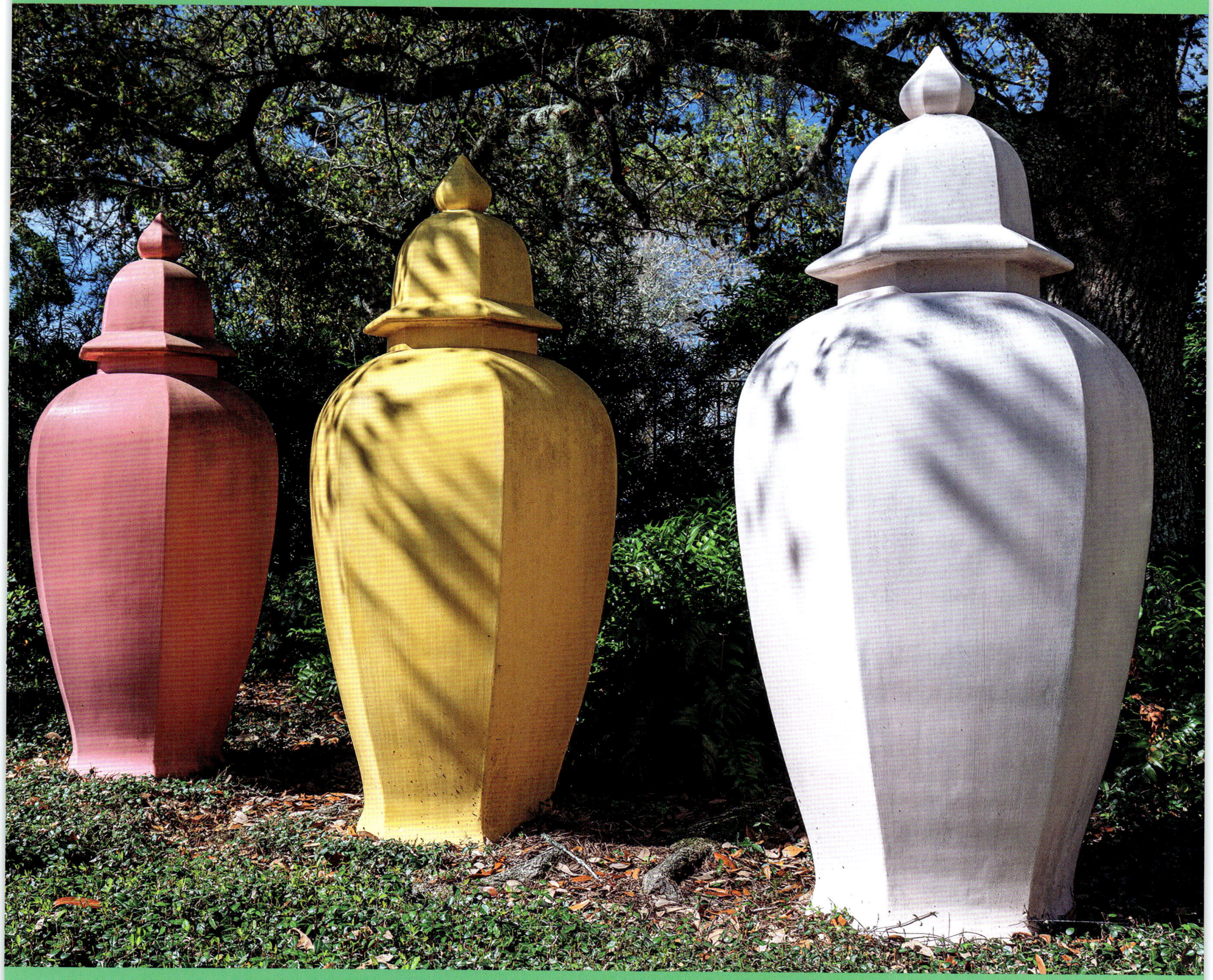

Gerold Miller

Verstärker 28, 2017

Like the New York Minimalists before him, Gerold Miller (b. 1961) understands the power an object placed in space has to entirely alter its surroundings. Working between drawing and sculpture, Miller's practice borders on architecture, with pieces that emphasize their construction and unapologetically take over a room, gallery, or courtyard. Part of Miller's first series of freestanding sculptures, 'Verstärker (amplifier),' visualizes the elements of three dimensions—height, width, and depth. The mirrored surface is seductive, drawing the viewer into the work, implicating them through their reflection, and simultaneously rendering the sculpture invisible—a reflective ripple in its surroundings, catching the light and shining it back, emphasizing all that preexists in its environment.

Miller studied sculpture at the State Academy of Visual Arts in Stuttgart, Germany, where he first learned about the Light and Space movement in California. Inspired by how artists such as Robert Irwin (1928–2023) and James Turrell (b. 1943) molded viewers' perceptions to the point that, how the work was understood, became as much a part of the piece as any of its concrete qualities, Miller applied these ideas to his wall-mounted objects. As he engaged more with the theories and principles of both West and East Coast Minimalism, Miller conceptualized his repetitive, serial sculptures as situated somewhere between painting and sculpture. This idea echoed Donald Judd's (1928–1994) loose definition of "specific objects," detailed in his eponymous 1964 essay as three-dimensional work that defies the neat classification of preexisting art forms. In 1989, Miller moved to Berlin where he fell in with an art scene remaking itself after the fall of the Wall, perhaps heightening the importance both physical place and social environment have within his work. Ultimately, Miller's objects are porous to the space in which they are displayed, interacting with and subtly modifying the boundaries of a room. Perhaps none more so than *Verstärker 28*, installed in the Sydney and Walda Besthoff Sculpture Garden, its glassy, silver surface constantly catching fractured bits of grass, trees, and sky.—*MH*

Stainless steel, 126 × 36 × 40 ½ in. (320 × 91.4 × 102.9 cm), Museum purchase with funds provided by Sydney and Walda Besthoff, 2018

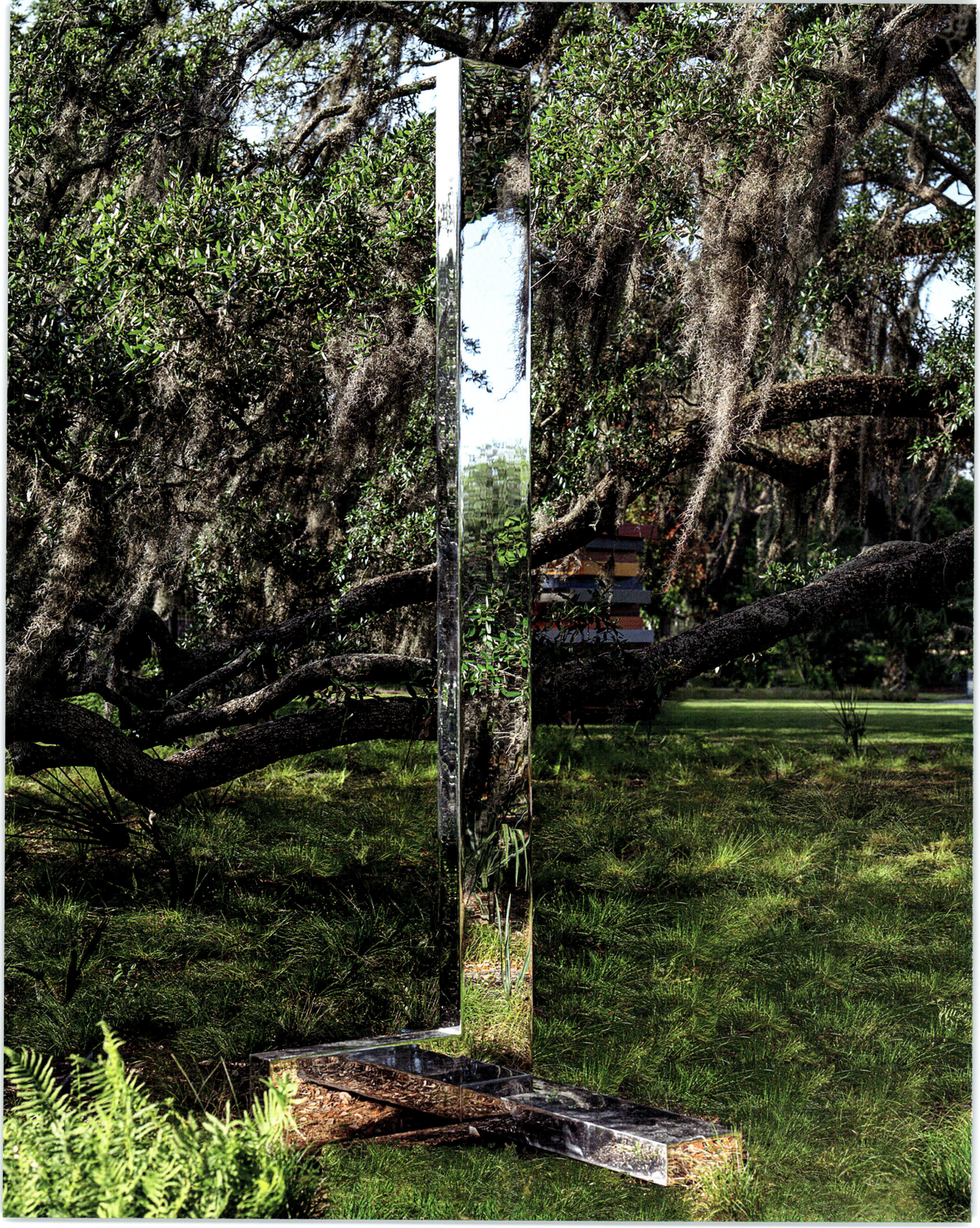

Henry Moore

Reclining Mother and Child,
1975; cast 1977

A singularly influential figure in modern British Art, Henry Moore (1898–1986) is renowned internationally for his semi-abstract, organic sculptures. Working in stone, wood, and cast bronze, Moore developed a unique style that combined fluid, biomorphic shapes with open, interlocking forms. He consistently returned to a number of themes and motifs across his lifetime, namely simplified reclining figures and the image of the mother and child—both of which are blended here in his monumental bronze *Reclining Mother and Child*.

Passionate about sculpture from an early age, Moore's artistic education didn't formally begin until after his service in World War I when, supported by a rehabilitation grant, he enrolled at the Leeds School of Art. It was here that he first met fellow sculptor Barbara Hepworth, whose work is also exhibited in the Besthoff Sculpture Garden. The two would go on to develop similar interests in the effects of negative space and abstracted shape, and both became master practitioners of the direct carving method. Moore continued his studies at the Royal College of Art, moving in the avant-garde circles of Hampstead, London that included such artists and architects as Marcel Breuer (1902–1981), Lázszló Moholy-Nagy (1895–1946), Ben Nicholson (1894–1982), and Hepworth. Funded by a travel grant in 1925, Moore left London for six months, splitting time between Italy and France, where he first encountered plaster casts of precolonial Mayan carvings which he would forever cite as a chief source of inspiration.

After the birth of his daughter in 1946, Moore reprised his depictions of family groups, and especially of mothers and children. As he began reworking this subject matter during the postwar period, Moore's sculptures grew increasingly larger and ever more figurative. While never fully naturalistic, Moore edged back towards representation, crafting movement-filled shapes that gesture at loosely defined figures. Evidenced in *Reclining Mother and Child* (cast by H. Noak Berlin), the liquid-like contours of each figure form the distinct shape of a small child, visible against the woman's supine silhouette, the blurred edges capturing Moore's constant vacillation between representation and abstraction.—*MH*

Bronze, 94 ½ × 53 ½ × 47 ½ in. (240 × 135.9 × 120.7 cm),
Gift of the Sydney and Walda Besthoff Foundation, 1998

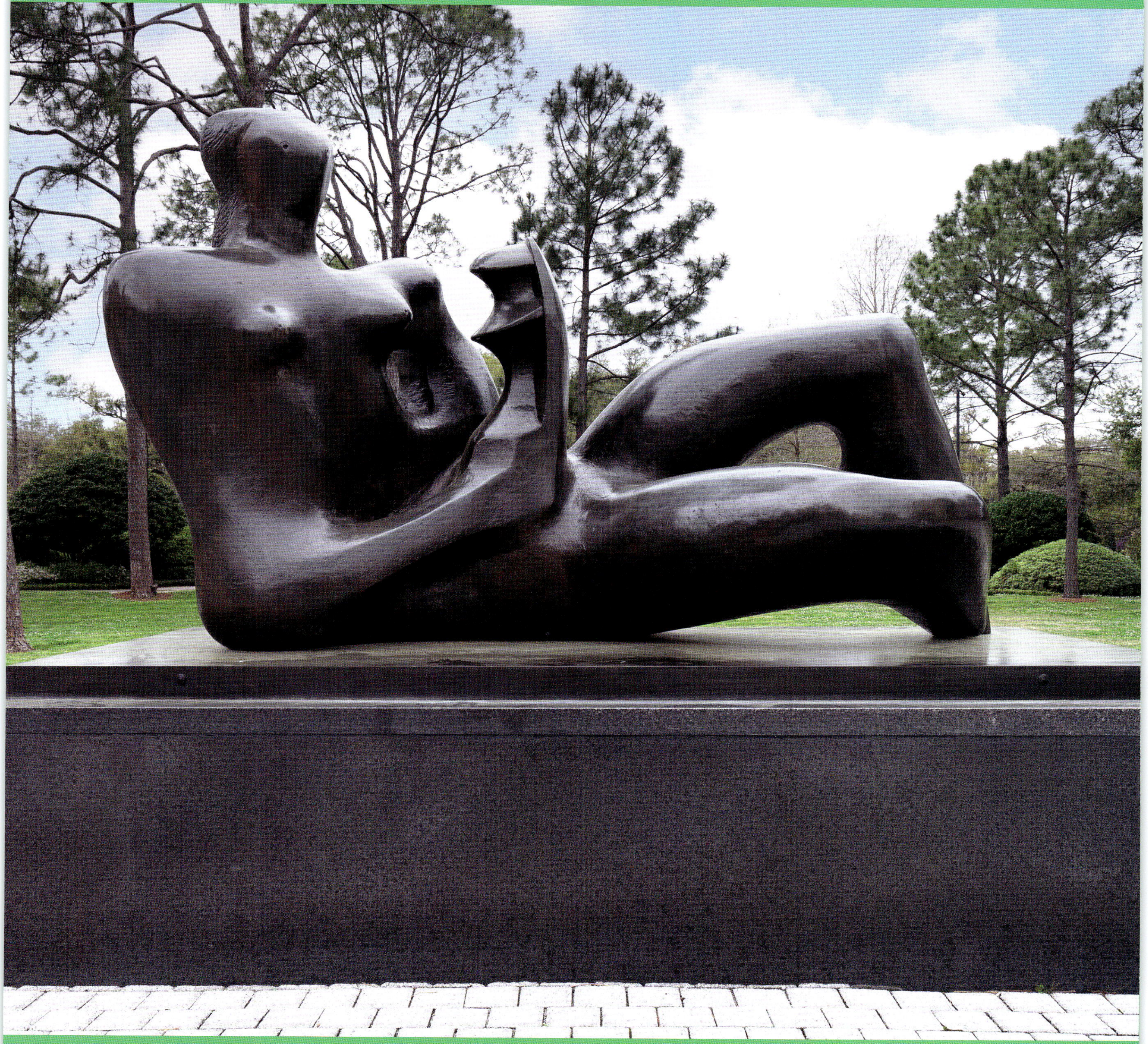

Jesús Bautista Moroles

Las Mesas Bench, 1989

Born in Corpus Christi, Texas, and residing in the state for most of his life, Jesús Bautista Moroles (1950–2015) set up his impressive sculpture studio in Rockport, where he worked almost exclusively with granite on a monumental scale. Moroles developed his creative practice and fascination with unyielding materials from a young age, receiving art classes in school and learning the craft of stonemasonry from his uncle as an adolescent. He received a bachelor of fine arts from North Texas University after serving in the air force as an electronic engineer. In the late 1970s, he apprenticed under the American sculptor Luis Jiménez (1940–2006). Soon after, he traveled to Pietrasanta, Italy, where he found inspiration in fifteenth-century quarries and refined his artistic vision. After probing various materials, including limestone and marble, the artist elected granite, despite the rock's complex and unpredictable qualities. All of these experiences helped form Moroles's distinct lexicon in which modernity, abstraction, and a sense of prehistory come together to form a cohesive whole.

While undeniably adopting a minimalist diction, Moroles's work calls for a deeper examination of humanity's symbiotic relationship with nature. He purposefully left elements of the stone in its rudimentary form, revealing a contrast between rough textures and smooth edges, between geometric shapes and organic lines, as present in *Las Mesas Bench*. Moreover, many of Moroles's structures are often installed near large bodies of water or as fountains for spectators to interact with. Such is the case for *Las Mesas Bench*—the sculpture sits atop a terrace surrounded by foliage and overlooking the garden's tranquil lagoon, further encouraging an appreciation for our environment.

In the 1980s, Moroles began rendering planes of granite and forming fluid patterns, sometimes stacking, interlacing, or overlapping them to create woven-like configurations. Although invoking pre-Columbian art and themes of spirituality, the pictured work is also imbued with a sense of futurity for its refined facades. Exemplifying Moroles's deft manipulation of granite and formal rigor, *Las Mesas Bench* weaves together stillness and movement in a radiant totemic composition.—*JM*

Granite, 13 ft. × 66 in. × 56 in. (3.9 m × 167.6 cm × 142.2 cm), Gift of the Sydney and Walda Besthoff Foundation, 2000

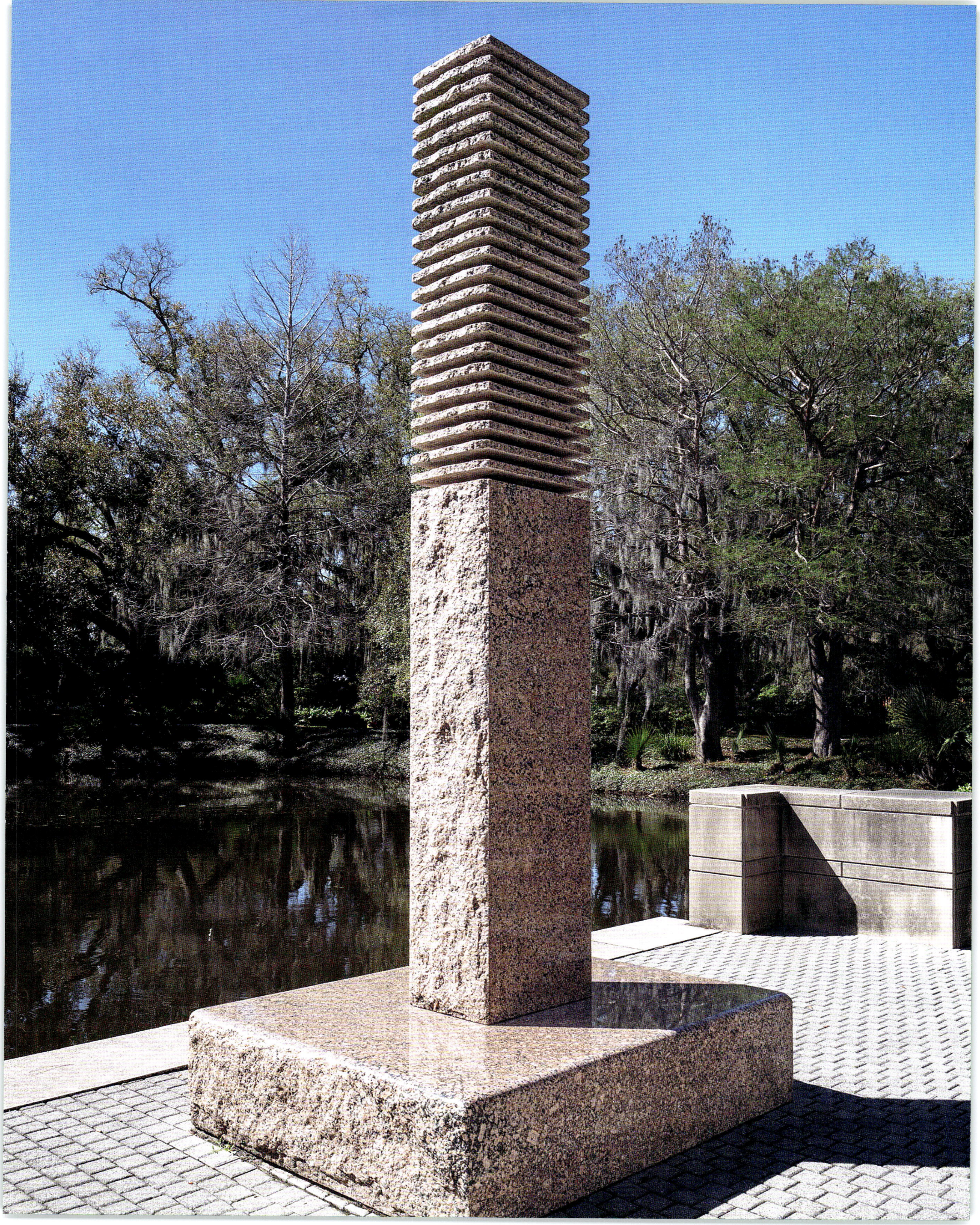

Wangechi Mutu

The Seated III, 2019

Known for her ability to seamlessly blend the mythic, the historic, and the otherworldly, Wangechi Mutu (b. 1972) creates sculptures situated at the edge of this world and the next. Working with traditions of both science fiction and Afrofuturism, she centers the female figure throughout her practice, often imagining matriarchal spaces where women are all-powerful, respected as essential links in the continuation of our species, and intrinsically connected to the natural world. In her sculptures, two-dimensional works, installations, and films, Mutu infuses history with many distinct potentials for a liberated future, combining the fantastical with the fabled to propose alternative ways for humanity to co-exist with nature and preserve the ecological wonders of the world.

One of four seated female figures, *The Seated III* was originally cast as part of Mutu's series The NewOnes, will free Us, designed as the inaugural facade commission for the Metropolitan Museum of Art. Refashioning the classical architectural fixture of the caryatid—a load-bearing column sculpted in the form of a standing female figure—Mutu's four women are at rest, enthroned and adorned, their elegant silhouettes at once futuristic and deeply historical. Each of the seated figures is constructed from a web of coils, a reference that evokes traditional tribal jewelry from the African continent. Additionally, the coils recall the most basic method for constructing a pot out of clay—alluding to how women have been cast as both metaphorical vessels for customs and culture, and more literally as the bearers and carriers of life. Positioned in erect, seated stances typically reserved for male monarchs, Mutu's spiraling figures nod to and dignify their legacy. Emblematic of the artist's uncanny talent for working across time—collapsing the present consequences of the past with the history that brought us here and the future we still hope to reach—the sinewy, graceful figure of *The Seated III* synthesizes the very best of Mutu's artistic agenda.—*MH*

Bronze, 82 7/8 × 37 3/4 × 33 3/4 in. (210.5 × 95.9 × 85.7 cm), edition 3 of 3 + 1 AP, Museum Purchase with Gifted Funds from Sydney and Walda Besthoff, 2021

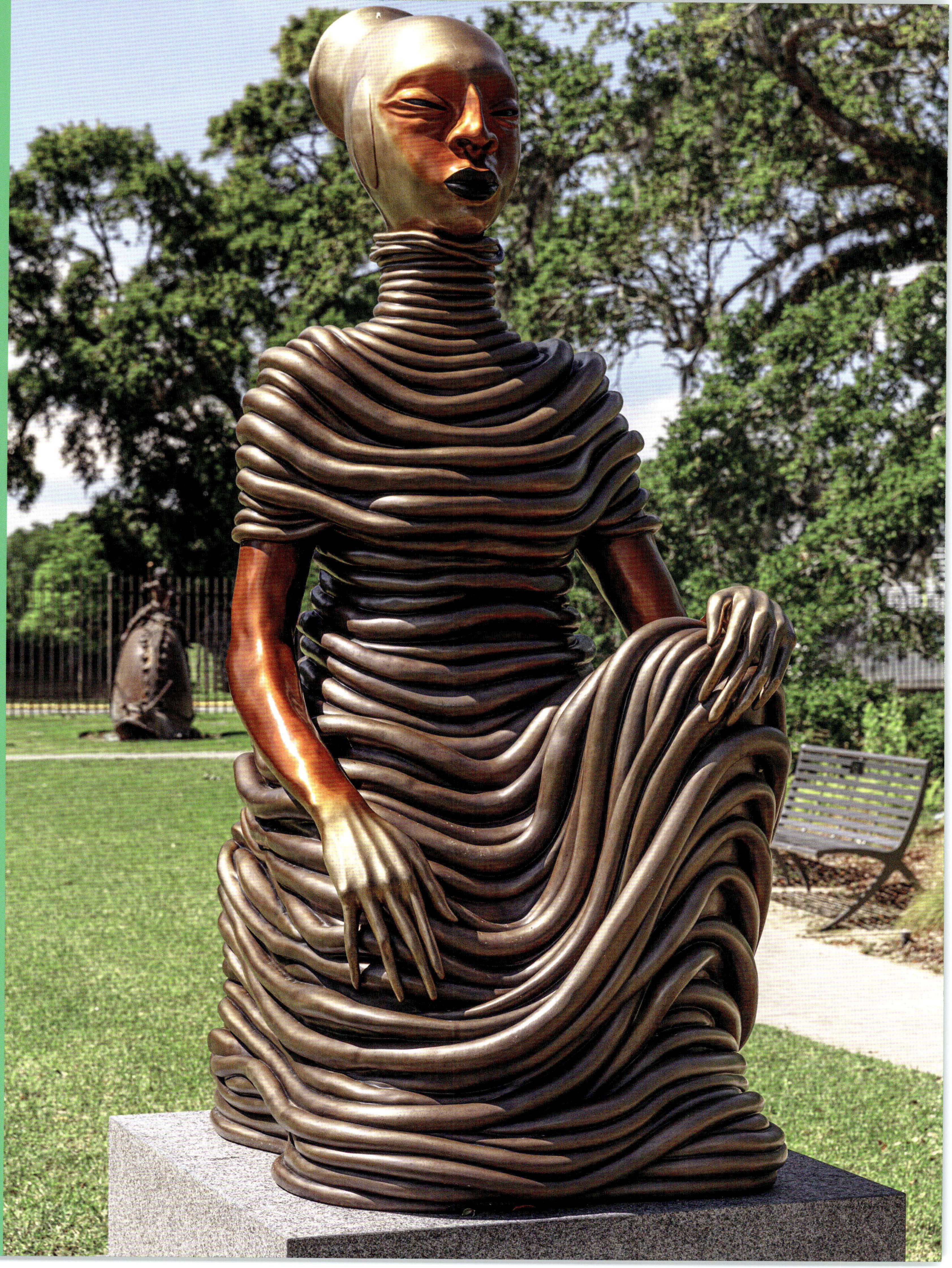

Wangechi Mutu

Crocodylus, 2020

Blending a diverse range of symbols—whether from sociology, history and archeology or science fiction, magic, and mythology—Mutu fabricates a world that is foreign yet eerily familiar to our own. Chipping away at harmful tropes used across Western art to represent Black women, Mutu's practice centers empowered, deity-like female figures, many of whom appear as hybrid animal-women. Such characters speak to the climate concerns plaguing contemporary life, and to centuries of civilization. Interpolated with themes of Afrofuturism, Mutu's idiosyncratic visual language ultimately collapses time through her careful integration of past, present, and future, about which the work is visionary. Known for her unique ability to braid a multitude of references into one coherent argument, Mutu's work furthers a political agenda of equity, conservation, and respect for the natural environment.

Taking the form of a signature hybrid animal-woman, *Crocodylus* blends a human figure straddling a crocodile into a single, otherworldly creature. Inspired by a fashion editorial that captured the supermodel Naomi Campbell (b. 1970) riding astride a crocodile for *Harper's Bazaar*, in Mutu's sculpture the human and beast become inseparable, covered in an intricate, geometric textile-like patterning of scales. An allusion to the prehistoric crocodile native to northern Kenya and to the alligators that prowl the American South, the crocodile evokes the painful dispossession and horrors of the slave trade. Taking part-human, part-animal form, *Crocodylus* is also equally symbolic of empowerment and mysticism. Drawing on the rich catalog of Egyptian deities, including several gods imagined in the guise of the crocodile, Mutu alludes to previous understandings of nature as divine. The sculpture is typical of the artist intertwining the feminine, the holy, and the ecological—potent concepts that comingle in her practice and her philosophy at large.—*MH*

Bronze, 48 in. × 14 ft. (121.9 cm × 4.3 m), Museum Purchase with Gifted Funds from Sydney and Walda Besthoff, 2021

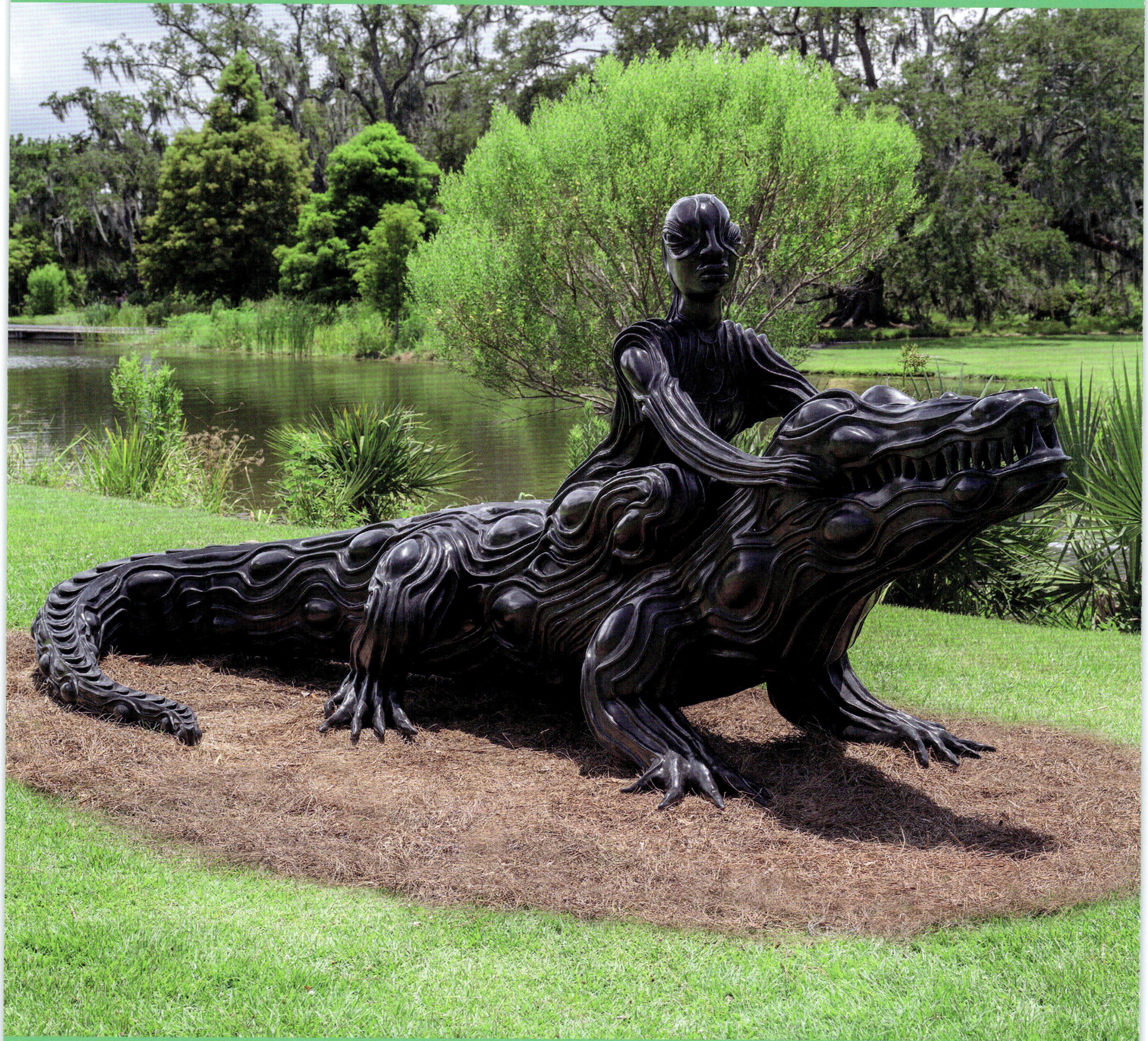

Masayuki Nagare

Bachi, 1979

Adhering closely to the traditional principles of Japanese aesthetics, Masayuki Nagare's (1923–2018) clean, abstracted forms juxtapose different finishes, creating a compelling tension between instances of high polish and shine and rougher patches where the chisel marks have been left intentionally visible in the stone surface. Favoring subtle, curvilinear silhouettes, the shapes of Nagare's sculptures draw references back to age-old Japanese crafts, from samurai swords to musical instruments.

Son of the founder of Ritsumeikan University, Nagare grew up in Kyoto, where he received a proper samurai's education: extensive training in the necessity of sport; practical lessons in ancient craft trades, including an apprenticeship with a master swordsmith; and teachings in both Buddhist and Shinto philosophies. After serving as a fighter pilot during the last years of World War II, Nagare retreated to the countryside, depleted by the experience of combat. Disturbed by the violence he had witnessed, in his solitude Nagare returned to his philosophical studies, traveling through small towns where he stayed largely with local farmers and industrial workers. He began exhibiting sculpture in 1955, and three years later, Aline Saarinen (1914–1972)—then the art critic for the *New York Times*—championed his work, praising Nagare to the upper echelons of New York's society collectors. The Rockefellers, Joseph Hirschhorn (1899–1981), and William Paley (1901–1990), all turned their attention to Nagare and began actively collecting his work, as did the architects Marcel Breuer (1902–1981) and Philip Johnson (1906–2005). By the 1960s, Nagare had received a number of notable commissions both in Japan and New York, exhibiting work at the 1964 World's Fair and later at the Carnegie International (1970).

In *Bachi*, Nagare's deft feel for texture and finish is apparent. The curved shape is a direct reference to the tool by the same name which is used to play the shamisen, a traditional Japanese stringed instrument. Enlarged beyond human scale, Nagare has honored the original form, perfectly reproducing its silhouette in a nod to the historical and artistic traditions of his homeland.—*MH*

Red granite, 72 × 30 × 8 in. (182.9 × 76.2 × 20.3 cm), Gift of the Sydney and Walda Besthoff Foundation, 1998

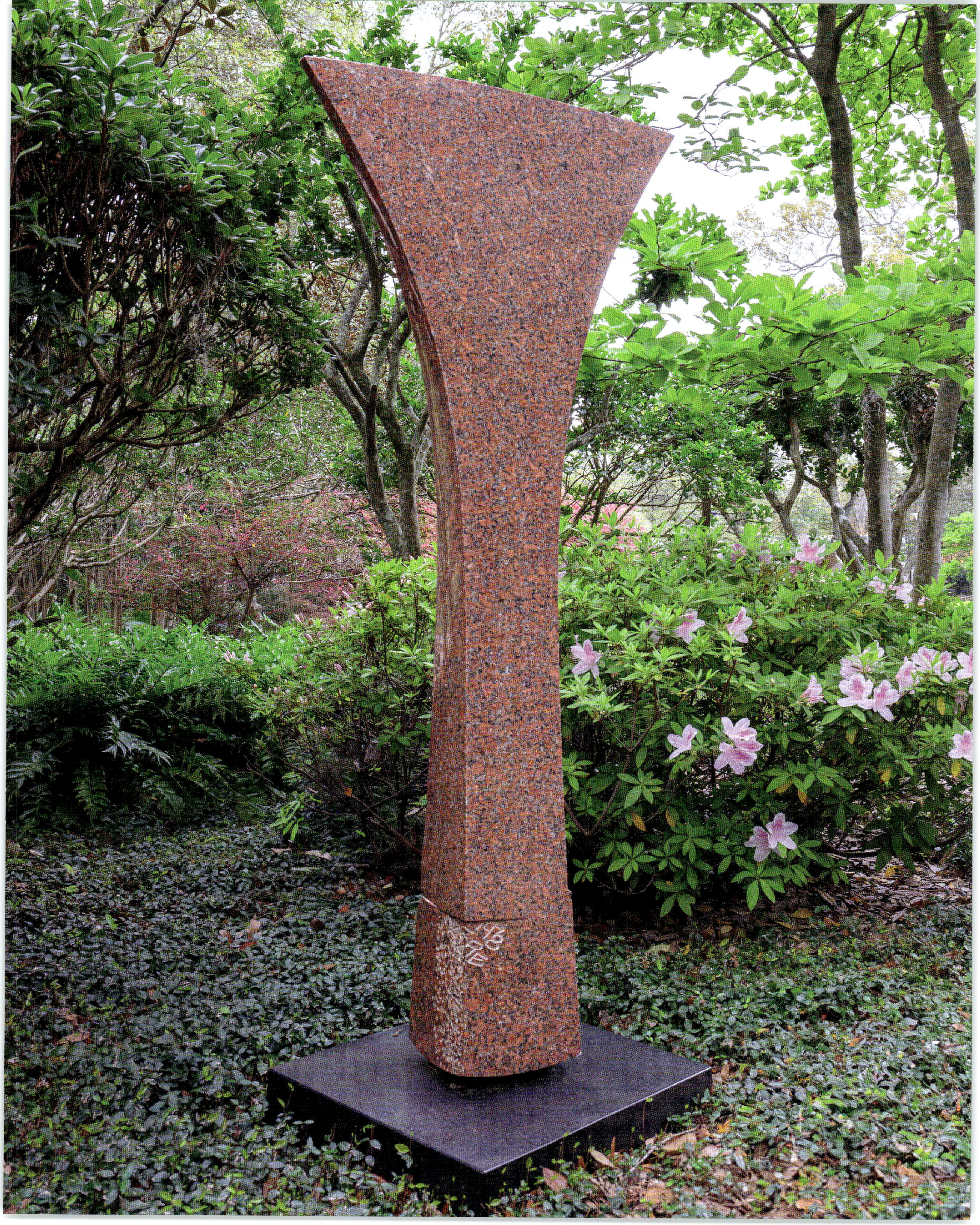

Minoru Niizuma

Castle of the Eye II, 1973

Known for his abstract, angular sculptures, Minoru Niizuma (1930–1998) always designed his artworks around his chosen material, often carving directly into the stone and shaping it in accordance with its preexisting veining, gradients, and physical properties to elevate its raw aesthetic beauty. This artistic philosophy, similar to that championed by his contemporary and friend Isamu Noguchi (1904–1988)—whose work is also featured in the garden—manifested in the simplified, geometric forms of his sculptures. Working frequently in series, Niizuma iterated the same silhouette or pattern across a wide variety of scales and materials, reinventing it each time according to the particularities of the stone used.

After a formal education at the Tokyo National University of Fine Arts, Niizuma moved to New York City. Immersed in the roiling postwar art scene, the artist witnessed firsthand the fracturing of aesthetic sensibilities as Minimalism and Pop art rose to the forefront of culture, each jockeying to fill the gap left by Abstract Expressionism. Niizuma's careful attention to form, and indeed his habit of working serially, links him with the tenets that began to define Minimalism, though he never associated himself formally with the movement. Instead, he took a job teaching, first at the Brooklyn Museum School before joining the arts faculty at Columbia University, where he would go on to teach for twelve years. During this time, he traveled to Portugal for various symposia, and on these trips became completely enchanted with the array of easily accessible stone. Niizuma increasingly spent time there, gaining traction in the artistic communities across the country and exhibiting in a number of shows.

Comprised of four stacked cubes, each carved with concentric squares, Castle of the Eye is Niizuma's best-known series and a form that he returned to numerous times in diverse materials. The sculpture balances repetition and geometry in a simple, but captivating form. Carved of white marble, *Castle of the Eye, II*, held in the Sydney and Walda Besthoff Sculpture Garden, uses the grain of the stone by incorporating it into the pattern and highlighting the natural beauty of the material itself.—*MH*

Marble, 112 × 25 × 25 in. (284.5 × 63.5 × 63.5 cm), Gift of the Sydney and Walda Besthoff Foundation, 1998

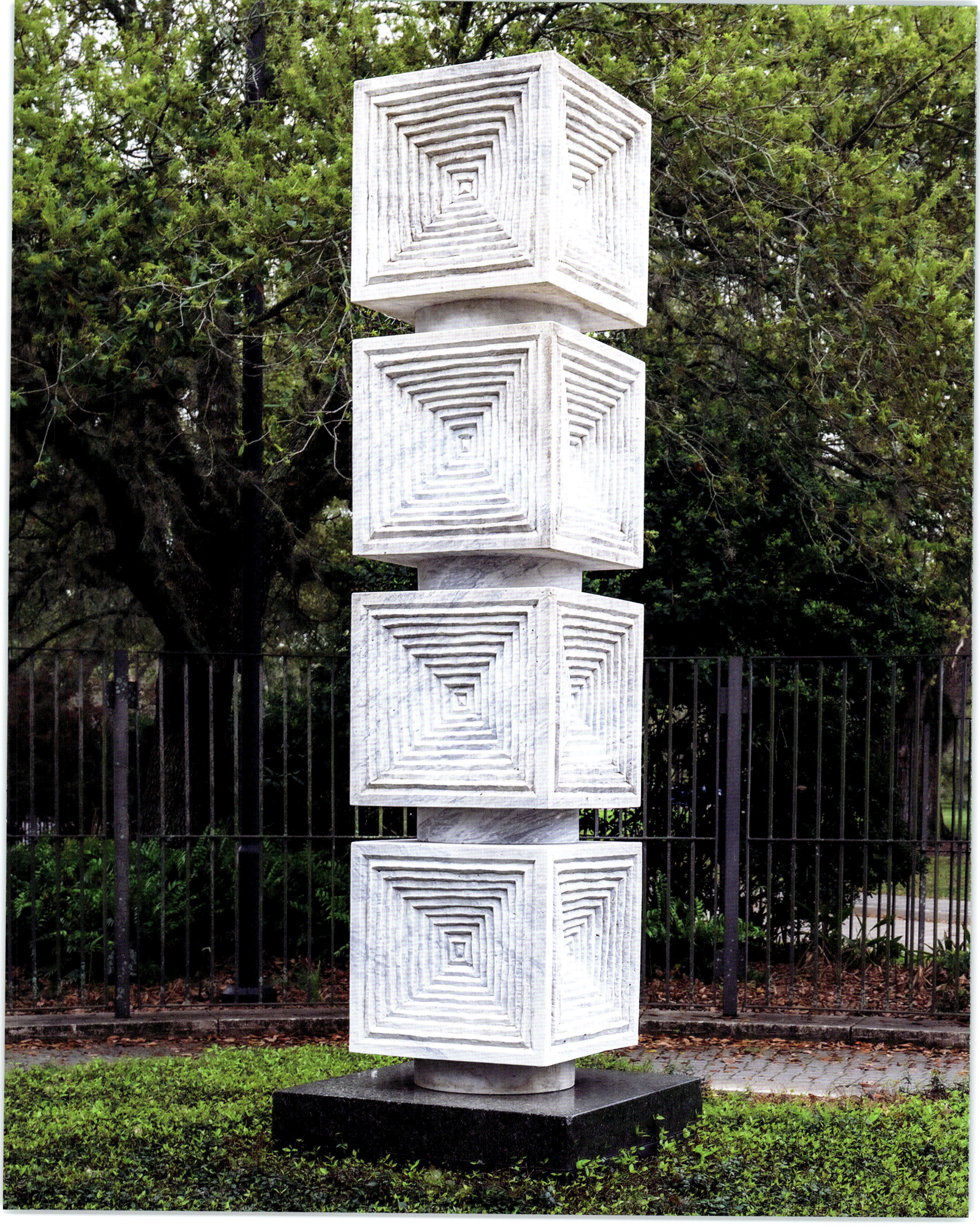

Isamu Noguchi

Rain Mountain, 1982

Few of Isamu Noguchi's (1904–1988) contemporaries pushed the boundaries of sculpture to the extent he did. Dismissing conventional differences between sculpture and design, Noguchi pursued an extremely wide-ranging practice that, sometimes crossing into architecture, included gardens, parks, playgrounds, plazas, stage sets, and furniture. Born in Los Angeles, Noguchi spent part of his childhood in Japan, a country whose history and aesthetic sensibilities remained important sources of inspiration.

While studying medicine at Columbia University in the early 1920s, he realized he had to become a sculptor and enrolled at the Leonardo da Vinci School in Greenwich Village. During this time, a Guggenheim Fellowship funded his first visit to Paris, where he was a studio assistant to sculptor Constantin Brancusi (1876–1960), a major influence. By the 1940s, his early portrait busts had given way to abstract and organic shapes, often of polished stone. Noguchi traveled extensively throughout his life and received multiple public commissions in both Japan and Europe. In 1985, he founded the Noguchi Museum in Queens, New York, the neighborhood where he had kept a studio since 1961.

From the mid-1960s to the early 1980s, Noguchi produced mountain-themed sculptures in various materials, including basalt, granite, obsidian, and travertine. *Rain Mountain* continued an interest in hot-dipped galvanized steel, a material he began working with around 1980. As with *Cloud Mountain* and *Mountains Forming*, two contemporaneous sculptures that similarly abstract from nature, *Rain Mountain* is composed of flat, upright, and rounded forms that are intersected with, and stabilized by, a single smaller perpendicular plane. *Rain Mountain* is the largest of about a dozen free-standing "mountain" works and among the largest of the hot-dipped galvanized steel pieces.—*AMT*

Hot-dipped galvanized steel, 95 ½ × 24 × 21 in. (242.6 × 60.9 × 53.3 cm), Gift of Mrs. P. Roussel Norman, 1991

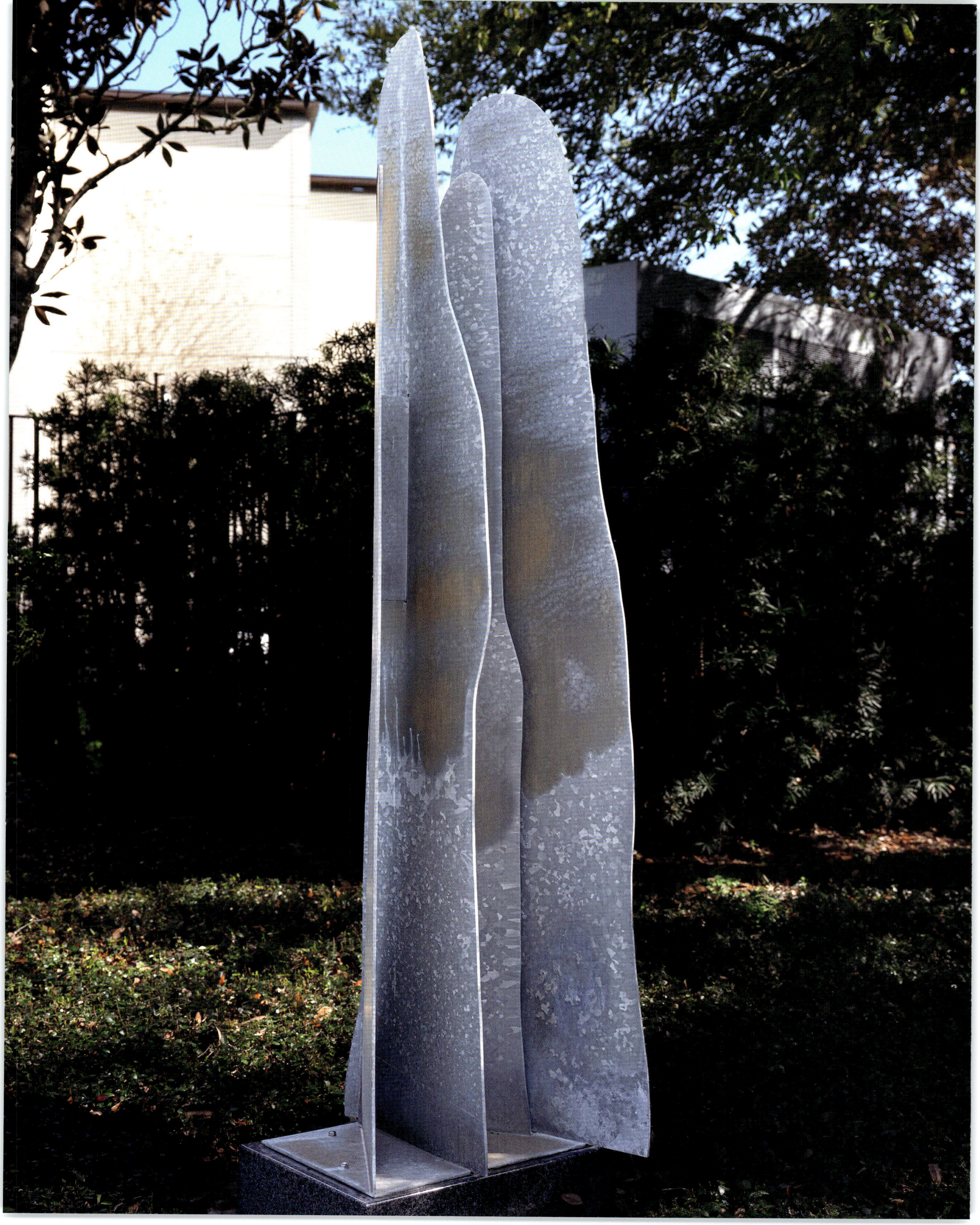

Claes Oldenburg + Coosje van Bruggen

Corridor Pin, Blue, 1999

The creative partnership between Claes Oldenburg (1929–2022) and Coosje van Bruggen (1942–2009) preceded their marriage in 1977. The duo met in 1970 and first worked together when van Bruggen, a Netherlandish writer and curator, advised on the installation of Oldenberg's *Trowel* (1971) on behalf of the Kröller-Müller Museum in Otterlo. Oldenberg had already forged a path adjacent to Pop art by replicating banal objects. Beginning as painted plaster and vinyl "soft" sculptures in the 1960s, his work continued to evolve as ever-larger outdoor iterations in metal, from the twenty-four-foot-tall *Lipstick (Ascending) on Caterpillar Tracks* (1969–74) at Yale University to the fourty-five-foot-tall *Clothespin* (1976) in central Philadelphia. Oldenburg's sculptures, arriving as they did with the burgeoning postwar consumer society, questioned the commodity status of works of art in strange and playful ways.

Over three decades, Oldenburg and van Bruggen collaborated on dozens of giant public monuments around the world: a pickaxe in Kassel, Germany (1982); a Swiss army knife–cum–gondola in Venice (1985); a bicycle in Paris (1990); shuttlecocks in Kansas City, Missouri (1993); and a saw in Tokyo (1996), to name a few. They called these works their "large-scale projects," all of which share some common characteristics, including bold colors, simplified forms, huge size, and responsiveness to the physical properties of each site. *Batcolumn*, his one-hundred-foot-high baseball bat in downtown Chicago is, fittingly, the tallest sculpture, since the Swedish-born Oldenburg grew up in the city from the age of seven. *Corridor Pin, Blue*, another enlargement of a common household object, has a weightless quality that distinguishes it from the innumerable oversized roadside attractions that dot the country. The safety pin, an American invention like the humble clothespin, is meant to fasten things together but here, unclasped, hints at a guillotine-like danger. Updating the Dada tradition of repurposing found and mass-produced objects, Oldenburg and van Bruggen elevate the mundane fixtures of everyday life via peculiar combinations of absurdity and wonder.—*AMT*

Stainless steel and aluminum with blue acrylic polyurethane enamel, 21 ft. 3 in. × 21 ft. 2 in. × 16 in. (6.5 m × 6.5 m × 40.6 cm), Museum purchase, Sydney and Walda Besthoff Foundation Fund, 2004

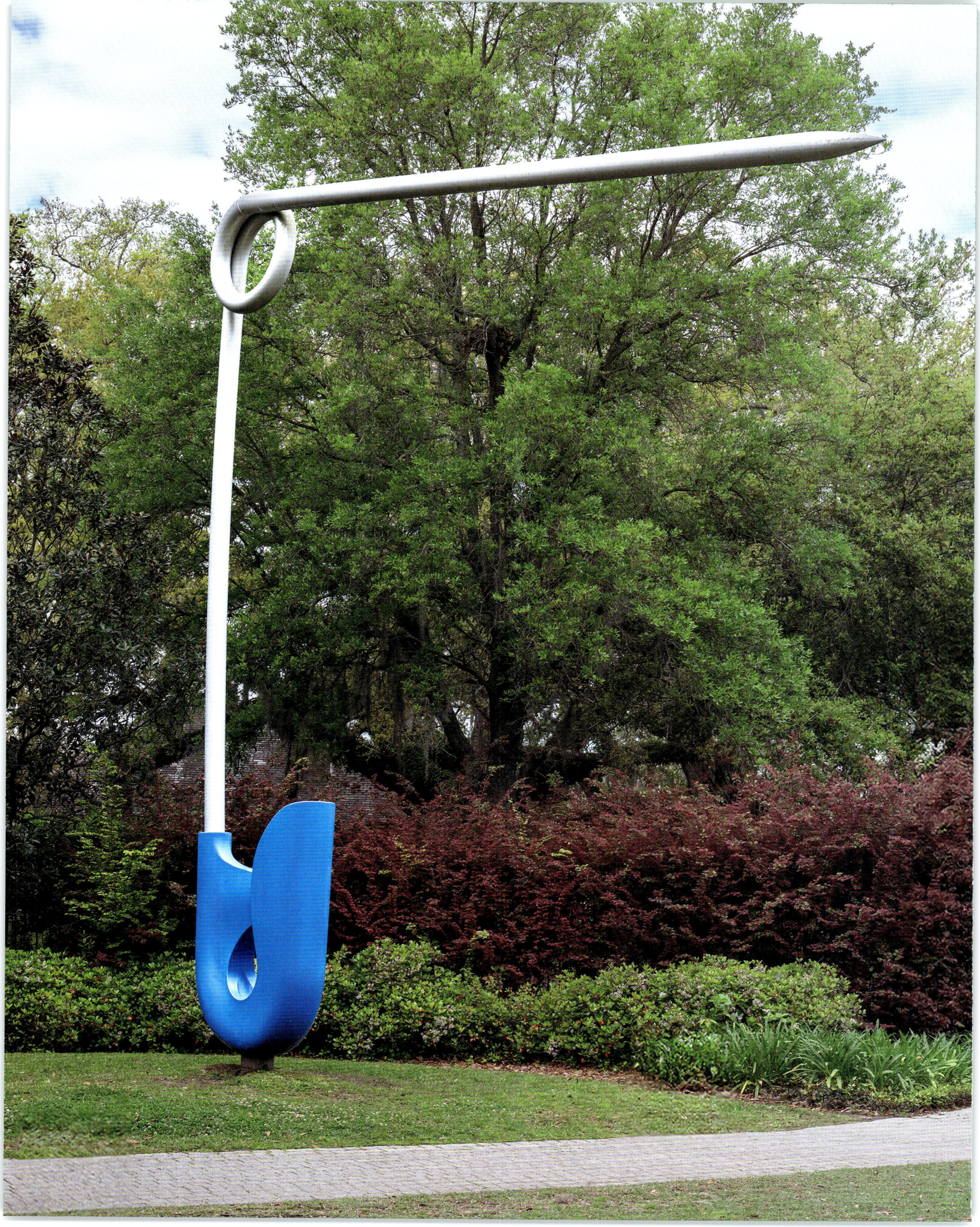

Jean-Michel Othoniel

L'Arbre aux Colliers (Tree of Necklaces), 2002

Widely acclaimed for his sculptures and installations, Jean-Michel Othoniel's (b. 1964) material-driven work investigates themes of beauty, transformation, and the environment. The artist lives and works in Paris, where he also creates using drawing, painting, performance, and photography. Coming of age in the late 1980s at the height of the HIV/AIDS epidemic, Othoniel initially deployed malleable materials such as sulfur and wax to poetically study concepts of fragility and ephemerality.

Since 1993, he has worked predominantly in glass, collaborating with artisan glassblowers in Murano, Italy, to produce brick surfaces, splendid orbs, and beaded compositions, for which he is most documented today. After completing a residency in 1996 at the Villa Medici in Rome, the artist switched his concentration to large-scale commissions, taking him beyond the confines of his studio and incorporating the aesthetic properties of landscape and architecture. From that point on, Othoniel has designed private and public monuments around the world, including the *Kiosque des Noctambules (Kiosk of the Night-walkers)* (1996–2000) at the entrance of the Palais Royal–Musée du Louvre metro station in Paris.

L'Arbre aux Colliers (Tree of Necklaces) demonstrates a continued interest in serial repetition and the examination of splendor in nature. Composed of glass and stainless steel crafted to resemble crystal, Othoniel acknowledges the unique possibilities of polished and reflective materials against a raw and unprocessed backdrop. The strings of beads gracefully dangle from the tree's branches, appearing precarious and delicate, and thus threatening a plausible rupture, perhaps acting as a metaphor for mankind's unpredictable interdependency with Mother Nature. Suggesting silence, motion, and defying systems of scale, Othoniel dwells on dichotomies of the monumental and the intimate, the geometric and the organic, the ornate and the minimal, and the bright and the obscure. What emerges is a type of beauty that occurs within domains of the everyday yet is only available for those who take a moment to look up.—*JM*

Opposite and following spread
Glass and stainless steel, six necklaces, 70 in. (177.8 cm), each, Museum purchase, Sydney and Walda Besthoff Foundation, and River Branch Foundation, 2002

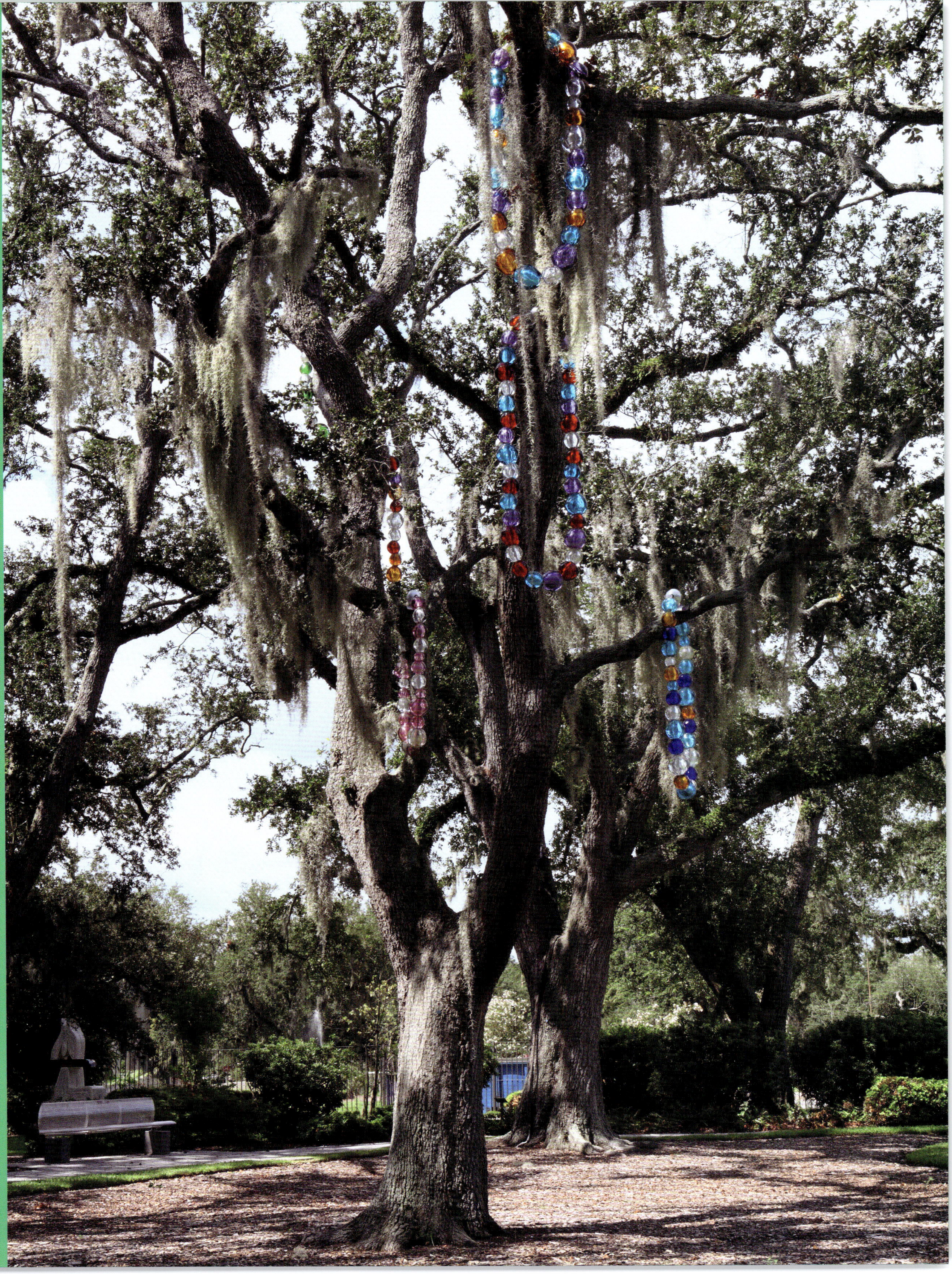

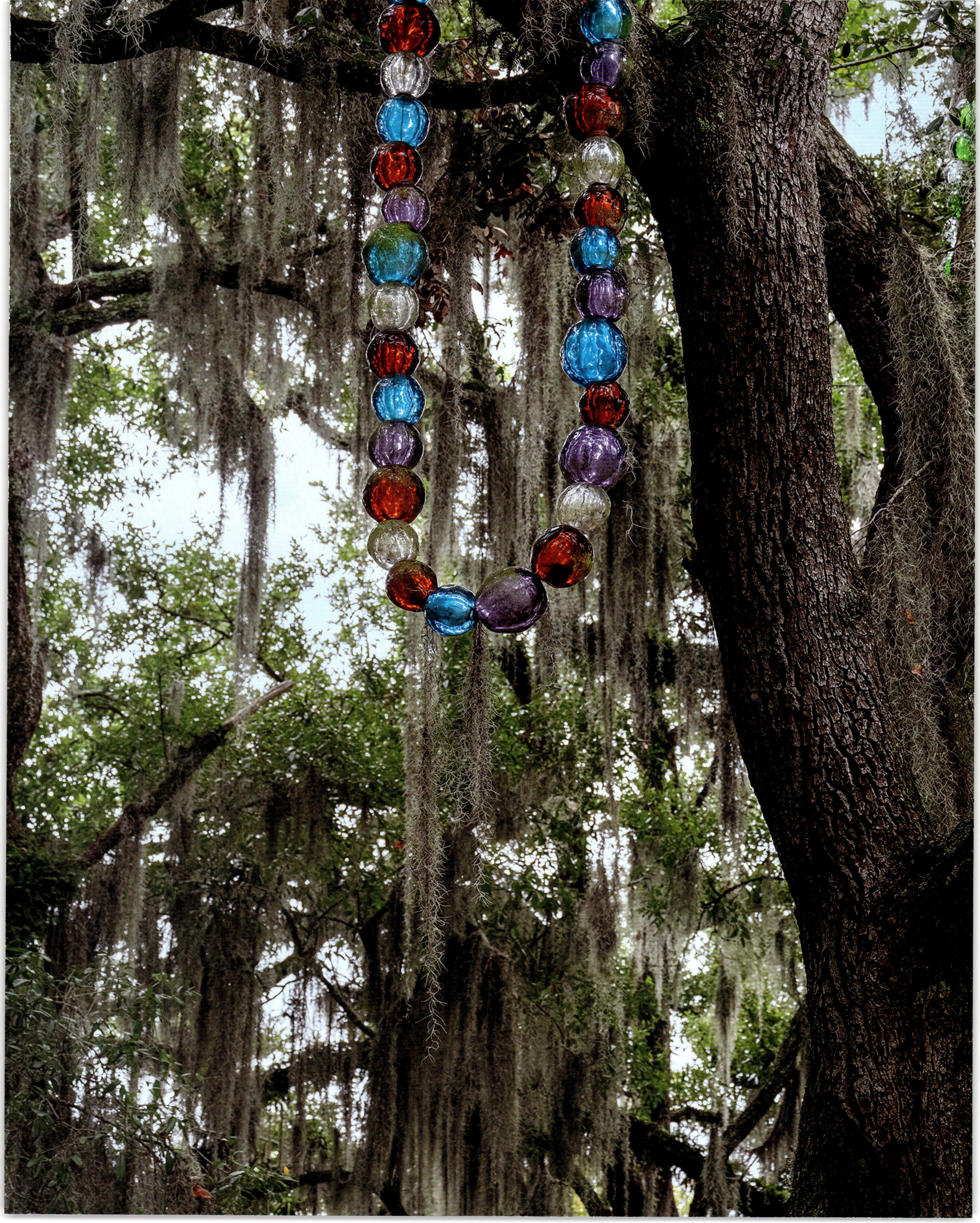

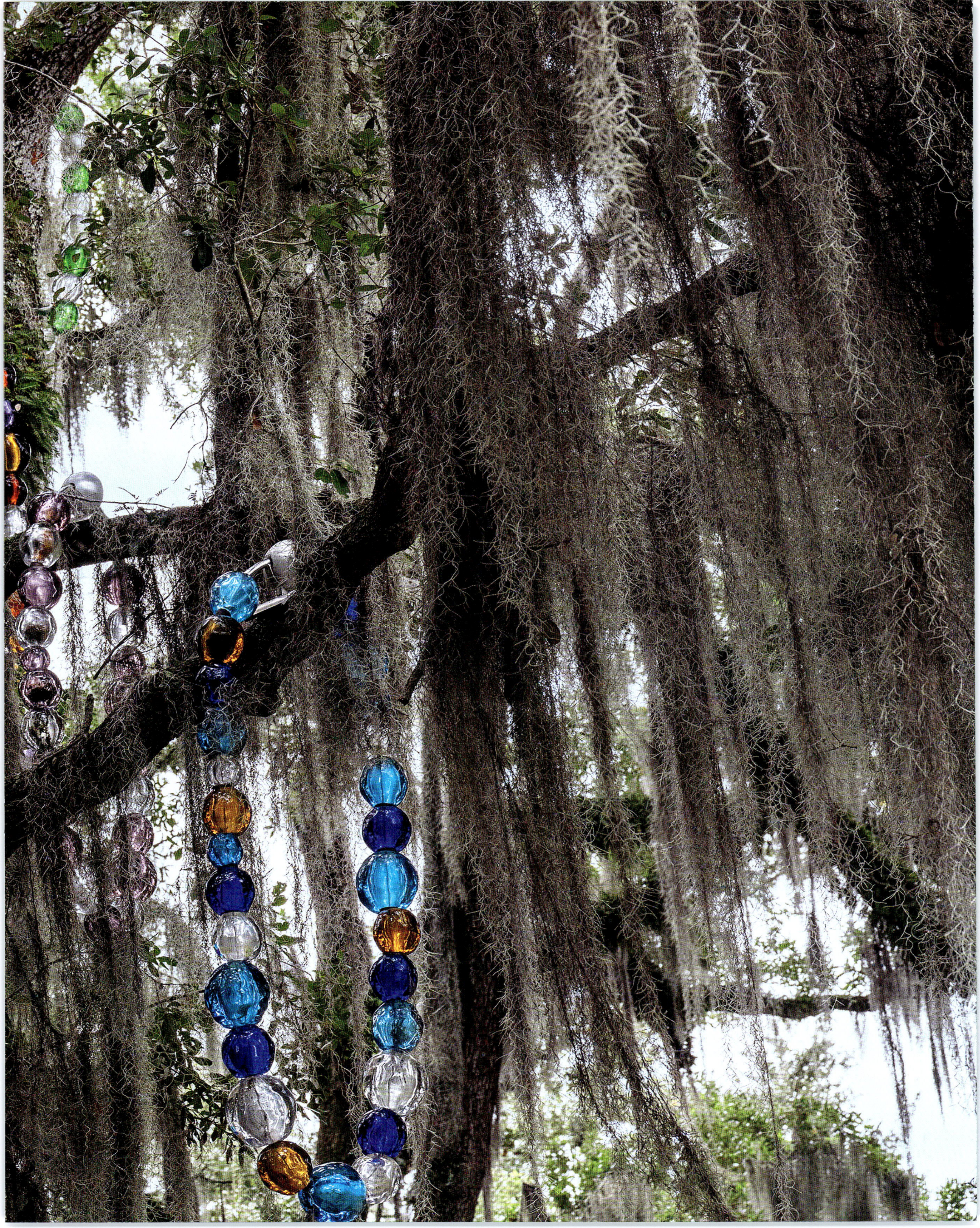

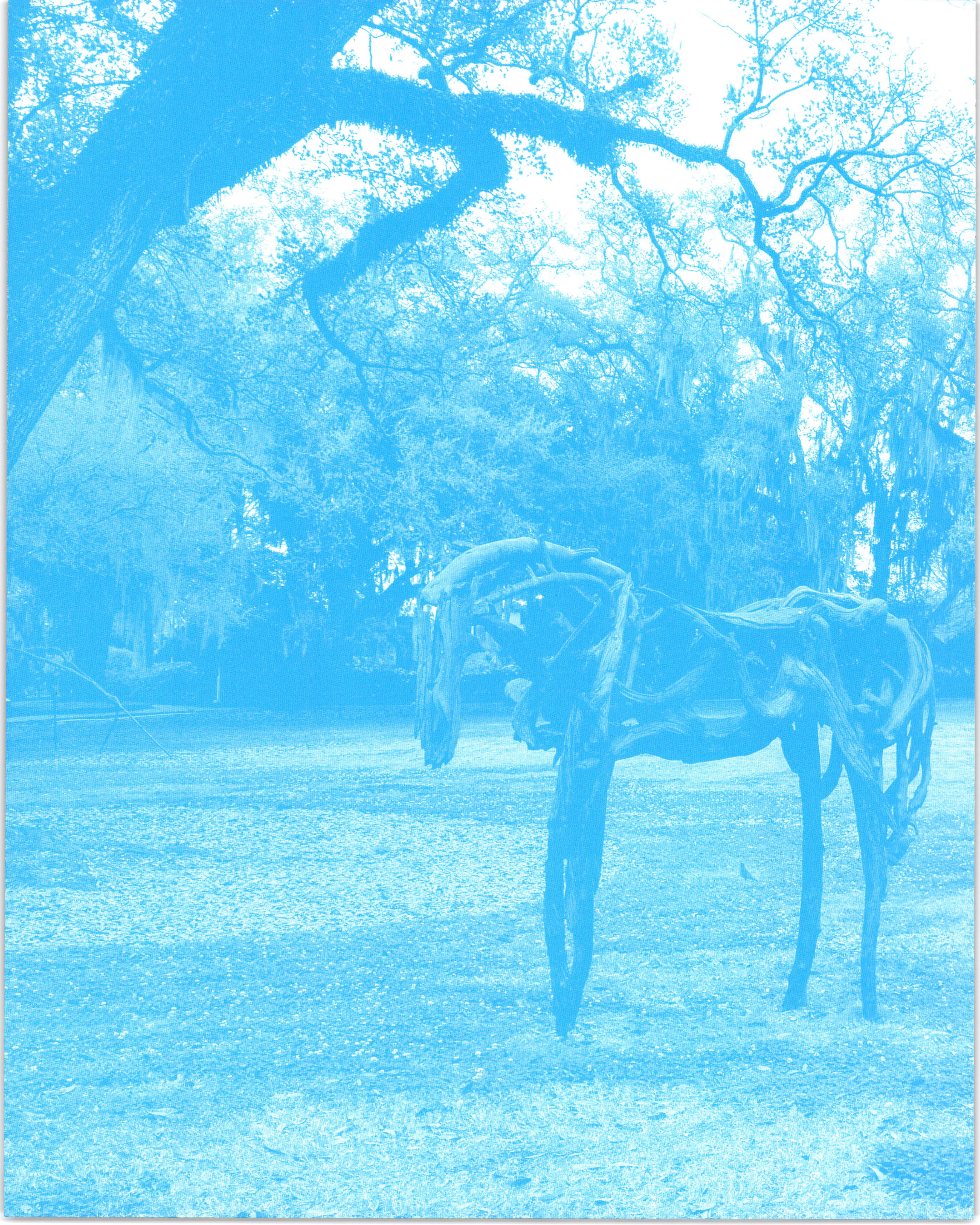

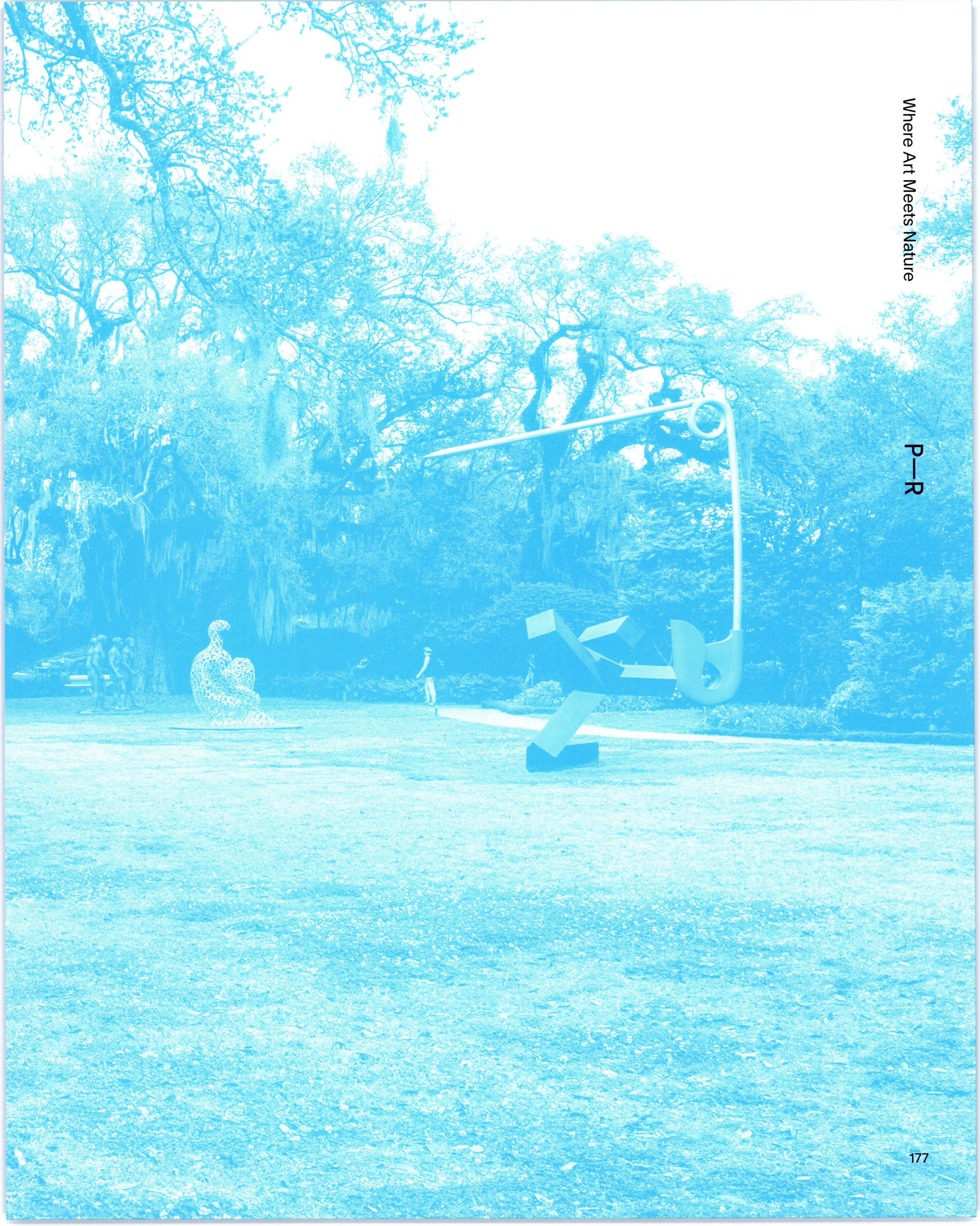

Mimmo Paladino

Caduto a ragione [Fallen for a Reason], 2008

Part of a group of postwar Italian artists who actively rejected the avant-garde's constant need for aesthetic innovation, Mimmo Paladino (b. 1948) instead takes artistic cues from art history. Looking to the patterns of ancient Egypt, the formality of Etruscan statuary, and the fluid drama of Greco-Roman art and architecture, the artist frequently references stories from classical mythology and Christianity in his practice, which spans painting, sculpture, and drawing.

He began his career primarily as a draughtsman, working and reworking allegorical scenes across various prints and drawings. In 1980, he exhibited at the Venice Biennale alongside Sandro Chia (b. 1946), Francesco Clemente (b. 1952), Enzo Cucchi (b. 1949), and Nicola de Maria (b. 1954), solidifying his association with the Transavanguardia movement. Coined by the critic Achille Bonito Oliva (b. 1939), Transavanguardia described a new set of Italian artists, who rejected the more conceptual work of the postwar avant-garde in favor of figurative painting. Alongside Arte Povera, the movement is widely considered one of the most significant of postwar Italian art.

For Paladino, this renewed fascination with representation manifested in primary, monochrome canvases, to which he increasingly added found objects or even components of his own sculpture. In 1982, he began working with cast bronze, developing the patina of each piece to create textured, dynamic surfaces that often mimic the effects of age, making his sculptures appear, at times, as though they date to the classical periods the artist so admires.

In *Caduto a ragione [Fallen for a Reason]*, the mottled surface of the figure appears burnished with time, its texture mimicking the classical bronzes of ancient Greece and Rome. Evoking the great myths that inspired Paladino, the figure, standing with arms outstretched and peppered with sparrows, recalls those mythological heroes perpetually plagued by themes of death, sacrifice, and regeneration.—*MH*

Bronze, 122 in × 55 in × 31 in. (309.9 × 139.7 × 78.7 cm),
Gift of Sydney and Walda Besthoff, 2014

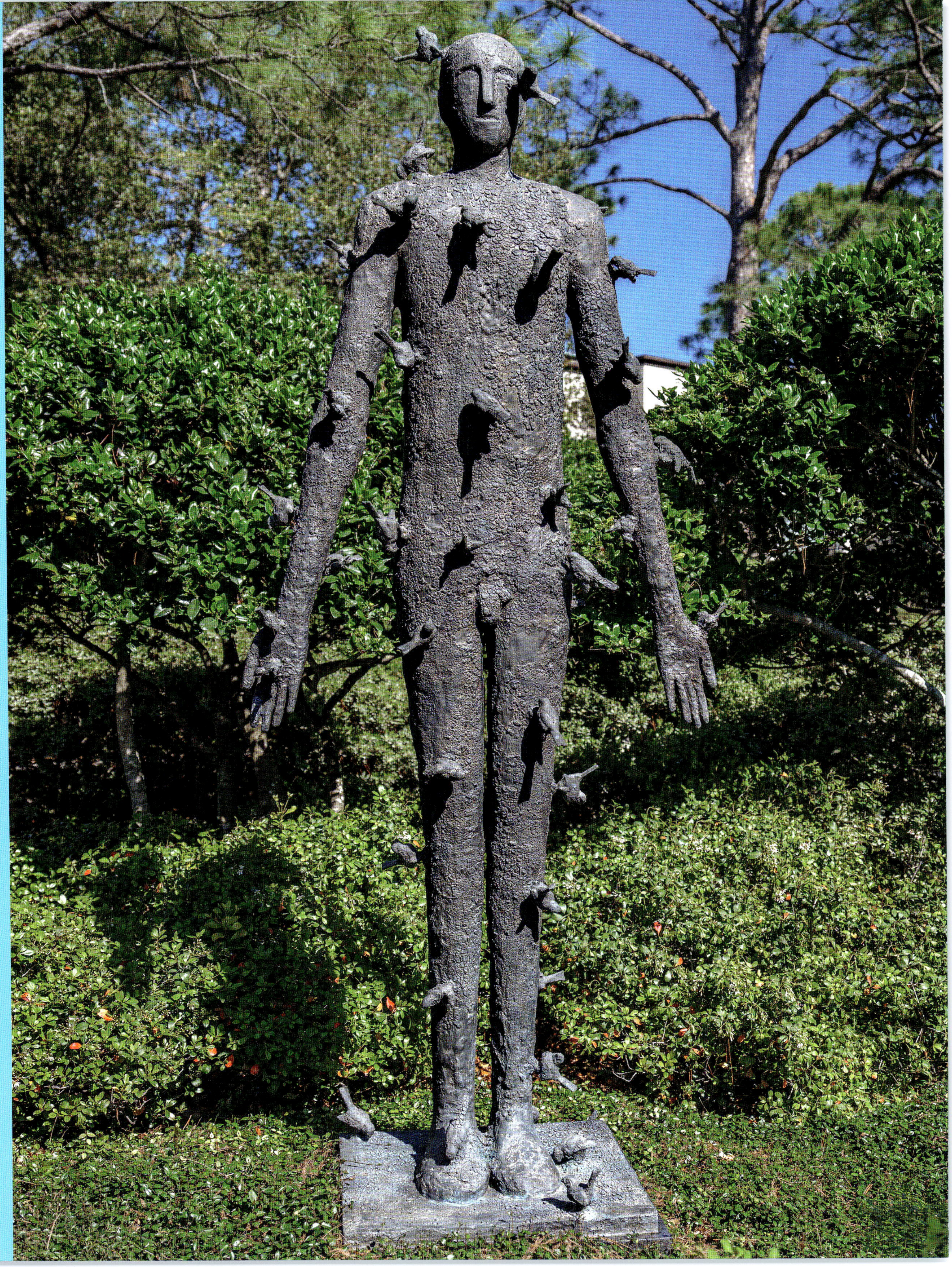

Beverly Pepper

Split Ritual II, 1996

Although Beverly Pepper (1922–2020) worked with a range of metals during her time, the artist's use of forged and cast iron remains unrivaled in postwar sculpture. Born in Brooklyn, she trained as a painter in New York, then France, before relocating to Italy in the 1950s. A 1960 trip to Angkor Wat, the enormous twelfth-century temple complex in Cambodia, changed her life—henceforth, she dedicated herself to sculpture.

Pepper initially became acquainted with iron in the early 1960s near Piombino, Italy, an area known for its plentiful iron deposits and Etruscan tradition of ironworking. Her iron and steel sculptures of this early period are curvy and organic. She was introduced to COR-TEN steel in the mid-1960s, and while she may have even been the first artist to experiment with it, she was certainly the only woman of her generation to give it monumental scale. COR-TEN, along with stainless steel, assumed a central place in Pepper's oeuvre—for the many wedges and broken circles that typify her style, for example—but iron held a special attraction because of its malleability and variegated surface. "I just love iron," Pepper affirmed in a 2009 oral history interview for the Archives of American Art, calling it her "favorite material."

In the late 1970s, a commission from John Deere in Moline, Illinois, brought her to ductile iron, the company's recent invention. It resulted in Pepper's work *Moline Markers* (1980), a set of thirteen totems ranging from about nine feet to over twelve feet. This watershed moment led to major outdoor public commissions, including *Palingenesis* (1993–94) in Zurich, an earthwork consisting of a 227-foot-long cast-iron wall embedded in a hillside fronted with seven steles, and *Manhattan Sentinels* (1993–96), four massive three-story cast-iron columns presiding over a New York plaza. *Split Ritual II* shares qualities with these earlier endeavors, albeit on a smaller scale. Due to its mutable patina, the upright forms are imprinted by the passage of time. Like tuning forks, rudimentary tools, or even male and female guardians, the pair in the featured artwork beguile, strike awe, and convey an archeological sensibility. Both before and after *Split Ritual II*, Pepper included the words "ritual" and "altar" in the titles of many sculptures, suggesting their affinity with the obelisks and ceremonial practices of the ancient Mediterranean of which she was so fond.—*AMT*

Cast iron, 120 × 96 × 96 in. (304.8 × 243.8 × 243.8 cm), overall, Museum purchase with funds provided by Sydney and Walda Besthoff, 2019

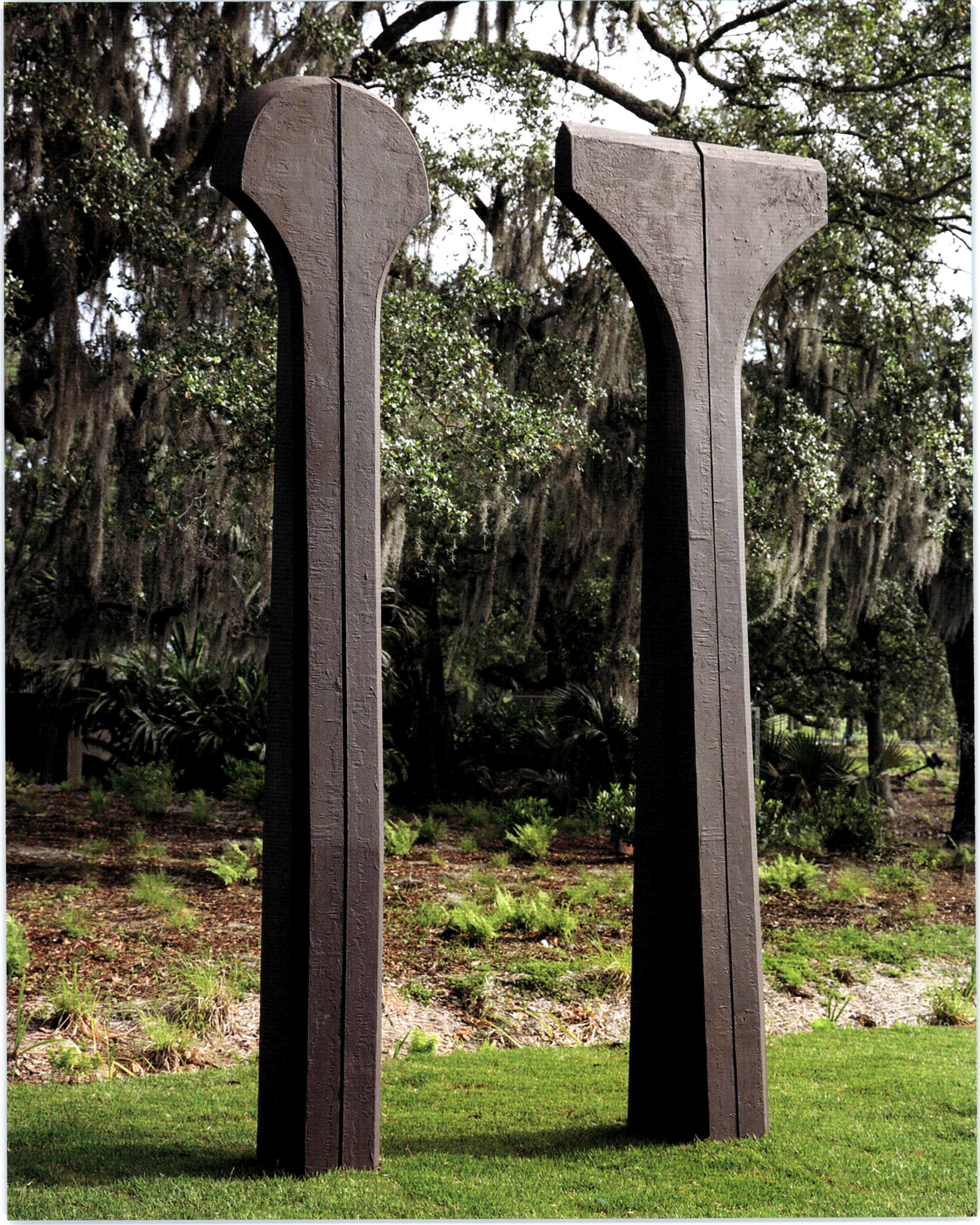

Jaume Plensa

Overflow, 2005

Through his conceptual approach and interdisciplinary practice, Jaume Plensa (b. 1955) collapses our understanding of human presence and its relationship to language. Plensa was born and raised in Barcelona, where he studied art and design, and later resided in various cities around Europe and the United States. He presently lives and works between Barcelona and Paris. Using a wide range of materials, including steel, bronze, and glass, and implementing various techniques, such as 3D scanning, glass blowing, and traditional casting, Plensa seeks to magnify the conceptual possibilities of the figurative tradition.

He rose to prominence in 2004 for designing *Crown Fountain*, a permanent interactive installation comprised of two videos and water fountains mounted on glass towers in Millennium Park, Chicago. He is broadly acknowledged for his colossal sculptures of elongated female heads molded and cast in a variety of mediums, most of which can be found in public spaces throughout the world. Shown with their eyes closed, implying slumber or meditation, many of these statues take on a spiritual and transcendental quality.

For Plensa, ideas are the foremost resource for creation and perhaps this is why language is central to his art. He pulls from a diverse array of lexical elements, alphabets, and dialects, as well as quotes and phrases from eminent authors and poets. All of these amalgamate in a series of larger-than-life figures, represented in introspective postures, as is the case in *Overflow*. The title of the piece suggests an excess or surplus, shown in formal attributes of the sculpture via a discharge of letters from the Latin alphabet. Although seemingly incomprehensible, the mixture of symbols implies an abundance of thoughts and ideas taking over the seated silhouette, trickling out into the world. Plensa's art conjures emotions, both universal and strange, and seeks to connect viewers from different backgrounds, regardless of religious, linguistic, or social disparities.—*JM*

Stainless steel, 88 × 96 × 100 in. (223.5 × 243.8 × 254 cm), Museum purchase, Sydney and Walda Besthoff Fund, 2008

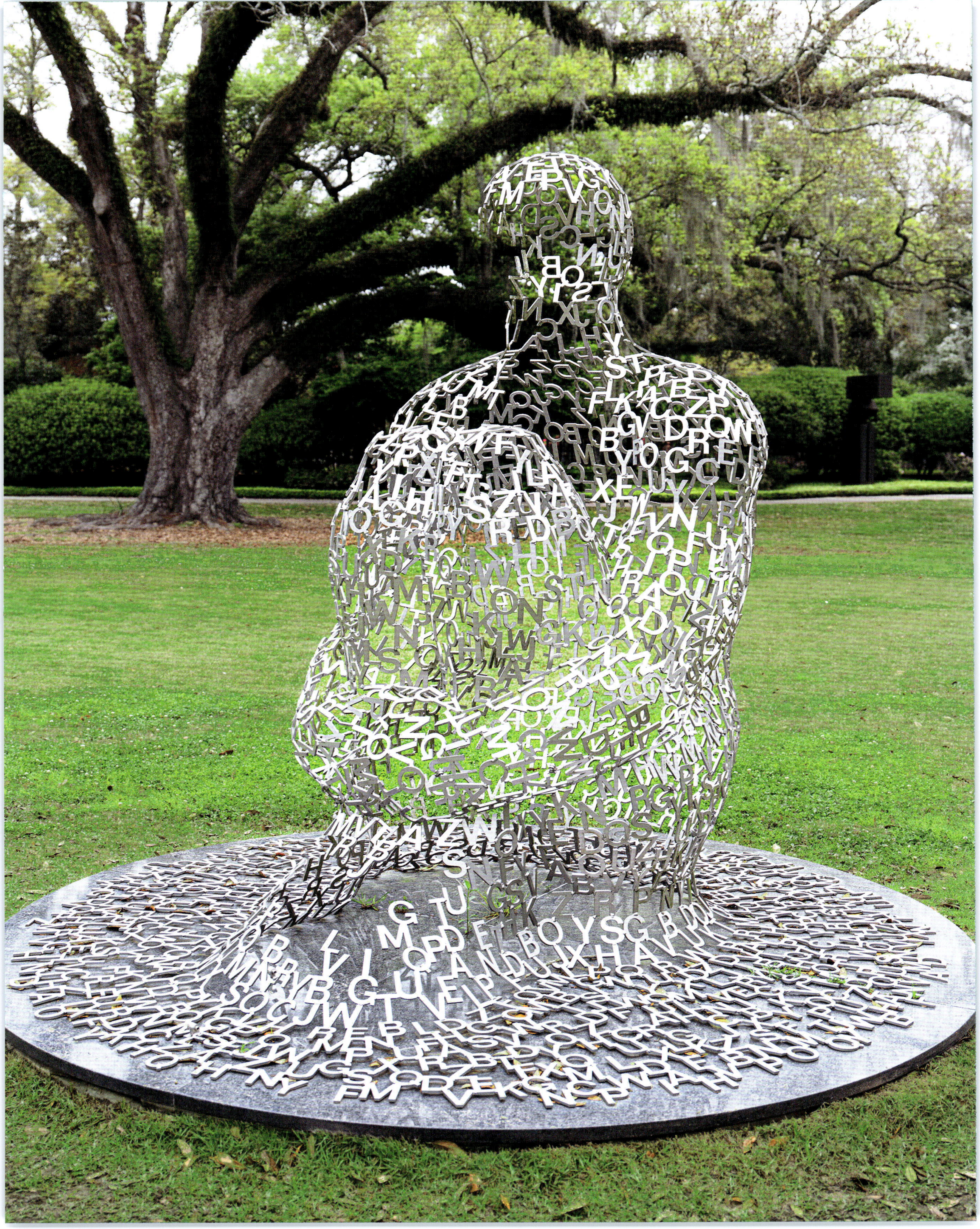

Arnaldo Pomodoro

Una Battaglia (A Battle), 1971

In Arnaldo Pomodoro's (b. 1926) sculptural work, we see an almost cyclical juxtaposition between deterioration and resurgence. Often made from polished metals such as bronze and stainless steel, Pomodoro's best-known sculptures portray geometric shapes, such as cubes, pyramids, and spheres, which appear corroded to reveal complex internal views. Activated by their natural surroundings, these objects often rely on elements from their built environment, such as wind and water. Informed by his studies in metalwork and scenography, as well as his efforts advising on the restoration of buildings in his native Italy, at their core, Pomodoro's sculptures educe concurrent senses of nostalgia and futurity. The formal qualities of Pomodoro's art bring to mind the aftermath of war-torn cityscapes, perhaps a reference to Europe's past.

Pomodoro was an instrumental player in the postwar Italian cultural milieu. Although living in Milan, throughout the 1950s he regularly visited New York, where he organized exhibitions and the elevated status of the art from his country. During this period and into the 1960s, he traveled extensively throughout Europe and had noteworthy encounters with artists such as Alberto Giacometti (1901–1966), Louise Nevelson (1899–1988), and Lucio Fontana (1899–1968). Pomodoro was a member of the Continuitá group, which sought to bridge Italy's cultural past with modernity. After a commission in 1966 for the Expo in Montreal, the artist shifted his focus to producing large-scale architectural constructions that can be seen in public spaces across the world.

The stark material contrast between the smooth and the jagged is characteristic of Pomodoro's practice. In *Una Battaglia*, the artist accomplishes a distinct architectonic quality by balancing a stainless steel column on a trapezoidal foundation. As the intricately carved base grounds the piece, the silvery mast grants the structure a delicate verticality. Although seemingly disparate elements, the pillar sits firmly atop the base, as if emerging from the ground, the upward movement instills feelings of hope and regeneration in the viewer. Melding spontaneous and synthetic components, in *Una Battaglia*, Pomodoro gestures towards a resilient future built on the chaotic underpinnings of the past.—*JM*

Bronze and stainless steel, 12 ft. 4 in. × 141 in. × 141 in. (3.8 m × 358.1 cm × 358.1 cm), Gift of the Sydney and Walda Besthoff Foundation, 1998

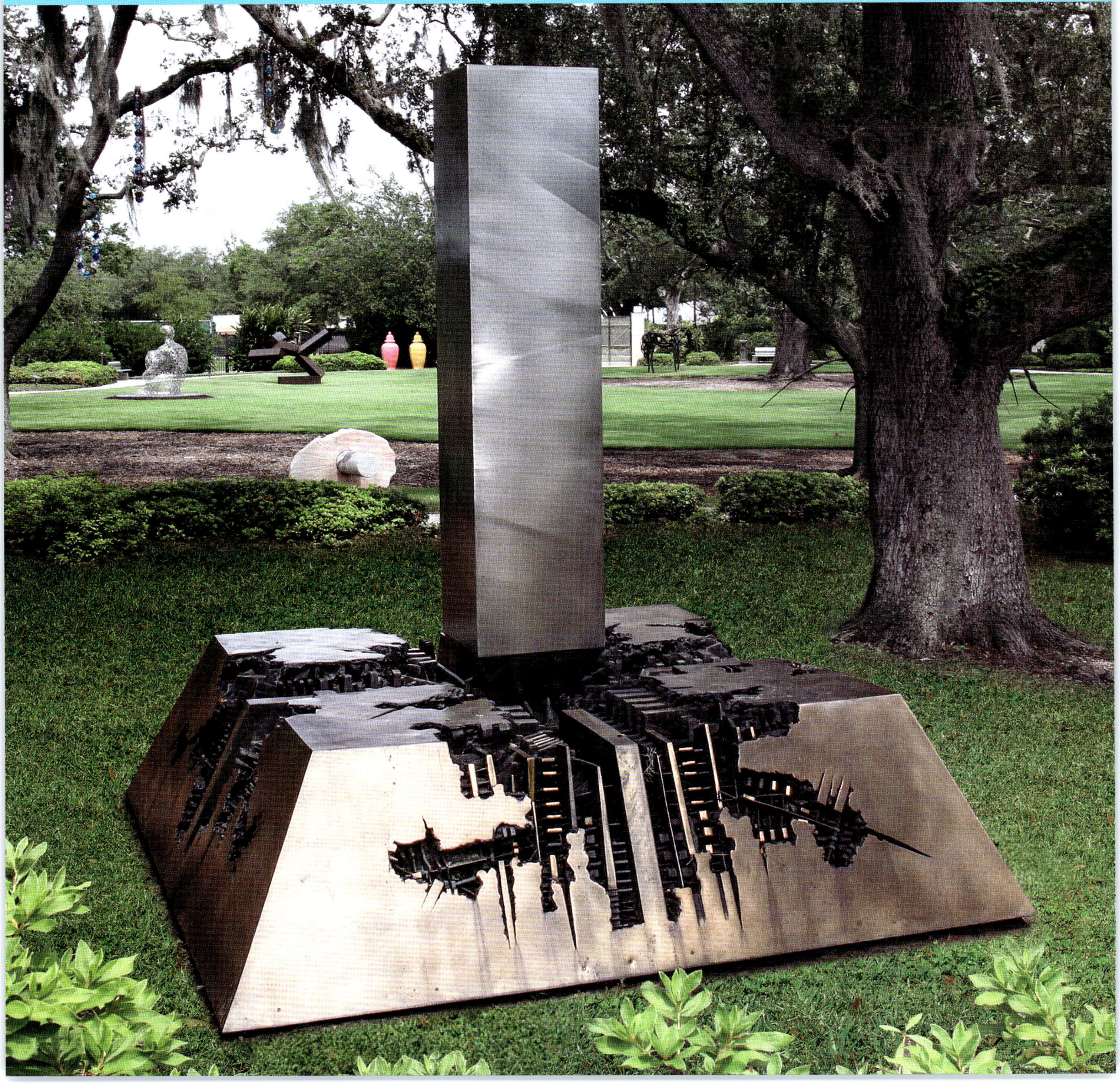

Rona Pondick

Monkeys, 1998–2001

Deeply engaged with theories of psychoanalysis, Rona Pondick (b. 1952) is best known for her striking, visceral, and at times disturbing, sculptural compositions. Having worked in an array of mediums from wax and resin to stainless steel, her practice remains first and foremost a study in metamorphosis. Pondick studied sculpture at Yale University. Following graduation, she moved to New York with her husband, the painter Robert Feintuch (b. 1953). It was here the artist first gained critical attention for combine-like works, constructed from such familiar objects as false teeth, mattresses, baby bottles, and high-heeled shoes. With a deft understanding of signification, Pondick's early sculptures fuse these disparate materials—each already laden with meaning—into a new shape, mutating and transforming both the object and its symbolism into something else entirely.

In 1998, Pondick began working with then-nascent 3D imaging technology, casting metal into hybrid human and animal forms. Studying historic appearances of such fragmented creatures, she drew inspiration from ancient Egyptian sphinxes to Greek centaurs. The artist was especially moved by Gregor Samsa's transformation into a cockroach in Franz Kafka's *The Metamorphosis* (1915), eventually making a life cast of her head and combining elements of her body with more abstracted animal silhouettes. *Monkeys* captures the uncanny contrast between human and animal, and the precision and abstraction, that would become a hallmark of Pondick's style. The creatures tumble over one another, their highly polished contours and fluid, frenzied motion simultaneously suggestive of science-forward futurism and the theatrical, contorted figures of baroque sculpture. The sinewy, buffed monkeys blend with outstretched human forearms, oversized and cast to render visible every pore, scar, or hair. The distorted scales conjoin to create haunting surrealism as gleaming, silver surfaces morph to become Pondick's own stern face, her eyes and lips sealed shut in eerie detail. Straddling attraction and revulsion, *Monkeys* captures the artist's lifelong fascination with the psychological and emotional components of her sculpture, existing as an object that is at once confusing and inexplicably compelling.—*MH*

Stainless steel, 41 ¼ × 66 × 85 ½ in. (104.8 × 167.6 × 217.2 cm), Gift of the Sydney and Walda Besthoff Foundation, 2003

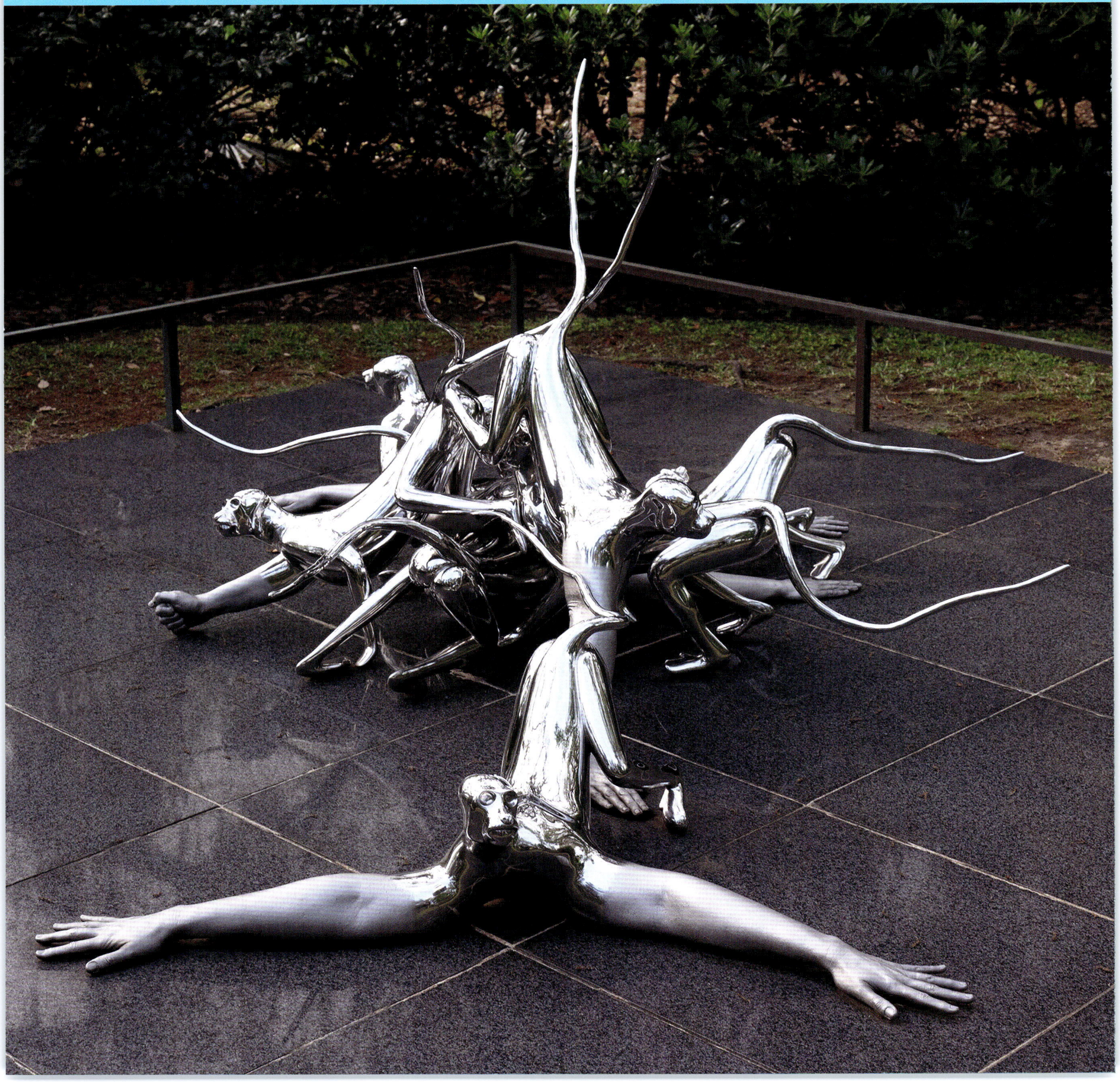

Thomas J Price

Time Unfolding, 2023

Best known for his monumental sculptures of standing figures, Thomas J Price's (b. 1981) artistic practice engages the history of sculpture itself, subverting traditional expectations around how three-dimensional work occupies public space. Often depicting people of color, Price is especially interested in challenging who and what is memorialized in our shared spaces; he frequently makes pieces that reverse or refute the minute aesthetic decisions which have traditionally lent monuments their gravitas and formality. Working with both digital renderings and traditional wax casting methods, Price inverts tropes associated with monuments to make public works that remain contemporary while also nodding to artistic traditions of the past.

Initially working in performance and film, Price's first sculptures were smaller-scale busts and three-quarter length figures. Over time, however, he became increasingly interested in how power and its systems are communicated through sculpture. Rather than being mounted on a plinth, Price's sculptures are placed unmediated on the ground so that the sheer largess of the figures forces the viewer's gaze up upon them, thus subverting any implication of hierarchy.

Time Unfolding captures the likeness of an unknown woman, standing, her hips tilted and arms crossed, looking down at her phone. Price has paid careful attention to the curls of her baby hairs, the edges finessed on her forehead, the necklace hanging below her collarbone, and the gentle pout of her lips—all characteristics that would outwardly appear to define her. However, in an intentional rebuke of public sculpture as exclusively commemorative, Price's figures are entirely fictional. Their facial features, postures, and silhouettes are conjured through a blended amalgam of references so that they become a kind of everyman—depicting the public over and above any singular hero of history. Price's sculptures have become a touchstone amid debates about the role of public monuments. Memorializing the quiet moments of the everyday, they capture the solitude increasingly associated with the digital realm, and in perhaps the most apt summation of our time, they stand alone, together.—*MH*

Opposite and following spread
Bronze, 108 × 34 ⅞ × 37 ½ in. (274.3 × 88.7 × 95.2 cm), edition 1 of 3 + 1 AP, Gift of the Sydney and Walda Besthoff Foundation, 2024

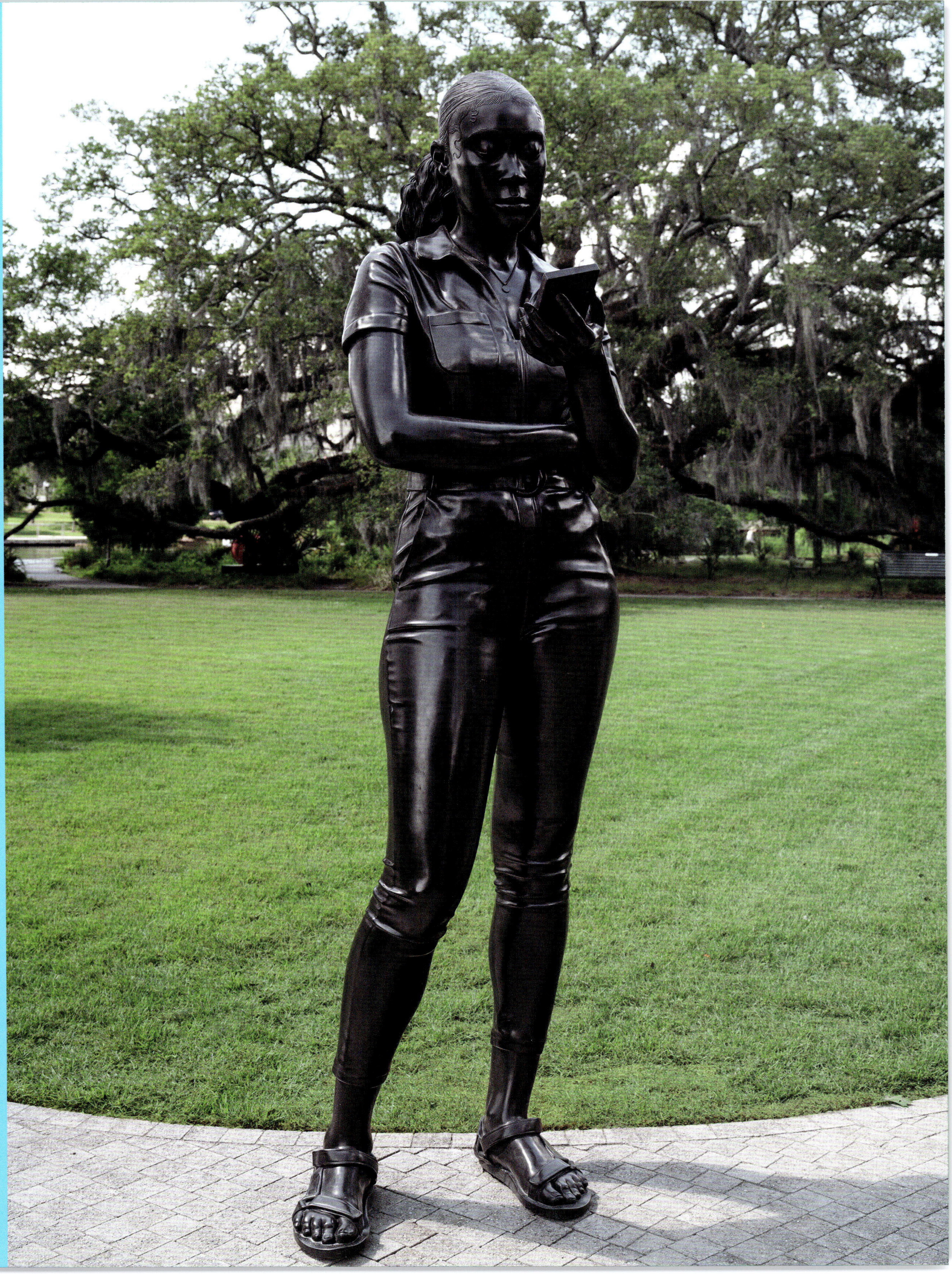

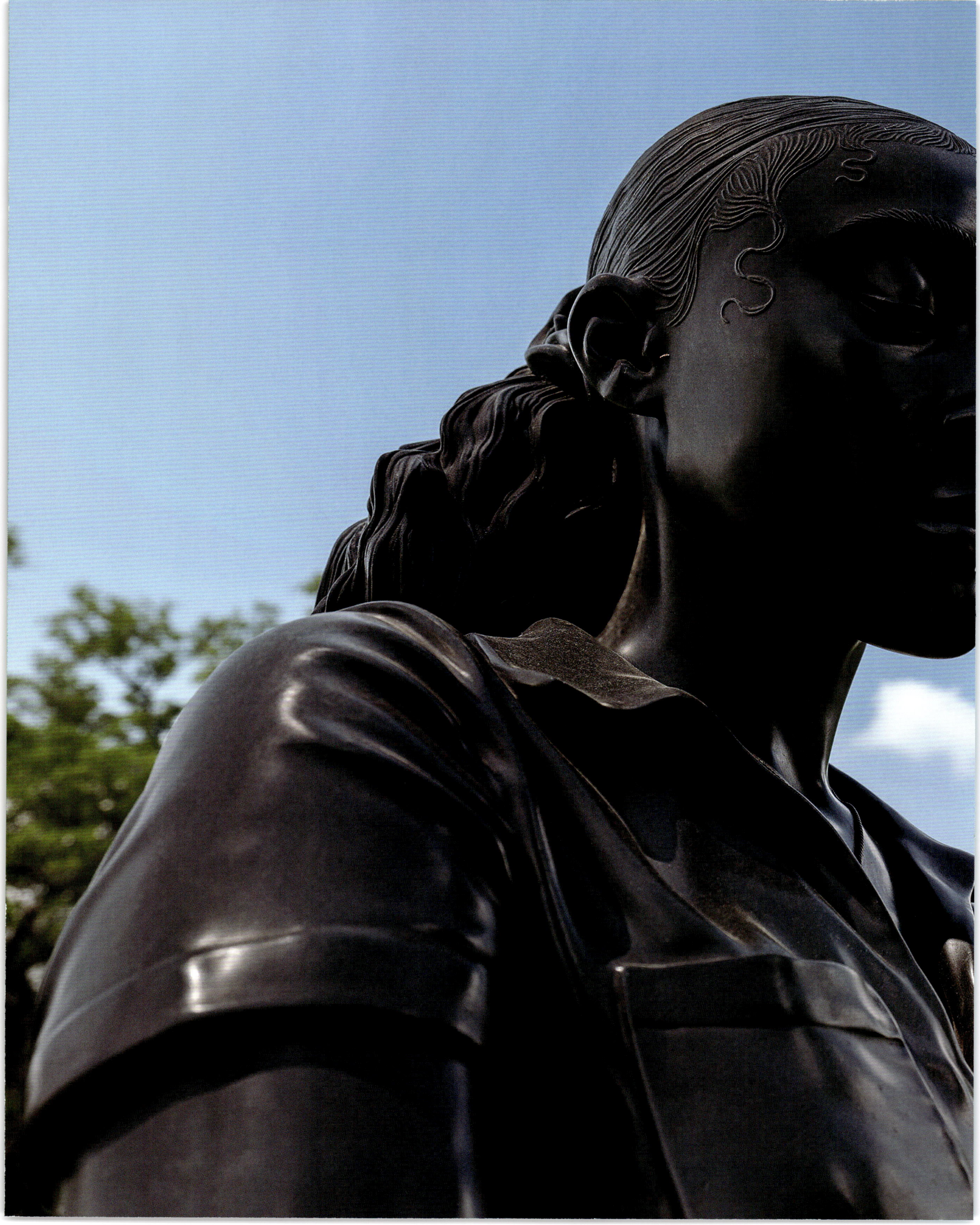

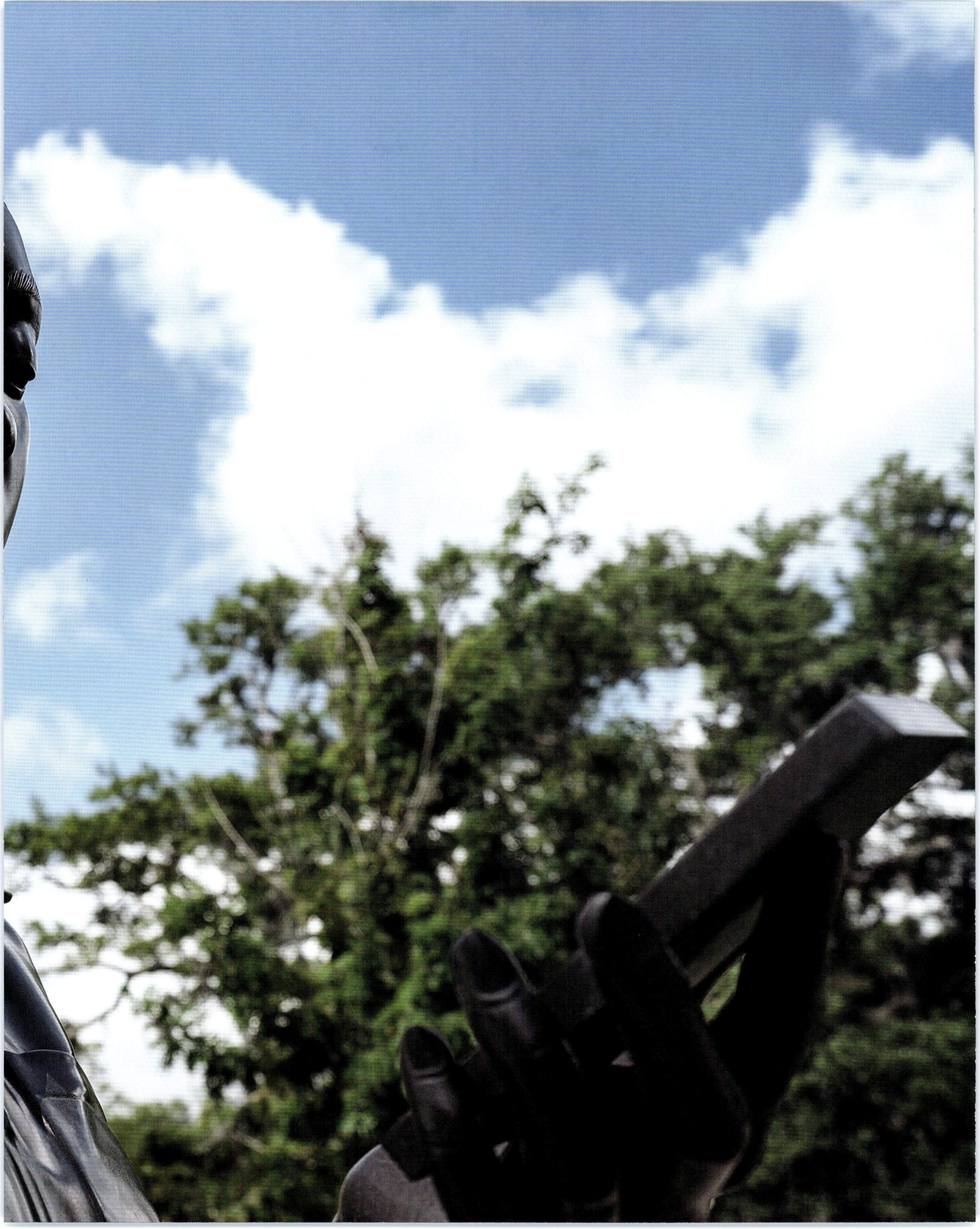

Laila Pullinen

The Wader, 1996

A central figure in Finnish modernism, Laila Pullinen (1933–2015) ushered an entirely novel abstract style of sculpture into Scandinavia, at once advocating for artistic freedom and a clean break from the formal constraints of representation. Attuned to the plasticity of shape and inspired by the pure abstractions of the European avant-garde, Pullinen worked chiefly in marble, cast bronze, and lesser-known native granites to create her fluid contours and curvilinear silhouettes.

In 1953, she enrolled at the Academy of Fine Arts in Helsinki, and though initially accepted as a painter, she quickly found her way to studying sculpture. Following her graduation, she pursued further education in Italy, where on a visit to the Venice Biennale, she first encountered more conceptual, nonrepresentational work. Taken with these new elastic geometries and uninhibited shapes, Pullinen began expanding her sculptural practice. For several years, she moved back and forth between Finland and Italy, welding together found objects collected from junkyards into collage-like pieces, exhibiting her work in galleries, and championing a more liberal, open-ended abstraction to her contemporaries back home. In Italy, Pullinen continued to develop her technical know-how. While studying at the Academy of Fine Arts in Rome, she worked with the Fonderia Arturo Bruni, where she received a proper education in metalwork, learning the diverse attributes of different metals and the traditional casting techniques best suited to each. As her visual language matured, Pullinen incorporated a variety of different materials and forms into her work—often building sculptures around a central tension created by two distinctive, juxtaposed elements.

Combining a base of Finnish granite with a roiling cast of bronze, *The Wader* exemplifies both Pullinen's unique approach to material and her uncompromising pursuit of organic abstraction. The veins of the granite complement the fossil-like ridges of the cast form, underscoring their material differences even as the fusion creates visual harmony, reaching the point of equilibrium that is typical of her practice.—*MH*

Cast bronze and Finnish granite, 60 × 23 ¼ × 15 ½ in. (152.4 × 59.1 × 39.2 cm), Gift of Dr. and Mrs. Herbert E. Kaufman, 2004

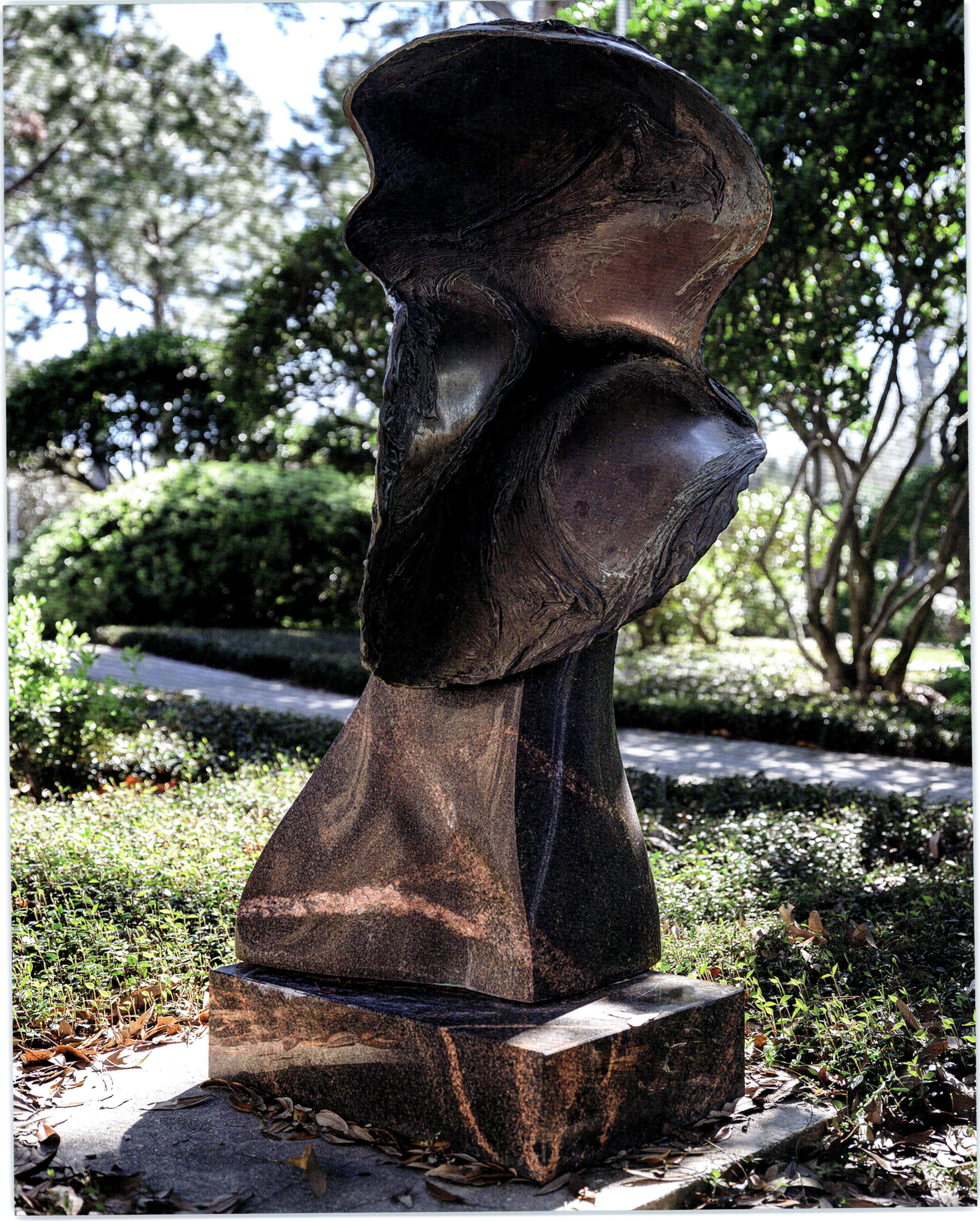

Pierre-Auguste Renoir

Venus Victrix (The Judgement of Paris), 1914

A founding member of the Impressionist movement, Pierre-Auguste Renoir (1841–1919) is considered one of the most influential French artists, greatly admired for his luminous depictions of modern Parisian life and people. Renoir began his career as a porcelain painter and studied at the École des Beaux-Arts in Paris, where he befriended many of his contemporaries, including Frédéric Bazille (1841–1870) and Claude Monet (1840–1926). He exhibited at the Impressionist salon numerous times before separating from the group in 1877. Unimpressed by the subjects and techniques favored by the Impressionists, Renoir turned to Old Masters and French eighteenth-century art for inspiration. In 1881, he traveled to Italy, where he became absorbed by the art of the Renaissance and refined his adherence to color by emphasizing form, line, and volume. It was during this time that Renoir began producing large-scale canvases of bathing nudes in the classical tradition.

Thanks to the encouragement of friend and art dealer Ambroise Vollard (1866–1939), Renoir started his journey as a sculptor after moving to the South of France in 1909. Physically debilitated by this time, Renoir hired the Catalan artist Richard Guino (1890–1973) to assist him in molding, casting, and executing sculptures based on figures from preexisting pictures, as was the case for *Venus Victrix (The Judgement of Paris)*. The nude female in this work is extracted from Renoir's previous oil painting *The Judgement of Paris*, (1913–14). It narrates the Greco-Roman myth in which Venus, the goddess of love, triumphs in a beauty contest against Juno and Minerva. She is rewarded with a golden apple from the Trojan prince, Paris, and in return, Venus promises Paris the most beautiful mortal woman for his wife: Helen of Troy. In the featured sculpture, Venus is rendered in Renoir's painting style—she is shown in the nude, in classical proportions, and celebrates a delicate youth and beauty. Flaunting her prize apple and striding confidently, Venus emanates a poised victory while maintaining an amiable demeanor.—*JM*

Bronze, 72 × 45 × 26 ¼ in. (182.9 × 114.3 × 66.7 cm), edition 4 of 8, Gift of the Sydney and Walda Besthoff Foundation, 2003

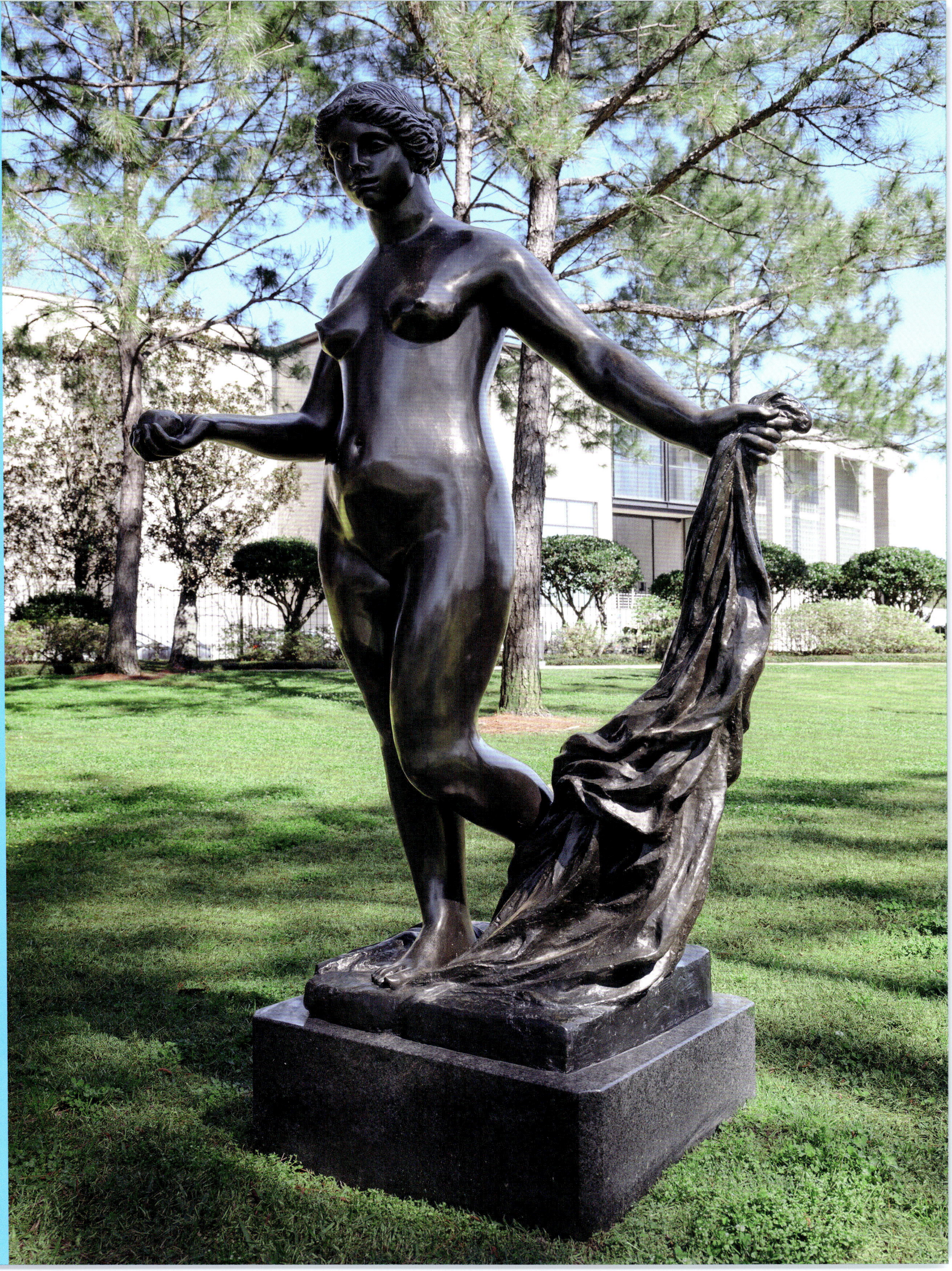

Pedro Reyes

Epicurus, 2017

Born and currently based in Mexico City, Pedro Reyes (b. 1972) operates at the intersection of sculpture, performance, and activism. Having earned a degree in architecture at the Ibero-American University, his work often engages with the built environment and how people interact within it. For example, in *Collective Hat* (2004), Reyes combined more than a dozen traditional Mexican wide-brimmed straw sombreros into one large hat, which he brought to different plazas in Mexico City and invited people to wear. Under the hat, the group had to communicate and collaborate in order to move together, and even so could only advance with great difficulty, suggestive of decision-making processes and the challenges of democracy.

For *Shovels for Guns* (2008), another project involving citizens, Reyes campaigned for the voluntary donation of guns, which were then melted and converted into shovels to be used to plant trees in other parts of the world. The transformation of destructive objects into productive ones is part of a tradition, in which Reyes is deeply invested, of art serving a social function.

In addition to these sorts of participatory, public projects—sometimes called "social sculpture"—that reflect on issues of inequality and violence, Reyes continues to craft more traditional objects. Beginning in 2014, he has carved the heads of historical figures—such as Socrates (c. 470–399 BCE), Karl Marx (1818–1883), and Frida Kahlo (1907–1954), to name a few—from volcanic stone. Their semiabstract visages recall colossal heads from pre-Columbian civilizations, notably the Olmec (c. 900 BCE), that were composed of the same material. Reyes's *Epicurus* pays homage to the ancient Greek philosopher of the same name, a key thinker who encouraged the pursuit of joy. Epicurus spawned an entire school of thought, known as Epicureanism, that advocated for pleasure, albeit in a manner ethically distinct from hedonism.—*AMT*

Volcanic stone, 100 × 39 × 32 in. (254 × 99.1 × 81.3 cm), Museum purchase with funds provided by Sydney and Walda Besthoff, 2017

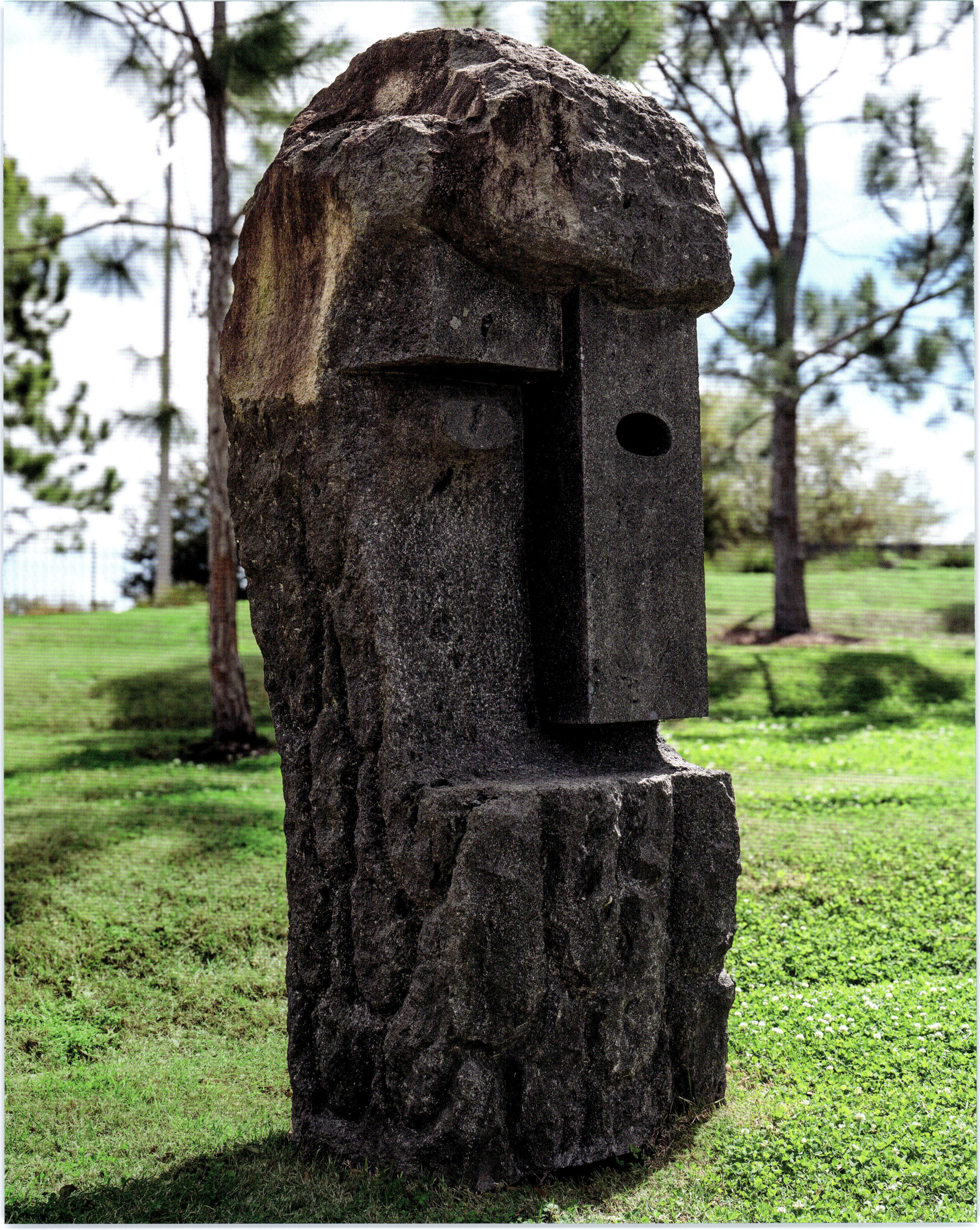

George Rickey

Four Lines Oblique, 1973–77; *Four Open Rectangles*, 1978

Perhaps the foremost kinetic sculptor of the second half of the twentieth century, George Rickey (1907–2002) devised simple yet energetic stainless-steel forms that gently bend, flutter, and whirl. After graduating from Oxford University in England with a degree in history in 1929, Rickey embarked on a path as a painter in Paris and New York City. He attended the Institute of Design, originally founded as the New Bauhaus, in Chicago in the late 1940s and encountered the sculpture of the Russian Constructivist and kinetic pioneer Naum Gabo (1890–1977), then a guest lecturer at the school. Soon Rickey was making mobiles, learning metalworking techniques, and adapting gimbals and rotors for sculptural purposes. Rickey taught art at several colleges and universities in Michigan and Pennsylvania, along with his home state of Indiana, before joining the faculty at Tulane University in New Orleans in 1955 and then Rensselaer Polytechnic Institute in Troy, New York. In 1966, he committed himself full-time to sculpting.

Much of the artist's work was created in rural East Chatham, New York, which remained the site of his studio until the mid-1980s. The appearance of Rickey's first "line"—also known as "blade"—sculptures began in 1961. These works usually comprised two, three, or four pendulums mounted in different configurations and titled with different qualifiers. *Four Lines Oblique* belongs to this group. As his technical knowledge of engineering and mechanics deepened, Rickey developed sculptures that behave according to several types of motion. Rickey's impractical machines—what he called "machines without use"—refuted the American obsession with efficiency and productivity. Air currents, gravity, and other environmental conditions activate these works—typically intended for outdoor spaces—in slow, graceful, and mesmerizing ways. *Four Open Rectangles* waves and dances as though living vegetation. The product of hours of labor, Rickey's sculptures would later become larger and more columnar in the 1980s and 1990s, as his practice developed.—*AMT*

Opposite
Four Open Rectangles, stainless steel, 39 ft. x 64 in. (11.9 m x 162.6 cm), overall, Gift of Sydney and Walda Besthoff Foundation, 2018

Following spread
Four Lines Oblique, stainless steel, height: 20 ft. (6.1 m); blades: 96 in. (243.8 cm), edition 2 of 3, Gift of the Sydney and Walda Besthoff Foundation, 1998

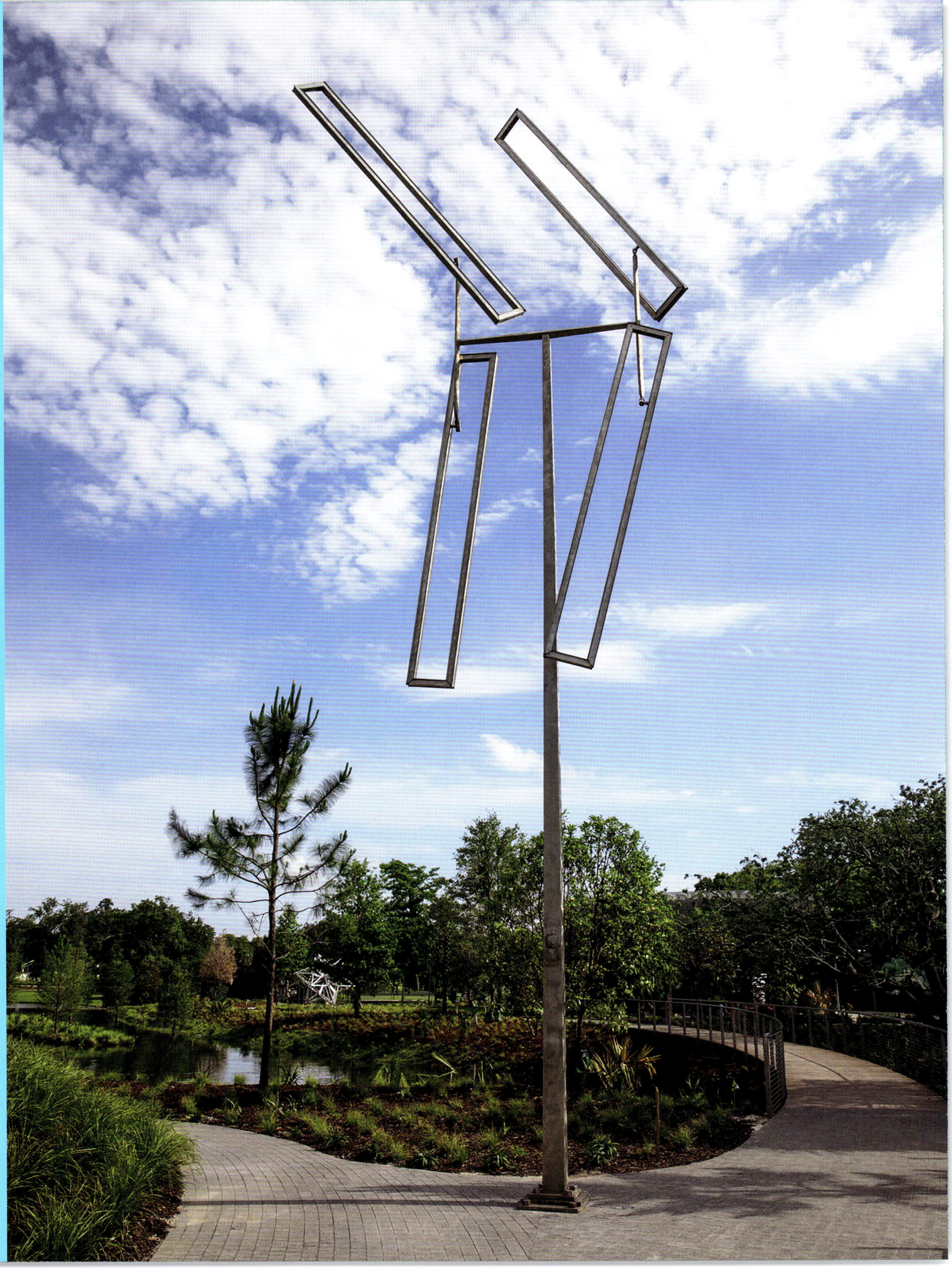

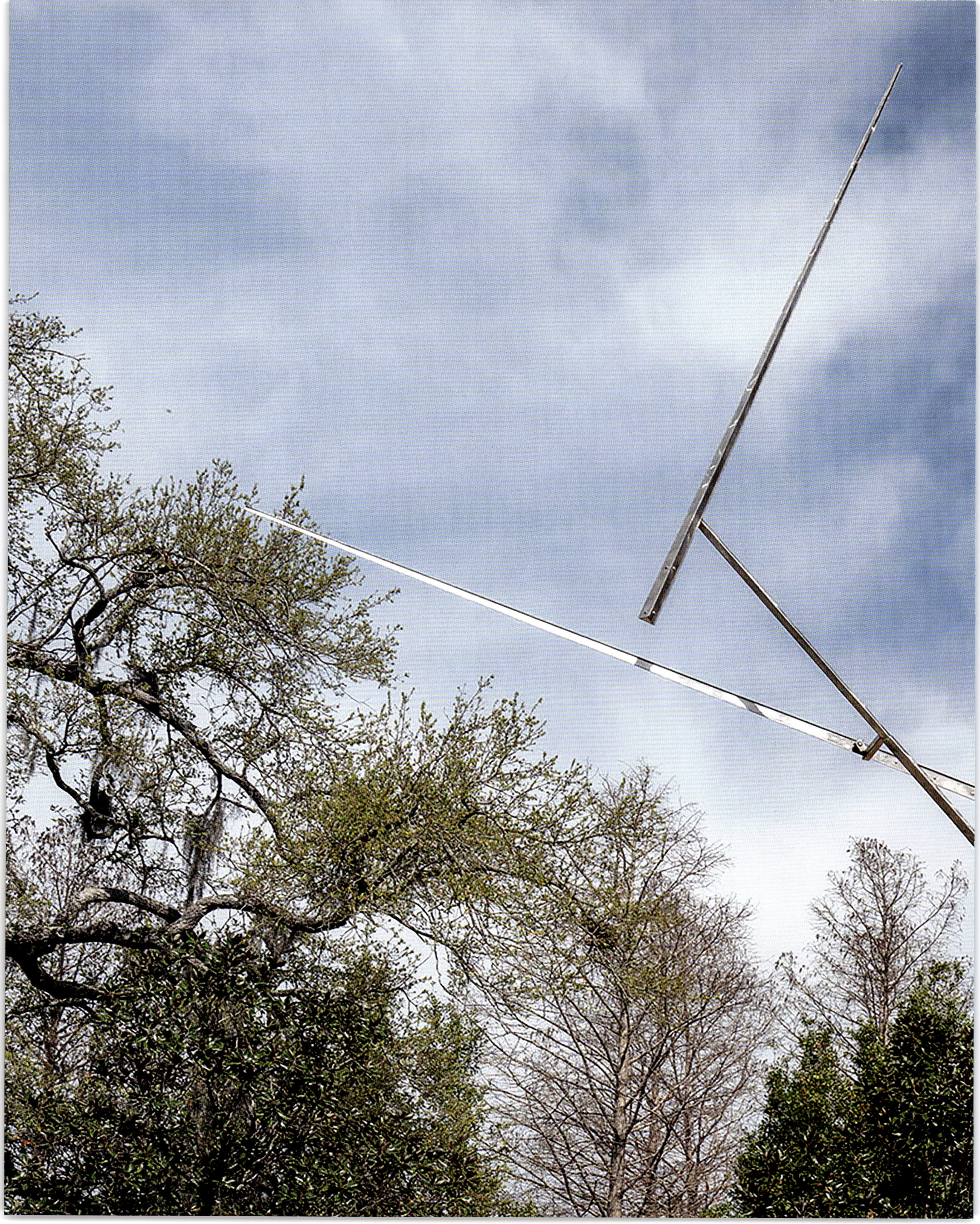

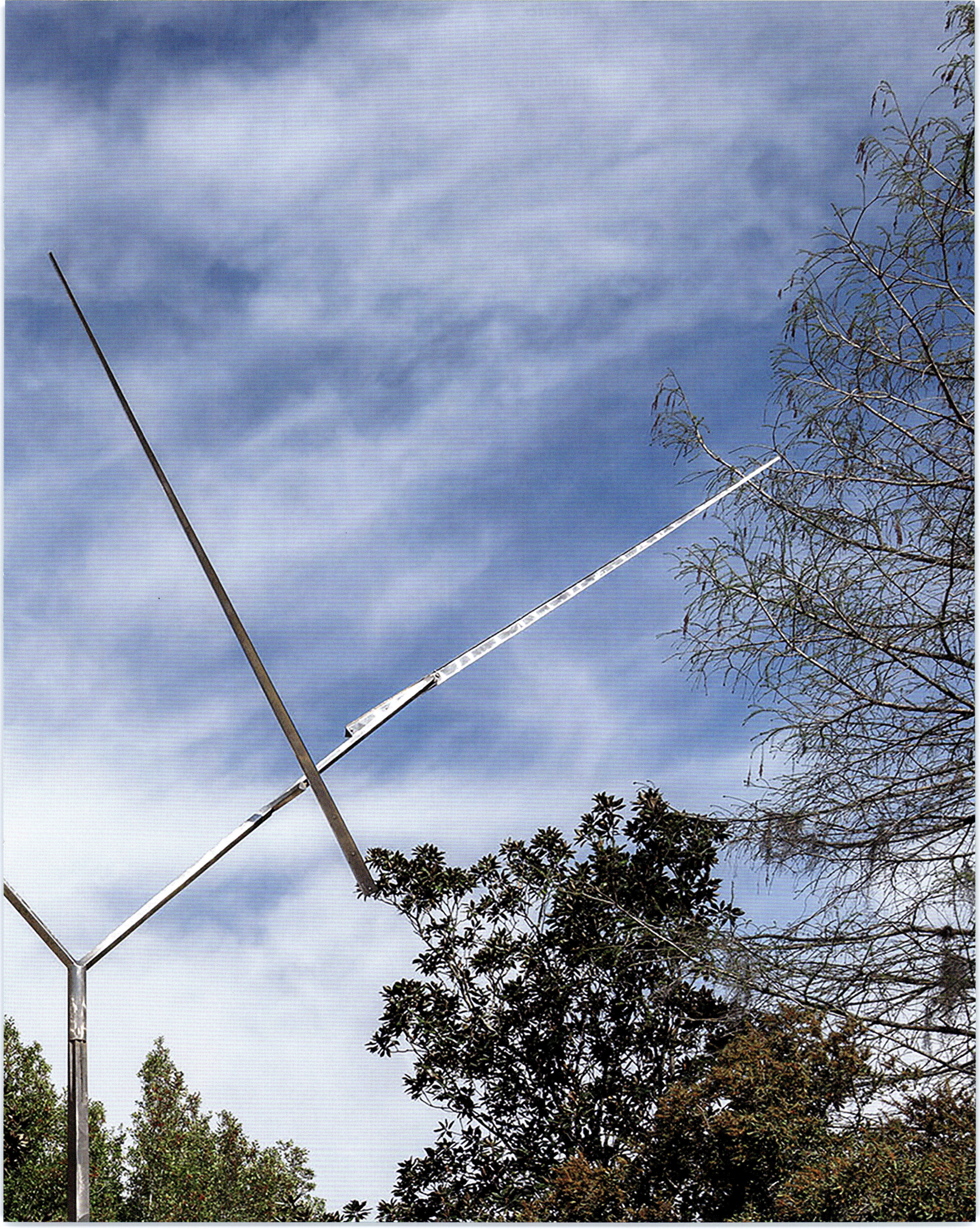

Auguste Rodin

Monumental Head of Jean d'Aire (from *The Burghers of Calais*), c. 1884–86; enlarged 1909–10

One of the most famous sculptors in Western art history, Auguste Rodin (1840–1917) gained acclaim at the end of the nineteenth century for his staunch rejection of rigidity, polish, and formalism—characteristics that defined the then-dominant style of academic sculpture. Instead of smoothly finished surfaces, Rodin favored more turbulent, fluid sculptural forms, and rough-hewn materials that captured the maker's every move. Be it sculpted in marble or cast in bronze, Rodin immortalized his making process by leaving patches of stone hatched with chisel marks or casting the hand-worked knots of his clay and plaster mock-ups permanently into the final metalwork. The resulting sculptures are emotionally charged, dynamic, and full of movement—in many ways the aesthetic opposite of the controlled and refined work coming out of the French academy, then the leading authority on artistic taste.

Rodin came to this trademark textured style later in life, and only after many years working under the tutelage of other artists. In 1875 he took a trip to Italy, where he was struck by the movement and emotion captured in Renaissance sculpture. Returning to France, Rodin immediately began developing his artistic voice, prioritizing motion and tension over carefully balanced compositions.

In 1884, Rodin received his first public commission for *The Burghers of Calais*, from which *Monumental Head of Jean d'Aire* derives. Looking for a way to boost patriotic morale following the Franco-Prussian War, the city of Calais fielded artist proposals for a statue commemorating the citizens who centuries prior—during the Hundred Years' War—had traded themselves to the English army of King Edward III in exchange for the liberation of the town. Contrary to the standardized form of a commemorative statue, which typically presented a single, allegorical or heroic figure, Rodin chose to depict all six of the men on their way to surrender to the English. Resigned, his figures appear as everyday citizens rather than mythic heroes, their facial expressions pained but resolved. Praised for the realism and raw emotion of the work, the commission spurred the public acceptance of, and taste for his singular style.—*MH*

Bronze, 26 ¾ × 19 ⅞ × 22 ½ in. (67.9 × 50.5 × 57.2 cm), Gift of the Iris and B. Gerald Cantor Foundation, 2009

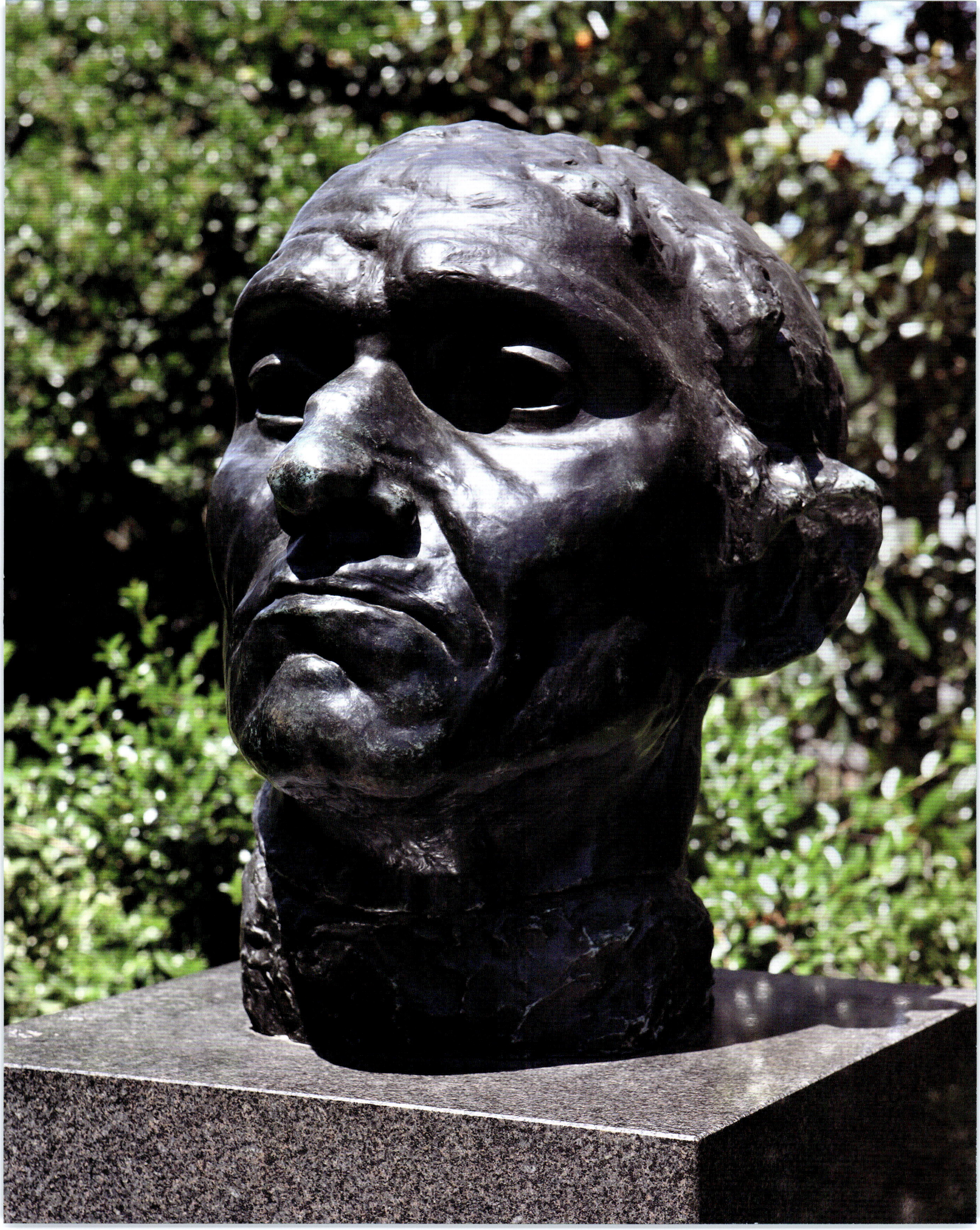

George Rodrigue

We Stand Together, 2005

A native of Southern Louisiana, George Rodrigue's (1944–2013) artistic career began as a result of his penchant to preserve the legacy of Cajun culture and heritage. Following a polio diagnosis that confined him to bed, Rodrigue began to draw and paint as a young boy, and eventually pursued a fine arts degree at the University of Louisiana at Lafayette and later at ArtCenter College of Design in Pasadena, California. After returning to Louisiana in 1968, he honed in on painting the swampy wetlands and oak trees inherent to the region, as well as prominent politicians, chefs, and artists with connections to the state.

In 1984, Rodrigue was commissioned to create a series of illustrations for a book of ghost stories, featuring the legendary creature loup-garou, best compared to the werewolf. Basing the portrayal on a black-and-white photograph of his canine companion, Tiffany, Rodrigue produced *Watch Dog* (1984), the first of his iconic Blue Dog paintings, for which he is widely recognized today. Since then, he has depicted cobalt, yellow-eyed mutts in countless settings and situations to observe complexities in our everyday existence. As the artist asserted in a 1988 *New York Times* interview, "It's not just a dog, but a dog trapped in that same uncertainty all people feel."

We Stand Together is unique for its multidimensional quality and gigantic size. Every facet of the sculpture shows a different canine, requiring active participation from the viewer to fully appreciate the entirety of the piece. Although each is rendered in a different primary color—red, blue, and yellow—the dogs are joined by their identical silhouettes, uncanny appearance, and amber stare. Retaining Rodrigue's quintessential naïve aesthetic, this sculpture is characteristic of his works from the early 2000s, for which he adopted a more minimalist vocabulary. The title, a unifying exclamation in the first person plural, implies a union among the three animals while evoking comprehensive themes of allegiance. It is also a nod to the artist's loyalty to his place of origin, and a reference to the aftermath of Hurricane Katrina in that community. Not only is Rodrigue's distinct vision brought to life against the verdant backdrop of the Besthoff Sculpture Garden, but also within his much-admired home state.—*JM*

Steel, aluminum, chrome and polychrome acrylic paint, 96 × 55 × 53 ¾ in. (243.8 × 139.7 × 136.5 cm), Gift in memory of Mignon McClanahan Wolfe, 2007

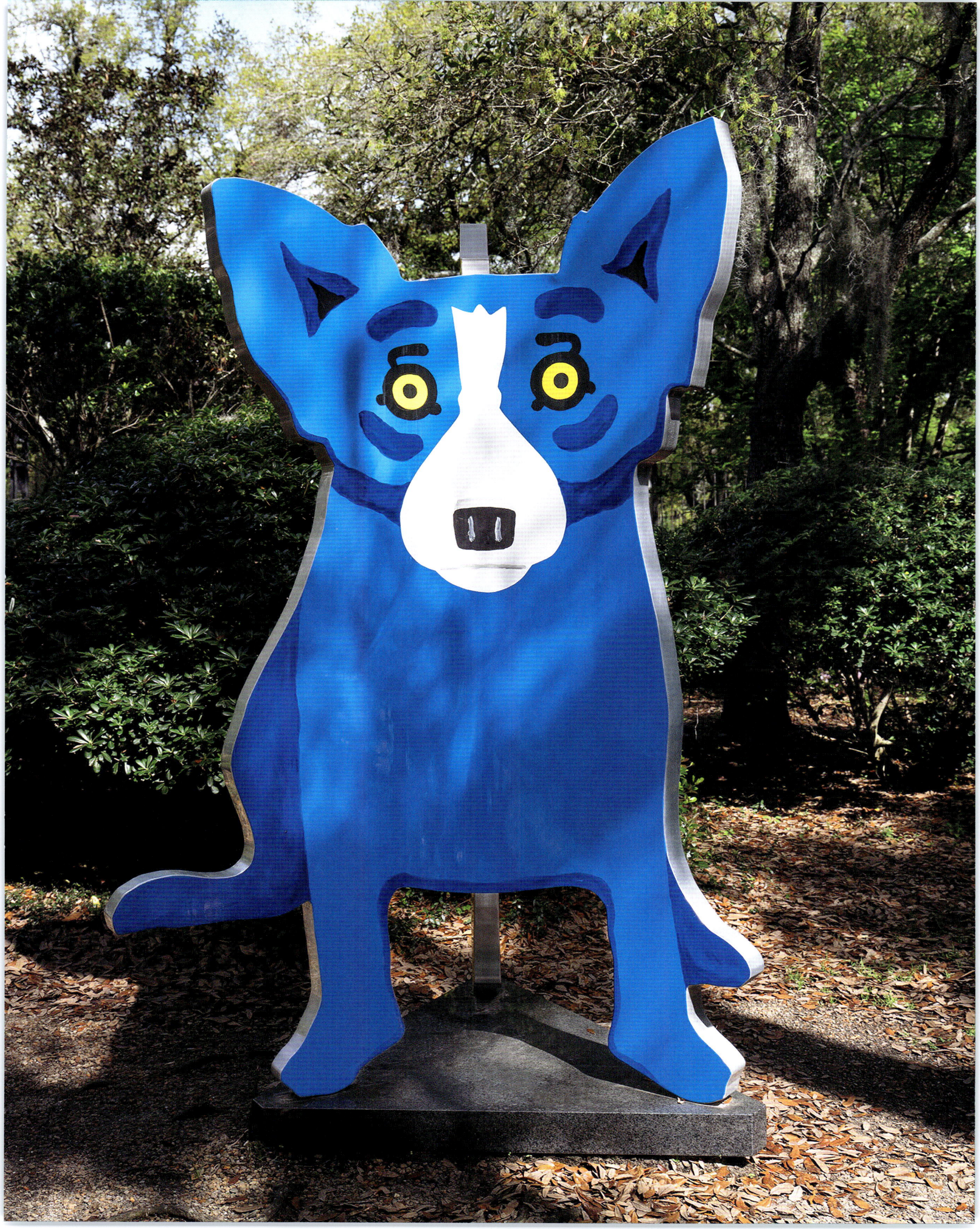

Ugo Rondinone

the sun, 2018

Images of both the sun and the moon play important roles in Ugo Rondinone's (b. 1964) repertoire. He directly or indirectly references the celestial bodies in more than a dozen projects in various media. For his sun paintings, which he began in 1992, hundreds of concentric rings of paint in various widths and colors are applied via a spray technique. His figurative sculpture series *moonrise. east* (2005) consists of twelve, painted-aluminum, ovoid masses—each representing a calendar month—that don "facial" expressions keyed to the waxing and waning phases of the moon. In a long-running series of aluminum sculptures cast from gnarled two-thousand-year-old olive trees, Rondinone utilizes titles such as *cold moon, flower moon*, and *snow moon* (all 2011). In 2019, Rondinone started *sunrisesunset*, a group of spare watercolor-on-canvas paintings showing the view across the Long Island Sound from his studio in Mattituck, New York. The Swiss-born artist studied in Vienna in the late 1980s before moving to the U.S. in 1998.

Like these bodies of work, *the sun* is part of Rondinone's engagement with the iconography and philosophy of German Romanticism. In the monograph *Ugo Rondinone* (2022), he noted how, in the wake of the death of his partner from AIDS in 1988, nature offered "a spiritual roadmap for solace, regeneration, and inspiration." Exalting elemental forces as well as questioning humanity's relationship to them, Rondinone manages to renew the investigation of age-old aesthetic tropes like the sublime in ways that are equally weighty and lighthearted, poetic and playful. A circular portal fashioned from cast bronze tree branches, *the sun* both evokes the sun and frames it. Its identically sized twin, *the moon* (2021), is covered in silver leaf. The two sculptures were exhibited together at the Storm King Art Center in New York in 2023, where they were aligned along an east-west axis. Together, they attune one to the unfathomable scale of the universe, cosmic time, to the relative brevity of civilization and individual human life on planet Earth.—*AMT*

Opposite and following spread
Gilded bronze, 16 ft. 1 in. × 17 ft. 6 in. × 21 in. (4.9 m × 5.4 m × 53.3 cm), overall, Museum purchase with funds provided by Sydney and Walda Besthoff, 2019

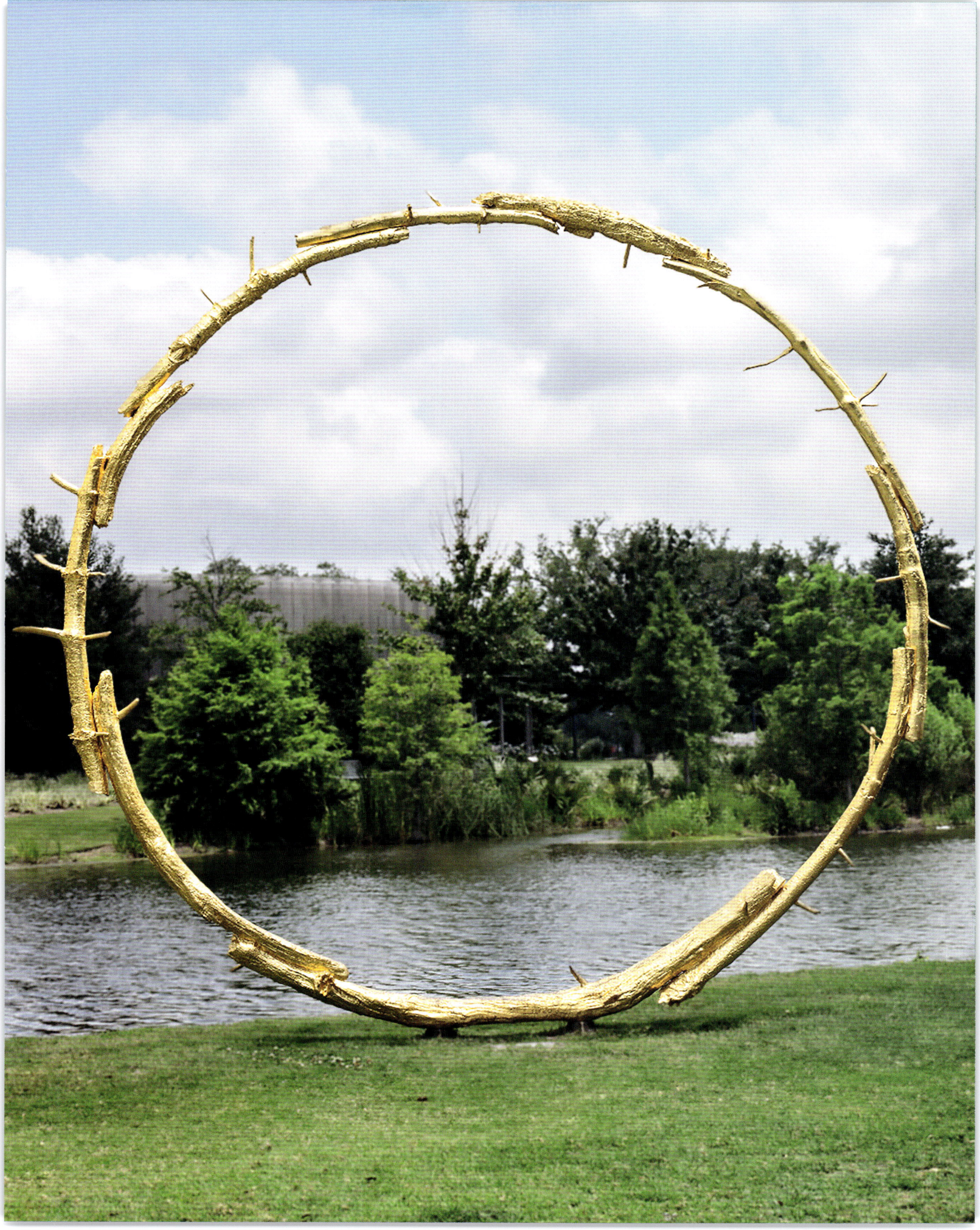

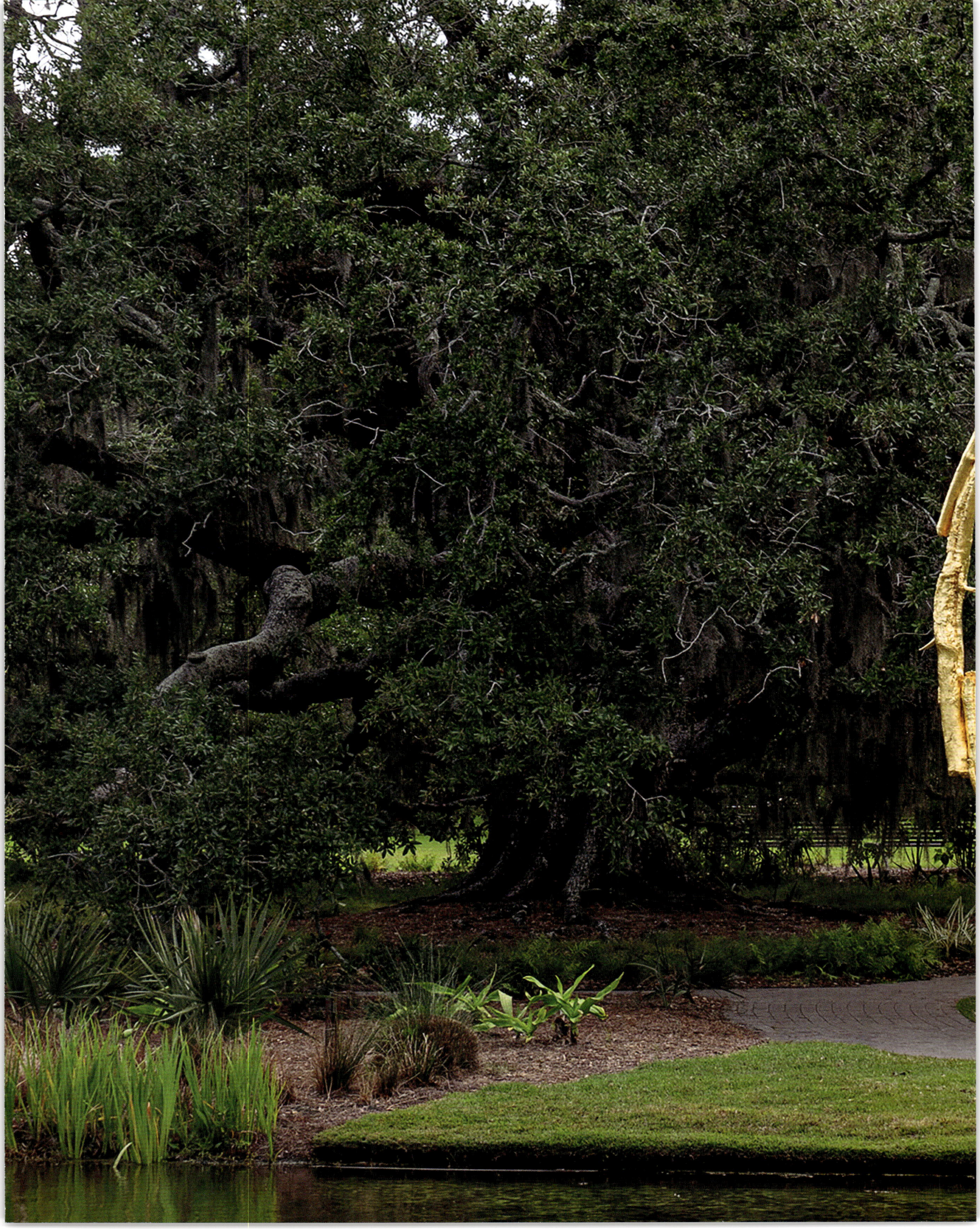

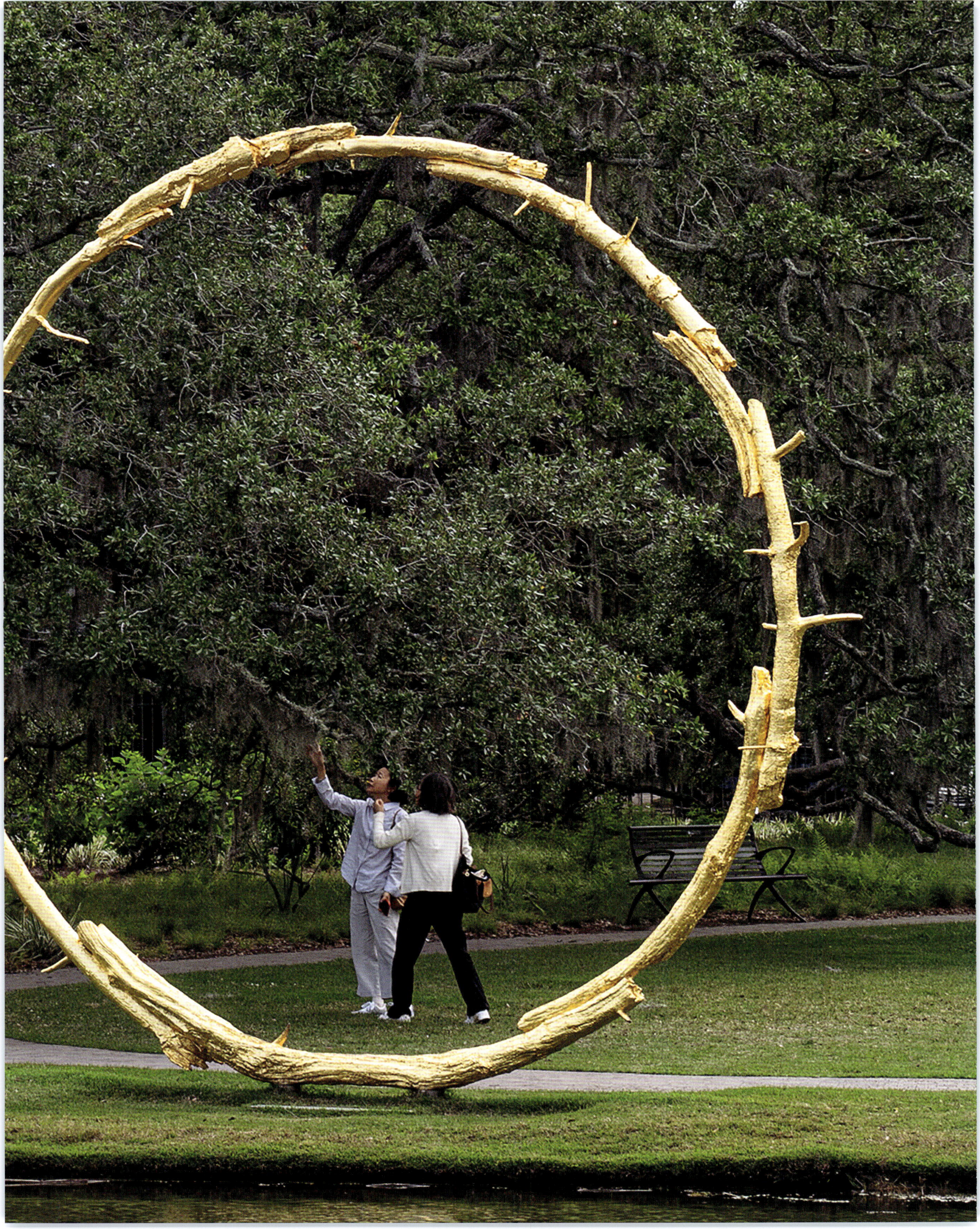

Richard Rosenblum

Adam, 1990–95

American artist and collector Richard Rosenblum (1940–2000) was celebrated for his art practice and collecting endeavors alike, both of which were driven by a fascination for wildlife, history, and geology. Throughout his life, Rosenblum amassed an internationally distinguished collection of Asian art, notably of Chinese scholars' rocks from the Tang dynasty. In 1997 and 1998, the Rosenblum Collection was shown as part of an exhibition organized by the Asia Society in New York at numerous institutions, including the Harvard University Art Museum and the Seattle Art Museum. Mesmerized by the mystical formations and patterns that animated the objects he acquired, Rosenblum found inspiration for his sculptural practice in his collecting habits and curiosities. He studied at the Cleveland Institute of Art in Ohio and the Cranbrook Academy in Michigan and his art was exhibited across several venues in the United States. Although perhaps more documented for his sculpture, in the 1990s, the artist also experimented with computer graphics to create digital collages.

Rosenblum deployed found tree branches and twigs to cast his sculptures, such as the one seen here. Through a combination of abstraction and figuration, by incorporating elements from the natural world these works evoke an arboreal character. They can best be described as a transmutation of dead branches into living ones, waiting to bloom again. Although blending in with the fertile background of the sculpture garden for its formal composition, *Adam* stands out for its humanlike presence. Almost double the height of an average person, the grandiose artwork towers over its surroundings; like a mystical being it confronts the viewer with conviction. Yet its rawness and sinuous form also project a tenderness. Simultaneously invoking the past and present, the organic and the inorganic, in both appearance and medium, *Adam* disrupts notions of temporality and illustrates a reciprocal tie between the human body and the environment. Rosenblum's art implies an appreciation for the cultural refinement of previous civilizations while interrogating our understanding of humanity's transient disposition and ephemerality.—*JM*

Bronze, 118 × 30 × 43 in. (299.7 × 76.2 × 109.2 cm),
Gift of Nancy L. Rosenblum, 2000

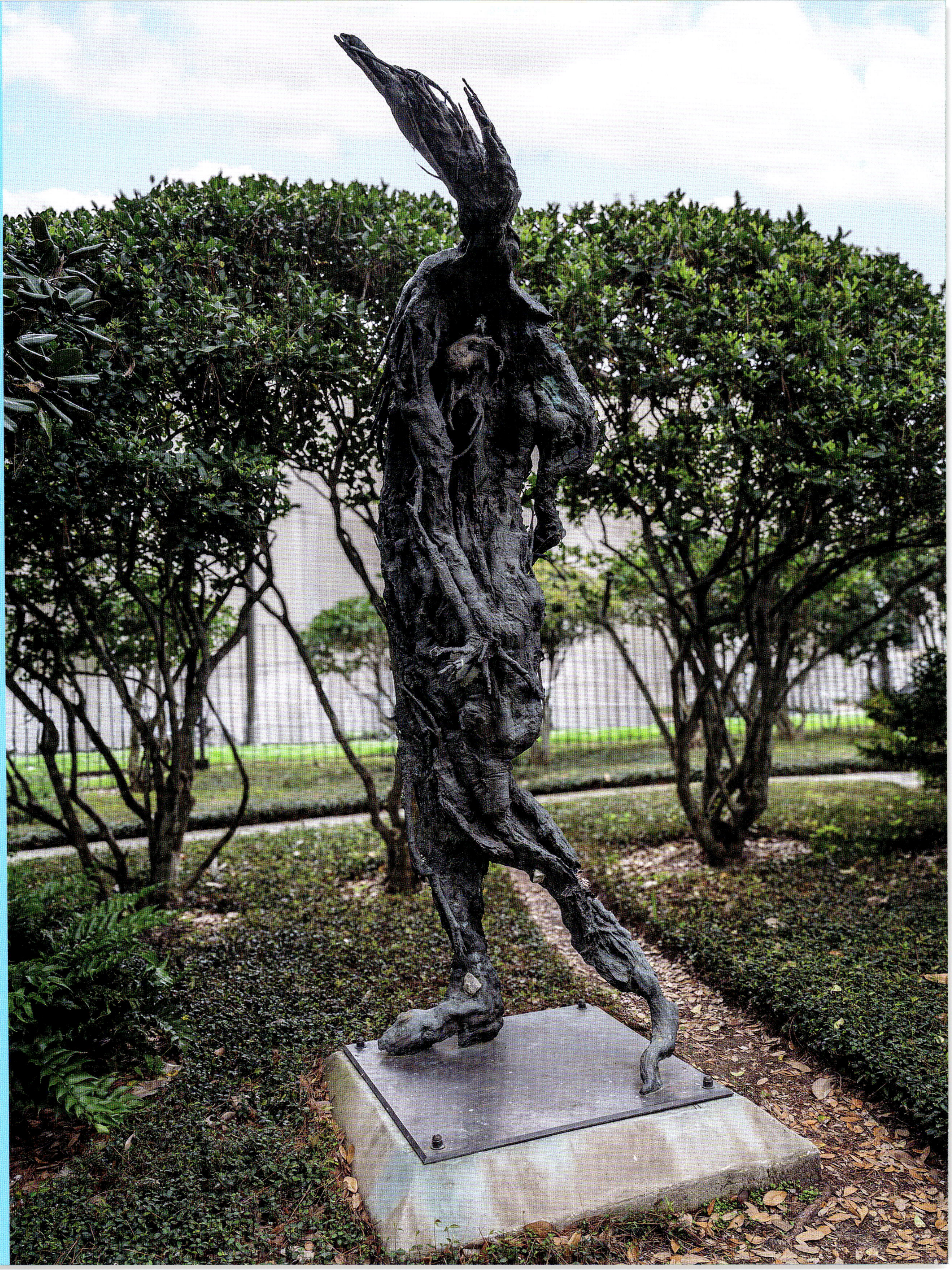

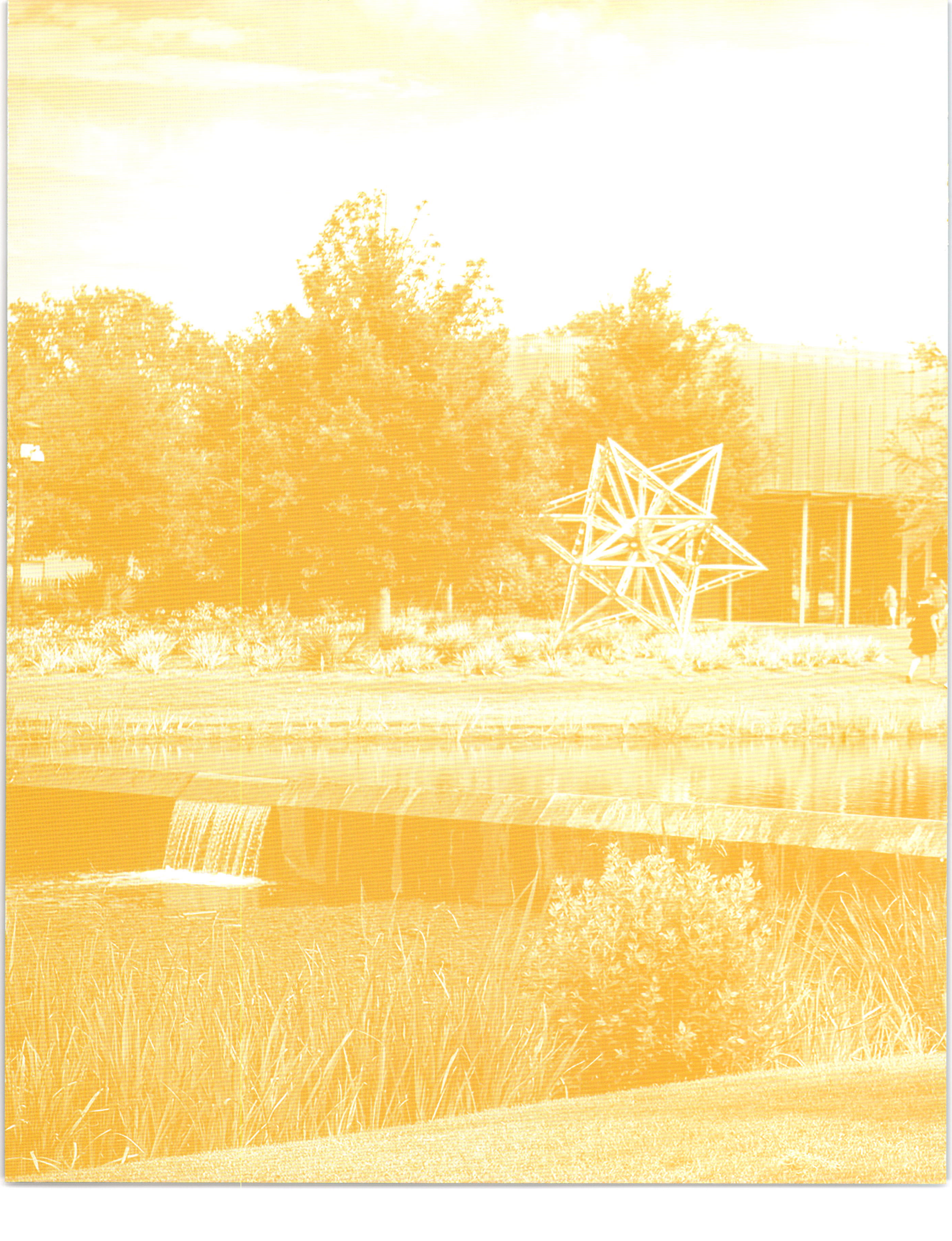

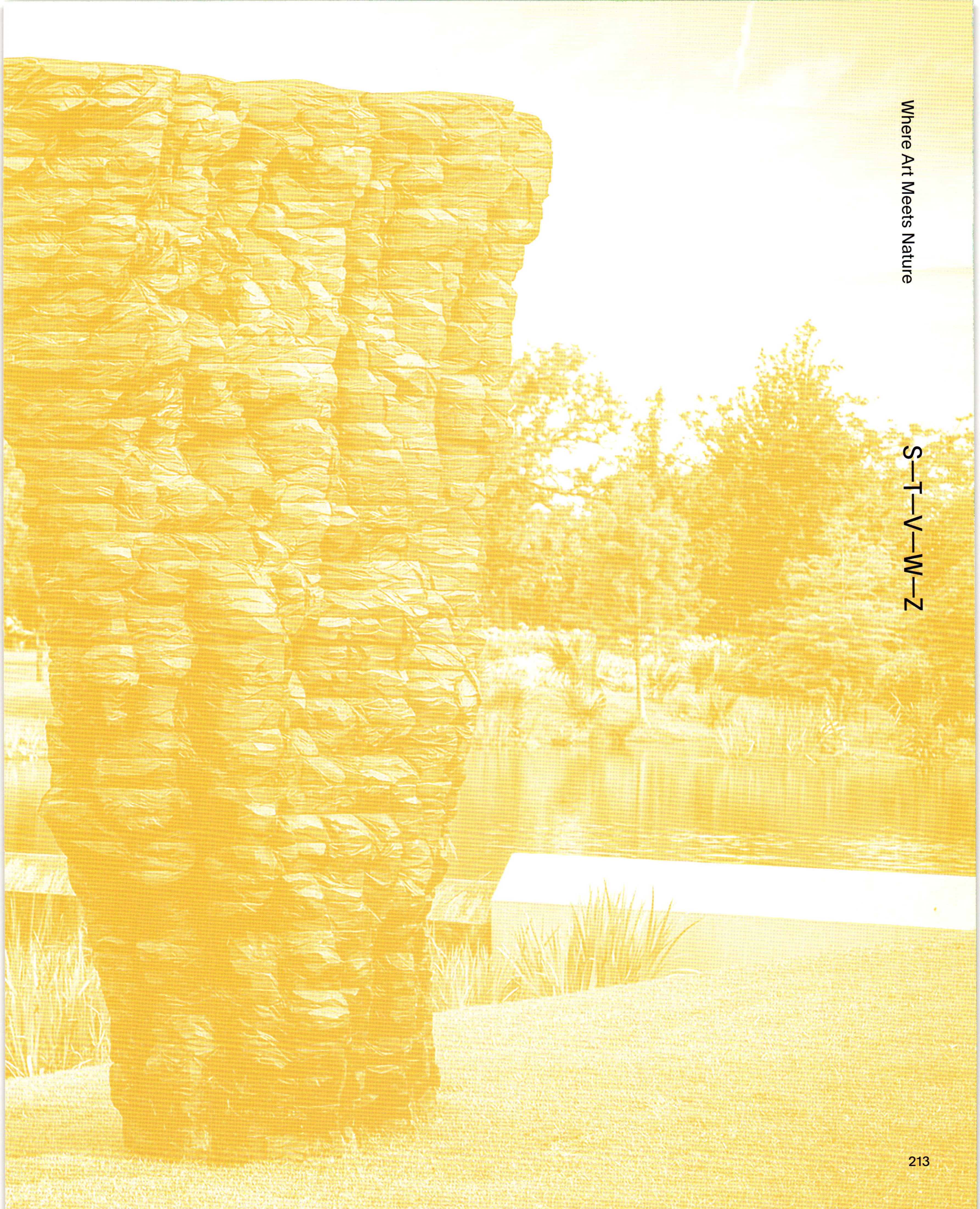

S—T—V—W—Z

Alison Saar

Travelin' Light, 1999

Through her multidisciplinary practice—encompassing sculpture, installation, printmaking, and drawing, among other media—Alison Saar (b. 1956) delves into the complexities of the African diasporic experience, addressing intersecting topics such as race, gender, history, and spirituality. Born and presently residing in Los Angeles, Saar received a BA from Scripps College and an MFA from Otis Art Institute in California. She grew up in a family of artists—her mother, Betye Saar (b. 1926), rose to prominence for her poignant collages that poetically challenge fixed notions of everyday symbols.

Expanding on her mother's legacy and the figurative canon, Alison Saar offers profoundly personal renditions of social, political, and cultural dynamics. Her sculptures—characterized by their powerful, emotive, and metaphorical depth—incorporate found objects and conventional media while drawing upon a myriad of motifs and visual references, namely classical statuary, Greek mythology, German Expressionism, and folk art. The resulting assemblages breathe contemporary resonance into historical narratives. Saar is perhaps most widely celebrated for her nude female statues that are at once imposing and tender and raise questions about the human spirit, encapsulating themes of pain, sorrow, loss, love, and collective memory.

Titled after the popular song by Billie Holiday (1915–1959), *Travelin' Light* portrays a man with a rigid stance suspended by his feet from a chain that is attached to a rectangular structure. Despite his precariously balanced position, the formally dressed individual exudes an aura of conviction and defiance, embodying courageous resilience in the face of adversity. Behind him, a cable produces a doleful chime when pulled by viewers, drawing inspiration from Japanese temple bells. Through this meticulously layered and interactive installation, Saar presents a poignant memorial to victims of violence and suffering, offering a compelling visual metaphor of a shared history that shapes and enriches our present experience.—*JM*

Opposite and following spread
Bronze, 82 × 24 × 18 in. (208.3 × 60.9 × 45.7 cm), overall,
Museum purchase, Mrs. P. Roussel (Sunny) Norman Ninetieth Birthday Fund from her family and friends, 2001

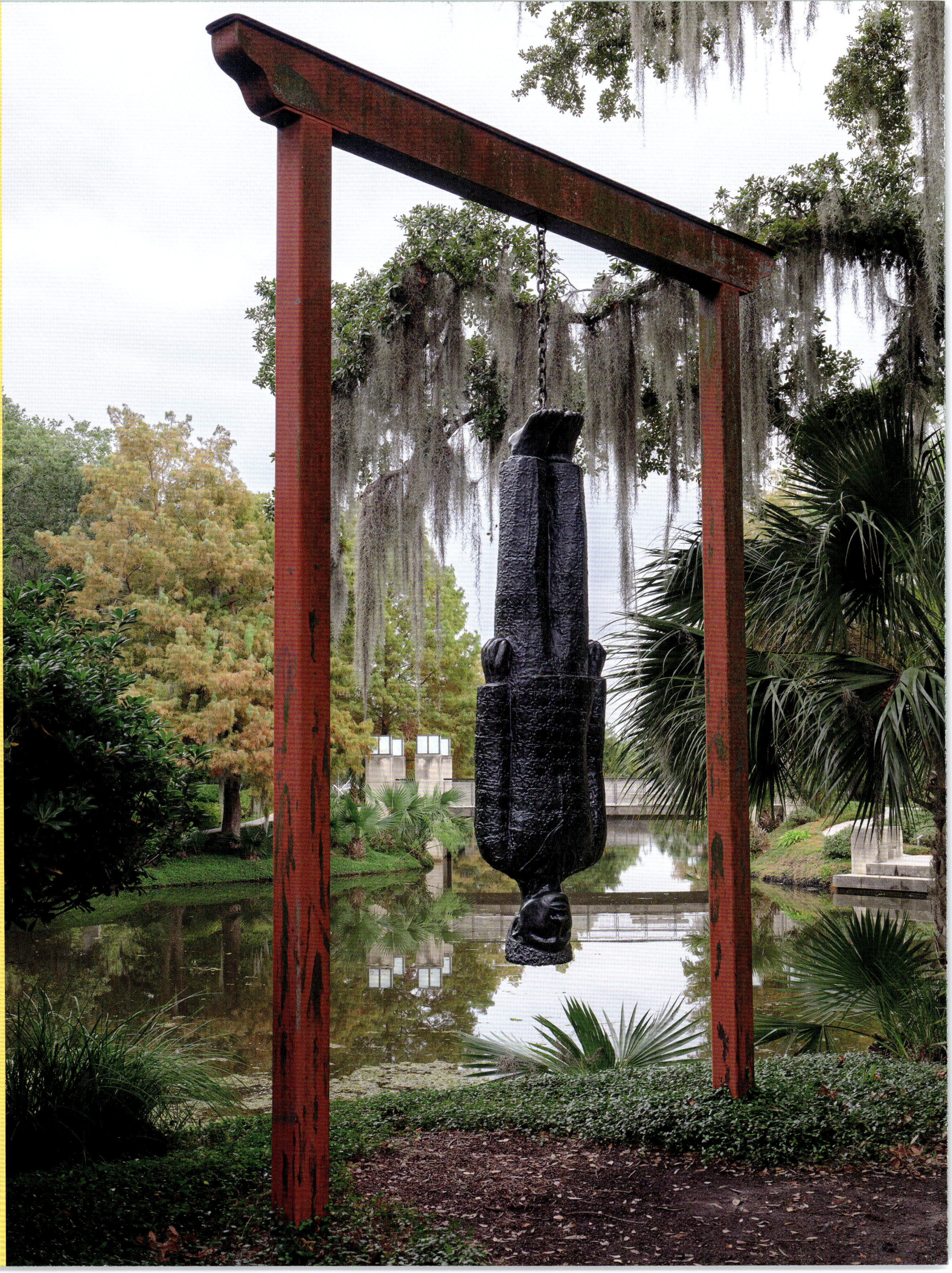

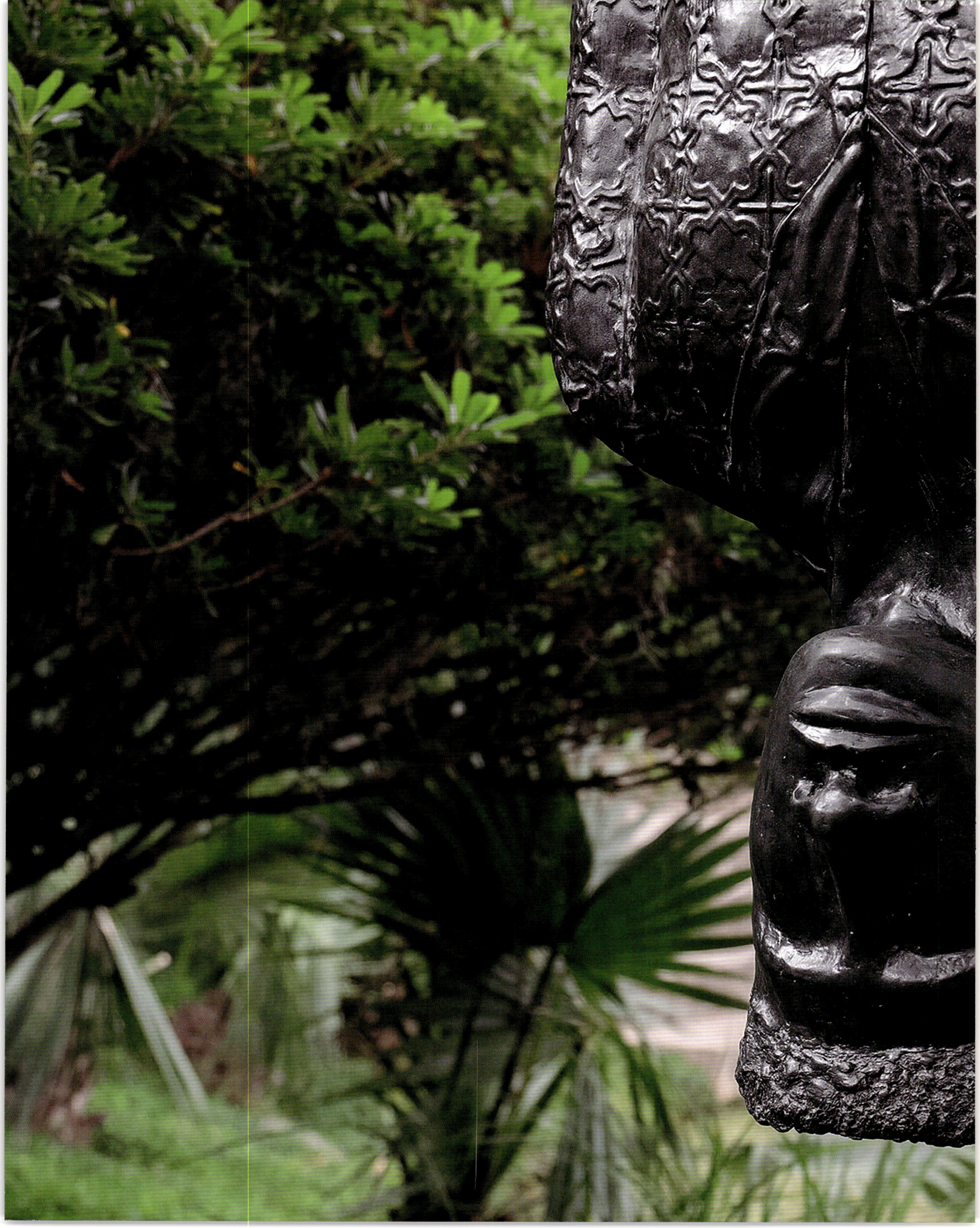

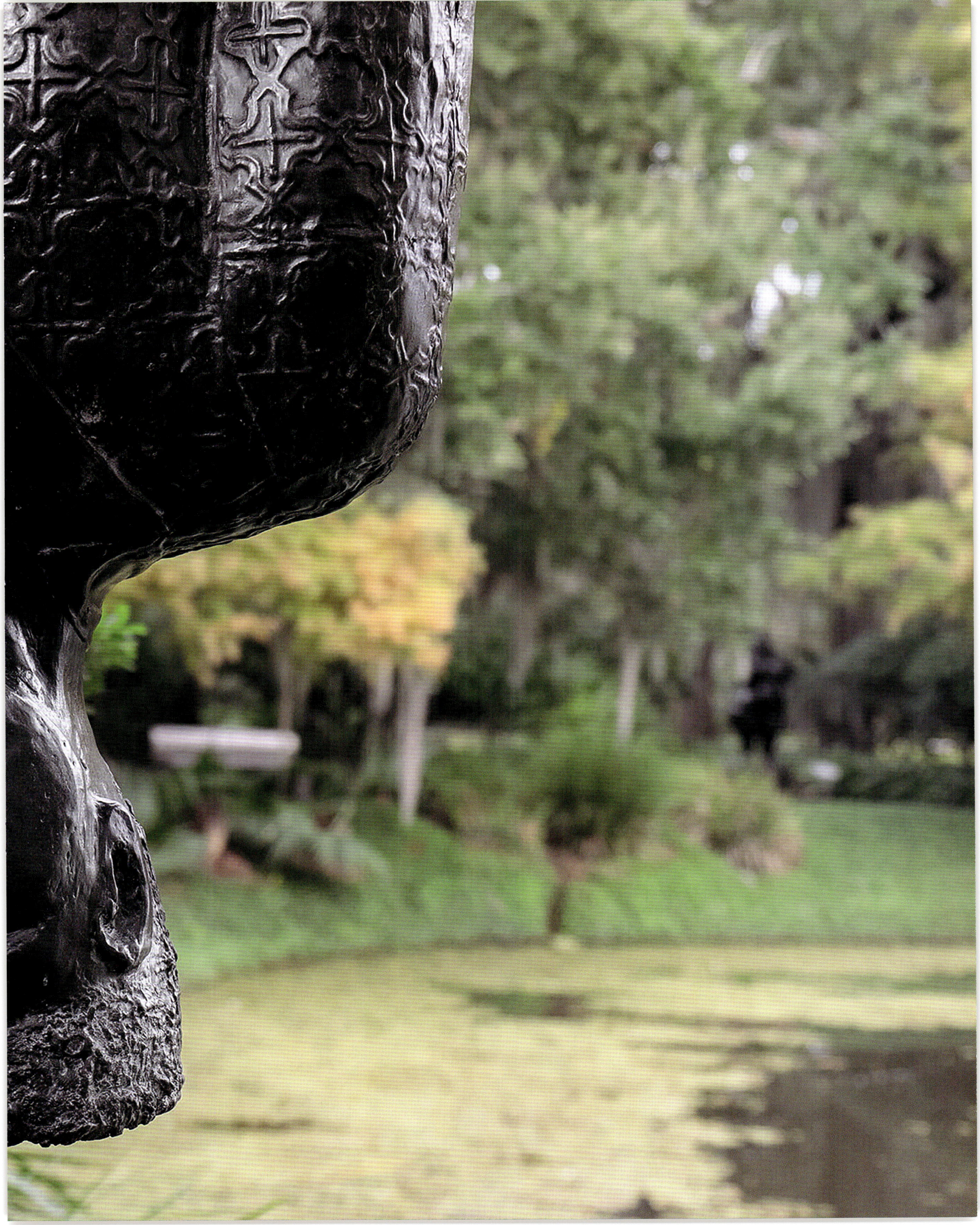

Augustus Saint-Gaudens

Diana, 1886; cast 1985

Diana, representing the Roman goddess of the hunt, is Augustus Saint-Gaudens's (1848–1907) most widely disseminated design. His only extant representation of a nude woman, the sculpture appeared in multiple sizes. Initially, his eighteen-foot commission capped New York City's Madison Square Garden, the building designed by friend and architect Stanford White (1853–1906). Set atop a nearly 350-foot tower, that sculpture was the highest point in the skyline when installed in 1891. A thirteen-foot version, now in the Philadelphia Museum of Art, replaced it in 1893, and almost a decade later the building itself was demolished.

Diana's steady pose and slender profile revised countless fuller-bodied precedents of the huntress, some of which Saint-Gaudens would have seen as a student in Paris in the late 1860s and as a copyist of antique busts in Rome in the early 1870s. In 1875, he returned home to New York, where the Irish-born sculptor had grown up. In the years that followed, the many portrait busts and reliefs he designed for domestic settings—often for prominent patrons in his cosmopolitan circle—had the effect of marketing him for larger, outdoor commissions.

Saint-Gaudens worked with White on his first major public commission: the *David Farragut Memorial* (1881), a bronze statue and stone exedra in Madison Square Park honoring its namesake, a distinguished naval officer from the Civil War. Saint-Gaudens became a specialist in memorials—particularly Civil War memorials—creating several of the most iconic and poignant of the era, including the *Abraham Lincoln Monument* (1887) in Chicago's Lincoln Park; the famous, multi-figured high-relief *Robert Gould Shaw and Massachusetts 54th Regiment Memorial* (1897) on Boston Common; and the *William T. Sherman Monument* (1903), an equestrian statue of the general led by an allegorical Victory, on the corner of Central Park in New York.—*AMT*

Gilt bronze sculpture (without base): 110 × 59 × 22 ½ in. (279.4 × 149.9 × 57.2 cm), first cast in an edition of 5 bronze casts, Museum purchase, Sydney and Walda Besthoff Fund, 2010

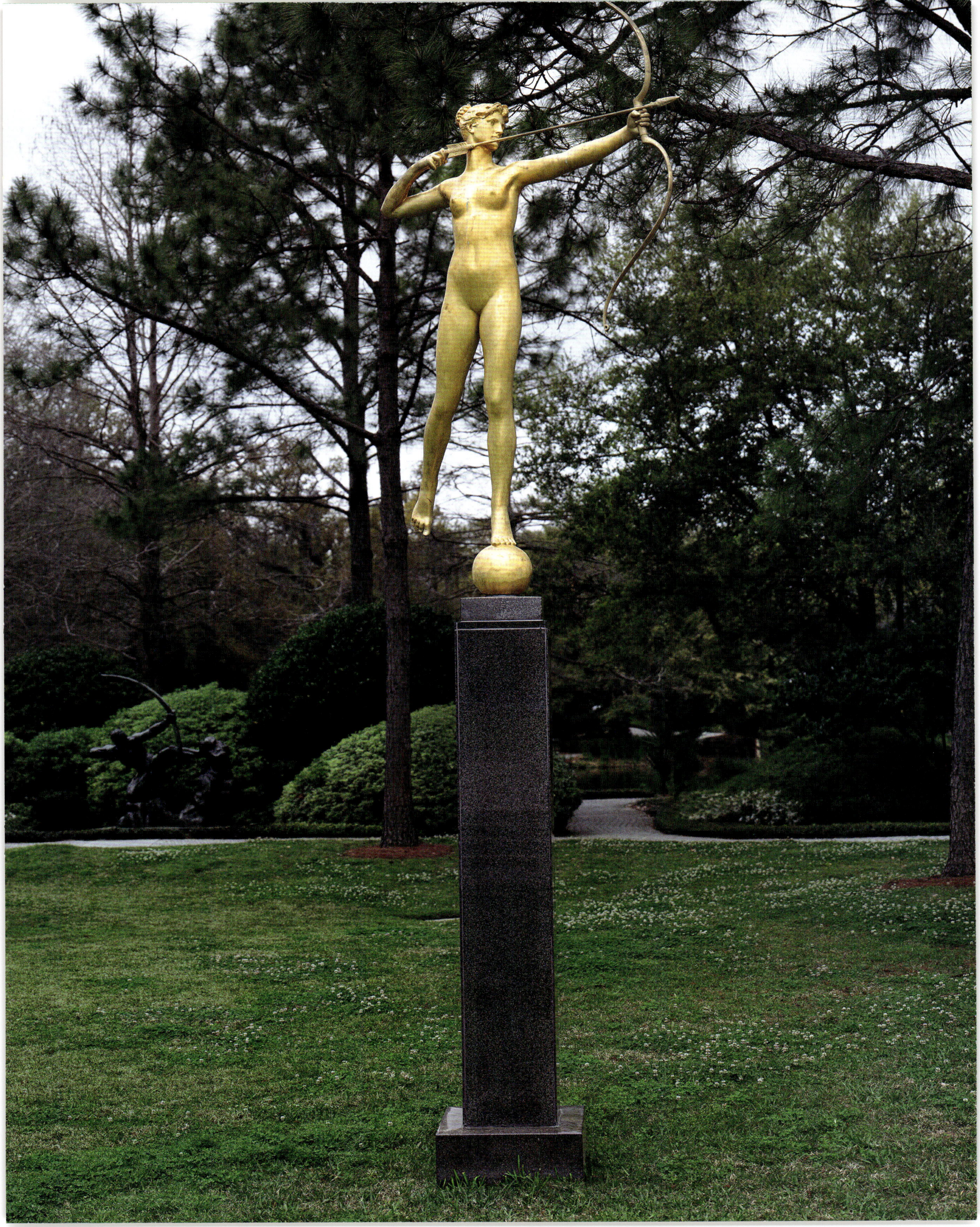

Michael Sandle

The Drummer, 1985

A British artist, Michael Sandle (b. 1936) is known foremost for his colossal bronze sculptures, reflecting on the chaos and complexity of modern civilization. Hailing from Dorset, England, Sandle completed his national service in the Royal Artillery before studying at the then-Douglass School of Art and Technology, Isle of Man, and later at the Slade School of Fine Art, London, where he focused on painting and printmaking. He lived temporarily in Paris as a lithographer before relocating to Karlsruhe, Germany, in 1973 to become a professor of sculpture at the Akademie der Bildenen Künste.

Initially working at a moderate scale to stretch the possibilities of abstraction and figuration, Sandle's practice soon moved towards more significant proportions. Paramount across his practice is his enduring concern for global conflicts and moral decay, particularly the catastrophic effects of war, corrupt exercises of authority, and the excesses of consumerism. Although working predominantly in bronze, he has also engaged with fiberglass and polyester resin alongside producing drawings, paintings, and etchings that revisit the motifs in his three-dimensional output. Perhaps his most notable sculpture, *Twentieth Century Memorial* (1971–78), depicts a bony Mickey Mouse commanding a shimmering assault weapon; it was presented as a critique of the United States' involvement in the Vietnam conflict.

A recurring subject of interest for the artist, *The Drummer* shows a marching, androgynous individual pounding the percussive instrument. The statue's framework comprises a skillful combination of abstract shapes in motion, combining a Cubist fragmentation of imagery with a Futurist execution of speed and technology. Hiding any indication of a human face behind a muzzle-like armature while sporting bands and straps that assimilate the body, the cyborg form emanates an avant-garde sensitivity. The figure's left arm forcefully beats the head of the drum with a stick, while the right hand holds a formation of six sequential batons, a deft photographic evocation of movement. Sandle found inspiration for this sculpture in a variety of sources, including the film *The Tin Drum* (1979), traditional German-Swiss *fasching* parades, and a painting he made in 1957 titled *The Three Magi*. In describing the work, Sandle has observed themes of death and destruction, conflating contradictions of progression and degeneration, machinery and humanity, and past and present.—*JM*

Bronze, 106 × 38 ½ × 55 in. (269.2 × 97.8 × 139.7 cm),
Gift of the Sydney and Walda Besthoff Foundation, 1998

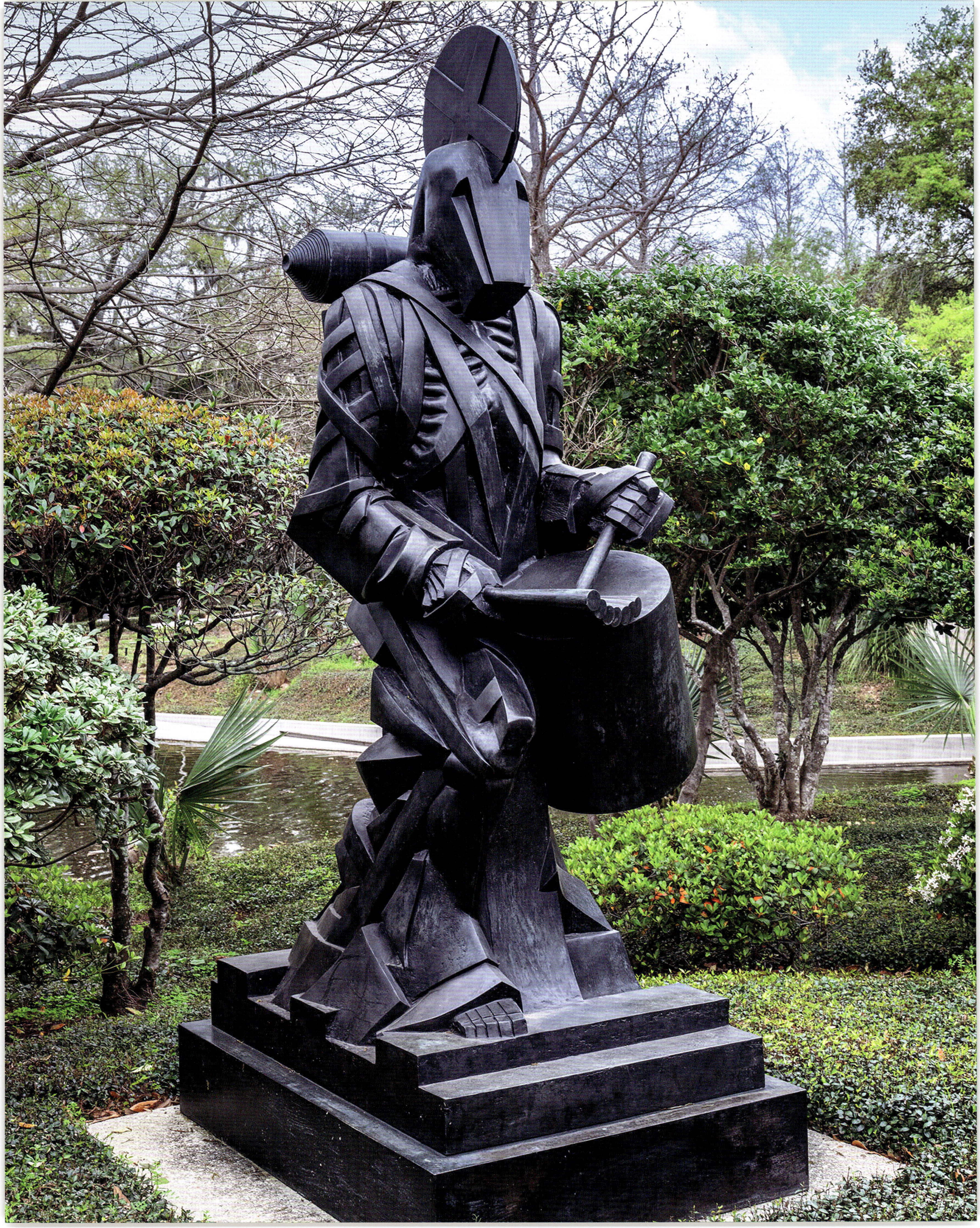

Sean Scully

Colored Stacked Frames, 2017

Primarily a painter, Irish-born and American-based artist Sean Scully (b. 1945) started making sculptures as an undergraduate student at Newcastle University in England from 1968 to 1972. It was not, however, until the 2000s that he fully embraced the pursuit. Even so, his paintings long exerted a powerful physical presence and their vibrating, interlocking, and brick-like rectangles drew comparisons to architecture. Scully, too, acknowledged the influence of the built environment on his reductive approach to abstract painting.

In the 1980s, trips to the ancient Mayan cities of Chichén Itzá and Palenque in Mexico left lasting impressions on him. Irregularly shaped canvases, projecting canvas elements, and a cycle of paintings whose titles reference structures—such as *Wall of Light*, which he began in 1998—all proposed the activation of three-dimensional space. Moreover, Scully's fascination with stone walls, fences, and mounds in remote parts of Ireland, where he was born, and the Isle of Aran, Scotland, where he made a series of photographs in 2005, provide considerable precedent behind his eventual move to sculpture.

Colored Stacked Frames extends this intermedia dialogue by carrying forth the emotive possibilities of the differing stripes from his paintings. In another callback, Scully turns frames—associated with painting and which usually hang on walls—into horizontal sculptural objects. The form of the stack conjures a difficult period in his life when, as a teenager in London, he took different jobs to support himself. Working in a cardboard factory, he recalls "creating these strange proletarian cardboard columns," as he noted in an interview in *Sean Scully: Sculpture* (2019). The strenuous and sometimes dangerous task of stacking cardboard aligns with Scully's subsequent artistic philosophy rooted in physical labor. Scully, who moved permanently to New York in 1975, has widely exhibited outdoor and indoor stacks composed of either metal, glass, or stone. In 2023, he installed his first permanent public sculpture in London, *Landline*, a tower of layers of colored marble.—*AMT*

Stainless steel with automotive paint, 120 × 96 × 96 in. (304.8 × 243.84 × 243.84 cm), overall, Museum purchase with funds provided by Sydney and Walda Besthoff, 2017

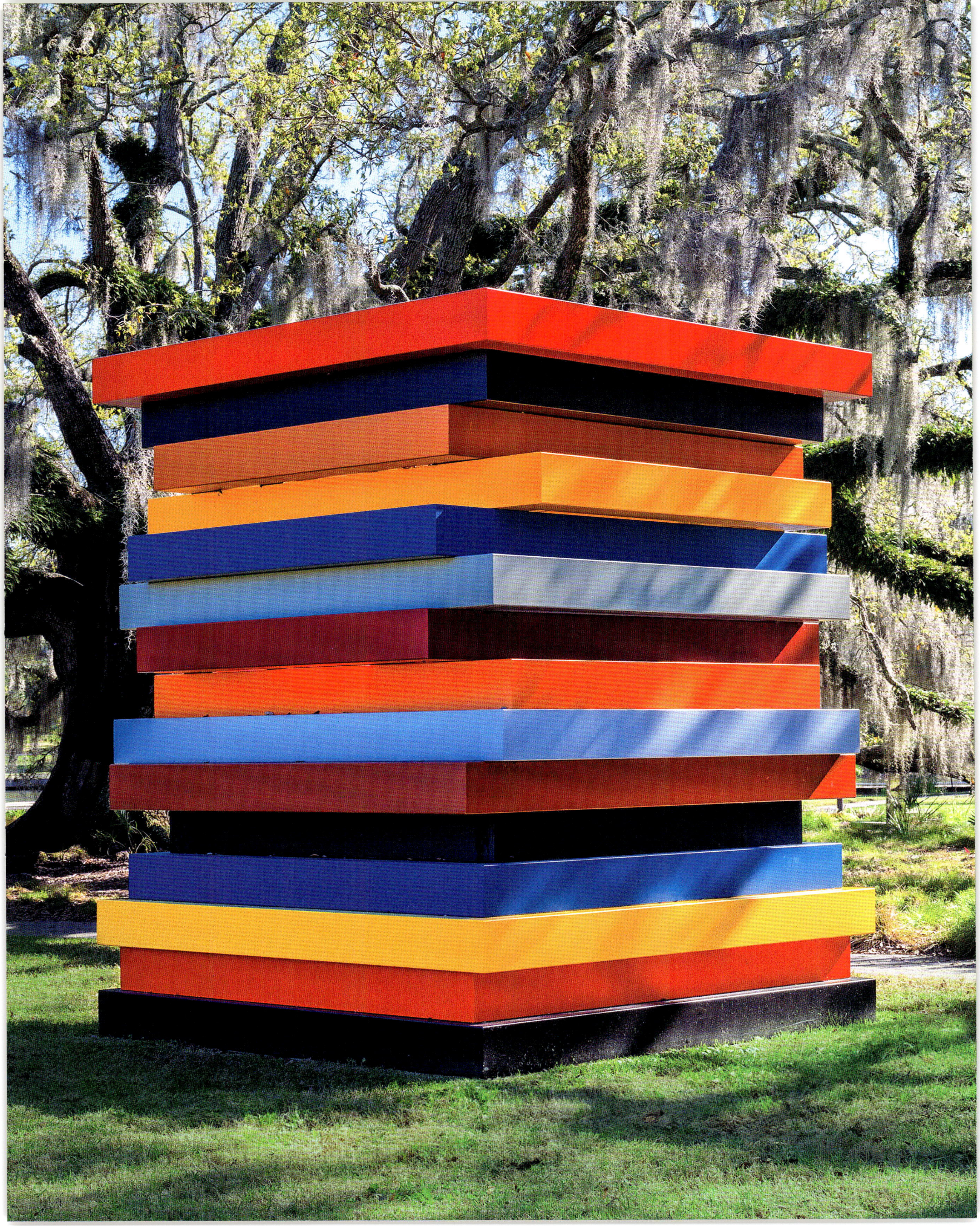

George Segal

Three Figures and Four Benches, 1979

Before creating a bronze sculpture, for more than a decade George Segal (1924–2000) worked largely in plaster. Plaster was a common material—inexpensive and widely available—that matched his predilection for ordinary subjects. It also lent itself to a process that, as a chicken farmer in New Jersey during the 1950s, suited Segal, seeing as he constructed and maintained coops. His first figures, completed in 1958, were made of plaster and burlap over an armature of chicken wire. Later he began—first on himself, then on his family and friends—to create full-body plaster casts by wrapping his model in strips, which he would remove and recombine for the finished sculpture. The resulting life-sized figure often had a lumpy, crude surface that showed the physical process of its production and that revealed little detail about the person. Thus, Segal's sculptures are less individuals than anonyms. Their homespun quality gives them a strange solemnity and an unexpected corporeal energy.

Segal soon built environments of real objects, marked by age, for his stark plaster figures to inhabit. His tableaux of simple circumstances—a butcher, a gas station attendant, diners, bus riders, and so on—imply a narrative. But the effect—reminiscent of Edward Hopper's (1882–1967) paintings, in which existential angst simmers in the most unremarkable scenarios—is more psychological, emphasizing withdrawal, alienation, and pensiveness. *Three Figures and Four Benches* captures the certain charge experienced between strangers in close proximity. With the advent of a new white patina in 1979, Segal was able to replicate the coloring of his plasters for his bronzes, which he had started producing in 1976. He achieved both continuity—by then the look of his figures was readily identified with him—and, in an unusual reversal, disguised an expensive material as a cheap one. Segal received numerous public commissions throughout his life, including *Holocaust Memorial* (1982) and *Depression Bread Line* (1991)—Segal was both Jewish and a product of the 1930s. Because of his interest in everyday life, Segal is frequently allied with Pop art, though the label fits uncomfortably. Like his friend Allan Kaprow (1927–2006), who performed the first one of his Happenings at the artist's chicken farm, Segal staged the meeting of art and life on more capacious terms.—*AMT*

Opposite and following spread
Painted bronze, 52 in. × 12 ft. × 58 in. (132.1 × 3.7 m × 147.3 cm), Gift of the Sydney and Walda Besthoff Foundation, 1998

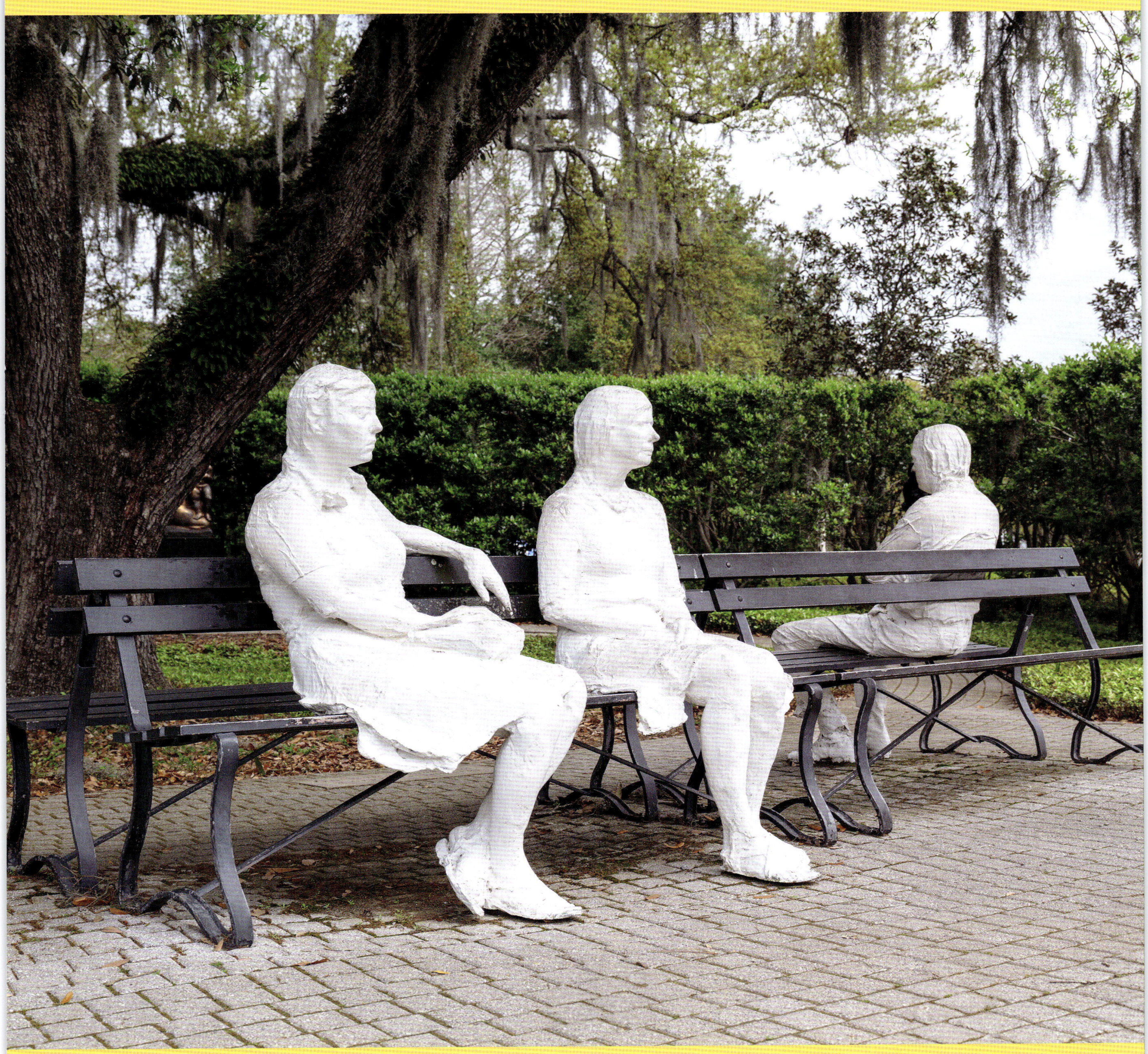

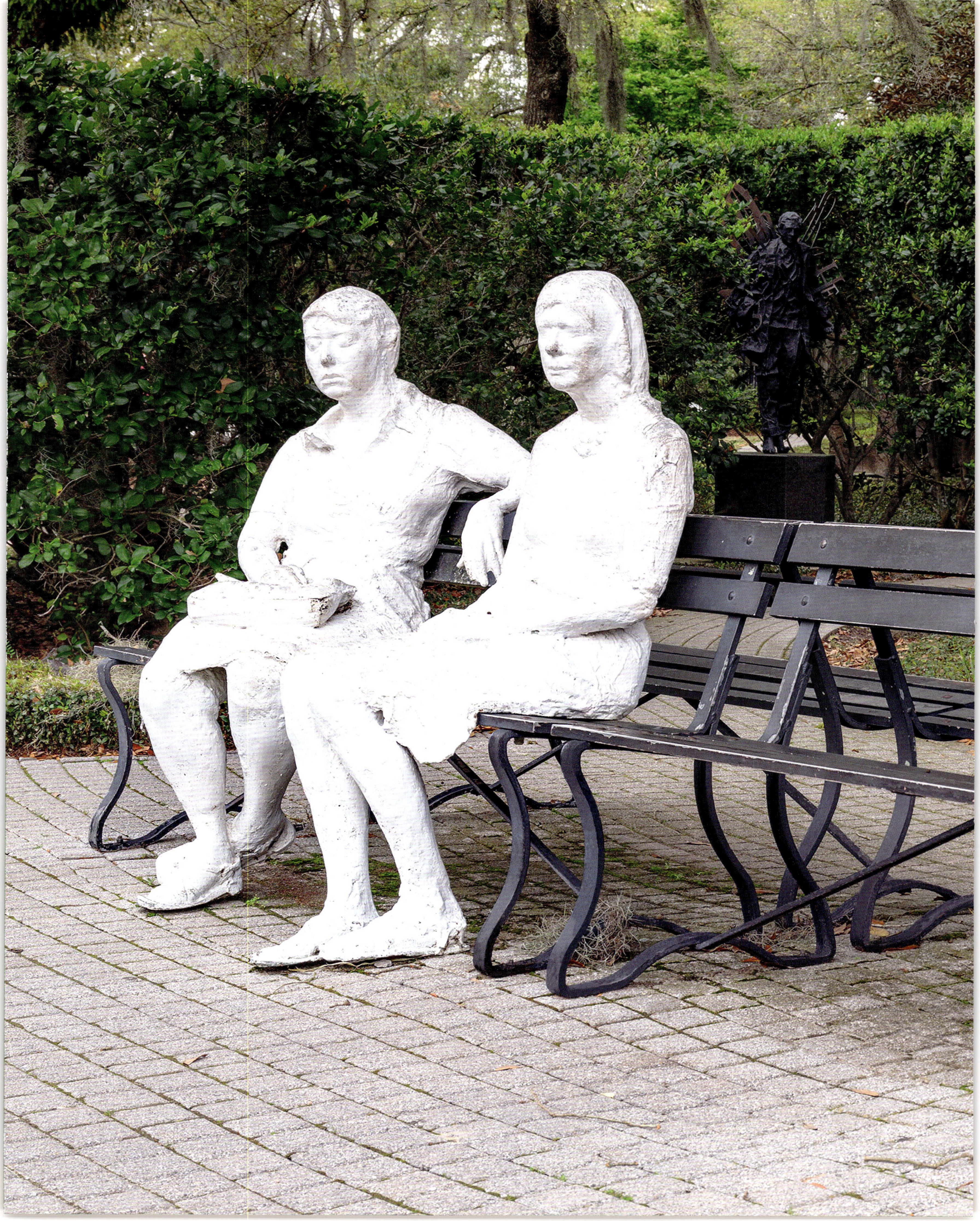

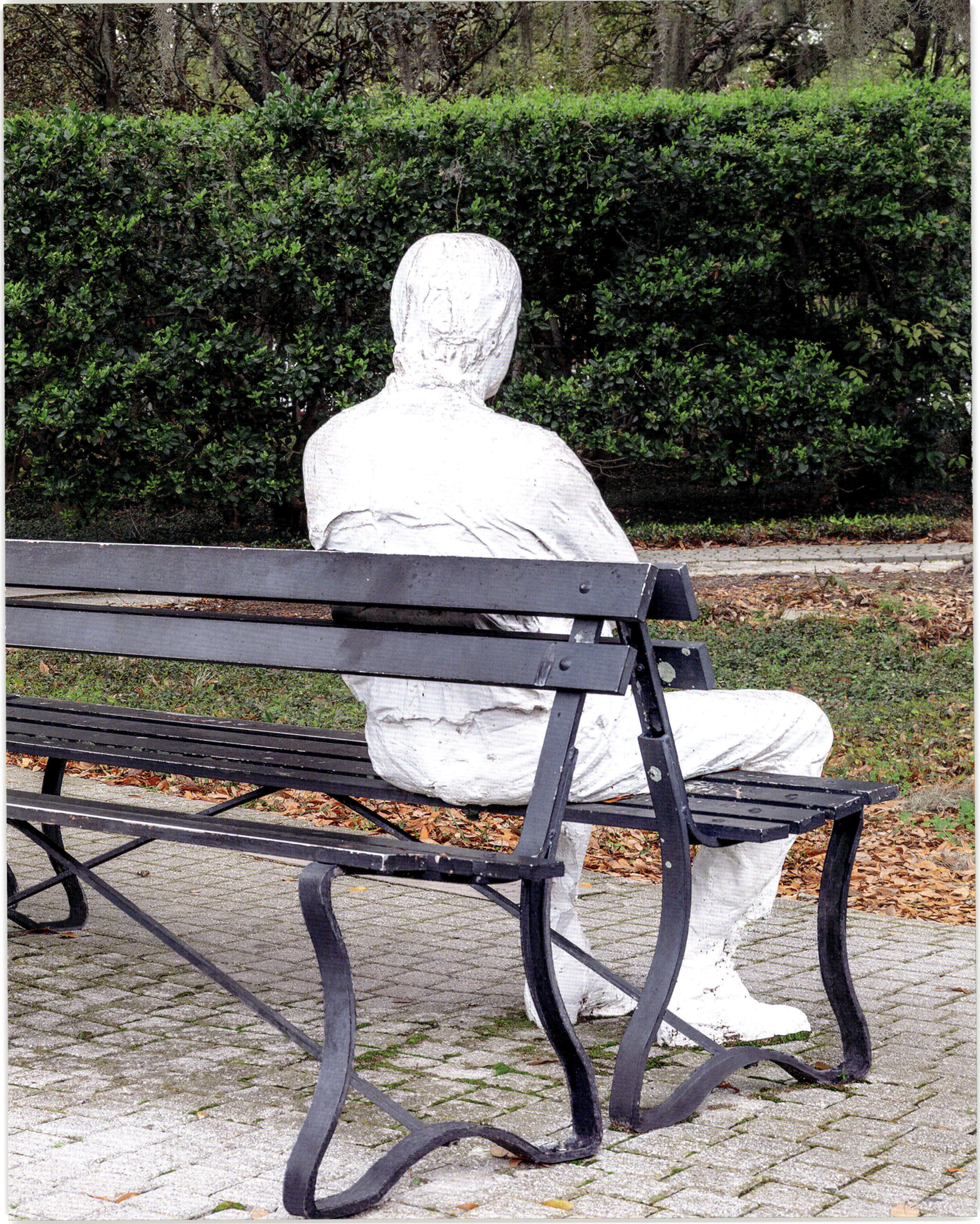

Joel Shapiro

Untitled, 1991

A lifelong fixture in New York City, Joel Shapiro (b. 1941) has been creating abstract geometric sculptures for more than five decades. He earned two degrees from New York University in the 1960s, and by the mid-1970s was pushing rectangular boxes away from the cool detachment associated with Minimalism and toward expressive ends. His wood and metal cuboid arrangements jut, balance, tumble, and gesture. At times, such compositions transmit a bodily energy, however schematic and sticklike their forms. Depending on the vantage point, one might vaguely resemble a pirouetting dancer, another a strutting pedestrian, another a splayed high jumper. As Shapiro summarized in the catalog for his 1982 Whitney Museum of Art solo exhibition, "I think it is important that a convincing piece of sculpture could be put together so simply and be figurative without having to get involved with literally describing human movement, but rather it describes one's idea of movement or one's internal feeling of movement."

The surfaces of Shapiro's large-scale bronzes, such as *Untitled*, record his working process. Their seams and warm patinas hew close to the original vision developed in preliminary, smaller wood studies. Drawing—in chalk, charcoal, and pastel, namely—has also played a key role in his practice. Color, though introduced periodically during the 1990s, became more predominant in his sculpture in the 2010s. In varying tones of red, yellow, and blue especially, these sculptures, slipping in and out of different skins, have given Shapiro a way to imbue a relatively simple repertoire of conjoined shapes with new kinds of emotional charge. Shapiro has received several major permanent outdoor commissions, including for the United States Holocaust Memorial Museum (1993) and the Kennedy Center for the Performing Arts (2019) in Washington, D.C.—*AMT*

Bronze, 84 × 125 × 54 in. (213.4 × 317.5 × 137.2 cm), Museum purchase, Sydney and Walda Besthoff Foundation Fund, 1998

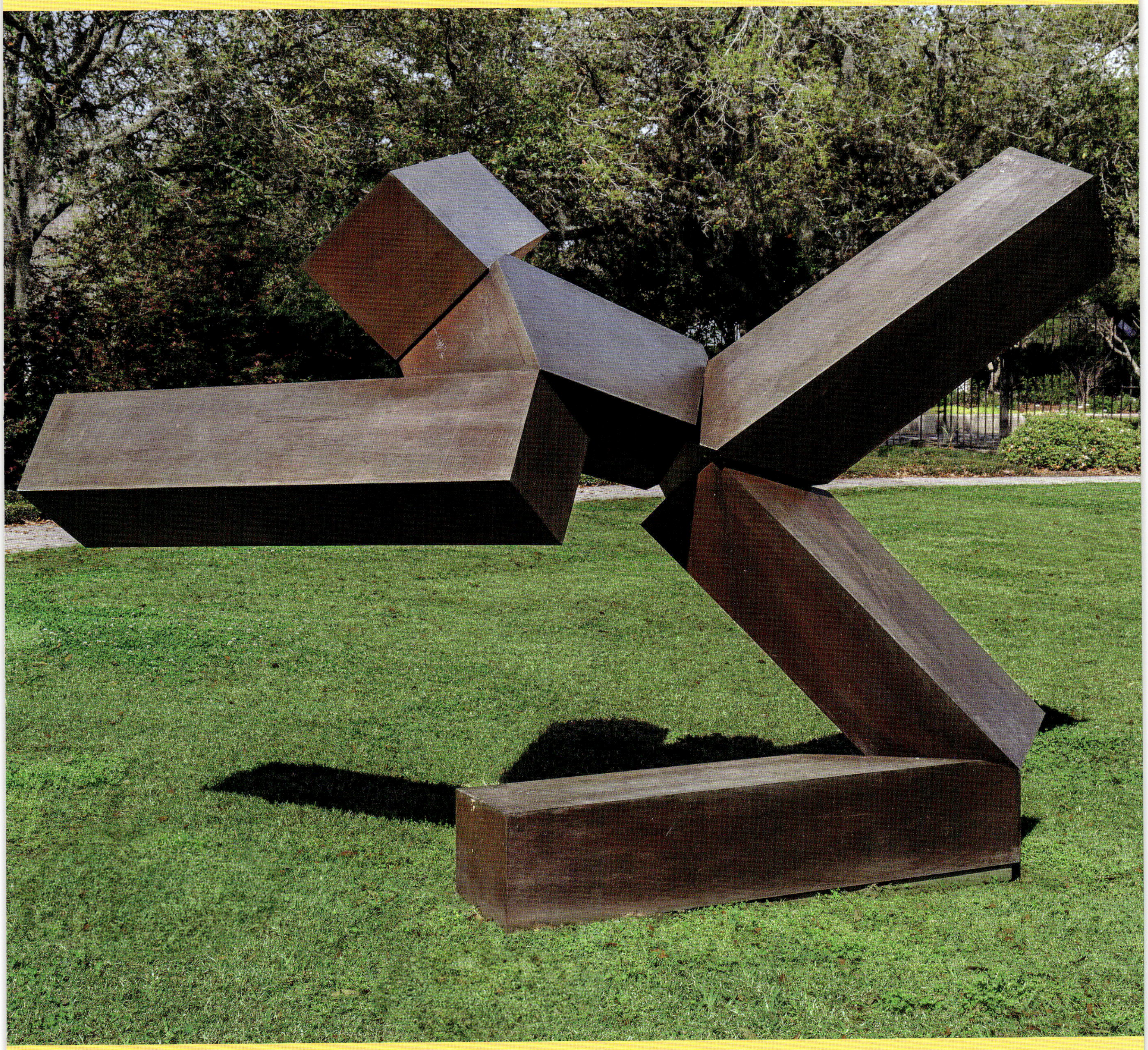

Yinka Shonibare

Wind Sculpture V, 2013

Known for his sharp, incisive interrogations into national identity, Yinka Shonibare's (b. 1962) sculptures draw on a range of evocative and often misunderstood symbols, cleverly combined to investigate themes of belonging, migration, and humanity's sense of place in the world.

Born in London and raised in Nigeria, Shonibare returned to the United Kingdom to study fine art, where he quickly developed a unique artistic voice pitched to examine the entangled colonial relationship between the two countries. Thoroughly researched, his work is frequently rooted in historical events, political conflicts, or obtuse references to Western art history. He is perhaps most recognized for his sculptures of headless mannequins dressed in ruffled colonial-era fashions, tailored from brightly patterned Batik fabrics. Emblematic today of the African continent, Batik textiles were, in fact, originally manufactured by the Dutch for Indonesian markets. However, the fabrics proved far less popular than planned and the Dutch began trading them in the West African colonies.

Many generations later, in the 1950s and 1960s, the vibrant, geometric patterns were adopted by leaders of the African liberation movements, cementing the textile's association with the region and transforming it into a worldwide export symbolic to many in the diaspora of their homeland. Shonibare uses the evolution of the fabric's meaning as a lens to examine how migration affects, contorts, and permanently alters not only a person's sense of belonging but also the idea of what it means to be from a place.

In 2013, the artist began making large-scale Wind Sculptures, such as *Wind Sculpture V*, on view at the Sydney and Walda Besthoff Sculpture Garden. Modeled from a swatch of fabric blowing in the breeze, the motion of the ripping sculpture recalls the wind in the sail of a boat. Such a reference to the slave trade and the marine conquests of the British Empire, was a theme Shonibare began exploring with his work *Nelson's Ship in a Bottle* (2010), made for the fourth plinth commission in Trafalgar Square, London. Patterned in Batik-like geometries of vivid reds, yellows, and greens, *Wind Sculpture V* is a monumental testament to Shonibare's enduring interest in the symbols that bind us to place.—*MH*

Steel armature and fiberglass resin cast, 20 ft. × 133 5/16 in. × 31 3/16 in. (6.1 m × 338.6 cm × 79.2 cm), Gift of Sydney and Walda Besthoff, 2014

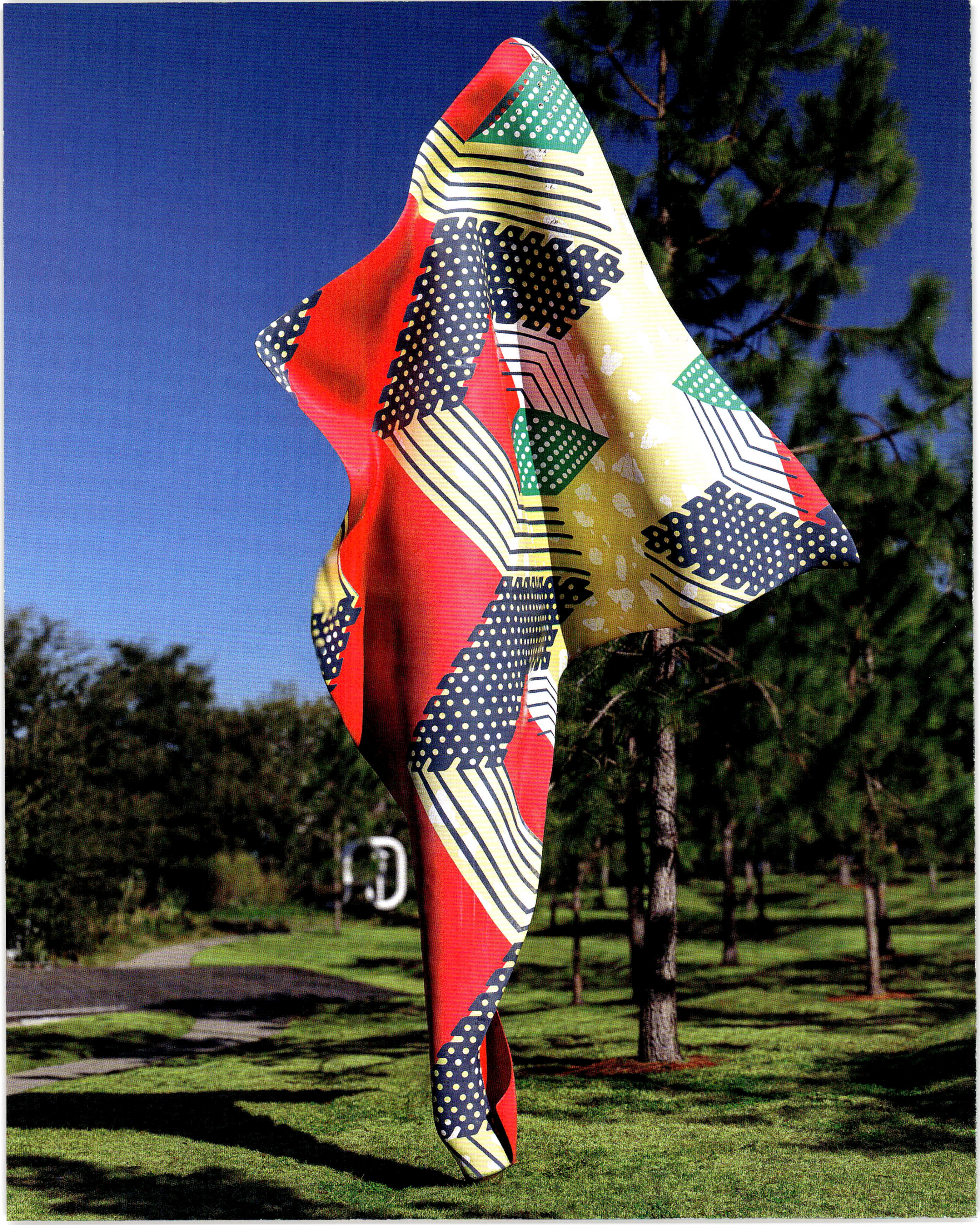

Kenneth Snelson

Virlane Tower, 1981

Made by threading together hollow aluminum tubes, Kenneth Snelson's (1927–2016) sculptures visualize principles of physics as ethereal, three-dimensional geometries. Working primarily with the tensions of equal and opposite forces, he constructed towers, arches, and other architectural designs from modular components. Snelson nurtured a passion for the visual arts from a young age and enrolled at Black Mountain College, North Carolina, after learning that the renowned artist and scholar Josef Albers (1888–1976) was serving as dean. Though he had left for college with every intention of becoming a painter, his plans changed when he arrived in the summer of 1948.

Richard Buckminster Fuller (1895–1983)—the architect and inventor who would go on to design the geodesic dome—was gaining a reputation among the students for his bombastic and thrilling theories of form and geometry. Thanks to Fuller's lectures, Snelson began his first experiments in sculpture and quickly took to working in three-dimensional space. He returned to North Carolina the following summer and began to further articulate Fuller's burgeoning idea of "tensegrity"—the concept of embedding tension into the structural integrity of an object—in his sculptures. Fuller more concretely defined this concept around the same time he exhibited one of Snelson's sculptures at the Museum of Modern Art in New York, conveniently forgetting to credit his pupil and creating a rift in their relationship that would linger for the remainder of Snelson's career.

Though Snelson's work relies heavily on scientific principles, he consistently rejected the critique that he was more of an engineer than an artist. Snelson insisted that at the heart of both science and engineering lies a problem to be solved, whereas his goal had always been an aesthetic one: a wandering exploration in pursuit only of form and beauty. Standing forty-five feet high, *Virlane Tower* exemplifies Snelson's architectural approach to sculpture. Impossibly vertical, the tension keeping the piece upright is undeniable and yet, despite the utter transparency of each structural component, the central force responsible for unifying the sculpture remains utterly mysterious. Above all, Snelson's practice is defined by his unique ability to conjure the forces that govern our world and make visible what to most is only imaginable.—*MH*

Stainless steel, 45 ft. × 13 ft. 6 in. × 13 ft. 6 in. (13.7 × 4.1 × 4.1 m), Gift of the Sydney and Walda Besthoff Foundation, 1998

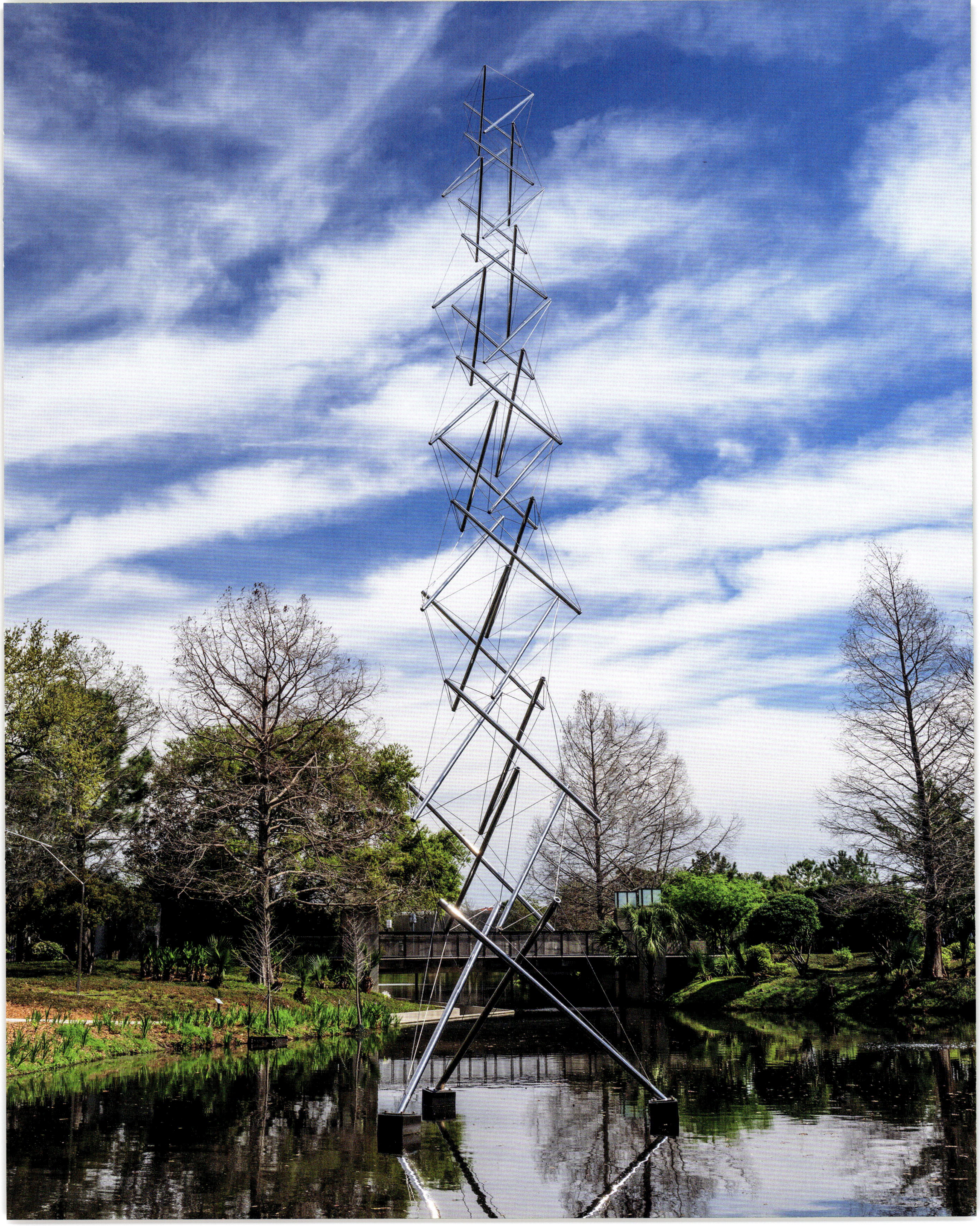

Frank Stella

Alu Truss Star, 2016

One of the most important artists of the twentieth century, Frank Stella's (1936–2024) work has evolved across decades from the pioneering shaped canvases of his early career, into his brightly patterned wall-relief works, and ultimately, into three-dimensional sculpture. Through every iteration, however, his practice has always been marked by an attention to form and the materials themselves. First gaining prominence in the 1960s and 1970s for his minimal stripe paintings, Stella has been both troubling and reifying the boundaries that separate painting and sculpture since his earliest days in New York.

Never formally trained as an artist, Stella moved to New York City in 1958 and found work painting houses to make ends meet while he developed his studio practice. A year later, he signed to the venerable Castelli Gallery, well-known for its roster of cutting-edge Minimalist and Pop painters. Working with simple patterns of concentric lines, Stella produced a series of Black Paintings, one of which was included in the groundbreaking group show *Sixteen Americans* (1959–60) at the Museum of Modern Art. The exhibition launched Stella's career and situated him center stage of a rapidly evolving art world. As the decade wore on, he began constructing shaped stretchers, morphing his canvases into geometric forms with circular edges, triangular angles, and notably, early starlike configurations.

Alu Truss Star belongs to a series of large-scale star sculptures, each markedly distinct in silhouette and style depending on the materials used to form them. Built out of milled aluminum, the angles of *Alu Truss Star* catch in the sunlight, multiplying the many points that converge into a visible knot at its center. Having experimented with relief-like works, Stella transitioned into more freestanding sculpture in the 1990s, and quickly took up the shape of the star, reproducing it at numerous scales and in varying materials. The aluminum lends the artwork an industrial undercurrent, while the open shape and many angles prevent the sculpture from becoming self-serious. With its playful, experimental attitude, the piece represents Stella's penchant to challenge our preconceived ideas about artistic genres.—*MH*

Milled aluminum, 14 × 14 × 14 ft. (4.3 × 4.3 × 4.3 m), overall, Museum purchase with funds provided by Sydney and Walda Besthoff, 2017

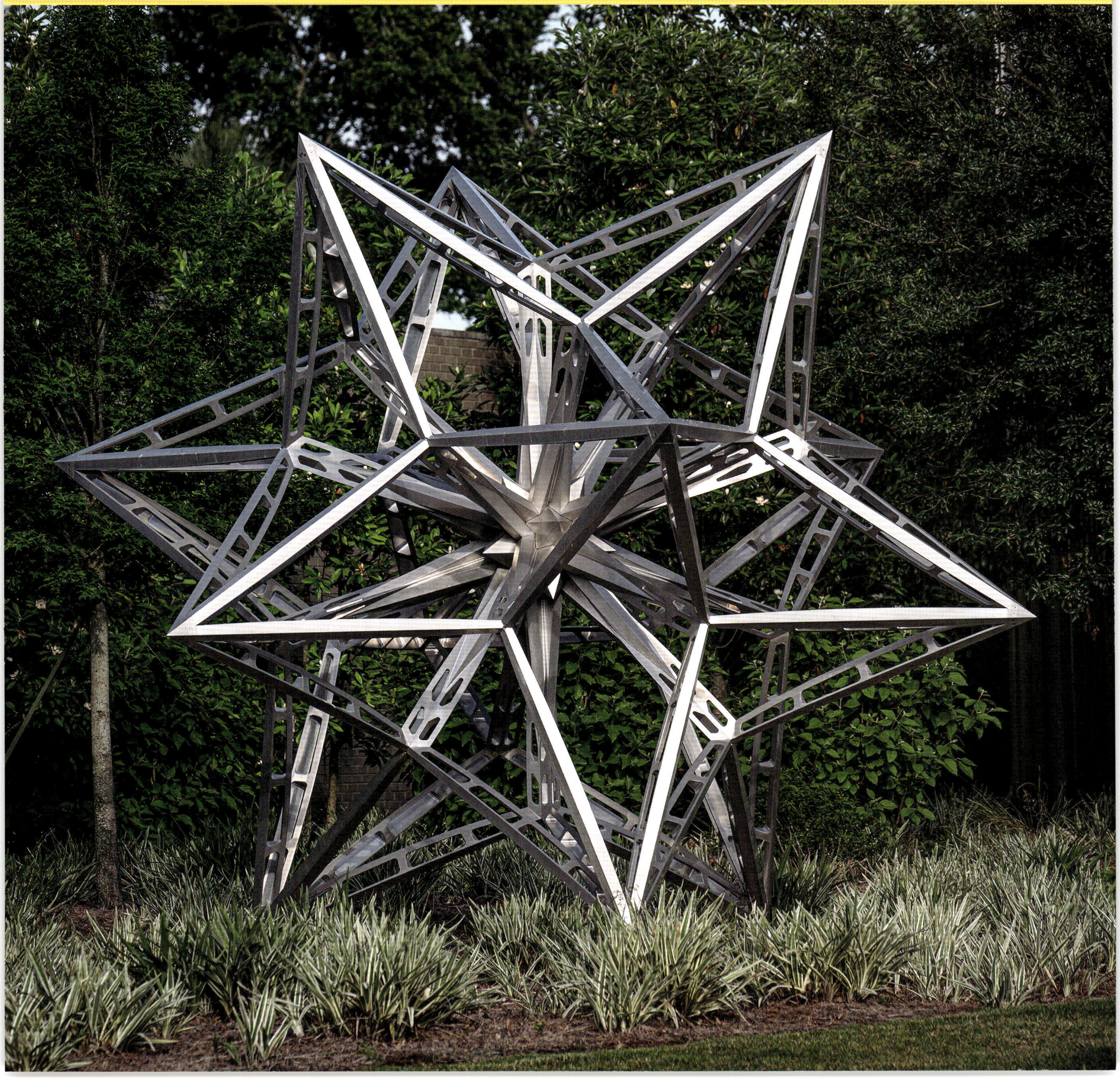

Do Ho Suh

Karma, 2011

Fascinated by memory, location, and the effects of displacement, Do Ho Suh's (b. 1962) sculpture captures the strange mix of pain, beauty, and longing that coalesces to form nostalgia. Best known for constructing precise, to-scale models of the various homes and apartments he has inhabited out of brightly colored diaphanous silks, Suh's work consistently questions what it means to belong to a place and how, through both distance and memory, we relate to the spaces we have left behind. Above all, these intense meditations on the concept of personal space seek to understand where the collective meets the individual and how the intimate world of one person is simultaneously reliant on, and determined by, the behaviors and systems of an interdependent society.

The son of a respected South Korean painter, Suh immigrated to the United States in 1991, enrolling in the Rhode Island School of Design. Having already received art training in Korea, Suh immediately began to tinker with ideas around the body within architecture, which quickly transformed into an interest in how a sense of self is shaped through place. From the beginning, Suh's practice framed identity as defined by and through its environment. Soon after, he began experimenting with concepts of reminiscence, yearning, desire, and loss—themes that continue to animate his work.

A striking silhouette, *Karma* takes the form of a solitary standing man, on whose shoulders sit a series of infinitely shrinking figures, curving up to the sky like a monumental tusk. Each man is perched on the shoulders of the previous figure, their hands reaching down to cover the eyes of the person below them, a remarkably simple and poetic composition that culminates in a total blindness. Though such literal representations of the human body remain somewhat of an outlier within Suh's oeuvre, the themes that *Karma* evokes cut straight to the artist's perennial preoccupation with the personal, the collective, and the near-constant expansion and contraction of the space that divides them.—*MH*

Brushed stainless steel, 23 ft. × 26 ¾ in. × 46 ½ in. (7 m × 67.9 cm × 118.1 cm), Museum purchase, funds from Dorothy B. Skau, and Gift of the Sydney and Walda Besthoff Foundation, 2011

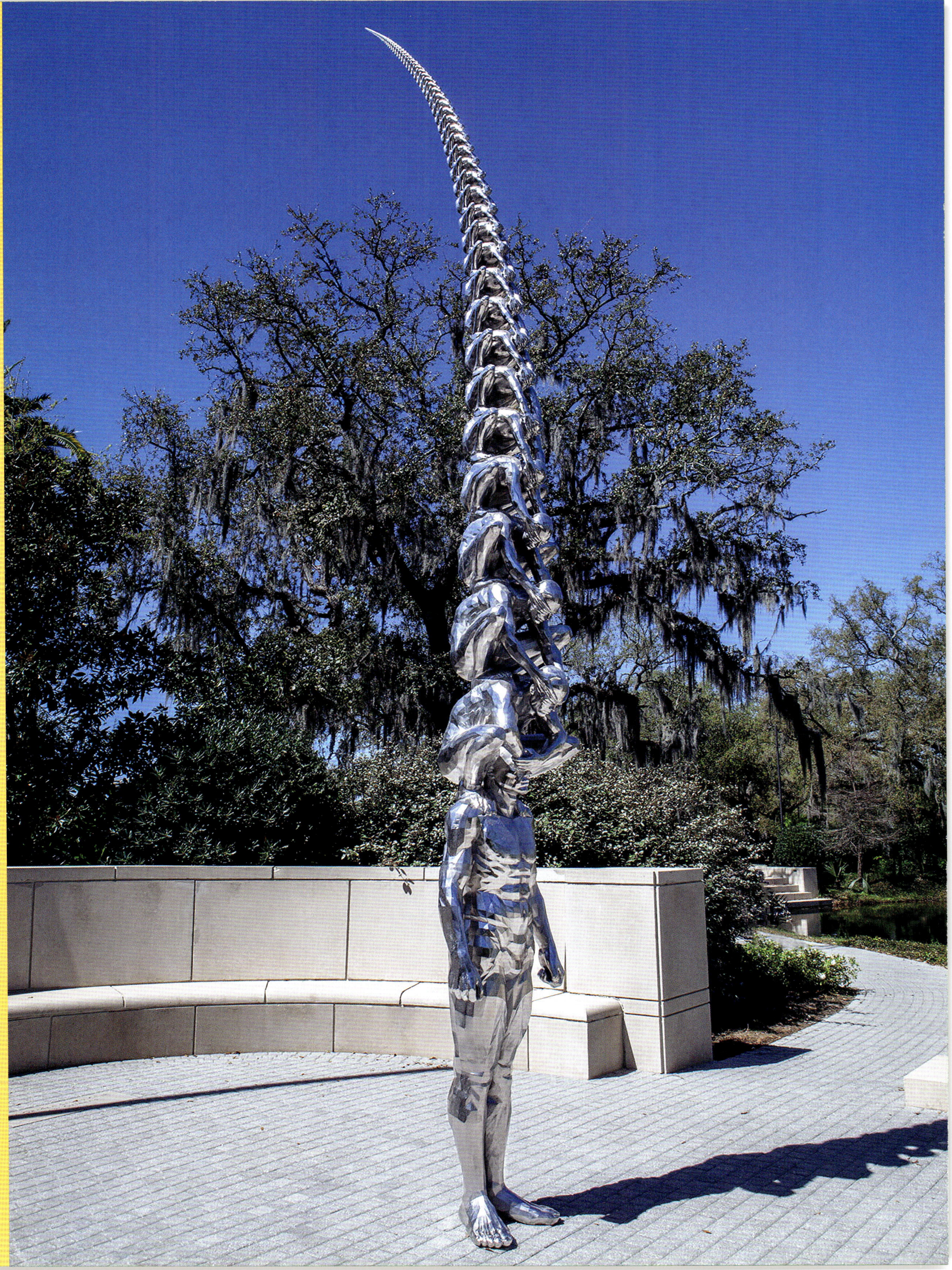

Sarah Sze

Certain Slant of Light, 2024

American artist Sarah Sze (b. 1969) uses a broad range of media to continuously expand and develop a dynamic body of work encompassing painting, sculpture, drawing, installation, and video. She is renowned for intricate installations that emulate the interconnectivity and chaos of contemporary life through a complex combination of found objects. Resisting systems of scale and often going beyond gallery walls, her assemblages—composed of electric fans, lamps, office supplies, and living plants, among other items—bring new meaning to the everyday. Engaging with video and multimedia work, Sze delves into the perpetual excess of the digital realm, exploring the junctions of consumption and production and their effects on our rapidly evolving world. Sze's multivalent practice is extensive in scope and diverse in form, yet she maintains an enduring commitment to investigating structures of information and collapsing our perceptions of time, memory, and place. Born in Boston and based in New York, where she teaches visual arts at Columbia University, Sze completed her studies at Yale University (1991) and the School of Visual Arts (1997).

Certain Slant of Light demonstrates the artist's masterful exploration of materiality, movement, and transformation, as well as her preoccupation with the environment. Made up of numerous glacial-like components executed in stainless steel, the piece appears to emerge organically from the grassy terrain, despite its refined exterior. The ruptured metal crescent simultaneously recalls spatial imagery and geological processes of erosion. It blurs the lines between the artificial and the natural, and the past, present and future. The sculpture's mirror-polished surfaces change depending on the surrounding environment, the season, and the time of day, capturing the passage of time through reflections of the sky, clouds, and trees above, and drawing analogies between planet Earth and celestial bodies above. Experimenting with variations of light to achieve a permanent state of mutability, Sze's *Certain Slant of Light* fosters a timeless sensibility and invites a new experience of the landscape around it.—*JM*

Stainless steel, 12 ft. x 12 ft. x 15 in. (3.7 m x 3.7 m x 38.1 cm), Museum Purchase with Gifted Funds from the Sydney and Walda Besthoff Foundation, 2024

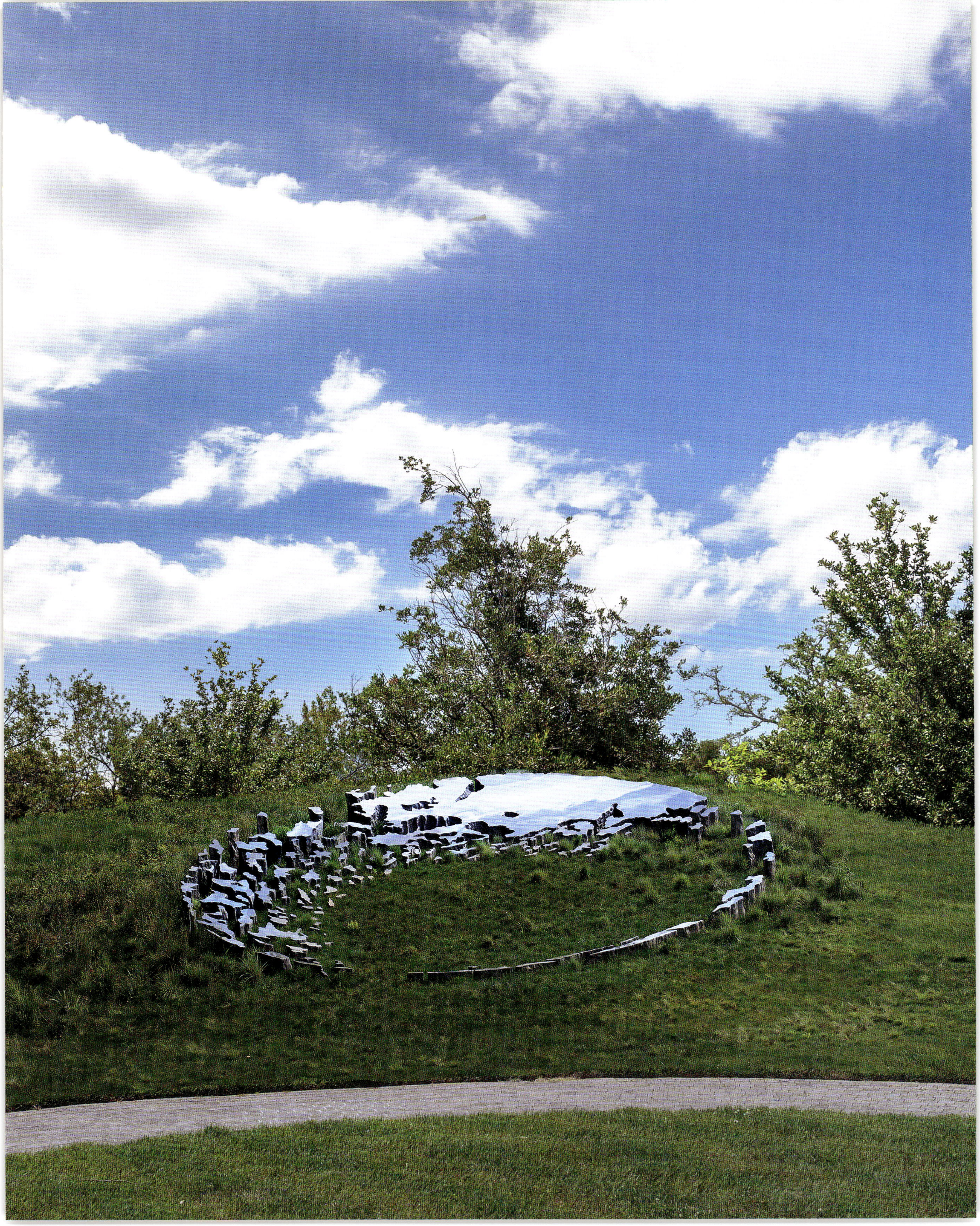

Hank Willis Thomas

History of the Conquest, 2017

For more than two decades, Hank Willis Thomas (b. 1976) has mined imagery and language from a broad swath of popular culture. Appropriating photographs, advertisements, and slogans, his work taps into the disturbing and all-too-common history of racist, sexist, and classist tropes that structure identity, desire, and commodification. His years at New York University and the California College of the Arts, where he earned a BFA (1998) and MFA (2004), respectively, focused on photography. But his approach to the medium has always been guided by the legacy of Conceptual art and the strategies of mass-media critique, from Pictures Generation artists in particular. For example, in *Branded* (2003), a trenchant early work, Thomas digitally altered the different body parts of a Black model, superimposing the Nike "swoosh" logo to propose links between corporate sponsorship, team ownership, and the labor of Black athletes and chattel slavery.

Thomas's bronze sculptures have also addressed issues of prejudice and subjugation. *Raise Up* (2014), at the National Memorial for Peace and Justice in Montgomery, Alabama, borrows from a photograph taken in apartheid-era South Africa. The ten heads and twenty arms on the plinth replicate the "hands up, don't shoot" gesture that originated in 2014 and has been widely used in protests against police killings of Black men. Thomas's *Embrace* (2022), a memorial based on a 1965 photograph of Dr. Martin Luther King hugging his wife, Coretta Scott King, is a twenty-foot tall, thirty-two-foot-wide bronze sculpture installed in Boston Common.

In *History of the Conquest*, Thomas presents a riff on a seventeenth-century German "curiosity," Jeremias Ritter's (1605–1646) *Nautilus Snail* (c. 1630). The enlargement both holds the racist iconography to account and subverts it—the "colonized" takes back the reins, in a sense. Thomas collaborated with the museum on a three-dimensional scan of the object for *History of the Conquest*, which debuted outside the New Orleans Jazz Museum during the triennial art event Prospect 4 in 2017. A counter-monument to Confederate equestrian statues—according to an interview of the artist in the exhibition catalog *Hank Willis Thomas: All Things Being Equal* (2018)—the sculpture resonates with "the context of New Orleans's history of Maroon communities of escaped slaves and Madame Marie Laveau—who was what we would call an early civic leader but was known then as the Voodoo Queen." *History of the Conquest* stands among numerous examples from his oeuvre that prod viewers to see how, to quote the 2017 text-based works of his, "history is present."—*AMT*

Bronze, 85 × 118 × 48 in. (215.9 × 299.7 × 121.9 cm), overall, Museum purchase with funds provided by Sydney and Walda Besthoff, 2018

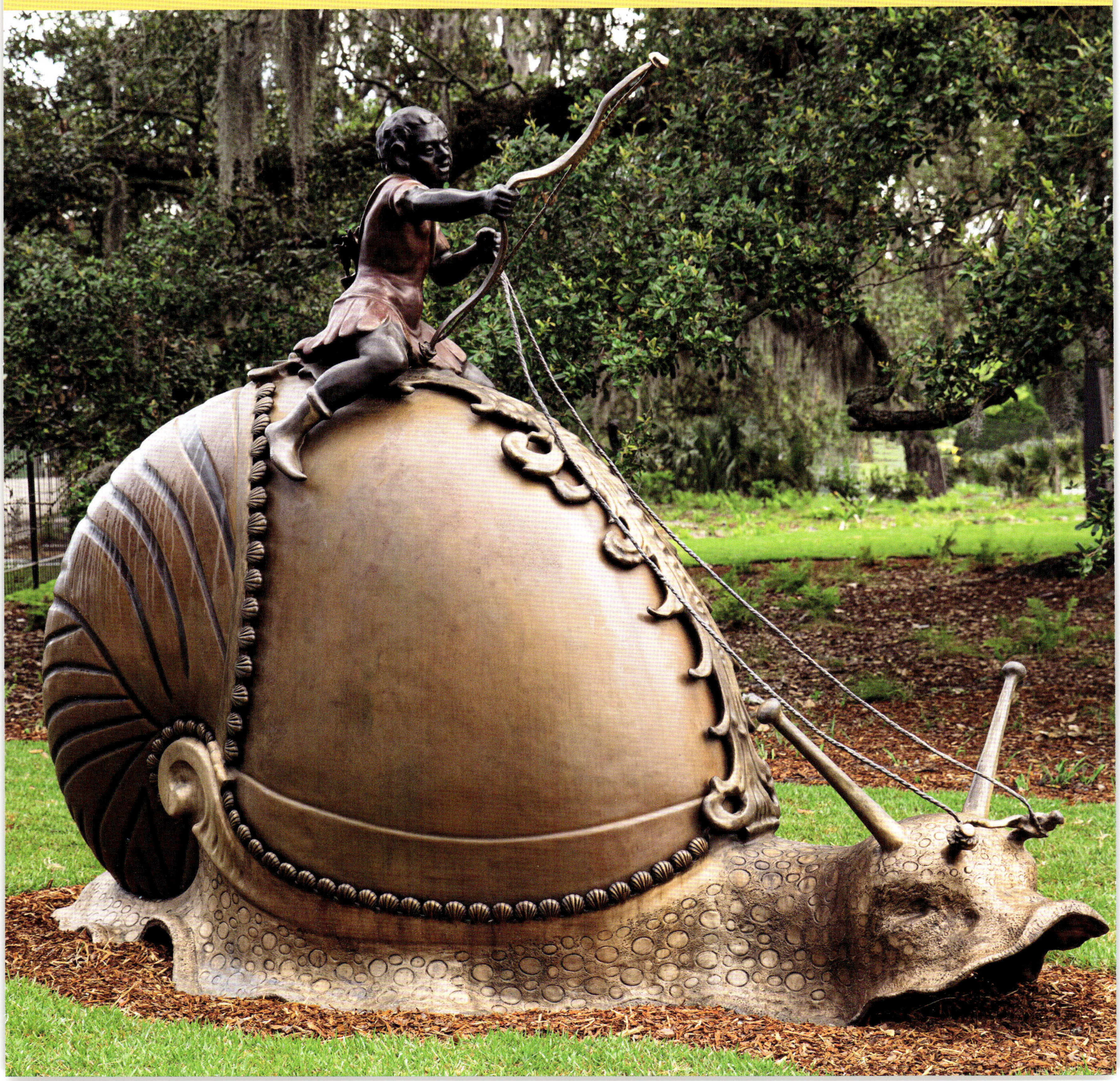

Bernar Venet

11 Acute Unequal Angles, 2016

Since the early 1980s, the trajectory of Bernar Venet's (b. 1941) sculpture has been guided by a small number of principles. The limits that he sets for himself are usually based on mathematical equations and plane geometry. His large-scale COR-TEN steel works—in straight lines, arcs, and angles—result from these rational formulations. *11 Acute Unequal Angles*, for example, is just what its title indicates: acute angles of varying heights and degrees. In the literalism of this Conceptual art gambit, the logical proposition that produces each sculpture is as much a part of the work as the finished product. The material form is even considered secondary to the thought form. Venet's coiled series of Indeterminate Lines (begun in the 1980s)—sculptures that embrace uncertainty and improvisation in their construction—is also a visual manifestation of a conceptual construct about the infinite variations of lines.

Born in the South of France, Venet gravitated to art at a young age. He began on his extreme anti-symbolic and anti-metaphorical path in the 1960s. His impersonal *Tar Paintings* (1961–63), consisting of black tar and industrial paint on cardboard, challenged the individualism associated with expressive abstraction. Similarly, *Pile of Coal* (1963) was a set of neutral protocols to be acted out to distribute shapeless heaps of coal. In this more purely conceptual phase of his career, virtually any formal elements were negated. Latching on to mathematics and physics in pursuit of the elimination of style and feeling from art, Venet saw his works as having only one meaning—as monosemic, as objective, and as not referring to anything outside of themselves. For a period the artist even gave up art, but resumed in 1977. Venet, who currently lives between New York City and France, often likens his artistic approach to that of a scientist: "In pursuit of research," as expressed in an eponymous 2007 monograph.—*AMT*

Opposite and following spread
COR-TEN steel, 97 5/8 in. × 14 ft. 1 in. × 47 5/8 in. (247.9 cm × 4.3 m × 120.9 cm), overall, Museum purchase with funds provided by Sydney and Walda Besthoff, 2016

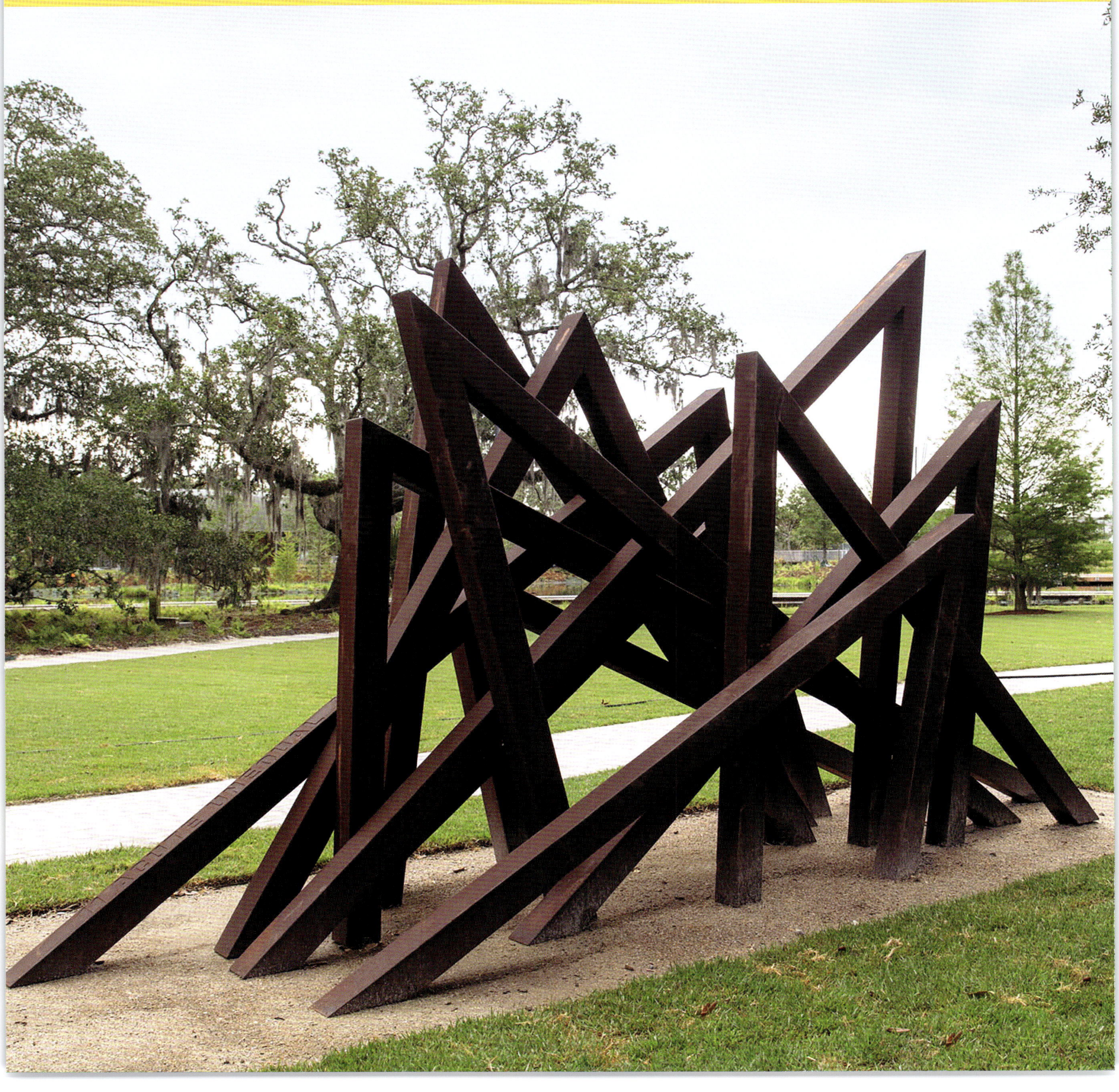

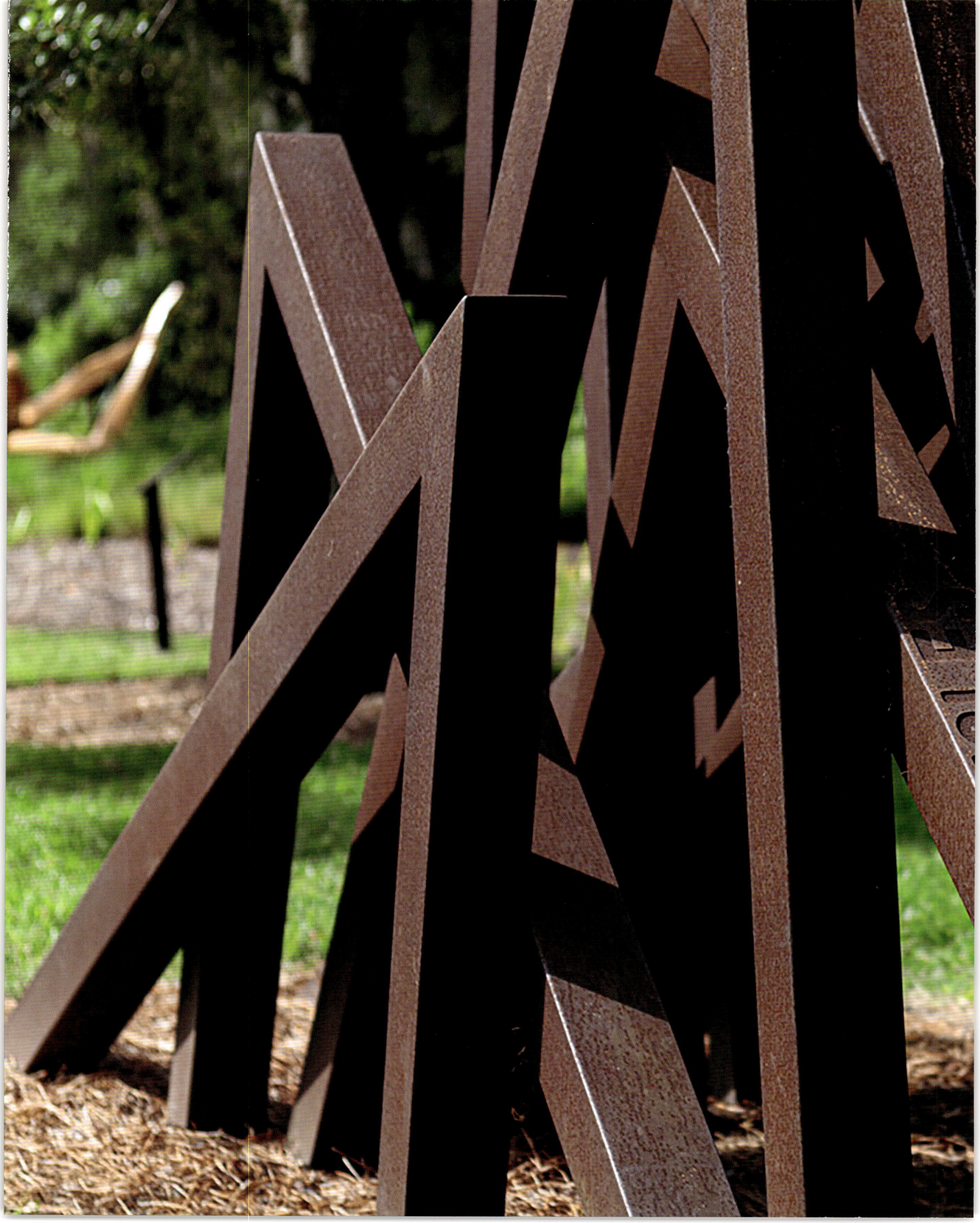

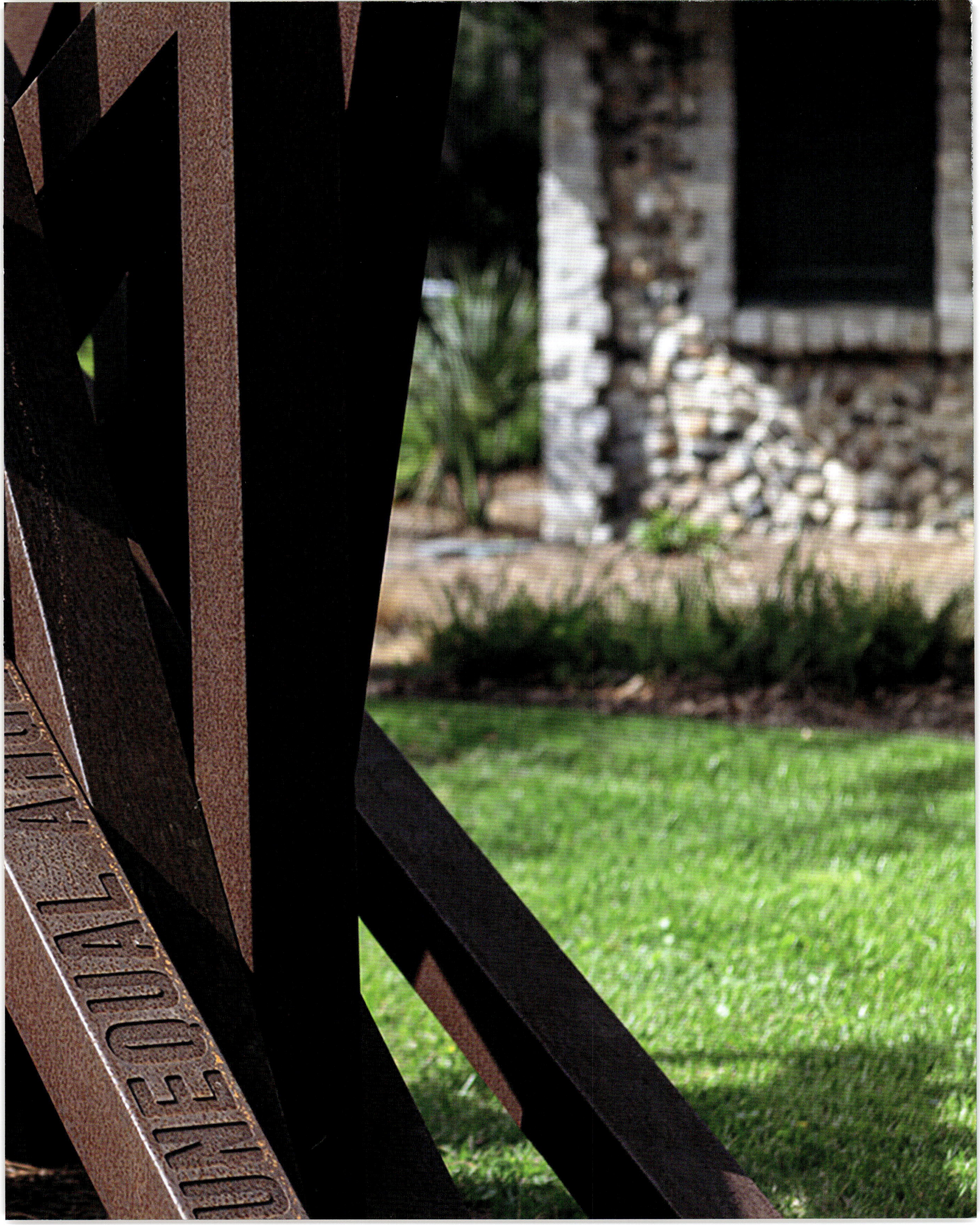
UNEQUAL

Ursula von Rydingsvard

Dumna, 2015

Not long after graduating from Columbia University in 1975 with an MFA, Ursula von Rydingsvard (b. 1942) began making sculptures from cedar wood. She experimented with variations in shape, including the box, cone, and pole forms. *Saint Martin's Dream* (1980), a site-specific public commission in the Battery Park City landfill, New York, was a turning point for von Rydingsvard in terms of both scale and recognition. One of several works from the period with titles referencing saints—her upbringing was Catholic—the more than 250-foot-long fence of posts, some topped with driftwood-like carved wings, seemed to flutter on the hillside. By the late-1980s, she settled on a distinctive working method: clamping, gluing, and planing four-by-four-inch cedar planks together. The carefully assembled hunk is then sanded, sawed, and gouged into an often imposing mass. Lastly, von Rydingsvard will scar and rub the uneven surface with graphite to attain a burnished and weathered patina.

From the repetition of the standard unit and the responsiveness of the softwood, von Rydingsvard creates numerous unique shapes. Although she has refined the process over the years—she now employs a team of assistants and imports cedar beams from Vancouver, Canada, to her Brooklyn studio—it has always been extremely labor intensive. The process, however, is cathartic for von Rydingsvard and linked to childhood memories. She was born on a farm in northern Germany during World War II to a Polish mother and a Ukrainian father who had worked as a woodcutter when he was young. Her displaced family shuttled through eight different refugee camps before immigrating to the United States in 1950. There is a primal, agricultural, and peasant mythos to her sculptures which—with the help of power tools—are constructed by hand and regularly situated in fields and parks. These craggy monoliths resemble knobby gourds, giant fossils, and stone outcroppings of grottos and canyons. In recent years, von Rydingsvard has translated their honeycomb texture into new materials, notably bronze, to resist the elements. Her large bronzes, such as the majestic *Dumna*, are cast from full-scale cedar models. Von Rydingsvard sometimes identifies sculptures in her ancestral language, and the title is perhaps an allusion to the Polish word for "proud."—*AMT*

Bronze, 130 × 97 × 64 ½ in. (330.2 × 246.4 × 163.8 cm), overall, Museum purchase with funds provided by Sydney and Walda Besthoff, 2019

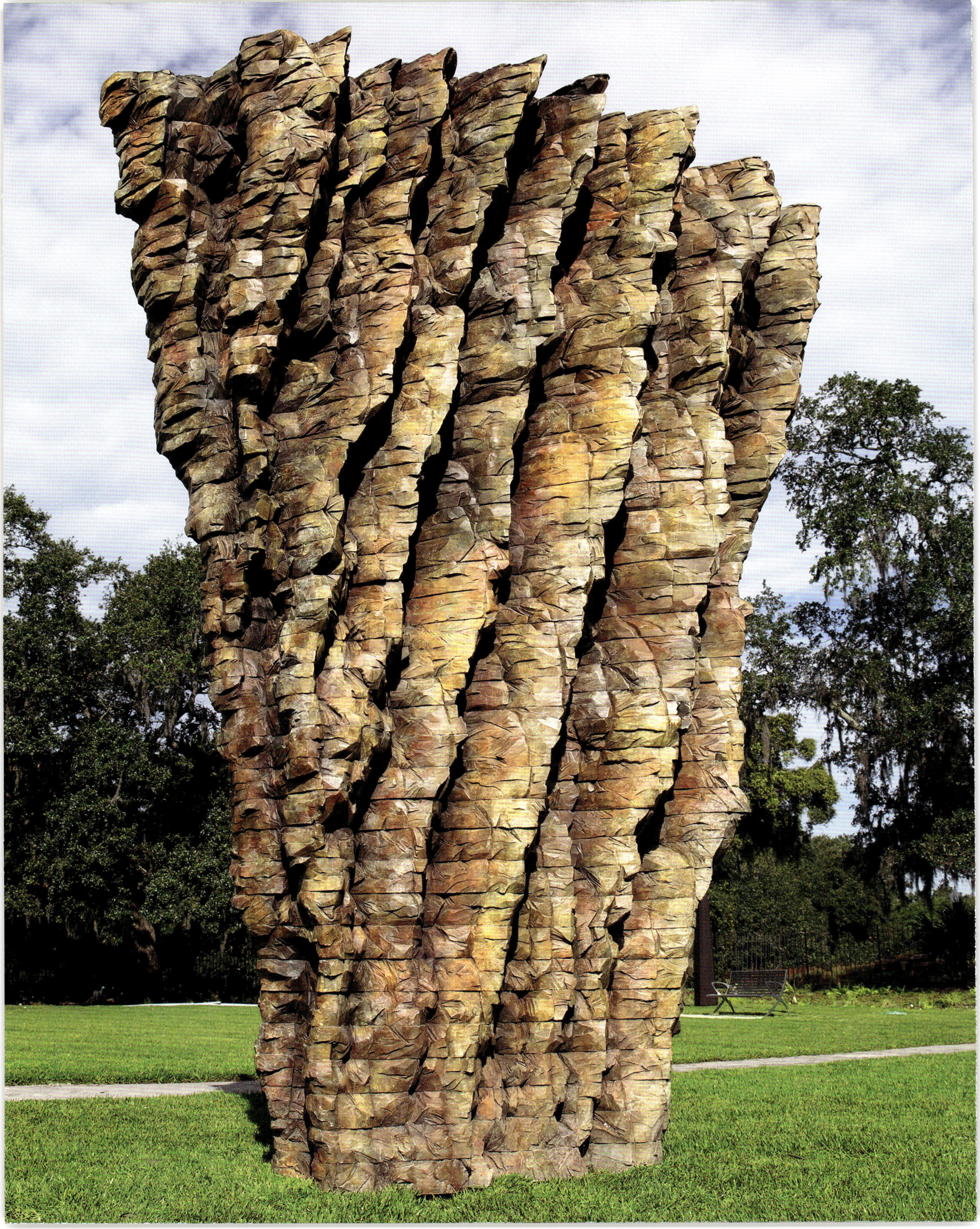

Fred Wilson

The Mete of the Muse, 2006

As one of the art world's most incisive commentators on race, Fred Wilson (b. 1954) has been less occupied with crafting objects than with recontextualizing existing ones. He grew up in New York City and earned a BFA in 1976 from the State University of New York in Purchase, where he also worked as a guard at the Neuberger Museum of Art while a student. As a freelance educator at several institutions, including the Metropolitan Museum of Art and the American Museum of Natural History, Wilson continued to hone his sensitivity to the role of politics, privilege, power, and prejudice in the display of art and artifacts. His seminal *Mining the Museum* (1992) at the Maryland Historical Society problematized the conventional distinction between these terms. By juxtaposing silver decorative art objects and slave shackles from the same era, most famously, Wilson unsettled institutional hierarchies, canonical narratives, and repressed meanings. This radical reshuffling forcefully demonstrated how white "refinement" was predicated on Black subjugation. Although informed by earlier Conceptual art strands of institutional critique, the project put Wilson at the cutting edge of a new museological impulse in art.

Wilson has worked with a range of media in different spheres to shed light on the ways history, culture, and race are constructed. His work *Collectibles* (1995–96) consisted of hundreds of racists figurines collected from thrift stores and antique shops to show the pervasive profiteering off demeaning Black imagery in the not-so-distant past. Wilson has long "been interested in these representations of black people by white people," as he explained in the exhibition catalog *Fred Wilson: Black Like Me* (2006). He often deftly engages the past to remark on the present. Comparing two things side by side, as he does in *The Mete of the Muse*, is also a recurrent strategy. One meaning of "mete" is a boundary. Through these two dissimilar, ancient representations of the human body, Wilson suggests that both Egypt and Greece are foundational to Western European culture. Yet even if Egyptian culture precedes that of Greece, its African origins are often dismissed or ignored. Wilson has investigated attitudes towards Egypt, where he lived briefly with his father, for several projects, including *Re:Claiming Egypt* at the Cairo Biennale in 1992.—*AMT*

Bronze with black patina and bronze with white paint; European figure: 61 × 18 × 20 in. (154.9 × 45.7 × 50.8 cm); African figure: 65 × 26 × 14 in. (165.1 × 66 × 35.6 cm), edition 4 of 5 + 2 APs, Museum purchase with funds provided by Sydney and Walda Besthoff, 2017

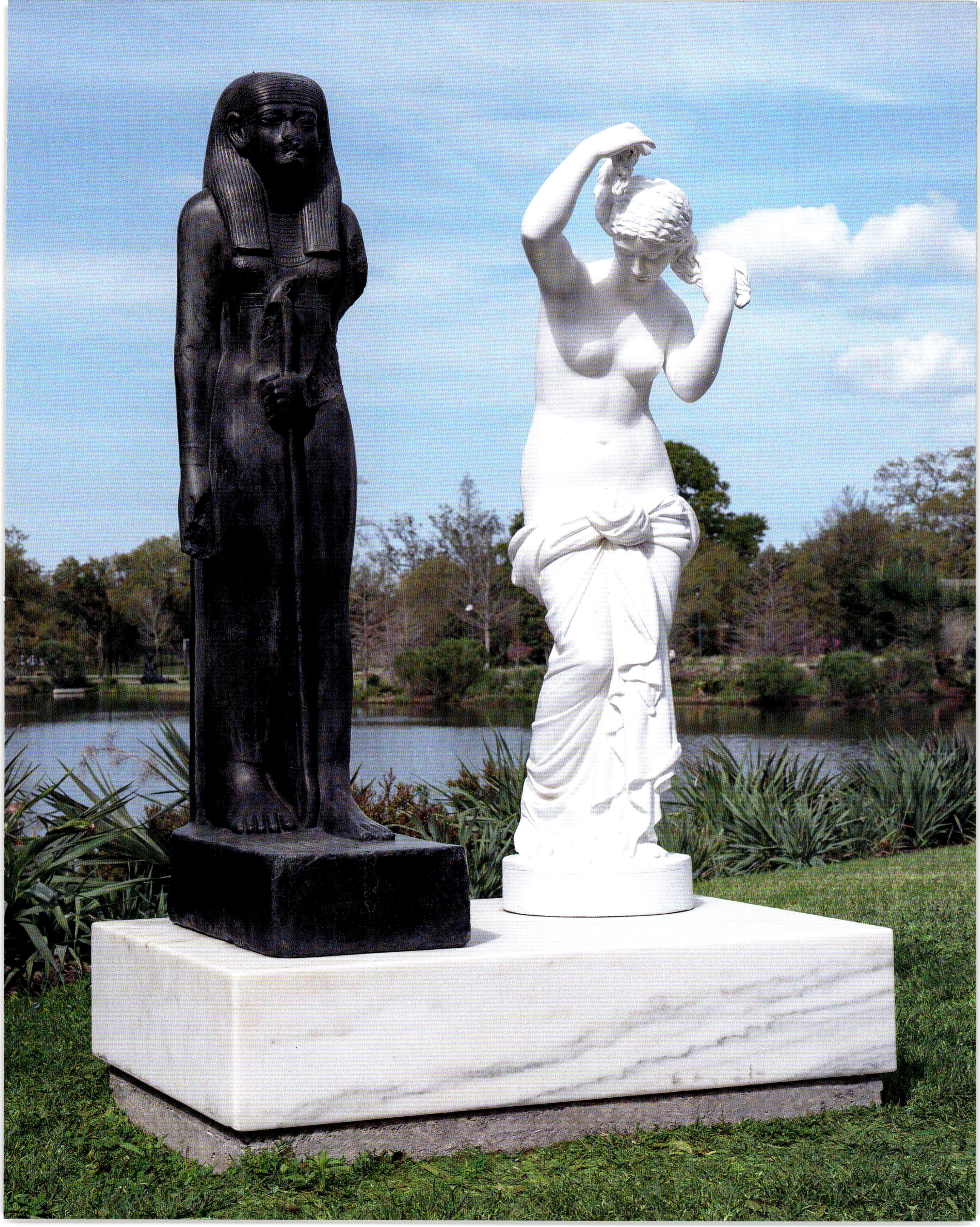

Ossip Zadkine

La Poétesse, 1953

Known for his elongated figures and Cubist-inspired geometries, Ossip Zadkine (1888–1967) remains one of the foremost sculptors of the early twentieth-century avant-garde. Blending the unlikely aesthetic influences of Auguste Rodin (1840–1917) and Pablo Picasso (1881–1973), Zadkine developed a unique style designed to capture and express emotion through right angles, abstract shapes, and combine-like sculptural tableaux. His sculpture is marked by an innate appreciation for the material qualities of the mediums he worked with, be it stone, wood, or cast bronze. In his stone and wood works especially, he became a huge proponent of the direct carving methods that would later be championed by modern British artists such as Barbara Hepworth (1903–1975) and Henry Moore (1898–1986), whose sculptures also feature in the Besthoff collection.

At an early age, Zadkine was sent from France to live with relatives in England, where he enrolled in art school and first began tinkering with woodcarving before moving to London to apprentice with a woodworker. In 1909, Zadkine moved to Paris, studying briefly at the École des Beaux-Arts, before giving up formal training and dedicating himself entirely to his work. He lived in La Ruche, a building in Montparnasse famous for its affordable artist studios, and quickly fell in with the key members of the Parisian avant-garde, notably becoming friendly with Picasso, from whom Zadkine picked up his trademark Cubist-inspired style. Having begun to work more consistently with bronze, in the 1930s, Zadkine began experimenting with negative space, designing figures around holes and other open, linear forms intended to give movement and fluidity to the pieces. As World War II encroached, the artist went into exile, teaching at the Art Students League in New York and becoming an active member of the artist-émigré community. *La Poétesse* depicts a subject that recurs across Zadkine's oeuvre. Articulated through his characteristic combination of angles, forms, and vague representational silhouettes, the sculpture serves as an homage to the writers, artists, and musicians of the creative set, among whom Zadkine made his life.—*MH*

Bronze, 31 × 64 × 24 in. (78.7 × 162.6 × 60.9 cm), Gift of the Sydney and Walda Besthoff Foundation, 1998

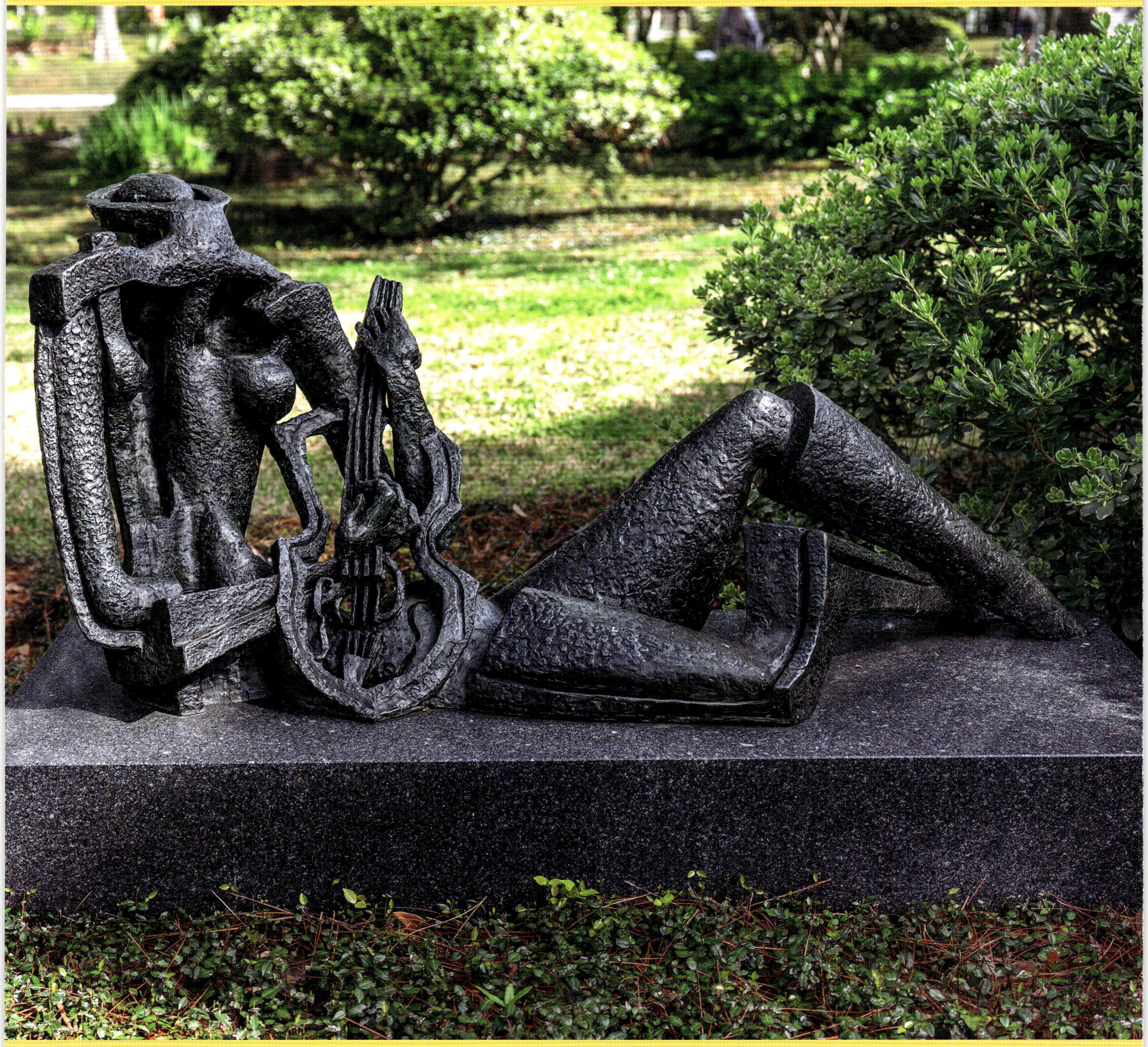

Elyn Zimmerman

Mississippi Meanders, 2019

Since 1984, American artist Elyn Zimmerman (b. 1945) has realized more than forty site-specific sculptural installations. Although born in Philadelphia, the artist grew up in Los Angeles, where she studied with abstract painter Richard Diebenkorn (1922–1993) and assisted Light and Space artist James Turrell (b. 1943) at UCLA, completing her MFA in 1972. A fellowship from the National Endowment for the Arts enabled her to travel to India. There, the rock-cut Buddhist caves at Ajanta and the Hindu temple complex at Ellora had a profound effect on her thinking about architectural scale, stone as a material, and the physicality of place.

Zimmerman's sanctuaries, plazas, and parklike settings often incorporate giant boulders and water elements, such as reflecting pools or cascades. Among her many projects are *Marabar* (1984), an urban oasis at the National Geographic headquarters—though reformulated in 2023 as *Sudama* at the American University—in Washington, D.C.; the multiuse sculpture garden at the Birmingham Museum of Art (1993); the *World Trade Center Memorial* (1995), a tumulus-like fountain honoring the deceased of the 1993 bombing; and *Freefall* (2003), a series of stone tiers and waterfalls down an embankment at a cancer center in New Brunswick, New Jersey.

Mississippi Meanders is another work meant to be experienced. Based on the colored bands from a 1940s geological survey that revealed alterations in the course of the river over thousands of years, the walkway calls attention to the depth of time, human efforts to control nature, and ecological precarity. Consulting with architects and engineers has been a unique and successful method to bring Zimmerman's vision to fruition within her landscape endeavors.—*AMT*

Opposite and following spread
Laminated tempered glass, steel, and aluminum supports, 80 ft. × 84 in. (24.4 m × 213.4 cm), overall, Gift of Sydney and Walda Besthoff, 2019

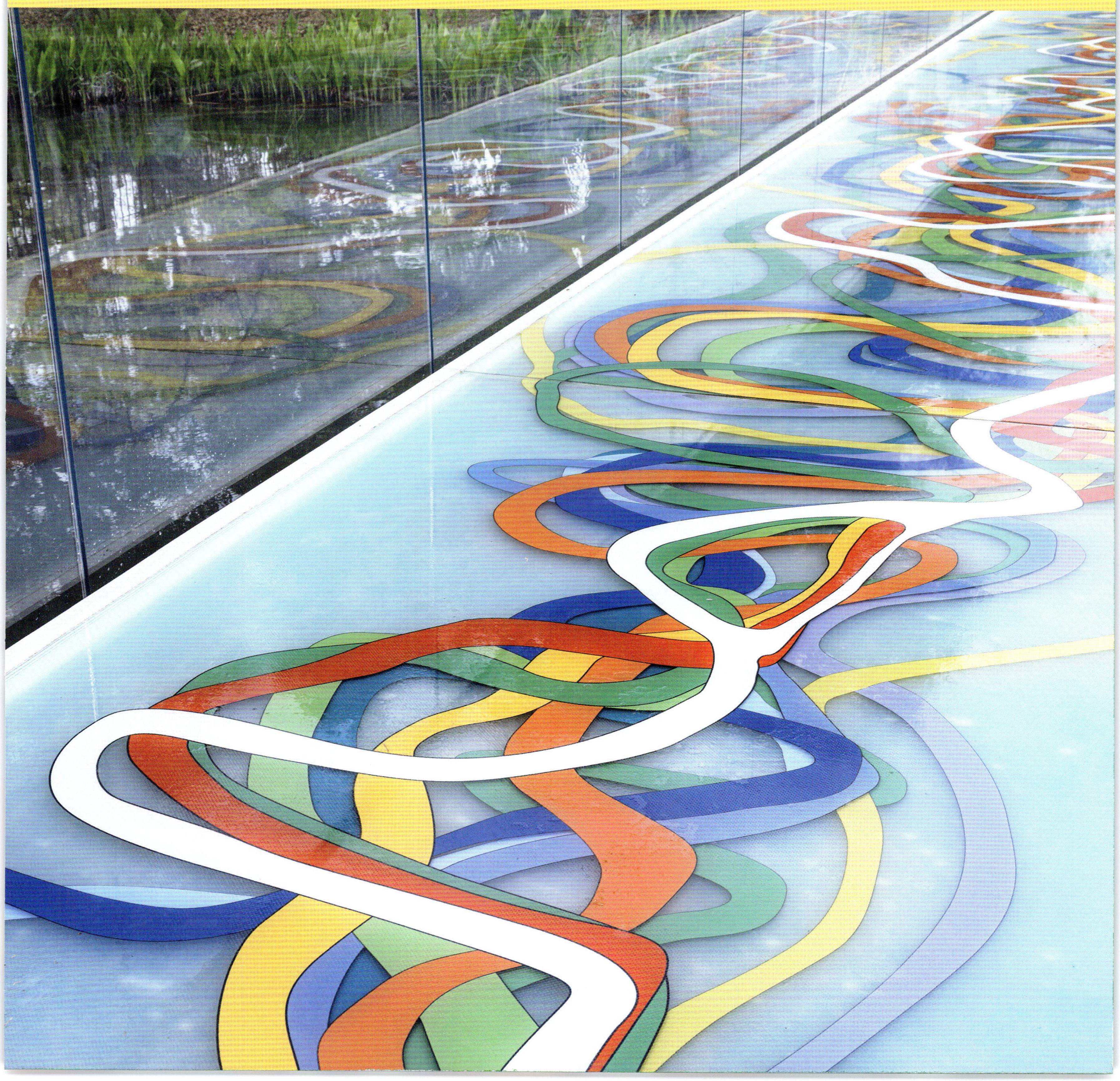

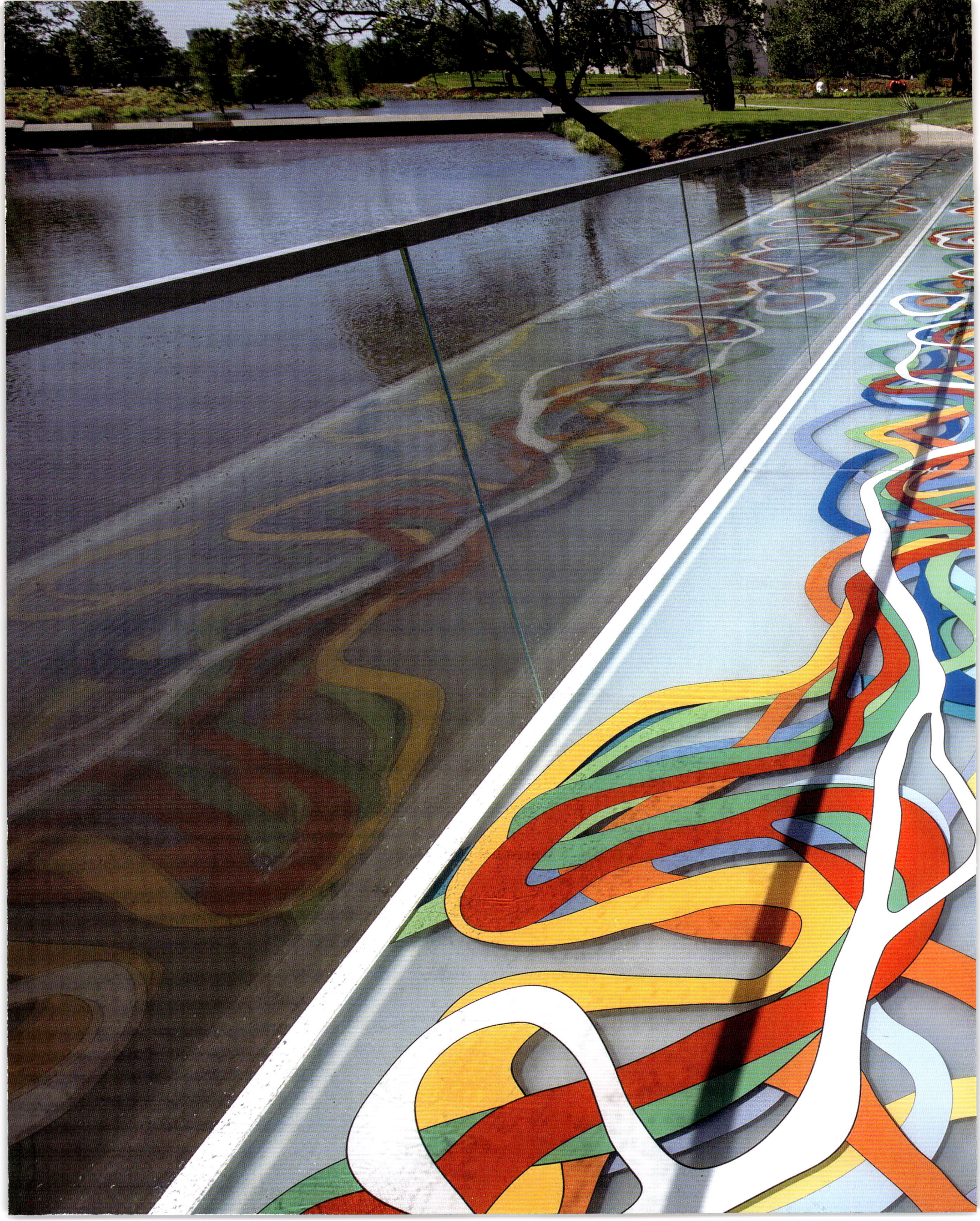

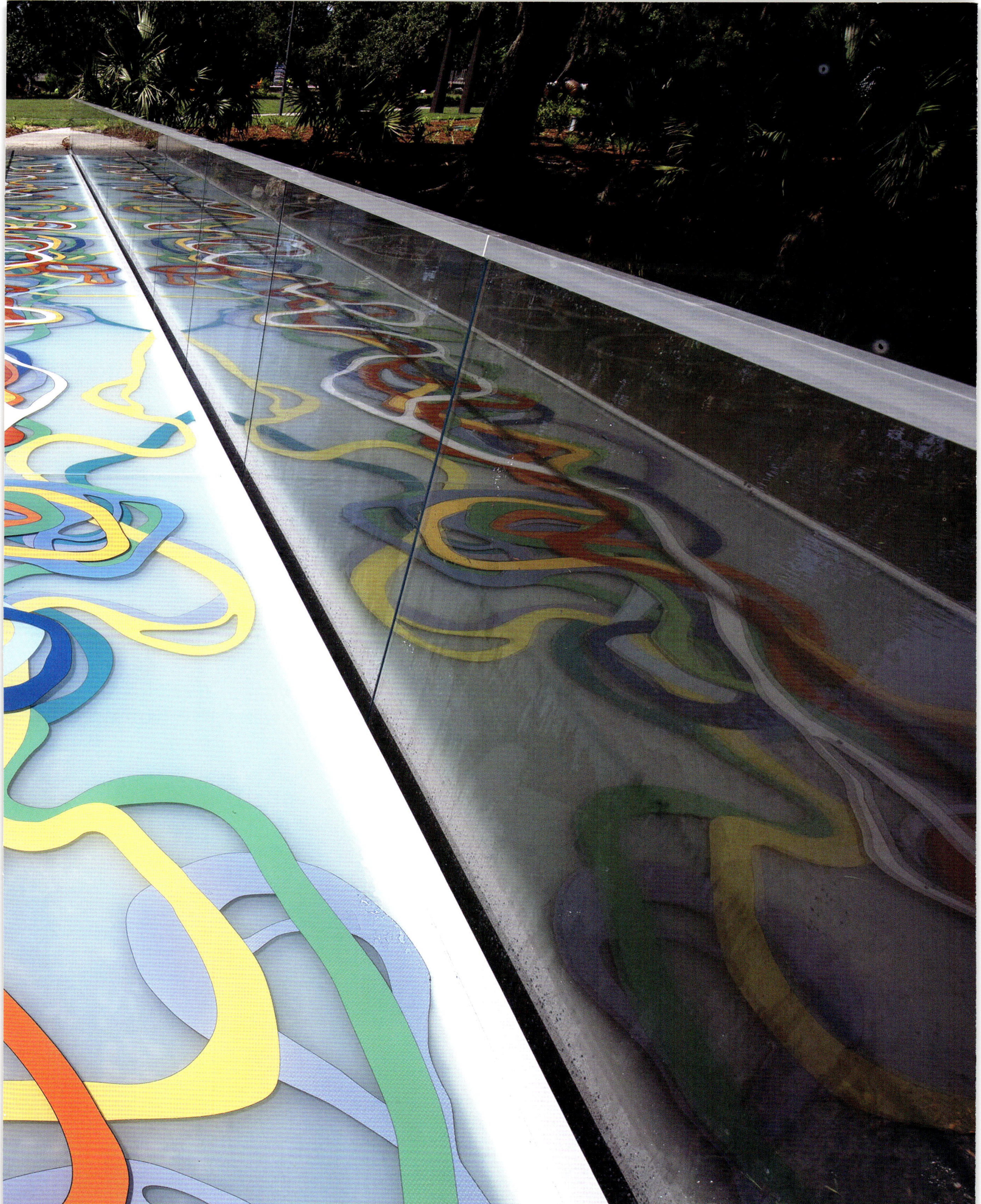

William Zorach

Future Generations, 1942–47

In 1917, William Zorach (1887–1966), a painter steeped in the latest modernist art movements, turned to sculpture. He received no formal training in this practice, though he studied painting at the National Academy of Design in New York before heading to Paris in 1910 for further education. Zorach painted in a Cubist- and Fauvist-inflected style for the next decade but—while he remained dedicated to watercolors—abandoned oil painting in the early 1920s. At three feet high, his mahogany *Mother and Child* (1922) was the largest of the ten or so freestanding wood figures he had produced in the direct-carving method up to that point. It was also one of his first attempts at a subject that would occupy him for his entire life and that he had addressed in paintings of a few years earlier, such as *Interior and Exterior* (1919). His proximity to maternal devotion may have motivated his passion for the subject: his wife, Marguerite Thompson Zorach (1887–1868), an accomplished artist in her own right, gave birth to a son in 1915 and a daughter in 1917. The two had met in Paris and married in New York in 1912.

Mother and child sculptures in various materials followed. His largest rendition, a sixty-five-inch high marble (1927–30), earned him accolades. A series of photographs by Charles Sheeler (1883–1965) document the arduous process of carving—without recourse to a preparatory plaster model—the three-ton block that Zorach imported from Spain. Although it may represent two siblings, *Future Generations* is a similar arrangement to these depictions—the woman is usually kneeling or seated and in close contact with the child. Indeed, the figures are inseparable, suggesting the strength of their bond. With full curves, the sturdy, simplified, and compact figures offer a generalized vision of the fundamental human relationships that so interested Zorach. Although he created other types of sculpture—animals, heads, nude women, and embracing couples—mother and child pairings were among his most enduring and tender. An identically sized marble version of *Future Generations* is in the Whitney Museum of American Art, which organized a retrospective exhibition of his work in 1959.—*AMT*

Bronze, 39 × 19 × 14 in. (99.1 × 48.3 × 35.6 cm), overall, Museum purchase, the Richard Koch Estate, by exchange, 2002

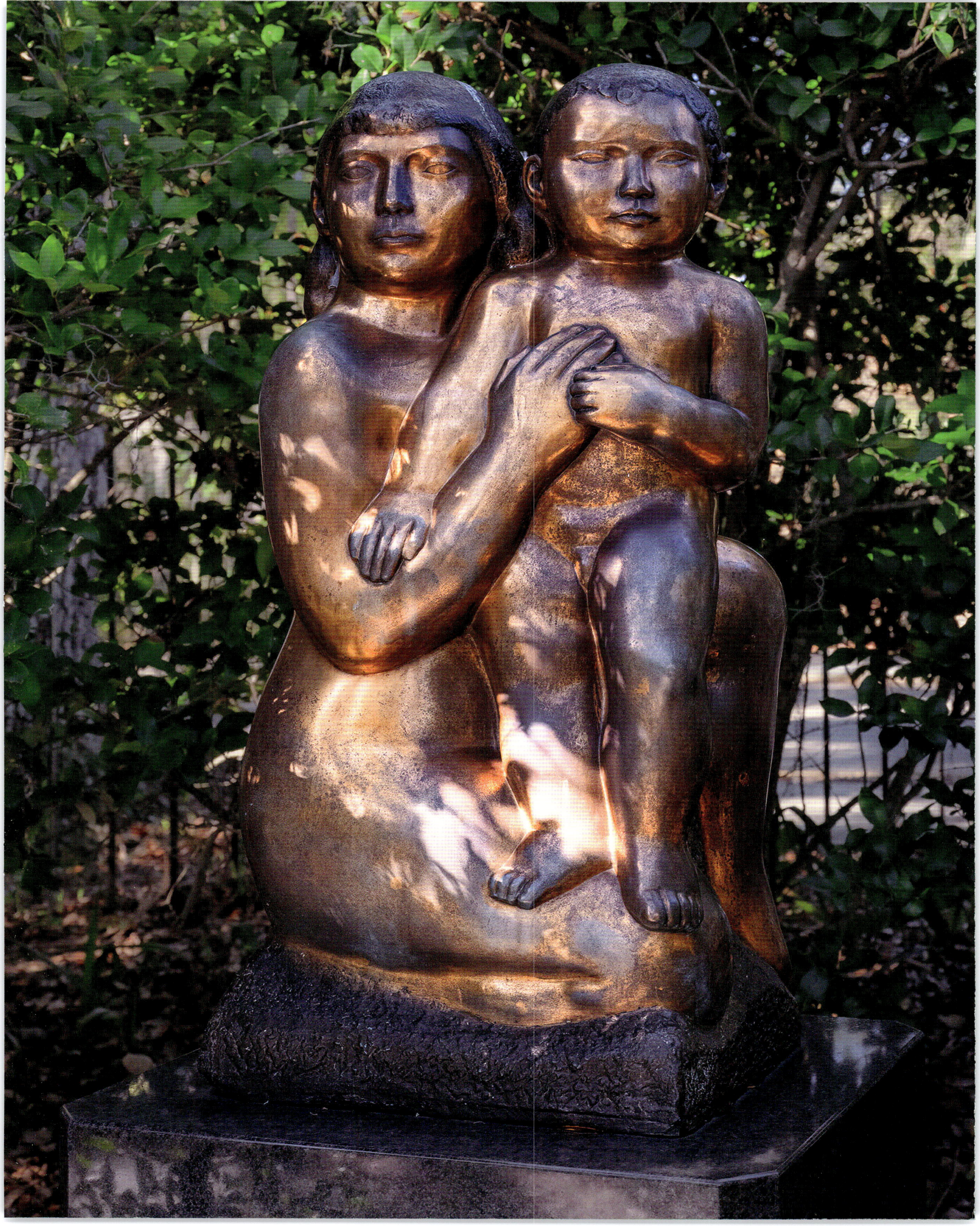

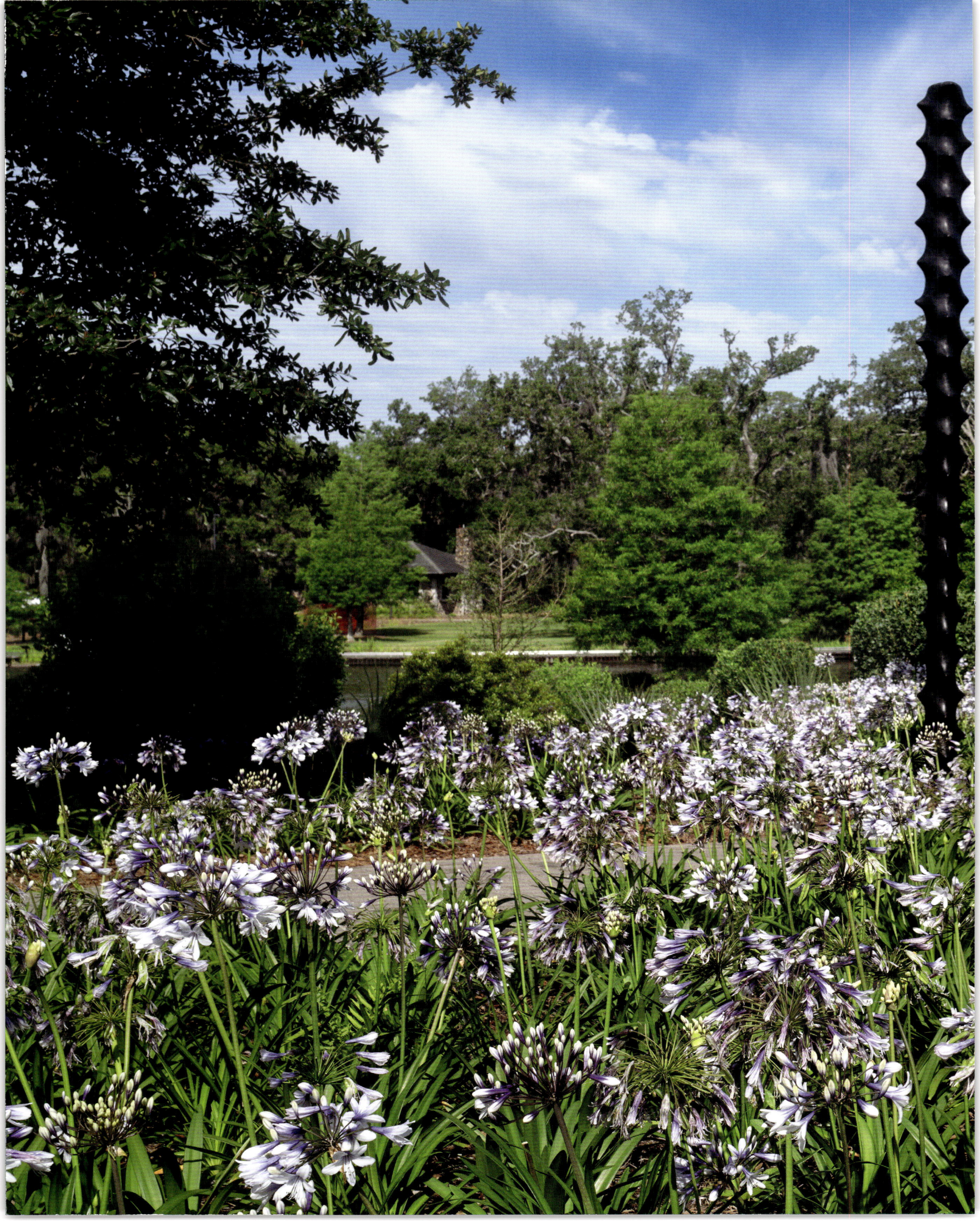

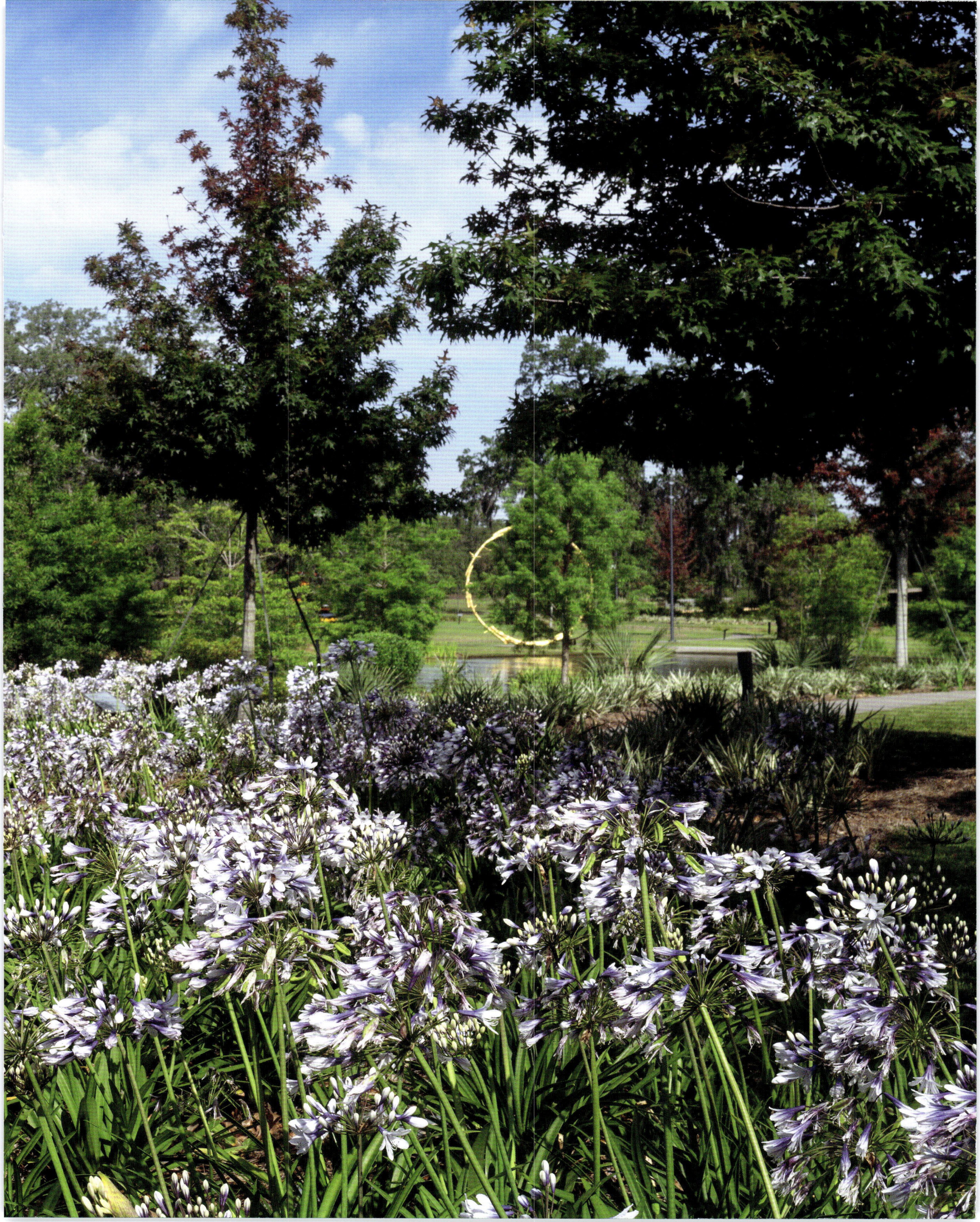

Acknowledgments

It is only fitting that we cap off the New Orleans Museum of Art's yearlong celebration of the Sydney and Walda Besthoff Sculpture Garden's twentieth anniversary with this stunning publication. It is the first in over a decade to focus solely on this important destination and the only book to both review its conception and opening in 2003 and highlight the monumental expansion in 2019. Thank you to all the trustees, patrons, staff, and visitors for your commitment, your care, and your pride in this remarkable, one-of-a-kind space where art meets nature.

Gratitude is due first to Walda Besthoff and her late husband, Sydney, whose vision and determination have single-handedly made this endeavor possible. Now with one hundred large-scale sculptures from the nineteenth to the twenty-first centuries, the Besthoff Sculpture Garden is truly a gift to the city and people of New Orleans. We thank them for entrusting NOMA with their passion and commitment.

I'd like to acknowledge the entire team at Monacelli and Phaidon, who have brought this book to life. Keith Fox, Sean Newcott, Holly La Due, Philip Ruppel, Michael Vagnetti, Jenny Mutch, and the designer Peter Ahlberg took on the complicated task of representing the experience, history, and splendor of twelve acres of magnificent landscape and world-class sculpture in these pages. Thanks are also due to Suzanne Turner for her written contribution that considers the garden's place in the history of City Park and its historic landscape, and Maddie Hampton, Juliana Mascolo, and Adam M. Thomas for their insightful contributions about all of the works in the garden.

Our thanks to Charlie Tatum, director of marketing and communications, for helping steer this project forward, and Sesthasak Boonchai, digital projects manager, for the remarkable photography that brings the garden to life in print. We also recognize the photography of Roman Alokhin and Richard Sexton, whose images are included.

Acknowledgement is also due to Ingrid Seyb, conservator of objects, for her attention to all the sculptures in the museum's collection and for embarking on a major conservation project in preparation for the anniversary and this book. In her role as NOMA's deputy director for curatorial affairs, Lisa Rotondo-McCord has watched the Besthoff Sculpture Garden grow from the very beginning and has ensured that this special place is an extension of our indoor galleries.

This project would not be possible without the museum staff who maintain the sculpture garden on a daily basis. Thanks go to Pam Buckman, sculpture garden manager, and Thomas Torres, sculpture garden assistant manager, for their thorough knowledge of native plants and trees, and the garden's landmark live oaks; all of their work reflects a dedication to the landscape and the space that make the Besthoff Sculpture Garden so unique.

We are also grateful to all the designers, architects, horticulturalists, and environmental experts for their roles in the development of the garden, including Lee Ledbetter Architects, Sawyer/Berson Architecture and Landscape Architecture, and Reed Hildebrand, among many others.

And most importantly, I would like to recognize and celebrate the artists whose work is on view in the Sydney and Walda Besthoff Sculpture Garden. Thank you for being part of a vision to create a place of respite, wonder, and discovery for all visitors—now and for generations to come.

—Susan M. Taylor

Contributors

Walda Besthoff, a native of New Orleans, Louisiana, is a longstanding supporter of the arts and a local philanthropist. She has observed a lifelong commitment to the performing arts, particularly theater and dance, as a performer, staffer, and patron. Throughout the late 1960s and '70s, she served in administrative and institutional advancement positions for various local ballet groups. She had also served on the board of the Contemporary Arts Center (CAC), New Orleans, in the 1980s, chairing the Capital Campaign for the expansion of the CAC. She currently serves on the board of trustees of the New Orleans Museum of Art.

Susan M. Taylor has served as the Montine McDaniel Freeman Director of the New Orleans Museum of Art since 2013. In this role, Taylor led the museum's major expansion of the Sydney and Walda Besthoff Sculpture Garden, which opened to the public in 2019.

Suzanne Turner is principal of Suzanne Turner Associates, a research and design firm. Turner has worked as a consultant for a number of historic and cultural landscapes, properties of the National Park Service, and numerous other house and museum properties.

Maddie Hampton is a writer based in New York. An alum of the Whitney Independent Study Program, her writing has appeared in *The Brooklyn Rail*, *Art Review*, *frieze*, and e-flux Criticism.

Juliana Mascolo is a writer based in New York and London. She currently works at Artsy. Her texts have been featured in publications including *Great Women Sculptors* (Phaidon, 2024) and *Latin American Artists* (Phaidon, 2023).

Adam M. Thomas is curator at the Resnick Center for Herbert Bayer Studies in Aspen, Colorado. He is a contributor to, most recently, *Great Women Sculptors* (Phaidon, 2024).

Credits

Photography
All photos by Sesthasak Boonchai unless noted otherwise.

Photos by Richard Sexton: 8–9, 33, 36–37, 45–47, 56–57, 75, 95, 103–05, 109, 119, 125, 127, 129, 131, 137, 145, 155, 159, 161, 173, 181, 199, 203, 208–09, 212–13, 235, 237, 241, 243–45, 247, 258–59, endsheets

Captions cont'd:

2: Jean-Michel Othoniel, *L'Arbre aux Colliers (Tree of Necklaces)*, 2002

4–5: (sculptures from left to right) Mimmo Paladino, *Caduto a ragione [Fallen for a Reason]*, 2008; Saul Baizerman, *Aurora*, 1950–57

258–59: (sculptures from left to right) Johan Cretan, *Massu II*, 2015; Ugo Rondinone, *the sun*, 2018

Library of Congress Control Number: 2024939409

ISBN 978-1-58093-649-1
10 9 8 7 6 5 4 3 2 1

Printed in China

Design by Dandelion

Monacelli
A Phaidon Company
111 Broadway
New York, NY 10006

monacellipress.com

New Orleans
Museum of Art
One Collins C. Diboll Circle,
City Park
New Orleans, LA 70124

noma.org

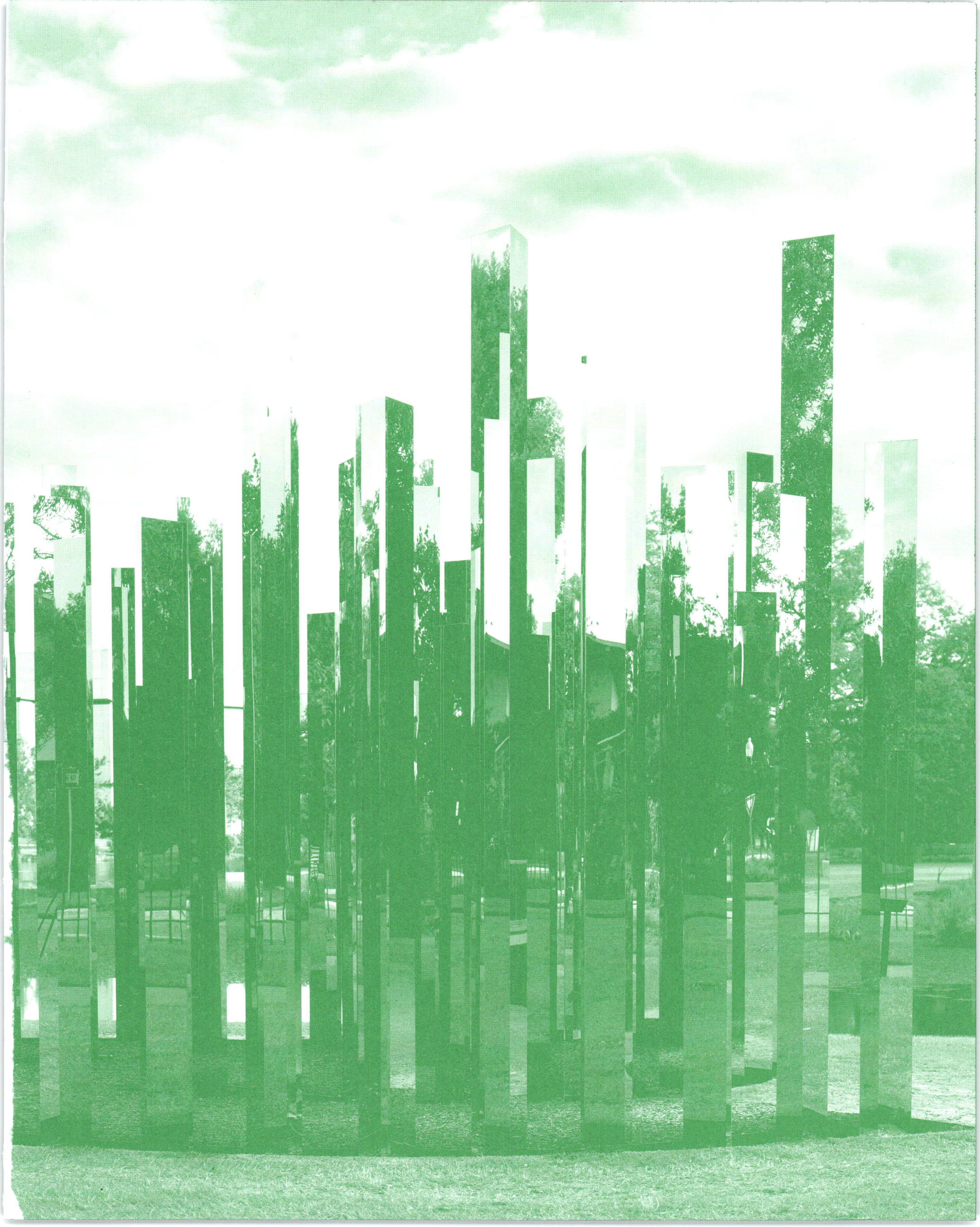

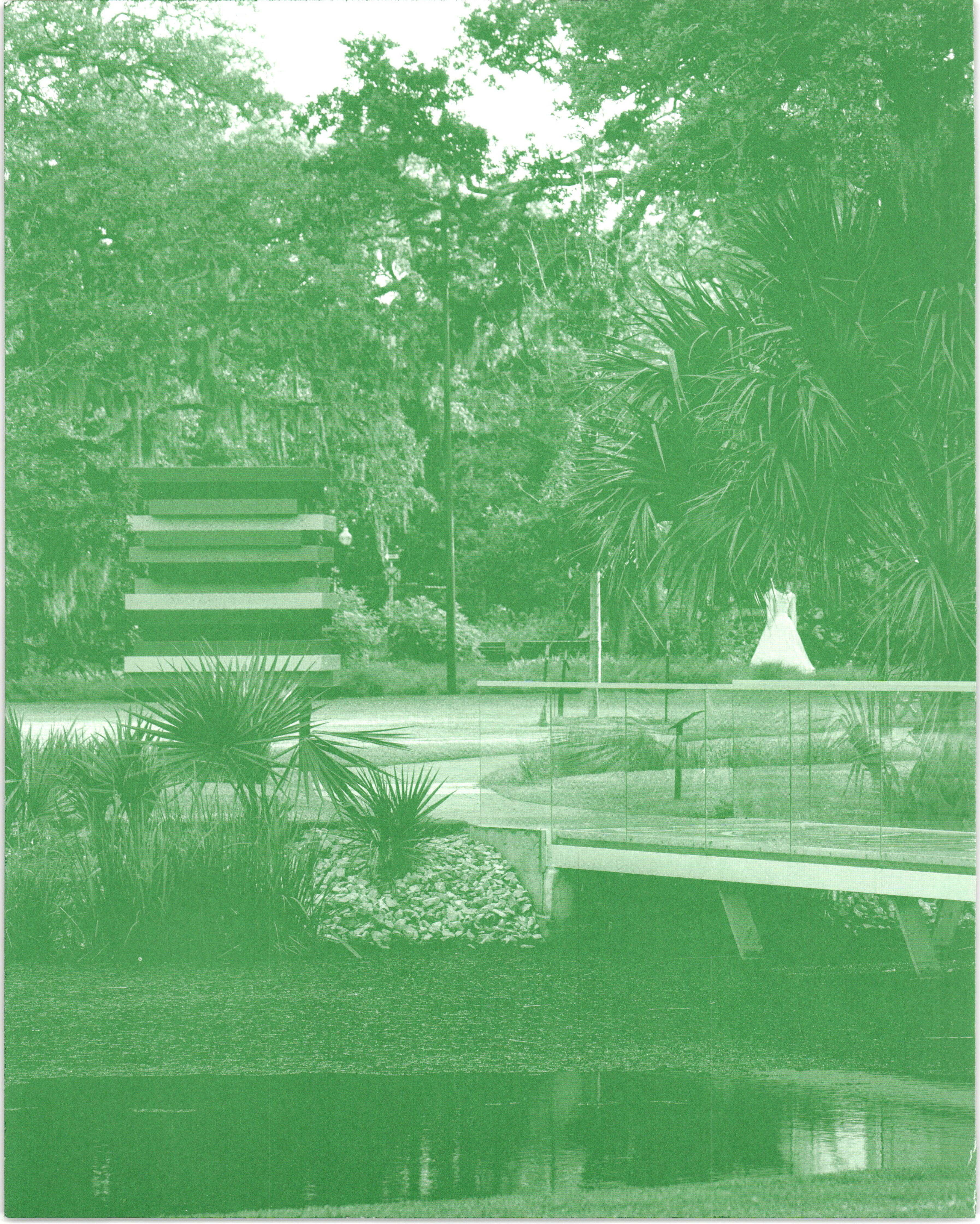